The American Dream

of a

Gay European Guy

The American Dream

of a

Gay European Guy

Marzio Deodato

THE REGENCY
PUBLISHERS

ISBN: 978-1-957724-68-3 (Paperback Edition)
ISBN: 978-1-957724-67-6 (Hardcover Edition)
ISBN: 978-1-957724-69-0 (E-book Edition)

Book Ordering Information

Phone Number: 315-537-3088
Email: info@theregencypublishers.com
The Regency Publishers, US
www.theregencypublishers.com

Printed in the United States of America

Contents

Chapter 1

THE AMERICAN DREAM OF A GAY EUROPEAN GUY

It must have been a cold night that 3rd of February 1947 when I was born! Maybe that's why I don't like cold weather. My parents had one child, a girl, nine and a half years earlier, then there was the second world war, and only after the war was over, maybe also because that nine years old girl insisted she would have loved a little sister, my parents must have decided that one wasn't enough…so there I was, but not a girl, a baby boy!

My childhood started very well. I was born at home, according to the fashion of the time, in a nice, comfortable house on Lido, that's the main island in front of Venezia, and the only one that has real traffic with cars, buses and motorcycles. It is connected to the mainland by a ferryboat several times a day.

My yard became a polar attraction in the neighborhood and since I was 3 I remember having friends over all the time to play. I also remember taking my first steps in the yard when I was just less than one year old.

In winter we had snow many times and I learned how to build snowmen with my friends. In spring the garden was all in bloom and I remember my grandmother taking big pride in her rosebushes, the palm trees, the jasmine and all the flowers that the soil would produce thanks to all the love that she would put into it,

Several times she won first price for the best yard in Lido and that was my world from the early October to the beginning of June.

As much as I love Venezia, I never spent a summer there because the family had a mountain retreat in the Dolomites, the mountain chain located in the northeast in an area that, until 1918, used to be part of the Austrian empire.

It was my mother's father that discovered that secluded village back in 1930 and decided to build a house in 1935 in the very spot where, together with his family, they used to sit to contemplate the high plane, surrounded by higher mountains, and see the sun setting behind the higher peek. We would go there by car and in those days it was a journey that took several hours. The roads were not really wide, the traffic was slow and there were not many cars around. Before the curbs the chauffeur had to blow the horn to make sure that incoming vehicles, mainly buses, stayed on their side of the road.

The arrival in Lavarone was always a big even for me. First of all I had to explore the house, a three story, surrounded by pines, birches and hazelnut bushes, not too far from the main square yet in a very isolated area. The second thing I would do was running to the main square were there was the house of my best friend who lived in Roma to see if him and his family had already arrived. I was sometimes disappointed to find out that the house had all the shutters closed. At that point I had to go to the next door hotel to inquire about the date of arrival since it was customary for them to send somebody over to clean and let fresh air go in a couple of days prior to the arrival. In those days the hotels and a few bars had a telephone service. Most people had a telephone at home but almost nobody had one installed in their second home. To make a simple phone call out of the area we had to go to the phone "station", call the operator, list the call that could take from a few minutes to hours to go through. In an emergency the cost would triple but we probably had to sit there until the phone would ring back. The communication wasn't always that clear and some people would scream making their business public.

When my friend Luigi was arriving it was one of the best days of the year. We would get together and make the projects for the months to come. Every year the group of youngsters would grow with guys and girls coming from different Italian cities, some renting a house for the hot months, some having a house built and some just spending the whole time in the local hotels. We were a happy bunch, the number never exceeded 16, some came for a few years and then changed their habits and sold their house and moved to a different place, some kept coming year after year. This village is divided in different "fractions" each one distant maybe 1 mile from the other, so every fraction had a different group of youngsters and sometimes we were rivals, so to speak, meaning we would not allow member of different groups to mingle with us, to build huts, to go to the lake to swim and take sun or to go mountain hiking and have snacks in the woods. We would however make some "war expeditions" to huts of different groups to destroy them while the members were not in sight, not before hiding ours with branches in order to escape the inevitable revenge.

We did not mingle with the local guys considered ignorant and not of our level. On the other hand they were not coming around because they were considering us "different" and they didn't particularly like the fact that we were invading their territory for three months of the year.

The parents of my best friend were of the conservative type: they did not allow Luigi and his sister to leave the house after dinner. That obliged us to go in force to beg them to let them go to the local cinema or just to hang with us in front of the main hotel in the square. More were the times that we were unsuccessful, but somehow it was all fun.

All that was coming to an end when the families would leave Lavarone and for nine long months they would reside in their city of origin. Exceptionally I was allowed to call Luigi in Rome once a month from the house phone and that was making me a very happy camper.

One week before the "voyage" back we would regroup and go to certain areas of the forest and collect big bags of hazelnuts. The right time was after the second week in September when they would start falling on the ground. In those days the mountain people lived a decent but poor life. Some women would walk for miles in the woods to pick up small strawberries, raspberries, mushrooms of different kind then walk from house to house trying to sell their finds. The milk was taken daily to the store were it was sold by the liter, still warm, between 7 and 8pm. Some people owned barns in the area and they were producing fresh ricotta, asiago, vezzena cheese and tasty butter. They were also going from house to house to offer their products and they would always sell every bit of it. So while our parents would buy fresh products to take back to their city homes, we were packing big amounts of hazelnuts to eat during the weeks to come.

The return to the city was somewhat fun thinking of the friends and the habits forgotten for months. The best time was the stop in a restaurant , always the same, to break that trip that seemed so long. By the way, I didn't like to travel, the motion of the vehicle made me sick most of the times.

Once back in Lido I had to go see my friends and make sure they knew I was back! The months ahead were going to be dense of things to do, games to play, tricks to play to my family, my sister and her friends.

My family was not very conservative. My father, a naval engineer, was in partnership with two other ship owners. He was always traveling, mostly abroad. I think he was spending at home two, maybe three months out of the year. My mother, half Swiss, half Italian, loved to travel and she was often following my father. My grandmother, 100% Swiss, was living in the upper apartment and my sister and I were in the very good hands of our nanny, Concetta.

My grandmother remained widow in 1946 and the company that my grandfather owned in Venice passed on to their nephew. My mother and her sister never had interest in importing dried fruits and vegetables. Fortunately my grandfather believed in the "brick" and left his wife a rich landlady. Married when she came to Italy in 1905, she was brought up by very open minded parents and very progressive for that time. But most German-Swiss families have always been that way. My mother and her sister grew up in the same liberal atmosphere, studying in Swiss boarding schools and eager to travel and take care of themselves from a very young age.

Concetta was just from a different world. Born in the countryside of Venice, she started working for my family when she was 15 years old taking care of my mother, my sister and, finally, myself. My idols were my grandmother Frieda and Concetta. My sister too, but she had her friends, and I guess the difference of age played on the fact that her habits and mine differed.

Concetta took care of me, washed me, paid attention to my needs and was always making sure I had plenty to eat. She was an exceptional cook. Frieda had thought her also some Swiss dishes like "spaetzli" and I believe her skills increased so much during the years that several so called friends tried to bribe her to serve in their household.

Those first 6 years of my life were really happy. I had very good communication skills and my little friends were always ringing the bell to see what I was up to. My yard was our kingdom, the trees were a hiding place and so was the big basement of the house.

I have always been intrigued by semi dark areas and I knew all the good places to hide when playing hide seek. I have never been fond of spiders and their webs. Even one of a small size will scare me to death. On the contrary I could handle lizards, rats, ants and all those insects that are found among grass and dirt.

Across the street lived Sergio and Alfredo, my same age. Next door there was Massimo and Gloria, I could say my very first girl friend. She was actually living in the city but her family would spend in Lido every week end and also all Summer, when we were gone.

In the early 1950's we did not have television and everything was rotating around the radio. During the afternoons there were some music programs. Then some famous voice of those days would read one chapter of some famous romance. Needless to say that at a chapter a day it took one month to hear the whole book. I got hooked on some and made sure to be there at that certain time to listen to the developments of the story.

In the evening, after dinner, I had to go to bed at 8,30 sharp but…often I was not in the mood to go to sleep that early. After they had turned off the central light I would turn on the one on the night table and start taking the sheets off, filling them with clothes, shoes and whatever I could find in the wardrobe. Eventually Concetta would hear the noise and find out that I had messed up the room again.

Next door was also living the family doctor that assisted my mother when I was born. He played a big role during my first years because I had almost all the typical infective illnesses that youngsters usually get. I must confess those days were nice and relaxing. In bed, listening to the radio, served for anything I could possibly want! But…

It all came to an end with my first school day.

Chapter 2

I was going to turn six on the second month of 1953 so my parents enrolled me in school that was starting on October the first. The first elementary class was a big happening but I had no idea on what was going to happen in that classroom. The preparation started fifteen days earlier with buying the black coverall, the pencils, the colors, the pens, the copybooks, the few books and a briefcase to carry all that stuff. I was kind of excited but also kind of worried because I had to wake up earlier than usual for six days a week and stay away from home for 5 hours in a strange environment.

My mother took me to the school where there were many children with their respective mothers or fathers waiting for the gate to open. At 8 o'clock the bell rang and we were in the classroom to find a suitable and well positioned desk to sit at. The teacher, a middle age lady, walked in, introduced herself, called each pupil by name and said a few words of welcoming. During the following weeks I learned that all the free time I had enjoyed was gone forever. Lessons in the morning and homework in the afternoon kept me busy for most of the day. The good thing was that I met new friends and soon enough my house was like a port of call. As I was saying earlier, my yard was a bit the center of all the activities going on with my friends. In the back of the house there were, and still are, some of the largest bushes of hydrangea. I considered Gloria, my week end neighbor, to be also my girlfriend and I would cut some of the large flowers and deliver them to her doorsteps. This would make my grandmother mad because she cared too much about the plants and it would make Gloria's mother smile to the fact that her daughter had such a young admirer. Soon there was a small group of schoolmates coming over every afternoon to study, do the homework together and, very big novelty for that time…to watch TV. The regular programs started daily in 1953 at 5pm sharp with the TV for the youngsters mainly short dubbed American movies such as Zorro and some western serials. Concetta would serve hot coco and cookies or some freshly baked cakes. Around 6,30 everybody was returning home living me alone to wait for dinner time that was always at 7,30. At 8,30 there was the curfew and I had to go to bed, no matter what. There was a popular commercial program on TV called "carosello" that lasted 12 minutes and it was said that after "carosello" all children had to go to bed. My household was no exception.

Saturday became the best day of the week for me. Sunday too, but in the late afternoon I had to think that the next day was a school day and I had to start a whole new long week. Since then I started hating Sundays.

Twice a month we had a lady tailor coming to the house to cut material and sew dresses for my mother, grandmother and, often, some of their regular friends. This was an occasion that would happen every day around 5pm when my mother was around. It was a kind of tea/chat/politic discussions, sometimes gossip. I was always around listening to every word, looking at their faces, studying their expressions and soon enough I started foreseeing their reactions. After a few years they became like an open book. I could tell what was going on just looking at them from a distance. Seldom I would also intervene in some talks amusing the ladies that such a little boy had something to say.

Once a month there was a male hairdresser coming over to cut and fix everybody's hair. The thought of the meticulous work with the scissors, sitting on a chair for 30 to 40 minutes drove me nuts. He was doing excellent work but I couldn't sit still for such a long time.

During one of those busy afternoons with the tailor I remember pulling out my dick, going to Angelina (that was her name) and ask her to cut some of it because I thought it was to long. That would make everybody laugh. I had no idea that the penis would play such a big role in my future life!

At school I was learning fast to write, read, count. I started having some knowledge of history, geography and religion. Everything was starting to make sense in my mind but I was very thirsty for knowledge and I had an enormous number of questions to ask. My teacher, Mrs. Gina, a widow of an engineer, had devoted her life to teaching. She had a twin sister, Mrs. Lina, also a widow, and they lived together on Sant'Elena island, in between Venezia and Lido.

I soon found out that my least favorite subject was mathematic while I was excelling in all the others. There was a schoolmate who was good with all the subjects, his name was Walter. Soon we became rivals: he was surpassing me in math, I was surpassing him in the other subjects. I loved learning the Italian grammar and soon enough we had to put our thoughts in writing.

The second year was even better. We started writing short compositions. I had a big fantasy and I must admit my compositions were pretty good. As a matter of fact even the teachers thought so and it happened several times that they were red to the students of higher classes.

I took pride of my studies. At the end of the school year, the beginning of June, the teacher would give us some summer work for the 4 months ahead. I never waited too long to do it, I was usually done within a fortnight thus enabling me to be carefree for the rest of my vacation.

Lido has a very nice beach. My parents used to get a cabin for a few weeks next to the private beach of the Hotel des Bains, the same one where Dirk Bogard shot the movie "death in Venice". I loved to swim in the sea. Play with the sand, keep away from the crabs, build sandcastles and run around with my friends. After that short period we would leave for Lavarone where I would regroup with my "summer friends" exchanging ideas and opinions about the school and comparing how far in the program we were. The rest of the time was spent as usual building huts and fighting the other groups.

It was during the summer break of the second year that I started playing with a couple of native guys lightly older than me. Near my house there is a very dark forest crossed by a little creek. Every morning there was this guy taking care of some cows so we started talking about life in the mountains and life in the city. He had never been out of Lavarone except a few times to go to Trento (just 25 miles away, capital of the Trentino region). One day we were chatting and walking and suddenly we found ourselves in a very dark secluded area. The curiosity was obviously mutual and we started with touching our hands, arms, comparing our legs and eventually we ended up comparing other anatomies of our bodies. We were naked, both with an erection, touching, studying, comparing and with many questions but no answers. Too scared or ashamed to ask some other people we swore not to say a word to anyone and so we did. Needless to say we met several times to play doctor and this was procuring us some kind of excitement combined with the fear that some foreign eyes could see us.

The following summer we resumed those acts but in the meantime there was also another local boy that joined us. He probably knew more than he wanted to let us know, but he never said anything and we never asked.

My curiosity was increasing and since I noticed that we all had a different shape and different size penis, I wanted to see those of my best friends to compare and also because I enjoyed looking and even touching.

There were those two guys on my street, Sergio and Alfredo, that looked promising so one cloudy afternoon I dragged one to my basement and there we started playing doctor. He was cooperating just like the boy in Lavarone and that became our hiding place. Once Concetta almost discovered us but she probably thought we were hiding from her as a joke. Sergio started playing with me too, but probably his interest came to an end pretty soon because we only did it a few times. For some reasons it gave me pleasure to be naked with another boy, touch him, be touched, getting an erection and wondering what the penis of a grown man would look like.

During a Sunday afternoon one of my female cousin from Venezia came to visit. That day I decided to play doctor with her. Instead of going to the basement, I locked the door of my room and undressed her (she was my age) on the rug. There was not much to see or touch because she did not have anything between her legs. I remember being disappointed to see a little crack where something else was supposed to hang. I lost quickly interest and decided that guys were far more appealing. Even during that occasion we swore not to say a word to anyone and for a few days I lived in fear that she would have blabbed it to her parents.

My family was somewhat religious. My mother's father was catholic, my grandmother was Methodist. The two daughters were brought up protestant. Big deal in Italy where 80% of the people are roman catholic, even considering that my mother's great uncle was pope Pius X at the turn of the century.

On my father side they switched to protestant in the seventeenth century after being catholic since 1193. My father's brother was a pastor in charge for two terms of the Valdesi, a protestant movement very active in the west side part of Italy.

I was getting a catholic teaching in the school. A priest was having 1 hour of catechism class once a week. But when I turned 6 my father insisted that I go to the protestant church in Venezia for the study and reading of the bible. So I would take the waterbus, cross the calli and bridges and reach the house of the pastor located on the side of the church. I found all that interesting…but somehow I was not really involved with the Christian religion and I started developing my own ideas about live, Christ, God, fear of God and all that stuff.

There was a lot of talking about the atomic bomb in the early fifties, the so called "H" bomb and we had seen all the devastation that the Americans had caused in Japan just a few years earlier. My idea was: "why does God allow children to be born if there are such catastrophes happening" and "if there is going to be an end of the world wouldn't people stop having children?" after all they were all innocent in the eyes of God so why would He want them to suffer physical pain and violent death!

The more we were reading the bible and learning from the mouth of the pastor about what happened to the "bad" people in the bible, the more I was afraid that what I was doing with my boyfriends was something sinful and one day I would have been punished for it.

Chapter 3

My life had been until now a lot of fun. Good family, nice friends, nice environment, winter in the city, summer at the sea and in the mountains to escape the heath. I was running wild in the fields and the forests of Lavarone, hiking, swimming in the lake and a group of very nice guys to hang around with.

The only thing I was really missing was the presence of my father and often the absence of my mother that was going with dad on many trips.

I was frequenting the families of my close friends to find out that they were really united. I guess I was growing up missing all that. I reversed most of my love in my grandmother Frieda and, of course, in my dear sister Wilma.

Also in the mountain there was the tea time with my mom's friends and even there sometimes I would mingle to listen to what they were talking about. Sometimes my father had to take care of some shipyard works in France, Belgium, Holland or Germany, so we would take a trip there and spend a couple of weeks in a foreign city like Bremen, Hamburg, Antwerp, Amsterdam, Rouen.

Besides the attention that I was paying to the countryside, the buildings, the windmills and all the other beautiful things that those country had to offer, I was also paying attention to the look of the people that we would get in touch with. I thought the Germans were very handsome but even some Dutch and French were not bad. I was always fantasizing how they would look naked.

It was during one of those trips, exactly to Wegesack, the port of Bremen, that my father and his two partners decided to move their company to Genova. Venezia was not a busy port and Genova was the first or the second most important port in the Mediterranean sea.

It was the summer of 1955. One year later my mom and I were in Genova looking for a house to buy. We spent there a couple of weeks checking out the possible areas. Every house the realtor was showing us seemed way too small compared to the one in Lido. Finally we found one facing the sea in an area called Lido of Genova. When my mom saw the morning sun reflected in the marble floor she decided that was it. The return to Venezia was not too happy for me because I really didn't like Genova and I really was not in the mood to say goodbye to all my friends, the school, my home and to the city that I adored.

Still we had to spend the summer in the mountains, go back to Lido at the beginning of September, arrange for the movers to ship the furniture, pack and move.

That month went by very fast. The last two days I asked my father to take me to the top of the bell tower in the San Marco square to enjoy the aerial view of my hometown and while we were up there the bells started playing like they were saying "goodbye".

The trip to Genova was long. My dad and mom were leading in their car, my sister and I were following in hers. It took all day, with the usual stop for lunch. My mom had put some of her plants in both cars and one of them, a cactus, hit my leg when my sister had to break for a red light.

We got there during the early evening. Concetta was waiting for us. She had prepared a nice dinner and cleaned the house. We spent the first night not really sleeping well because we were tired of the trip and we had to get used to that new home.

The inhabitants of Genova have never been too friendly. The city, big rival of Venezia for centuries for the dominium of the sea and for the trading from the orient, is built on a long and narrow strip of land surrounded by hills and some higher mountains.

I cannot say it is an ugly city, but one has to divide it in three: the east section is very residential with nice houses and villas, well kept, clean and green, facing the beaches that are rocky and not really as pretty as the one on the Adriatic sea. The Downtown is the historical district. Very narrow streets, building closed together and sometimes connected by small elevated passages used during the middle ages in order to escape the pirates that could invade the city for robberies. The ancient port is in the heart of the old district. Of course, being an international port, it welcomes people and sailors from all over the world and that attracts all kind of people like prostitutes, transvestites, homosexuals, robbers, drug attics, black market traders and so on. We could say it is like one of those kasbah that one would expect to find in Casablanca or Tunis.

The west side of town is the industrial one with factories, offices, shipyards, and a very large port divided in sections for oil tankers, different merchandises, passenger ships, ferryboats and so on. Not a very nice area to visit. From Nervi, the extreme east side, to Voltri, the extreme west side, the city is about 40 kms long but only 7 or 8 kms wide in the widest point with about 1.500.000 people. Very different from the beautiful Venice, big attraction for people worldwide and with 90.000 inhabitants at the most.

In a way the downtown area was very attractive for a nine year old. In those years it was quite safe to walk around prostitutes, pimps, drug dealers and such. The area has many fancy stores, ancient buildings dating from the 12th century on and a big variety of people shopping, browsing, walking, looking, chatting. When some American ships were in port there were groups of nice sailors walking around, always guarded by the military police to prevent riots.

I got accustomed to the city but I didn't know anyone. My moods started changing. My sister didn't like it either but she was gone for several months at the time to study in England, then Germany, Spain and France. I was left with Concetta, sometimes my mother and seldom my father. The only time the family got together was during the summer in Lavarone or to take our usual trips to northern Europe.

The 1ˢᵗ year was tough. My parents chose a private German school because they did not trust the public system. So the school bus came to pick me up every morning at 7,30 and left me at my doorsteps at 1,30. The atmosphere was not exactly the same as in the public school of Lido. We had 4 different teachers for different subjects and almost everything was carried on in German. I met several nice guys and girls but not everybody was living in the same neighborhood so it became difficult to get together after the school hours. We were still too young to be allowed to go far from our block or to ride public buses.

I would get home, eat, play some card games with Concetta, do my homework, watch TV, have dinner and go to bed. This routine became kind of boring and in some subjects I wasn't doing so well because they did not polarize my attention. But I passed the year and there I was, back in the mountains, among my old friends and still fouling around with the two mountain guys in our little forest.

It was after one of those encounters that going home I had the surprise to find my dad talking to my mom about me. They took the decision to send me to a boarding school in Germany so I could perfect my German and be among guys of all ages. The school in Germany was starting one month earlier than in Italy and for me that meant one month less with my friends, no hazelnuts, and away from home, form my toys, books and all the things that I loved.

Needless to say that those weeks went quickly. There I was on a train traveling to Bonndorf, a beautiful village in the black forest, not too far from Freiburg, to meet my new destiny.

We arrived in the early afternoon and checked into a nice hotel. We walked to the college where we were greeted by Mrs. Lange, the director. She welcomed me with a big hug and she assured me I would be very happy there.

There were 4 buildings on the premises: one for kids my age, one for older kids, one strictly for girls and one with the classrooms, dining rooms, playrooms and study areas. There was a large swimming pool, tennis courts, feather ball courts and a small playing ground with sand and a little stream. The whole compound was surrounded by the darkest forest I had ever seen.

My mom, unexpectedly, left the very next day and I was left alone 1000 kms from home. My German was pretty good but there were some words that I had not learned yet. Obviously I was obliged to learn fast because there was no other Italian in sight that I could turn to for help!

The food was ok, the classes were interesting and quite easy actually, except for my hated subject: mathematic.

This was my 4th year of elementary school and I found out that in Germany there are only four years instead of five. That meant that the following year I would have been in 1st medium high.

Now there was nothing else to do than study, get to know my new friends and wait for the Christmas break to go home.

I must have been very hot blooded because during that September I managed to swim in the pool with a water temperature of 62F! The guys were nice and so were the girls. I already had my eyes on a guy 3 years older than me, typical German, blonde, blue eyes, named Hermann. There was also this girl from Berlin that was after me, her name Brigitte. I played games with her but I was always keeping an eye on Hermann.

Every day we were taking a shower but everybody was wearing a bathing suit and there was a monitor in the looker room making sure nobody exposed himself. That was probably because boys of different ages were showering together and we were not supposed to find out about pubic hair.

This aroused my curiosity: were German guys made the same way as the Italians?

The bulge under the bikini bathing suit indicated so…but I was not 100% sure. The fact is that during my 2 years of permanence in Bonndorf I could never find out because I never saw anybody totally naked.

The school was going on well during the 1st year. During the 2nd we started studying Latin translating it from German and into German. I did pretty good considering. The subject to keep an eye on was math; especially now that we started studying algebra.

Back in Lavarone in summer my usual friends were asking me all kind of questions about my permanence abroad and some were envious because they wanted to escape the daily routine of their life in the cities.

After the 2nd year I really had enough of Bonndorf and I was craving for something different. The occasion came when my dad got some brochures of a boarding school in Paris and my mom said she wouldn't mind if I could speak some French. There was only one little problem: France medium school did not recognize the German school system and I would have to start from the 1st class again.

I had heard about Paris since I was a little boy. We had been through there going to Rouen and I know I was fascinated by the boulevards, the squares and the tour Eiffel. It was an entire new world to be discovered so I was kind of excited about it. After all I had lived in a forest for 2 long school terms and that was enough.

The day arrived soon and we were all in my dad's car on the way to Paris.

The trip took 2 days. We slept in a wonderful hotel in Lyon and had dinner surrounded by waiters making sure our glasses were always filled and our dishes were promptly removed. I have always been very fond of desserts and that evening I had 3 different ones. The next afternoon we arrived in Paris where we had two rooms booked at the hotel de la Ville near Notre Dame. We dined at Chez Maxime with a very famous pianist sitting at the table next to ours, Arthur Rubinstein, who at the end of his dinner smoked a big Havana cigar.

The city was intriguing me. I knew it was called "la ville lumiere" but I had never seen so many lights dazzling all over.

The next morning we were on the way to Charenton where the boarding school was located. Charenton is a district famous for its schools and it's in between the downtown area and the Porte de Clignancourt, site of a very big flea market.

Chapter 4

Paris 1961

The building was nice and impressive shaped like a big T. A higher tower was in the center of this construction. On the left side there were younger boys from the 1st elementary class to the 3rd medium high class; on the right there were the young men going to the 5 years of high school. The tower was just for show and the back of the building hosted the dining room, the indoor pool, the studying room, the kitchen and the apartments of the monitors, the cleaning people and the apartment of the "director", Monsieur Doctor Girardet. He is the one that greeted my parents in his office. After the acquaintance a nice woman in her late twenties showed us my room, my armoire, my bed, and introduced me to Jean Louis, my roommate. She was in charge with all the young boys living there. On the other side there were the older guys with a male monitor looking after them.

Ms. Girardet suggested my parents to leave while I was introduced to my new friends and so they did. Even though I had been alone before, that was like something traumatic happening in my life. Now I was over 1500 kms from home and it would take me 15 hours by train to go home! Planes in those days were not too safe and then besides Genova did not have an airport, I should have gone through Milano and ride a train from there.

The director had a degree in psychology and was running the compound with very modern ideas for the times. The school was located next door. We had access through a gate on the left side. Our living area was for male students only, the school was mixed including students from that section of town. In my class there were 26 pupils. The teachers were nice except for…you guessed it! The prof. Of math!

It didn't take a long time to figure out where everything was and to get around in the building. There was a game room, a cinema, a TV room and a music room.

In the morning the loudspeakers were broadcasting classical music to wake us up. Breakfast was at 7,30 and consisted in a croissant, butter, jam, coffee and milk or hot coco. Then off to school until 1pm. Lunch was served at 1,30. Intermission until 4pm. From 4 to 6 everybody had to study and do the homework, supervised by a couple of monitors ready to answer any question concerning different subjects. From 6 to 7,30 we were usually in the game room or in the pool area until a bell would announce the serving of the dinner. Curfew was at 10 when everybody had to be in bed with the lights turned off. The older guys could stay up until 11pm.

The big novelty was that we all were given a certain number of "points" every week: 30 to go out and about and 16 to watch TV programs between 8 and 10.

Each point to leave the place was worth 15 minutes; to watch TV was worth 20 minutes.

If we had a punishment of any kind we would be penalized by losing points. During the weekend we could take off providing we were picked up by relatives or friends of the family known to the director. In this case everybody had to be back by 7,30 pm on Sunday.

Every Saturday at 3pm there was a line of guys in front of the Director's office who would give us a weekly allowance agreed with each family but never to exceed 10 NFs, the equivalent of 5$. We could get more if we had to buy stuff like toothpaste, soap etc. at the internal store that was open daily for1 hour.

I started studying the guys around my age to see which one was more interesting for a possible close friendship but frankly I found them rather ignorant and not too attractive. Some older guy was catching my attention and soon I started going around with them leaving the others to their childish games. Charles was just stunning: 4 inches taller than me, nice body, black hair and sky blue eyes. There were at least nine that I was attracted to but of course I never did or said anything to make somebody suspicious. I was, as the Director put it, like a piece of furniture that never changed or got scratched by the elements surrounding it.

I was missing home but I was getting over that quickly. If they didn't want me around…fine, I had other things that kept my mind occupied and first of all I wanted to explore that city so big and fascinating.

On a Saturday afternoon I would use all my weekly points to go around. I bought myself a map and learned how to use the subway system. I walked all over, visited museums, got special permits to go even further, to Versailles. Spent entire days in the palace, the gardens, the petit trianon imagining all the parties and intrigues that had happen there, thinking about Marie Antoinette chatting and gossiping with the courtesans and imagining the fear of having the people invading the salons to take the king and his family prisoners. The Louvre was one of my favorite spots. I wasn't much impressed by the Monna Lisa but there was a painting that I was particularly crazy about, it was an old man carrying a candle. The light of the flame was shining creating some shadows in the room. It was stunning.

A few times I managed to go out with my new cute friend Charles, trying to impress him and to find out if there was some remote mutual understanding similar to the one of my mountain friend. It never came to anything and I understood he was dating a girl that was in his same class. (I learned a few years ago that they had married and settled in Beauvais, a city 60 kms north of Paris).

The passion for classical music and opera was probably inherited from my mother's genes. She was a soprano and had a very good voice. She had a teacher in Venezia called Toti dal Monte, very famous soprano in the 30's and 40's. We often went to "la Fenice", the most famous theater in Venezia, to see full scale operas and to hear several concerts. I'm saying all this because waking up to classical music every morning reinforced in me the desire of going to the Opera' in Paris. Fortunately the Director liked the arts too and I convinced him to form groups of students who wanted to go to see some good performances. There was a bus on the premises that was used occasionally for daily trips to interesting sites such as Waterloo and Fontainebleau. The evening of the performance a small group of students was conducted to the theater. It was always a success. I also managed to see a good performance of Callas in "Tosca" and a memorable "Boheme" sung by Renata Tebaldi.

One night, coming back from the theater, I heard some gossip about two older guys that had been expelled because they had been caught masturbating each other. The news made a big sensation. I still didn't know much about sex and my curiosity was increasing. The more I was asking the more the other guys were smiling, laughing and thinking I was joking on the matter. All my doubts were cleared when, a few days later, the Director called a meeting with the guys of my age in his private apartment.

He started talking about flowers, pollen, bees, and explained to us how the plants were reproducing. Then he talked about the male and female anatomy showing slides of the reproduction organs and how everything was taking place. When he talked about reaching orgasm I did not know what he was talking about…so I made the famous question: I understand all that, but…after the male has inserted his penis in the vagina of the female, how long does he have to wait to fecundate the egg? He smiled and said that I had not reached puberty yet, so I would find out in due time.

That night I thought for several hours before falling asleep about the orgasm and what it really physically meant, wondering what was Charles feeling when he was sleeping with his girlfriend. Was it something that could be reached only if a girl was present? I was feeling too stupid to ask somebody so I kept quiet for weeks.

One night I had to go to pee after curfew so I went to the bathroom making sure I didn't wake up anybody. The light in the room of the monitor was on. When I reached the urinal I saw there was a guy standing there stroking his hard penis. Very excited by that vision I approached him and started looking when he invited me to touch it. So I did. He started touching me and I immediately got an erection. Almost at the same time the monitor walked into the bathroom to see what was going on. Each one of us went straight to bed hoping the incident had finished there.

The Director did not say anything to me during the next three days, but the other guy was expelled never to be seen again. Finally the Director called me to his office and told me that he was not proceeding against me because I still didn't know about ejaculation (remembering my question) but he had to inform my father of the incident for my own good.

My father came to Paris a few weeks later, had the talk with Ms. Girardet, than took me out to lunch but did not mention a word about the matter. Was this a good or a bad sign? I had never really had a dialogue with my dad; he was seldom there and when he was he did not have much to say. Everything passed over like a very fast wind and I went back to my usual life.

My parents had some close friends in Paris. Sometimes I was invited to spend the weekend at their home located in Montparnasse, by the Moulin Rouge. This area is very beautiful inhabited by artists. The church of Sacre Coeur is just a few blocks away and also the most famous show of transvestites is in the neighborhood: Chez Madame Arthur.

One Sunday afternoon I went out for a walk and passed by the "gay" theater. I noticed that upstairs they had an atelier. Some windows were open and I heard some people chatting and laughing loud. Curious, I went upstairs where I saw a bunch of older men cutting material, sewing and making embroideries. This was the atelier where the costumes for the transvestites were made. When they saw me they invited me in, they asked my age, and they told me about their vocation in life. It was interesting but I felt sorry for them because they didn't really look like men nor women. Some had a 2 day beard but was wearing make up and mascara and they had a shrill voice. One was probably trying to understand if I could be one of them or just somebody there by mistake. When I told them I was Italian they started talking about Farinelli and the famous "white voices" at the Vatican in the 15th century.

I left them promising I would go back there to see their new costumes. And so I did… but id didn't happen until about 15 years later.

Walking up the hill to the church of Sacre Coeur I noticed something was going on around the bushes and I did notice a really handsome guy looking at me and touching his crotch. It was just after dark on a Saturday evening and not many people were around. With my heart pounding I left the paved walkway and sneaked away in the direction of that bush. Sure enough there was this 30 years old guy asking me to get closer. My face was all red and my blood pressure was rising. He started hugging me, touching and finally he unzipped his pants revealing his big and hard penis. He put my hand on it and told me to stroke it gently, then he let my pants go down to my knees and was doing the same thing with mine. Not many words were said but suddenly he started moaning and he ejaculated on the grass. Finally I had seen what everybody was talking about. They guy seemed to have a pleasure mask on his face. As soon as he cleaned my hand he pulled up his pants and disappeared without saying a word. I didn't reach the so called orgasm but that adventure had put me in a very different mood willing to see and do more.

That night, as you may remember I was a guest over my family's friends, I didn't sleep well because I was thinking about the bible, God, who had seen it all, and the punishment that I would have incurred one day when this fact would become public knowledge. My fear was also that somebody could have witness what happened and would tell the Director…you never know!

The rest of the school year went by pretty fast, studying and socializing with some of the guys. I became pretty close to Jean, a cute 16 year old on the 2nd year of high school. Once his parents took me out to lunch and invited me to spend a weekend in their country house south of Paris, a village called Melun.

I was not sure if Jean was so friendly because he expected something to happen or just because he was a nice guy…anyway one month later we did go to Melun. I expected to sleep in his room, but I was in a guest room and much to my surprise a girl showed up to spend the weekend with the family. She turned out to be Jean's girlfriend from 2 summers before. There died my hope and I concentrated on having a good time with that nice and cute couple. Eventually we became good friends and we were still talking a few years ago.

It was the end of the school year. I had done well in every subject, except in math where I was barely sufficient. It was time to say goodbye to books and school for the next three months and enjoy the company of my old friends in Lavarone.

I got on the train very happy to leave everything behind and found a seat near a cute older guy. The trip was long…why not trying! Nothing happened.

Concetta was happy to see me; she was so happy she had cooked my favorite meal, potatoes gnocchi, and my favorite dessert, crepes suzettes. My friends gave a very warm welcome and told me they had been missing me a lot during those few weeks (the school in France ended later than in Italy). One day to adapt and recover from the 12 hours trip and I was running wild on the fields and in the woods. I had too hook up in some spare time with my two local friends to tell them about my adventures in Paris but, surprise-surprise, one had a girlfriend and the other had gone to work in Trento for the summer.

Not much happened during the summer. Soon it was time to close the mountain house and to go back to Genova where I would have gone shopping with my mom for new clothes and go back to Paris.

It was during those two weeks that I was soaking in the tub in my bathroom, reading a comic and touching my hard penis going up and down as I had seen the guys in Paris doing. Well, all of a sudden I felt something like I never felt before. A deep pleasure pervaded my whole body and some sperm kept coming out clouding the water and making it stick to my skin. I remember that I had to clean and scrub the tub well before I got out of that bathroom since I didn't want anyone to even think what went on. From that day on, masturbation became a daily routine.

The trip back to Paris was quite pleasant due to the fact that my sister drove me there. She was going to spend a few months in England but she stayed in Paris for a week. Because she was a relative I was allowed by the Director to spend my free time with her and we went around the city visiting even more museums and exploring areas where I had never been. My favorite spot besides Montmartre became Saint Germain des Pres also known as the Latin quarter. I was fond of French history and I knew what went on there in the 17th century when the underground area was occupied by the "court of miracles" and not even the police dared to raid that site. Then there was the sadly famous "place de greves", now place de ville, where hundreds of people were executed burned at the stake or by the guillotine. The narrow streets are a reminder of what the older Paris used to be before the great fire and the re-built ordered by Napoleon.

The structure of the city is magnificent. The large boulevards can accommodate all the heavy traffic in both directions. The "peripherique" is a loop around the "arrondissements" that form the numerous sections of town enabling to drive fast from one part to the other. The "place de la Concorde" at the foot of the Champs Elysees is very wide indeed and the palaces with their characteristic roofs are imposing.

The only thing I did not get used to was the freezing wind in winter and the cold weather almost all year round. By nature I'm always cold and sometimes the heavy coat, scarf and gloves were not enough.

At some corners they were selling hot omelettes a' la confiture, basically crepes. I used to spend a lot of money on them. The bistros are really good restaurants and I could warm up just having a soupe a' l'oignon covered with melted cheese over bread. Sometimes I could sneak out in the morning during the weekends and have some full French breakfast with crunchy bread, warm croissants and any kind of jam I wanted. Did I ever mentioned that I love everything that is sweet?

Back at the boarding school I found more or less the same guys of the previous school year except for those that had completed the 5th year of high school. Everybody was talking about their holidays, some had photos to show around. Everything went back to normal after the 1st week.

On every Sunday afternoon they were showing a movie on the big screen, mostly gags with Charlot or Stan Laurel and Oliver Hardy, but sometimes there were good films followed up by a general discussion lead by a monitor. There was one film that they were showing periodically: Titanic. We came to the conclusion that they must have bought that movie because it was always breaking in the same two segments.

I was spending some of my free time with Charles and with him I started talking about sex and the experience that I had at home. He laughed and said: "so you finally reached the stage of puberty! Good for you! Did you start growing hair in your pubic area?" I was noticing that something was slowly changing in my body. Hair was growing on my forearms, under my armpits, on my legs and in the pubic area and I also was experiencing acne on my face, sign, I guessed, that my beard was coming out. The most annoying thing was happening at night, during my sleep: I was having night pollutions due to the fact that having erotic dreams I was ejaculating in my pajama and through that on the sheets. That was embarrassing and also messy. They were changing the linens once a week and I thought that with all the sheets they were washing they couldn't tell mine from the others, still I hated that so I started going to bed wearing my underwear too in order not to mess up the sheets. That didn't help much.

I talked to Jean about it and he said that it was a natural occurrence, nothing to be worried about. The people in the laundry were accustomed to it and it was happening to them as well. That reassured me but I still thought it was a messy business. I certainly couldn't let that happen at home with Concetta, she would have told my mother, father and who knows what. In my family I never heard anybody talking about sex, not even a dirty word was ever pronounced. So, I came up with a solution to the problem: before going to bed I would wrap my penis in a small plastic bag and put a small rubber band around the base. The system worked fine except for the mess to clean up the next morning. This was becoming a nightly event. I liked to have erotic dreams but hated the mess that they were causing. I thought that daily masturbation would have helped but it seldom did. I talked about the matter to Charles and he also told me not to worry and enjoy it. He said that girls had a worse problem than guys for a few days every month, so we were lucky in comparison and pleasant too.

The real surprise got me a few weeks later when I was called to the office of the Director.

He started asking me if I was experiencing some physical changes and if finally, I started having orgasms. After my affirmative answer he told me that, due to his studies on the juvenile puberty, he had to take some pictures of me…naked. He was a nice person to talk to but not at all physically appealing and I was kind of reluctant to submit. On the other hand I didn't have any problems in allowing him to proceed and I went to his apartment. He had a room with a sealed window arranged with big reflectors. He took several pictures and disappeared in the dark room telling me to get dressed. That was all and he never ever talked about it again. I didn't tell that to a living soul but after several years I learned that the Director was fired from his position because suspected of being a pedophile. That's why he was often coming to the shower room, sit on a chair, and look at all the guys washing! Probably he was running upstairs, looking at god knows how many pictures and masturbate leaving his fantasies running wild.

After the 1ˢᵗ quarter, when I came back from the Christmas holiday, there was a new student, 16 years old, who had moved to Paris from Toronto. Tall, slim, dirty blonde, green eyes and with a killer smile. His father was a diplomat, his mother had died in a plane crash, and he was basically a loner, misunderstood (he thought) by his dad. Moving so much he didn't have time to cultivate the friendship with other guys his age and he was basically a loner, a bit like me after I moved out of Venezia.

The encounter was casual while I was leaving for a weekend and he was coming out from the TV room. Our eyes met, we smiled, said "hi" and didn't see each other for three days. I saw him in the game room one afternoon, he was reading a magazine, I was playing chess with Jean. Finished the game, I walked over to him, smiled and introduced myself. His name was Alan. His mom died when he was 6 and he had been living in South Africa, Holland, Brazil and now Paris. We started talking and the time just went by so fast that we had to say goodnight and go to our respective rooms. I was very excited because I found somebody who knew what I was feeling inside since he had more or less had the same experiences.

He was very mature for his age and didn't like to mingle with other guys because he found them too superficial and interested only in childish amusements. The weeks in the class with homework and all were going fast and we were saving our points to go out walking in the big town on Saturday and Sunday afternoons. His father was never around but that didn't bother him, he was used to it. It was like we had met a long time before and now we were together for some peculiar design of destiny. The surprise was also that his birthday was on January 27, just one week before mine.

I never dared to talk about sex but I was curious to know what he thought about it, being three years older and all. We started talking about religion and agreed on certain aspect of the teaching of Christ. The fact that Martin Luther broke with the Catholic Church and started the protestant movement in Germany was very understandable considering those days in which the pope was the absolute ruler in Europe above kings, princes and dukes. We agreed on the fact that the bible was written by wise people and also that the various translations from Hebrew into Greek, Latin and consequently all the other languages added different meanings to the original text and maybe was tailor made to suit the clergy and the aristocrats at the expenses of the masses. He didn't like the fact that the Vatican kept the people in the dark and prevented people like Galilei to express their theories and opinions and told me that other religions were much more open and permissive than the Christian like the Buddhist, for instance. At that point I became very interested in knowing more about it so he loaned me some books that he had red on the subject.

I had heard about Tibet and knew about the Chinese invasion in that pacific country. What I didn't know was that they were Buddhist, had a spiritual leader, the Dalai Lahma, who was forced into exile by the Chinese army. Reading about the lamas, the theory of reincarnation, the life of Buddha, was like a dream come true! I often thought of past lives, reincarnation, the meaning of this life. Questions like: where are we coming, why are we here, where are we going, what's going to happen after death and so on were popping in my mind continuously. It was like a volcano erupting without control. I had passed sleepless nights because I kept thinking endlessly. Now Alan had opened a window from which I couldn't see a horizon but a lot of light.

Alan and I became inseparable. Even Jean complained that I was not spending much time with him, but he was spending most of his free time with his girlfriend anyway and I knew there could never been much between us.

The school year went by in a swift and there came the day of departure. Alan was going to some country with his dad but didn't have any plans for august. I asked him if he wanted to come to Lavarone to visit me and he accepted gladly.

Back at home I had the usual great welcome. I had passed all the school tests with honor except for a "just sufficient" in math. Not that I cared anyway: I hated that subject with passion.

After spending fifteen days with my sister in Torre del Mare, a beautiful resort on the Riviera where my dad had just bought a house, we went to Lavarone where I finally got reunited with my friends. One year older, one year wiser, our usual habits were starting to change. Almost all the guys now had a girlfriend carefully selected among the usual group. We were going to the disco in the evening, going home late at night, some were disappearing along the way with their g/friend in the woods.

The schedule was: meeting by the Cervo Hotel after breakfast, meaning 10,30-11am, hanging around chatting and deciding what to do in the afternoon after lunch, meeting at the same place around 2pm, going for a walk in the woods. Go home for dinner and meeting again at the same place around 8,30 or 9pm. That's when the real plans for the evening were made. Sometimes we did not reach a unanimous decision at midnight when it was time to go back home.

The routine stopped with the arrival of Alan on the 1st week of august. I was so excited that I convinced my sister to drive to Trento to pick him up at the train station. For the occasion Concetta cooked a French dinner surprising Alan. My mother welcomed him like another son and they prepared the room next to mine on the 3rd floor.

After dinner we walked to the square to meet my friends. Some spoke French, some English making it easy on him. Two of the girls were already taken by his looks and that made me kind of jealous. Now it was the time to see what his attitude was about girls.

We had a great time walking around. I had to show him the woods, the special spots, the "Belem" a little natural terrace overlooking the "Valsugana" 1000 meters below (a valley with 2 lakes). He liked good food and Concetta made sure that by the end of august he had tried all the possible Italian specialties.

Alan was very courteous with everybody but he didn't seem to be more interested in girls so I finally had to ask him. His answer was: "I like everybody as long as they have something interesting to say but I think that sex and love are two different things. If I love somebody I don't care about looks, age or gender. When the time will come I will fall in love and that will be the right person".

I did not inquire further but I was happy to have his friendship and was hoping to be friends for life.

We organized a long walk in the woods and all the way to the top of a mountain. All my friends were coming. Everybody was carrying food like bread, cheese, ham, chicken, fruits, veggies and a lot of drinks. Concetta prepared for the two of us some cheese crepes, caviar on bread butter and lemon and of course a chilled bottle of champagne with some crème caramel to eat as dessert. It was about 1pm when we found a nice spot on a field and sat to eat. When the others saw what we had in the rucksack they went nuts: that lunch became the famous tale for years to come! even now they remember it as very funny and distinguished. At the end of the walk, at least 20 kms long, we were exhausted but very happy to have accomplished it. My feet hurt for a couple of days and poor Alan had to go buy another pair of shoes because his broke down.

I forgot to tell that during the hike up the valley we found a hand bomb, residue from the 2nd world war. We didn't touch it but signed the area and informed the police about it. The following week it was recovered and an officer told us they made it explode. It looked like a tube with some kind of a handle.

August was slowly ending and Alan was preparing to leave. The separation would have been a short one because in two weeks we would have been together in Paris once more. That would be the 3rd and last year of my permanence at the boarding school. I was turning 13.

At the end of the school year there were the final examinations for the junior high school and I knew it was going to be tough. I did not apply myself too much on the subjects that I loved such as literature, history, geography, English, civic education and Latin, but I was concentrating more on math, physics and chemistry that I cordially hated.

Alan managed to sit next to my desk in the studying room so he could give me tips and help me if I needed it.

Each year the number of "TV " and "free exit" points were increasing so we could spend more time going around in the city. We spent endless days at the flea market where I wanted to buy a lot of stuff. I always had a passion for antiques and started collecting items since I was 6. I must say that besides the money that the Director was giving me every Saturday I also was getting money from my grandmother, my mother and my father enabling me to spend much more that a kid my age could. The fact is that everybody was contributing something without knowing that others were doing the same. I got away with it for years! The cash was flowing through the friends of my family in Paris because at the school we were not supposed to have more than the set amount. I had a money belt hidden under the vest.

That last year was full of events. The Director organized a trip to the south of France to visit Montecarlo, Nice and Cannes. There were 30 of us on the bus but Alan was not among us because it was reserved to the students of the 3rd year. We went to the Isles de Lerins and visited the fortress where the man of the iron mask was kept prisoner (it seems he was the unwonted brother of Louis XIV, the king Sun. We also went to see a monastery where the monks had their own winery with dwarf plants of grapes. We sunbathed on the rocks and some, the most courageous, ventured to swim in the cold sea.

Nice was a very nice, colorful city with nice wide streets and the world famous "promenade des Anglais" by the sea. The botanical garden was also very famous and so was the sea museum in Montecarlo.

On the bus on the way back they were singing French country songs accompanied by a guy that was playing the guitar. I must say the trip was very well organized and the hotels were excellent as much as the food.

Back in my room I noticed that clothes and personal belongings of my roommate were gone. The monitor told me that his father had a stroke and she doubted he would be back. There were still four and a half months left to the end of the school year, plus another 15 days for the final examinations. That meant I would be the only one in that room for the rest of the term…not bad at all.

The only relevant thing that happened during those last months was the encounter with an 18 year old guy from the other wing. He had looked at me several times in a certain way I couldn't miss. One Sunday evening almost everybody was watching a soccer game on TV and he asked me to meet him in the game room. He told me to follow him and we went to the laundry where he opened a linen closet and pulled me in. We fooled around for about half an hour and for the first time my orgasm was caused by a foreign hand. That experience was so "different" that I had to replicate it whenever possible. To add more suspense there was the fear that someone could have caught us. Fortunately there wasn't a soul around.

When school finally ended I had one week to seriously prepare for the examinations. First we had those in writing, then the orals. My preoccupation was just for math, physics and chemistry as for all the other subjects I could make the tests being blind.

Alan was leaving for the Summer, the following term would have been his last in high school. We were both sad to part and swore that no matter what we would have kept in touch for the rest of our lives. I invited him to spend some time in Lavarone but his father had plans to go to Australia. He promised he would do the impossible to come over for the Christmas holiday.

I was under stress. The written tests were quite easy but the scientific subjects were just too odd. The oral was much better: I had the ability to guide the teachers to ask me just what I wanted to be asked. I passed with the average of 7.

My sister joined me in Paris and my mother arrived a couple of days later. They helped me pack everything and on that June 16th 1960 I finally said "goodbye" to that boarding school, the monitors, the Directors and to that room with the uncomfortable little bed!

We headed back to Genova stopping in Geneve Switzerland where we visited some relatives.

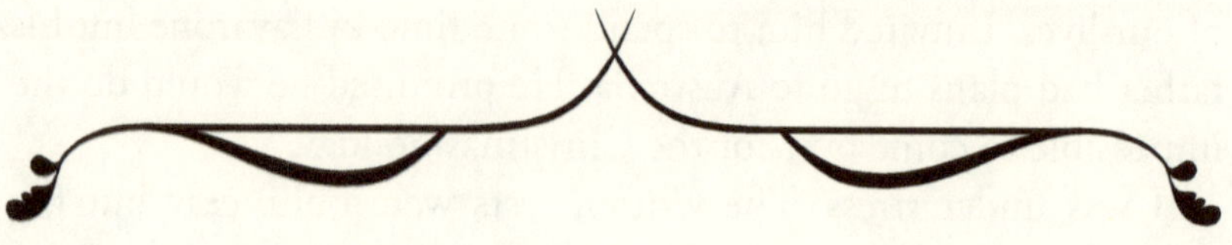

Chapter 5

Genova

Concetta was by the gate welcoming us with a big hug and complimenting me on the recent promotion. My father was in New York taking care of business but he did send me a telegram for the occasion. At that point I just wanted to amuse myself, enjoy the summer without thinking of school works and think about what I wanted to do next. In the Italian system after the medium high we can chose the "classic" the "scientific" the "maritime" the "hotel" and the "avviamento" (kind of general notions of different subjects with specific input to skills like carpentry, mechanical, construction etc.).

I knew that if I had gone for one of the first two I would have probably ended in another boarding school and that was to be avoided categorically. The maritime was only in Genova or Venezia in the north of Italy. My dad had gone to the one in Genova and the present dean had been his professor of math back in 1922. There was no reason why my parents would send me to a different city.

My sister was dating a guy 17 years older than she was that she had met in Torino at a fashion show. He was very charming, handsome, 6'3" tall but absolutely not sexually appealing to me. I was wondering why she fell for him with all the cute nice boyfriends she had around. My father was not too happy because of the age difference, in the meantime my grandmother was in Milano to inquire about his family.

Wilma, my sister, and I went to spend the usual two week in Torre del Mare on the Riviera. Bruno, that was his name, was driving there from Milano almost every afternoon to take us out for dinner, then drive back home. One hundred ten miles each way! At the speed of at least 100 miles/h since in those days there was no speed limit.

Around sunset he was arriving and calling my sister from the intercom, we would go out for dinner and by midnight he would go back to Milano. He was nice enough but I whished she had dated that nice Dutch guy she had met in Madrid the previous year.

We went up to Lavarone at the beginning of July and I reunited with my friends.

There was somebody new in our company, Roberto, a guy my age from Genova. Red hair, glasses, kind of cute, very straight. We became good friends and incidentally we were living just a few blocks away in the city.

Meeting him changed my life in Genova. He was born there, was going to school there and had a bunch of friends. We had many things in common, loved the mountains, the sea, horseback riding, tennis, playing cards and had the same ideas in politic. He was going to the classic high school just one block from the maritime high and he was good mathematically inclined.

Being from Genova I had the pleasure to introduce him to the rest of the gang. When he met Anna, my friend from Bologna, it was love at first sight! (they are still married today and have 2 daughters and 1 son).

The summer months became more relaxed. We were meeting at the usual bar three times a day and we were still endlessly deciding what to do and where to go but the big happening was in the evening. Lavarone has 1200 inhabitants but during the holidays the hotels and the rental houses get filled with many people passing the 5000 units. We had a mini golf, tennis courts, horse stables, the lake to swim with two little beaches, plenty of walks in the woods and several night clubs. We had out favorite clubs and we would walk from one to the other according to our moods. The music of the fifties in Italy was mellow but some great singers appeared on the horizon at the beginning of the sixties like Mina, Gianni Morandi, little Tony, Celentano and Rita Pavone. Many English and American singers were also very popular. Some songs became bestsellers and the vinyl records were selling like hotcakes. Our favorite hang out place was "la ruota" a disco in the basement of a big hotel owned by the father of Ketty, a girl of our company. The good thing was that we never paid cover charge, the music was good, the place was dark and the dance floor big enough to accommodate a lot of couples. Being part of the group I was playing along and had my girlfriend, Paolalberta. She was a very pretty red haired girl, exactly my age, and we had known each other since we were 5. I have always been a practical joker. I remember when one night I put the empty bottle of a coke in my pants and I invited her to dance. Those were slow dances, shake had not been invented and the only fast dances were the hally galli and the twist. I started getting close to her and half way into the song, I had her crotch pressing on the "hard" and quite large bottle. She tried to get away with a disgusted look on her face. The whole thing did not remain unnoticed by our friends and everybody was laughing like crazy. Another time she was wearing a toupee' and when I tickled her on her waist she made a movement that threw her toupee on the floor. One night, at the cinema I tried to kiss her in the mouth, she refused and slapped my face. Everybody heard the slap but before they understood what was really going on, I said: "this is just a taste of what you'll get if you'll do that again"!

In spite of all that we were still, and are, great friends.

Often after the disco we were going to have a pizza at the "Pom" and then back to the silent square sitting around the tables of the bar chatting until 2 or 3 in the morning.

In the village there was not much to get in trouble. The policemen knew us and were closing an eye if we were not behaving too properly. Among us there was also the nephew of a national hero who died on a mission against the Austrians during the 1st world war (every town in Italy has a street named after him).

We had discovered a restaurant way up on a mountain where they were cooking the best steaks and several times we had to beg somebody who had a car and driver license to take us there. The food was exceptional and very cheap. We would spend hours eating, drinking, chatting, telling jokes around the fireplace. Some morning we were going to take sun at the lake and some of us, the most foolhardy, were swimming in the freezing water. For your information it is a natural lake and it's up to 75' deep in the center.

The summer was slowly coming to an end and it was time to say goodbye once again but…there was a novelty: the community of Lavarone was building five long slopes and for the 1st time they were going to have a winter season for skiing and ice skating. Most of us did not have a central heating at home and before leaving we had to make sure there was no water left in the plumbing because the temperature was going well below freezing during the winter. So the only logical solution was to reserve a room at the "Cervo" for the 15 days of Christmas holiday. It would be a lot of fun to meet again and spend some quality time together on the snow for a change.

My father was exceptionally in town for two weeks and tried to dissuade me to go to maritime school. I knew he was right even because that involved a lot of math… but I did not change my mind so we went to the secretary and registered. The class was starting on the 3rd of October. I had to buy the books and get ready for this new task. In those days that was an only male lyceum. The subjects were: Math, Italian, English, chemistry, design, physics, maritime arts, astronomy and navigation, history, geography and Morse Code. After the 1st three years we would get rid of Morse, geography, maritime arts, design (except for those that chose construction and planning), physics and chemistry because we had to concentrate on the remaining subjects with emphasis on trigonometry.

Each subject had a different professor who thought his or her subject was the most important in the program. The whole picture sounded tough as hell.

I knew I had to concentrate on math and company because on the others my background was pretty strong.

This is not a private school so I had to take the streetcar or the bus every morning and in 10 minutes I was at the school. The class was from 8am till 1pm and twice a week in the afternoon from 3 till 6.

In Italy we could not drive a car before the age of 18 but at 14 we could have a motorcycle (Vespa) with a maximum of 50cc engine. Its maximum speed could not, in theory, exceed 50Km/h. I had to wait until February in order to get it even though it was way too cold in winter to drive such a vehicle. Of course a Vespa was synonymous of "freedom" and that was what everybody my age wanted.

My new friend Roberto who was starting the 1st classic lyceum introduced me to his friends and soon I was a happy camper because it was very difficult to enter a close group of friends in Genova. We all lived in the same area and we were meeting at the bar Tonitto, famous for the best ice creams in town. I became one of the guys and that legacy is still going on these days.

School started and we met all the professors. Between Miss Foco, the Italian/history teacher, and I, was love at first sight. She was knowledgeable and knew how to teach. Mrs. Munna, Math., was not that nice and, of course, she didn't know how to teach. Mrs. Marescotti, physics, was peculiar: she was tall and skinny with a heavy Tuscan accent, and she would go crazy talking about Galilei, Da Vinci and others. Mrs. Ghisaura, geography, was a real "character". She would spend hours talking about her subjects while the class was totally out of control: some were chatting, some using rubber bands to through pieces of paper, some were listening to the radio and some were constantly asking to go to the loo so they could smoke a cigarette in the hallway! It was a complete anarchy. Mr. Bartolini, naval art, would not allow anyone to whisper. He was explaining, then ask someone to repeat the lesson: if the unfortunate did not repeat word by word, he would write an insufficient vote on the register. Mr. Gulli was teaching maritime art, knots, sailing, rowing and anything concerning the equipment of a vessel. He had 4 hours every Saturday morning and if the weather was cooperating we would go to the port to row on the two big boats that the school owned. It is memorable the fact that once everybody was on board and he took too much time to step into the boat: he fell into the frigid water leaving his hat floating! Fortunately he was promptly rescued and taken to a nearby office to change and dry.

Once a week, in the afternoon, we had to go to the gymnasium with Mr. Caffaretto. He was a good teacher but he was a soccer maniac. I hate soccer with passion but we were obliged to form the teams and play because even his votes had a certain importance on the general average. The dean, Mr. Levi, was a short little fat character and would pop in from time to time to check on our preparation in the various subjects.

During the 20 minute morning breaks some guys were talking to the teachers, others would go outside to smoke a cigarette and some would wait for the most shy guys to go to the bathroom, hold them, pull their pants down, and sign their name on the guy's ass. This practice was so common in that school that even the teachers did not intervene or even talk about it.

Everything started smooth. The homework was kind of heavy but nothing really impossible to fulfill. I befriended three schoolmates that lived in my neighborhood and we often go together to study in the afternoon. During the weekends I was getting together with my friend Roberto, the one I met in Lavarone, and with other guys we would spend long evenings playing cards or going to the piper. The piper was a famous newly opened disco very popular among teenagers.

Some Saturday nights we would go to dine out and then we would raid the semi-deserted narrow streets of the old downtown filled with prostitutes and their pimps. I remember one of us carrying a big magnifying lens, approaching some old lady, taking a close look and screaming: "look, this is an old mummy from the 3rd dynasty"! while she was screaming: "1$ for a blowjob in the hallway or 3$ for a fuck in my room"!

During the nice rarely warm winter Sundays, if my father was in town, we had to go to short car trips to Portofino, Santa Margherita and other locations on the Ligurian Riviera. You should know that the Riviera back then had only one main road, the Roman built Aurelia, running from Roma to Marseille. The traffic was horrendous, bumper to bumper for hours during the week ends also due to the fact that people from Milano and other cities were coming to the see to enjoy the scenery. If I had a choice I would spend my day at home relaxing, watching TV or together with my friends but my father was very offended if that had been my choice. Of course I hated Mondays because I had to start the week all over again, going to school and getting up early.

At school most guys were smoking and I had to try what that was like. During a morning break I finally inhaled some smoke and started coughing. I did not like the taste of it and it made my throat itch. I gave it up for the time being. Back then most people had that bad habit and for us teenagers it was a way to overcome a sense of insecurity due to our age and to overcome shyness. Nobody was smoking in my family except for my sister who used to smoke one after meals. Her story with Bruno was unfolding so well that they decided to get married at the end of February 1961. The respective families had met once in Milano, once in Genova. He was leader in the perfume industry. Had the agency for Italy of the famous Lubin company based in Paris and he had 19 sub agents in Italy selling perfumes, beauty creams and custom jewelry.

His father, a 1st world war hero, had built a five story building in Milano where the whole family resided. On the ground floor there were his offices and the laboratory. Needless to say that I was showered with cologne and after shave.

My grandmother came to visit before the wedding and she took me on a shopping spree to prepare for the wedding. Among clothes, shoes and other things she bought me my first golden watch and a matching ring with the coat of arm of my family. I had wanted a ring since I was five and I was so happy about that.

Christmas arrived and so did our two weeks break from school. Strong of the results obtained in those first three months I convinced my parents to let me go to Lavarone to ski with my friends and I left with Roberto, his mother and his two sisters. That was going to be a vacation to remember!

I had gone skiing before with my family in Andermatt, Switzerland. The difference was that this time I was staying at the Cervo in a room all by myself surrounded by all my best friends and god knows what we could do!

A typical day: Wake up late, have breakfast in bed, go downstairs to see who had got up.

We would finally regroup and get ready to catch the small free bus to go to the base of the ski-lift and then up to the big slopes.

The trees were loaded with the white fluffy snow, the sky was blue, the temperature was freezing but it felt good with the protection of the well-insulated uniform. It was a must to wear goggles to protect the eyes from the reflection of the sun. I also had a blue helmet.

We were skiing until about 1,30, then had lunch at the "Tana Incantata" then back to the slopes until sunset. The last descent was the nicest down the Blue slope. It was not as difficult as the Green but it was awesome. It was winding among the forest for about three miles. The silence was interrupted only by the screech of some birds or by the noise of the heavier blocks of snow falling from the branches stretched out to the sky like invoking God. Tired but happy we would arrive to the end of our ski-run and meet at the bar by the Cimone Hotel where we would sit and drink a hot chocolate.

Back to the Cervo it was shower time and we would get in some more comfortable clothes in order to make a good appearance at the dinner table.

Since there were 18 of us, the management had set up a long U table. The rest of the guests were family groups with many kids. The menu was varied and plentiful. Sometimes we were driving the waitresses crazy with strange and out of the ordinary requests. When the long dinner was over we had the difficult task of deciding what to do in the long evening ahead. The Ruota was always the logical choice but sometimes we were playing cards or going bar- hopping with the natives. Paolalberta's room was next to mine. Several times I tried to attempt to her "purity" more for fun then for desire. She let me kiss and touch her but she never let me go further than that. It was understood by the group that her and I were coupled. How were they wrong!

One steady couple was forming there between Roberto and Anna, my friend from Bologna, there was something more than friendship going on.

The last day of 1960 was approaching and the preparation for the big dinner was on. I had brought my tuxedo for the occasion. All the girls were having their hair done while the electric breakers of the hotel were switching off every ten minutes for the large demand of power. The dinner started at ten and it consisted of consommé' of tortellini, pork with lentils, spinach and roasted potatoes (lentils are a symbol of plenty for the new year), various desserts and bottles of Dom Perignon to be opened at the strike of midnight. None of us was a big drinker but the wine to accompany the meal and the champagne at the end was a must. After the greetings we were on the way to the Ruota to party until daybreak.

That early morning we were walking around the main square chanting obscene songs when someone got the idea of going to the Catholic church for the 6am mass. Gigi, a friend from Padova, wanted to smoke a cigarette and did not hesitate to go to one of the minor altars to light it on a candle. That was recorded in history like one of the most sacrilegious act committed in Lavarone.

We went to sleep around 7 and did not wake up until dinnertime. On the 3rd we were saying goodbye to go back to civilization.

The schools were reopening on the 7th and the normal routine would win again. But it was so much fun that Lavarone for Christmas would become our habit for years to come.

At home there were big preparations for my sister's wedding. The tailor, the list of the guests, the "bomboniere" (sterling silver bowls with five nougat candies), the booking of the church, the restaurant for the wedding dinner and so on. The house was a port of call but everybody seemed to have a good time.

The most excited about this event was our next door friend, Lina. She was a beautiful lady who's husband was the photographer on board the Andrea Doria when the ship sank.

He was always on a cruise ship and she was home looking after their son 3 years my junior. Often I was going to visit because I guess she was like the mom I seldom had. Concetta was all right but with her I could chat about different things with no shame.

The set day arrived. My sister looked stunning in her wedding gown. The limousines came to pick us up and with a perfect timing we were delivered to the church's doorsteps. Bruno was catholic but he was marrying Wilma who was Valdese in a protestant church. Because of that he got an excommunication from the Catholic Church! In the 1960's!!! Not that he cared much! The pastor made a nice simple speech and they were married. My father was very moved and it showed. During the party at the Plaza Hotel we had a great time, the food was great and the cake even better. Around 3pm we took the newly wed to the port where they embarked on a ship to cruise the Mediterranean from Egypt to Greece. That was a memorable day that Lina's husband immortalized on a 16mm film. For me it was also a sad event because my sister was moving to Milano, almost 2 hours drive north of Genova.

The next day everybody had left, my parents too, and the house was more or less back to normal.

Now at 14 my hormones were boiling and I was not satisfied of the daily masturbation sessions, I was in need of some body contact and started to go to places where I knew something erotic was taking place: cheap cinemas.

The most famous cinema in Genova was the Roma, incidentally owned by one of my dad's partners.

I was going there in the spare time to find a helping hand in the darkness of the house. If the guy approaching was of my taste I would let him touch and let him jerk me off. If he wasn't my type

I was pinching his hand with a toothpick that I always carried with me. I stabbed many hands. After the service was performed I was leaving the cinema, making sure nobody was following me, get on the bus and go home. There were also other cinemas where these kind of things were going on, but I always had the best of luck at the Roma. My kind of guy was slim, with a nice smile and in his 30's or 40's.

Another place where I was going if I was desperate was the public toilet, or vespasian. There was one under the old wall of the city, 100 yards for the house of Cristoforo Colombo. There was always somebody in there. I was standing outside and go in only if someone I liked was entering the dark place. It was just a quick hand job and I was gone like the wind. At that point I had never had a full sexual encounter but I was really ready to try.

The occasion came on a Sunday afternoon while I was walking through the deserted streets of the old city. On a Sunday only a few bars and restaurants are open so people usually go for a walk near the beach or in the public parks. That day I noticed a guy in his mid 30's following and staring at me. He was nothing special but not really ugly and besides there was nobody else around except for prostitutes.

I was looking at some shoes in a window when he finally started talking to me asking what I was up to. When h did that I got overly excited and my face became so red that he immediately noticed it. He must have also noticed an instant erection under my pants and that must have given him the courage to insist in his purpose.

He said that I was cute and asked me if I had to be home at a set time, then he said he had to go visit a friend nearby and invited me to follow him. With the hearth beating fast in my chest I started following him looking around to make sure that nobody I knew was passing by. We arrived at the building # 3 in Vico Usodimare and started going up two fly. An old man came to the door, they said something in dialect that I did not understand, and we went in. The old man was renting rooms by the hour. The room was bare, small, ugly furniture and a small twin bed was against the wall. Silvio, that was his name, locked the door and started hugging me trying to kiss me in the mouth. I pushed him away but he charged again starting to take my clothes off and undressing himself until he remained naked. At that point I thought I had enough. I quickly regained my clothes, opened the door and ran away from that awful apartment.

I got home and took a long bath thinking that God was going to punish me for what I had tried to do that day.

The school, the homework with some of my new schoolmates, the busy Saturday night playing cards or wondering around town and the weeks were passing by fast.

Even with some fear of God I was still going to the cinema Roma and satisfy my needs almost every day.

Now, at that time, I was getting some money allowance from my mom, some from my dad, occasionally from my grandmother and my brother in law. The fact was that one of my father's friend and also a marine part supplier loved children but his wife could not have any. He had his shipyard on the west side of town and lived close to the west city limit, some 20 kms away. Every time I was visiting him he would give me money, but not just a few lire… 10, 20, even 50.000 lire (1$ was equal to 650 lire). Mr. and Mrs. Passalacqua, that was their name, had bought a house next to our in Torre del Mare. Several times during the winter we would go there just for the day to escape from the city and enjoy the view of the sea and the gulf from our beautiful terrace. For me it was always a pleasure to see the Passalacqua because my walled would be refilled for several days to come. Whenever I was getting too low on cash I would get on the bus to the other end of town and go visit that old generous friend and that went on until I turned 18.

I had turned 14 and it was time for me to get some transportation. April was a good month because the temperature was increasing. I caught the chance that my father was at home for one week and we went to the Vespa dealer that was located just 2 blocks away.

I remember my dad paid 150.000 lire for that 50cc scooter and I proudly drove it home.

Dad recommended me not to drive it until the insurance company had issued a policy. Never then less the same afternoon I had to take a ride in the area. I was so happy that I didn't realize that the tracks of the streetcar could be a threat to the small tires of my vehicle, so because of those and also because I was looking at a guy walking on the other side of the road, I fell breaking my pants and scratching my right knee. Fortunately the Vespa wasn't damaged. From that time on I learned to keep an eye on the road and not to look at nice guys walking by.

With a vehicle now I thought my life was going to be much easier. I didn't have to wait for buses, I could park almost anywhere, I could sleep an extra 20 minutes in the morning and I was free to cruise around with Roberto and my other friends of the bar Tonitto. At our age to have a Vespa was a must. Also to go to the cinema Roma became easier, in 1 hour I could go and be back at home.

At school the atmosphere was kind of heavy towards the end of the term. We did not have examinations until the end of the 5th year but the end of the term was when the professors would make up their mind about our preparation and the interrogations were frequent. My only difficulty was in Math but with the help of the dean my vote was just sufficient to pass.

Torre del Mare was waiting for me as soon as the school was over. My sister came from Milano to pick me up and with Concetta we went there to spend a few weeks.

Even at the sea I had a few friends. We would meet by the beach bar, hang around a tent protecting from the hot sun, listening to the new 45rpm records, playing cards, telling jokes, swimming, diving and drinking coke. Around sunset we were going back home and we would meet again at the bar in the little square on top of the hill to decide what to do during the long evening. The nearest discos were in Spotorno, a couple of miles away. We all had our motorcycle so it was easy to get around. I was also looking for some "action" but I could not detect anybody around. At night it's very common for the local people as well as for visitors to walk by the "lungomare" (boulevard by the sea). I was always trying to catch in the eyes of mature guys that look that would tell me they had some interest. The public toilet had a guardian day and night so that was out of the question. On the beach each family was renting a wooden cabin for the season and the one next to mine was rented by Salvatore and Alessandra, a cute couple in their early 30's. Those were the only naked people I saw in Torre del Mare during that month through a hole in the wood. I still remember he was stunning even because I saw him a few times masturbating while he was changing his bathing suit. The cinema Roma was not reachable and the next move was Lavarone. That meant I had to go dry until the end of September!

We went to the mountains after a two days stop in Milano at my sister's house. I had to go to the train station to ship the motorcycle to Rovereto, just 35 kms from Lavarone. All my friends had now the very same model of Vespa and our vehicles were taking most of the available parking in the square.

The schedule was more or less the same but at night we could now go to different villages, even more distant, where there was usually more going on. Being in a group our parents were confident that nothing bad was going to happen because we basically grew up together and we were always ready to help each other. I must say that in Italy we could drink at any age, anywhere and at any time. But nobody in the group was a drinker. Drugs were not really available like today but none of us was even thinking about drugs. Bad behavior was something more common among newcomers than among us and usually we would cut off the friendship with guys that we believed were not following our path.

Never than less we were practical jokers and we did play several jokes to visitors and residents. Here there are some examples.

Lavarone is a very quiet village 1200 mts above sea level and it's divided in 17 fractions.

Each one attracts a number of visitors for the summer season, mainly families with children because of the many walks in the woods. At night the children are in bed and the parents spend their time playing cards, talking politics, telling jokes, eating ice creams and zipping on drinks.

The guys like us form groups in the same age range that meet year after year. The disco, mini golf and bowling are some of the activities these groups get into but sometimes the night takes a different course and that's when we plan jokes to the expenses of the communities.

There are lines of buses connecting Lavarone with Trento, Rovereto and Vicenza and usually they leave early in the morning. One night we loaded the top of each bus with branches of trees.

The movie theater was run by the local Catholic priest and of course their budget was low so the movies shown were old, cut whenever there was a love scene, and the film would often break so that the spectators were forced to wait the usual five minutes for the repair. We used to sit still during the boring scenes and laugh or talk loud during the intense scenes, thus causing the wrath of the priest who, in the darkness, was trying to locate us the source of the noise.

We became more sophisticated when my dad brought me a walkie-talkie from New York. We would set one in an area of the cinema where there were many empty seats and someone else walk make strange noises from the outside or from the restroom area.

The best joke of the season happened in august, which is the notorious month in Italy when everybody is on vacation. The walkie-talkie had a regular radio incorporated that could be switched on by pushing a simple button. On Sundays there are a bunch of people coming from the cities to spend the day in the woods and to cook out. The area we picked up was very crowded that day and from the tags of the cars around we knew they were all from Padova, Vicenza and Verona. At 1o'clock sharp I turned on the radio and the speaker started reading the news. Suddenly I switched to my friend who was hiding half a mile away. He started reading some catastrophic weather report concerning the cities mentioned above: torrential rain, flooding, lightning, fallen trees and so on. Soon everybody was collecting seats, tables, dishes and ground covers to return to their homes to see what had happened. There was not a cloud in the sky.

That summer my parents and I took the usual trip to Austria and Germany. In Hamburg I went with my mother to visit the Ripperbahn in St. Pauli, the "forbidden" section of town with prostitutes, bars, night clubs and a lot of sexual explicit material. Somehow I managed to sneak out from the hotel after my parents had gone to bed. Just walking around the streets at night was interesting but for the German law I was underage and could not go to any public place that was appealing. I did find a public toilet and a few minutes were enough to see what was going on. I managed to get a hand job from an enough good looking guy and I was proud because that was my first "adventure" in Germany.

My vacation was slowly ending. It was time to go collect hazelnuts and say goodbye to all my friends with the promise to get together again for Christmas.

Back in Genova I had two weeks to get back to the usual school routine. I had to get together with my schoolmates and refresh my memory on the things we had learned during the previous term.

The professors were the same but from 36 students the number had dropped to 24. Some didn't make it, some dropped out or changed school. The result was kind of positive: less people, less noise, more attention…but also more interrogations!

My parents were leaving for Canada so I had a whole month by myself. Concetta was cooking all my favorite dishes. I was inviting over for dinner many of my friends and my room became a center of studies.

The subjects were becoming more interesting with the exception of Math that seemed more and more complicated.

During the fall I was getting more interested in music, all kind of music, from opera, classical to all the new Italian singers and, of course, the American and English. Roberto was always going to this fancy record store located downtown and he introduced me to the owner. On almost every Saturday afternoon I was going there to listen to the new records in order to make a selection and buy those that I liked more. I noticed that the owner was overly friendly but I never thought he could be gay. So one afternoon when I was the only customer in the store, he came inside the boot with the excuse to show me some recordings and started to touch me. He was a nice looking man and of course I let him go on. After that my record library was updated for free because he was refusing any money. The sex was great even though until that time I was not really reciprocating.

That happened after my 15th birthday when at the cinema Roma I met this guy named Marco who invited me to his apartment. I jumped in his convertible while my blood was boiling and we headed to my neighborhood. He was living just a few blocks away. He was an actor in one of the main theaters in town. His apartment was nice, tastefully furnished, comfortable, with a great view over the sea. He was calm, decided, light brown hair, green eyes and a killer smile. About 6 feet tall and with a very well toned body.

After offering me a drink that I firmly refused (I had heard of people getting drugged that way) he took me into his arms and started kissing me passionately. It was the first time that someone was kissing me. The impulse was to push him away but somehow I resisted that and I finally started liking it. The heath was mounting while we were slowly undressing each other. His hands were exploring my body and I was feeling something different from the usual hand jobs I was getting in those places. I came three different times during those two hours and the last one was in his mouth. Ha was kissing me all over, licking and sucking giving me a pleasure like I had never felt before. This was definitely a jump in quality and from that moment on I knew what I had to look for, now that the fear was overcome.

I left him with the promise that we would have got back together soon and I walked back home thinking about the hottest encounter of my life.

Christmas arrived and there I was, in Lavarone, with all my friends at the Cervo. There were some new faces since the place was becoming famous for its slopes and for the nice ski-lifts. We welcomed some new people in the group and we had the usual good time. It was during the holiday that I started smoking. The chosen brand was Kent. I remember having a cold and still smoking at least half a pack a day just because everybody else was doing so, I guess according to the fashion of the time.

I never really got hooked on nicotine but if I was around someone smoking I had to light a cigarette too. Just being by myself I was not thinking about it at all. It would be like that for all my life. I guess the general idea about having a cigarette in our hands gives us some sense of dignity and it helps to overcome a problem like shyness. That Christmas I had a terrible cold but I kept smoking like a chimney. Back in Genova, if my parents were around, I would smoke too but wearing gloves so that the smell of smoke could not be detected on my fingers. My mom never smoked, my dad gave it up during the 2nd world war when he was on board of submarines. During Easter we went to spend a few days in Torre del Mare with the Passalacqua. Useless to say that he was magnificent in dispensing money because, as he put it, a guy my age had growing necessities.

The end of the school term arrived fast and this time I would not be too lucky: I had to take Math class all Summer and pass the test in September in order to be admitted to the 3rd year. My dad said he saw it coming and blamed me for choosing to go to maritime high. After we spent three weeks in Torre del Mare, my dad proposed me to go on one of his ship for the month of July in order to exercise with navigation skills. I decided to go to break the routine, one month would have done me good.

The "Fiamma" was one of the largest oil tanker of the company. 25.000 Tons, 100 meters long, with a crew of 36 people and it was rented at that time by the Mobil oil Company. It was loading crude in Saida, Lebanon, and unloading in Livorno Italy. That's where I had to go to catch the ship.

I arrived in Livorno during a warm afternoon and a cab left me on the dock. I was welcomed by the captain who showed me my cabin located in the front bow. All the cabins in the front were occupied by the officers, those in the stern were occupied by the rest of the crew.

My duty was to work on the main bridge with the 1st officer from 4am to 8am and 4pm to 8pm. I had to be at the helm, take the coordinates through the sextant and eventually take orders to the other officers.

I was not supposed to be paid for that month, as my father told me, but I was going to have my meals with the captain and the officers.

Before the ship sailed off Livorno I went to buy candies, cookies and all the stuff that was not available on board. I was ready for this new adventure.

The Fiamma sailed south and the next day we were crossing the Messina narrows between Italy and Sicily. That was my 1st time traveling south.

A sailor was waking me up at 3,45 with a hot coffee and there I was on the bridge chatting with the 1st officer. The sky was covered with stars, the night was warm, the sea was calm and black with some lights indicating the presence of other floating vessels.

The officer showed me how to use the sextant and I must say it was much easier to do it for real than in the class. From that point on I could do it without help or supervision. After the shift I was having a nice breakfast and go back on the bridge to see what the 2nd officer was doing. Soon enough I became very familiar with every member of the crew. After dinner I would go to mingle with them in the stern while someone was playing a guitar, others were playing cards and the steward was passing around slices of watermelon and drinks. Cigarettes were available in cartons tax free because we were in international waters. At that time I switched from Kent to Peer, a brand that doesn't exist anymore. There was also a TV room picking up signals from some other Mediterranean countries besides Italy.

Among the crew I had already spotted a couple of guys that in my opinion could be interested, but, due to the fact that I was who I was, nothing was ever said or done. I was just dreaming that one of them would knock at my cabin one night to have some fun. That remained just a dream and, looking back, I'm glad it did because the consequences could have been disastrous.

It took 3 full days to reach Saida. I thought the ship would go to the dock to load the crude (it was taking about 26 hours) instead they had a big hose emerging from the sea. There was no way I would stay on board during the demurrage so I exceptionally obtained a permit from the captain to go on shore with the boat of the local ship provider.

I was walking the streets of this mid eastern city, looking at the shops, chatting with the local people in French, and even checking if there was some gay scene around. I tried to smoke the narghile' but the taste was really awful. I bought a bunch of postcards to send to all my friends. I managed to go to spend the night in Beirut, the capital, that at the time was considered the Montecarlo of the Middle East.

Before going back on board I asked the provider if he could put stamps on the postcards and mail them and I gave him some money. Guess what…never trust a mid eastern guy: no one postcard arrived to destination!

Back on the ship they had completed the loading and we were ready to sail. The news was that due to a strike in Livorno we had to go to Northern Europe to unload and that meant the harbor of Hamburg.

To cross the Mediterranean it would take one week and another one to go all the way to Hamburg. The adventure was getting more interesting.

The voyage was long and monotonous. For days there was no land in sight but we crossed path with many vessels of different flags and with a myriad of fishing boats with sailors waving at us.

I really got fed up with waking up that early but I had to go on doing it not to loose the respect of the crew. It was interesting to go through the Gibraltar narrows and then head North close to the Spanish and the Portuguese coasts. Seen from the sea the city of Lisbon was beautiful. I just regretted to pass by but not to be able to stop and explore.

So far the weather had been nice and warm but a surprise caught us when we crossed the gulf of Biscaglia from the coast of Spain to the French one. The sky had the color of lead, the wind was strong and the sea was force 7. The fully loaded oil tanker was rocking and rolling so much that it was kind of difficult to walk around and stand. I never got seasick before but during those two days I did. The only possible way to escape it was to lay in the bed and get up only if necessary. I hardly ate and of course I didn't dare to venture on the bridge. Close to the coast of Normandy the weather changed but the wind was brisk. We finally arrived in the port of Hamburg at midday and it was then that I decided to leave the ship and return home by train. To my big surprise the 3rd officer called me to his office and gave me the salary for the work I had done on board! It was quite a bit of money for those 22 days. I packed my suitcase and left in the car of the German ship supplier who was a dear friend of my dad.

Glad to be there by myself I took a room in a decent hotel downtown and after a shower I was ready to explore the St. Pauli area by myself. My father's friend had put at my disposal a white Mercedes with a chauffeur. He left me in front of the best Chinese restaurant in town and told me he was going to pick me up after dinner. Wisely I brought a small amount of Marks with me and I dressed just with jeans and a sweater. The maitre D looked at me with nonchalance and I took seat at a single table. When dinner was over I waited a while longer on purpose because I wanted to make sure the Mercedes was there when I was leaving the restaurant. I left a 5Dmks tip to the waiter and when the maitre D opened the door he saw the chauffeur waiving at me and let me in the car. That was my revenge since he was probably thinking I was just a "nobody".

At the St. Pauli I dismissed the car and started walking in that area that my mother had shown me the previous year. It was like Alice in wonderland. Bars, clubs, prostitutes, sexy shows, women fighting in mud, straight clubs, lesbian clubs and gay clubs! I walked for hours looking at the people right in their eyes and trying to understand what they were up to. There were many sailors from different countries sitting or standing but they all had one thing in common: they were drinking beer. I figured out that if I had waited too long everybody would have been drunk by midnight. So I took the bull by the horn and I ventured inside one of the gay clubs. Since I hardly drink because I don't like the taste of alcohol, I ordered a cider and started sipping it. Walking around the place I saw several cute men and some were looking at me wondering why such a young guy was in a place like that. Finally an older gentleman asked me some questions and introduced himself. I was absolutely not interested in him but to be polite I started a conversation. He was a doctor and of course he had been to Italy many times on vacation. He was very concerned about me being there and absolutely wanted to give me a ride back to the hotel. I saw my little big adventure go up in smoke but it was getting too late so I succumbed. Of course he asked me to spend the night over his house but I firmly declined. Now my only hope was to find some cute guy in the lobby or among the night personnel that was servicing the rooms. I didn't sleep well that night because I was paying attention to all the noise that was going on in the hallway and in the rooms next door.

I spent the next day guest of my dad's friend and his family and at 9,40pm I took the overnight train to Italy. I was heading to Trento, the closest station to the mountains. I got in a cab and when I arrived in Lavarone I asked my surprised mother paying for the taxi.

It was fun as usual to see all my friends but I also had to spend a couple of hours a day taking Math lessons from the ex mayor who was also a teacher.

This time I had to go back to Genova two weeks earlier than usual because the written test was during the 1st week in September and the oral was during the 2nd week. So I was at home all by myself with Candida, the maid, coming to clean the house in the morning and cook me lunch.

I passed the written test and to celebrate I went to the beach across the street. It was the end of the season and there were just a few people sunbathing. I noticed a cute guy and casually I went to sit very close to him. We started talking about different things and when it was clear that he was up to the same thing I was, I invited him home.

He was really what I had expected. We took a long shower together and then we spent a couple of hours rolling on my bed. I was appreciating more and more the effect that kissing did on me and he was so nice and passionate that I will always remember him with affection. A few minutes after he had left my father drove up and opened the gate. He was supposed to be in Antwerp until the end of the week. Thank God he did not arrive a little bit earlier.

After the oral examination I resumed the usual life with my almost daily stops at the cinema Roma. I really wanted to call Marco, the actor, but for some reason I was afraid to. I liked him a lot but I did not want to get involved in some kind of relationship that would have tight me down with just one guy.

The school year started a few days later thanks to a strike of the school janitors. The class had lost another seven students and we certainly did not miss them. There was more room and we could pay more attention to the lessons.

This was the last year for the studying of some subjects like physics, geography, chemistry and naval arts. The 4th and 5th years were more a concentration of the remaining subjects. The novelty was that the English teacher had changed. Now we had an elderly lady of Italian origin that moved back to Genova from Melbourne Australia. Her accent was really something else! We had to get accustomed to understand her.

Just before the end of the 1st term some voices started circulating about one of my schoolmates: it seemed he was having sex with older men for money and that's how he could afford new clothes and expensive accessories all the time. Nobody was blaming him… on the contrary: the guys considered him smart and not at all gay, just taking advantage of the situation. As a matter of fact I saw him a few time at the cinema fooling around with really older guys and receiving some money for it. I thought that wasn't right but when he told me once that he wasn't gay because he had a girlfriend I objected telling him that if he could get an erection with another man he had to consider himself bisexual, not heterosexual.

Luckily in those years the drug was not on people's mind and, if it was, it was kept so secretive that nobody suspected anything. The cigarettes were the big things to do for the grown ups. Alcoholic drinks were available at any time, any age and anywhere. In numerous families wine was and is commonly used to accompany the daily meals but I never saw anybody abusing of it. I did not know about alcoholism until I saw the movie with E. Taylor and R. Burton "Who's afraid of Virginia Wolf". My dad was the only member of my family who would drink a glass of wine while eating. Neither my mom, or my sister or I ever liked the taste of it.

That Christmas my sister and my brother in law came to Lavarone to ski. My dad had installed a heating system throughout the house and had instructed a resident to turn it on a couple of days before our arrival. We were just sleeping at the house because it was more convenient to go to eat at the Cervo rather than fooling in the kitchen. I was sitting at the table with all my friends and still giving a hard time to the waitress with our extravagant requests.

One night at the Ruota (the disco) I saw that there was a guy staring at me and I recognized him being one of the temporary staff of the Cervo. I left Paolalberta with the others and I started a conversation with him. We ended up going to a secluded place around the lake in his car and having sex on the back seat. That was a pleasant surprise as I would have never thought to find somebody in that village. We went out every night and I had to find excuses with my friends not to join them. His car was well heated because the temperature at night was subfreezing.

It was the beginning of the fabulous 60's when we went to sleep that early morning of January 1st. During the previous 15 years Italy had recovered from a disastrous war and from an empire with colonies overseas had become a small republic. The age of Mussolini and the baby boomers had ended. There was an economic "Bang", the electric and telephone cables had been buried underground, most people owned a car and the television was spreading fast taking the place of the surpassed radio. Mina was the greatest Italian singer, Maria Callas the most famous soprano, Elvis, Paul Anka, Gene Pitney, Connie Francis, Petula Clark, Neil Sedaka, Aznavour, Pat Boone and Edith Piaf were the most acclaimed artists on both sides of the Atlantic. Our President was sleeping with an actress who did commercial spots on TV, the 1st lady was sleeping with her chauffeur and nobody gave a damn. The bikini was taking the place of the old one piece bathing suit, the fashion had become a very important part of our culture with the Italian designers slowly taking over the French. Florence and Milan were becoming the international capitals of good taste. Even the shapes of cars were becoming more appealing and their maximum speeds were getting higher. Like Germany, Italy had built a wide net of "autobahns" enabling everybody to cut the driving time in half. It became a habit to leave town on Friday afternoon and come back on Sunday evening. Many Italians had a second home at the sea or in the mountains or both. With the booming of the economy we started having some traffic jams, some problems with pollution and many problems for disposing the garbage, so they built many incinerators serving the largest cities. Some chemical plants built in the proximities of rivers and lakes were polluting the water causing death to million of fish and many ugly building were made without regular construction permits. The government employees were usually lazy and very slow in producing documents and the paperwork was sitting on their desks for ages. It was a normal praxis to bribe the public servants with money and gifts in order to expedite the documents. The unions were becoming more powerful and the right to strike was recognized to the workers.

I was born one year after the king of Italy Umberto the 1st had been exiled.

The family on my mother side was half Venetian and half Swiss. My father was from a very old aristocratic family of Orvieto, a little town in central Italy just north of Roma. One of the first ancestor was Roberto, a knight serving king Pietro the 2nd as captain of the guards in the city of Orvieto from 1193 until 1208. The family became very powerful in Siracusa and Noto, cities in Sicily, trough many advantageous marriages. In the year 1665 they embraced the protestant religion and for that reason they were excommunicated by pope Alessando 7th and repaired in Geneve Switzerland until the mid 19th century. My grandmother became a widow when my dad was 7. Fortunately she was a wise businesswoman and managed the family fortune in a way that they never had to struggle. In those days to buy in properties was the best way of investment. They had lived in Genova not too far from our home. My dad went to the very same school that I was attending and then was drafted during the 2nd world war and served on board of submarines as Major (capitano di machine).

After the war him and two partners bought a few small tankers used to transport water from the mainland to the Italian islands. Then they signed a contract with a Polish company to transport coal from the Baltic sea to Genova. In 1952 they started building the oil tankers that were leased to companies like Exxon, Mobil, Shell etc.

My dad was going to church whenever it was possible, my mother was not so spiritual but she vas taking an active part in organizing charities on behalf of the protestant church. I had the moral obligation to go to catechism every Saturday afternoon but I think I can count on my fingers the times that I really attended to those meetings. I had not been baptized because protestants usually do that at the age of 16.

Now that you know the background of my family I must tell you that religion at that point had been an important part of my life. The pastors, the monitors, the mentors had always depicted God as an omnipresent entity ready to judge and condemn. The many Catholic priests and friends that I had met so far were even more bigot. There were several things that were not too clear to me. When Costantino in the year 313 decided to make Christianity the state religion it was the end of the pagan era and also the end of the way of life that Christ and his followers until that time had intended. The successors of Peter had yet to be called popes and had lived in hiding to avoid persecution and the multiplying Christians were meeting in the catacombs and in other secret places. One of the first gifts to the church was a heavy platinum chain that a rich widow gave with the idea of helping the poor. That donation was just the beginning of the famous Vatican treasure that during the next 17 centuries surpassed the imagination. The teachings of Christ were misinterpreted on purpose in order to gain power on the ignorant masses and make them work hard and pay for the benefit of the merging clergy. It all worked so well that until the end of the renaissance the pope was the most powerful man in the world, even more powerful than the emperor himself.

The temples and the statues of the old gods had been destroyed and on their ruins they had built Christian churches in the shape of the cross. The crucifix was above the altar and soon enough the statue of Christ was becoming a normal presence in every temple. Each church dedicated to one God was subdivided in smaller chapels each one dedicated to different saints, each one protecting a specific group of people. Even Mary, mother of Christ, started to be venerated as a goddess "mother of god" and during the famous council of Nicea in 325,the cardinals debated for days about her virginity. The truth was that the fall of the ancient gods there was replaced by the rise of many gods bearing different names. The people were happy, the clergy satisfied because they were acquiring more riches and power. The idea that God could see everything that was going on in somebody's life (and so did the priests through the confessionals) was scaring most people. Heaven was so difficult to reach while the gates of hell were ready to open for everybody. There was the general idea that God was extremely vengeful and only the clergy could intercede for a place in Heaven. Of course that would never happen if the villain had nothing tangible to give.

I'm talking about this because later on in life I will have some more spiritual moments. At this point I was still debating about wrong and right and the sense of guilt for my impure acts were upon me.

1963 was a good year, a nice one. The school was going well, Math was not, my friends were very nice and supportive and I joined the Genova junior swim team. For Christmas I had the very pleasant surprise of going to Lavarone with my dear friend Alan who had come to see me from Tanger where his father was stationed.

Everybody in the mountains was glad to see him. He was grown taller and cuter than I remembered, I could have fallen in love with him and so could the girls in the group!

There was just enough snow on the slopes to ski but we had a good time playing cards and socializing with newcomers. Sometimes Alan and I would mingle with Wilma, Bruno and their friends. It was a total different age group but Bruno loved to speak French and for some things it was kind of fun to be around them.

On new year's eve we had the usual big dinner at the Cervo topped with the usual Dom Perignon, then we went to the usual Rota to dance. Paolalberta was definitely interested in my friend and that was really making me mad. With Roberto, Anna and Luigi we started drinking shots of "Grappa" a typical hard liquor of the North-East. After the 12th shot I was not only buzzed but also sick: that was the first time I had gotten drunk. Alan had to get me home in a cab, I vomited several times, didn't sleep and had a hung over for the rest of the day. Even now I cannot stand the smell of Grappa.

We went back to Genova with Roberto in his mother's car. The short two weeks vacation was over and who knows when I would have seen Alan again. We promised to keep more in touch and he flew back to Morocco.

My parents had just come back from Port Said and strange enough they did not have any trip planned for the next month. I told mom that I wanted to have a big party for my 16th birthday and she totally agreed with me. Now I had something to plan, a project, and I was very excited about it. School resumed and so did my almost daily visits to the cinema. I was getting lucky almost every time but if the guys in the audience were not of my liking I was just locking myself in the toilet and jerk off. The guy at the record store was becoming something not too exciting to do so I was going there only in case of extreme necessity.

I had several invitations printed for my party. A catering service was booked for the day. I spent hours recording all the songs that I wanted on one of those first magneto phone with a three hours tape so that I wouldn't have to change the records all the time.

The day came. The party was starting around 4pm and my friends started arriving after 4,30. Some of the girls were accompanied by their mothers that wanted to make sure everything was fine. In total 42 people showed up. The party went on until around 8pm. Everybody had a great time, nobody got drunk, the food was good, I got many compliments for the choice of music and the place was a mess! Concetta was in distress but the next day she had the help of Candida to clean everything up.

Easter was just around the corner. My dad asked if I wanted to join him, mum, Wilma and Bruno to go to Canada for 10 days which would mean to loose at least 4 schooldays. I agreed reluctantly because I had never been on a plane before and I was kind of scared to board one. My mom insisted that we flew on Swissair as she didn't trust any other airline. I went to visit the Passalacqua and that move gave me a lot of extra money for the trip. We left from Zurich on a big propeller plane. My dad was filming everything on his 16mm Paillard camera. The flight was long, boring and bumpy. The food was very good and abundant served in china, crystal and sterling silverware. The crew was very friendly and a stewardess took me to visit the cockpit. The landing was the most crucial moment and even the best for me because I had enough of flying for that day that was already 6 hours longer than usual. Toronto looked like a large city from the air but it certainly seemed bigger once we left the airport terminal to reach the hotel downtown. The cars were much bigger than the European but the roads were wider too. We were on a limousine that could easily seat 12 with a driver that looked like Robert Taylor in his best days.

I guess everybody was tired from the flight because when I went to the lobby after changing clothes and a nice long shower I did not see anybody. I also had dinner by myself and it didn't even cross my mind to call my mom or my sister on the phone to see what they were up to. After dinner I started exploring the surroundings on foot making sure I knew where the hotel was located. A European city would have been filled with people walking around, in Toronto I did not see a soul on the sidewalks, just cars. The bright colored lights on the streets were not marking the presence of bars, nightclubs or cinemas but they belonged to different stores already closed for the day. The only thing I could do was to get back to the hotel, hang around in the lobby and see if there was some guy with the same interests. I had never been with a Canadian! The search was not successful. I suddenly got really sleeping and quickly retired to my room.

We spent three days in Toronto visiting the city, boarding a boat and going all the way to the Canadian side of Niagara Falls. The fourth day we flew to Vancouver, one of my father's favorite cities. It was early spring, everything was blooming. My mother, who loved plants, was asking names of trees and flowers and was driving us crazy with her "look at this" and "look at that".

The trip was reaching its end and I had not found one single Canadian to have sex with! On top of that I found out I was not allowed into clubs because of my age s I was feeling sorry for the guys my age living there: how were they surviving?

The flight back to Zurich took the whole night. I tried to sleep like my mom suggested but I was waking up every ten minutes. We reached home around 4pm, I took a shower, went to bed and didn't wake up until noon the next day.

I had to get together with some schoolmates to recuperate the three days I had missed at school, fortunately it wasn't much.

From Easter until the end of the school year it was just a short shot. Yes, you guessed it, I had to take Math to September again!

My parents were going to Japan while Concetta and I went to Torre del Mare and from there to Lavarone with my sister who was pregnant.

At the sea I became very familiar with the father of some friends of mine, Silvio, who wanted to live like a young guy but was rejected by all the groups meeting on the beach and by the bar on the little square. Hw was driving a fabulous sport car, a Ferrari 250GT, equipped with the most sophisticated stereo record player. It was a pleasure to ride and be seen in that car by anyone on the street. Going out with Silvio who had the reputation of being very active with women it gave me the chance of hooking up with some girl and made him feel good because he had my devoted friendship. The man, who was a widower, had a heart condition and according to what people were saying at 38 he didn't have much left to live. I would have liked to have some adventures with girls. I thought it would be cool to slowly undress each other and see what her reaction would be when we would be totally naked, kissing, touching, licking and sucking. Unfortunately I did not know how to handle girls. The only one I had tried to do something with, Paolalberta, was not the kind that was going to have sex just for the fun of it. Going around with Silvio it was different because he was a grown man who knew what he wanted and knew how to deal with women. We were going night club hopping and get acquainted with several ladies that wanted to have a good time and a few drinks. A few times we were very close to take some home but for a reason or another there were always some inconvenient arising. One night at the Copacabana, just one Km away from home, we found a couple of nice looking girls that were working as maids in Spotorno. Thanks to the eloquence of Silvio and after a few drinks they finally decided to follow us to his house. May be they were impressed by his villa, may be because they thought we were brothers, we succeeded in having sex with them. Silvio went to his bedroom leaving us sitting on a sofa in the living room. I was red like a lobster, shy, my hands were shaking. I thought the best thing to do was kissing her so I took her into my arms and did so. She was kind of surprised and told me nobody ever kissed her like that before. Usually guys were rough and wanted to get to the point quickly. It took me about 30 minutes to undress her, then I started licking her on the neck, the arms, the chest working my way down to her groin. In the meantime she was exploring my body feeling my penis with her soft hands. She did some oral sex but I must admit I had better from guys. We played for at least one hour before I decided to go one step further and insert my penis in that moist vagina. Being my very first time I was careful to do it gently but suddenly she pushed it in all the way and started moving up and down. She was moaning and breathing fast, I was sweating and was trying to control myself not to reach the orgasm while I was inside. In those days the pill was not around and I did not have a condom. I think she came at least twice so I decided to pull out and I came all over her belly. To my surprise she put her hands in it and even tasted it!

That sex was fun but I liked the guys better. There was something missing there or, maybe, there was not enough chemistry there to match mine. I felt good though just thinking I did what a straight guy was expected to do. At that point I just wanted to get out of there, go home and take a shower. Silvio and his girlfriend had fallen asleep because there was no noise coming from the bedroom. Not to be rude I started napping on the sofa until we all waked up around 10.

My sister was mad because I had spent the night out and I didn't even call to let her know. Fortunately my brother in law understood the situation and gave me some moral support. Concetta was not pleased and acted like she was mad for the following two days.

Before leaving for Lavarone I organized a little party on the terrace with my friends. We were all having a good time slow dancing in the very dim light. Patrizia was pressing her breast so much against my torso that I couldn't help it getting an erection. I thought I was going to repeat the experience of the previous night with her but when her sister got ready to leave she left too leaving me dry.

That was the last summer I saw Silvio because a few months later he was dead from a massive hearth attack.

In Lavarone I found my usual dearest friends, and also the ex mayor to give me those damn Math lessons.

We were all driving those Vespa but there were a couple of older guys with a car, one was driving a jaguar, the other a Lancia Sport Coupe. As a natural result these two guys became the center of the attention of the girls. In our opinion these two were so arrogant that they deserved some kind of punishment.

On the 14th of August, the night preceding "ferragosto" (big Italian holiday) I noticed that Luigi and Mario were acting in a strange way. Shortly after midnight they disappeared and when they came back about one hour later they were laughing. I knew that something was up but I did not know what until I walked to the Cervo on the morning after.

The two guys were cleaning their cars with a lot of newspapers. A small loud crowd was surrounding the, and all my friends were sitting at the outside bar observing the scene. Their windshields, windows, doors, handles, roof, trunk and hood were all covered with cow shit. I learned that they drove to the gas station but the attendant refused to wash them. So they were doing it themselves using all those newspapers. Even the local guard came to warn them not to leave trash on the ground. Some of the girls were upset with all of us and told us they would never take rides in those cars again. The revenge was painful for some and sweet for others.

The summer was coming to an end and it was time for me to go to Genova to take care of the Math examination. I passed with a kick and there I was starting my 4th year of maritime school. In the class there were now 18 students and the attitude of the professors had slightly changed in…better.

We felt older and wiser and were looking upon the younger guys starting from the 1st class. They were looking at us like gods. We had almost made it. We were in the best terms with the professors therefore we could take a few liberties that were denied to them.

I resumed my trips to the cinema and, even though I was very tempted to call Marco, I never did.

One afternoon hanging around a deceitful bar in the old section of town filled with American sailors (the Forestall was anchored in the gulf) I started talking to Maria, a nice cute little prostitute. She convinced me to follow her to her apartment promising heaven. I was really taken by some of the sailors but they were mostly drunk, paying attention to their beers and to the juke box than to me. So I followed Maria up the stairs of an old building and she let me into this small room. There was a sink, a bidet, a mid size bed and a night table. She asked me to wash while she was getting naked asking me if I had done it before. I said I had done it plenty of times but never with a prostitute. She helped me undress and she started sucking on my penis. She was better than the girl at the sea, but not as good as some of the guys I had been with. I fucked her without a condom and she insisted that I came inside because she was wearing some sponge and there was no danger for her to get pregnant. Her vagina was very moist but not so tight and it did not encounter my taste. I decided that girls were ok just for sex once in a while and only if they had approached me. I paid her 1500 Lire (the equivalent of 3 $) and left promising to go back whenever I wanted her again.

Somewhat I felt more hetero when I was talking to my friends and schoolmates. In the past my father had tried to draw my attention to girls passing by but I always pretended not to understand or not to pay any attention. With Bruno it was different, one could be open with him and sometimes even ashamed because he was saying some sexual sentences or dirty words while we were eating or in the car with my mother. She always pretended nothing was said but the whole thing was bothering me, not making me feel at ease.

My nephew was born on that November 14th in Milano so we went there to see him and pay our respects. He was a little tiny fellow and in my opinion didn't look either like Wilma or Bruno. I have never been fond of babies nor children at least until they were over 20. I was really hoping that Wilma would stop after this one that was named Alberto.

1964 was at the gate. Christmas in Lavarone was always a must. It was relaxing to go there to ski, hang around my friends, talk about our studies and about…politics. At this stage in our life politics was taking most part of our talks. We had always complaining that our TV news reports had too much politic involved, and now we were carefully listening to everything the Italian and even the foreign politicians were saying. Italy had many parties in the sixties and they were always fighting each other. We were slowly understanding more and taking well defined directions. At school most of my schoolmates were in the left wing, meaning socialist and communist parties. My real friends were more for the right wing, liberal, democratic and even "missini" the survived fascist party. I considered myself liberal and Malagodi, the secretary of the "partito liberale italiano" was my role model.

Back to Genova and to the old school routine I was goofing off with my friends one afternoon when I saw coming towards me Marco. He looked gorgeous and I couldn't help showing signs of redness on my face. He said hi and we talked about trivial things. He was going to be in a play starting in February at the Duse, one of the most prestigious theaters in Genova and wanted me to go see him.

I almost forgot the whole thing until the day before the premiere. I tried to get a ticket but it was sold out so I resolved to call and tell him I was not going to be there. He brought me a complimentary ticket and there I was enjoying that play and Marco's acting. I knew one day he would be very famous.

Going to the theater was a habit that I had lost from the times of Venice and Paris. I really liked doing that and I started keeping track of what was interesting and I didn't want to miss. I would have loved to go with one or more friends to share the emotions that a play or an opera were giving me but nobody wanted or had ever time to go. In those days I was sticking to the classics like Giacosa, Pirandello, D'Annunzio, Goldoni, Verdi, Puccini, Mascagni and others. Maria Callas was more involved with stupid Onassis than in singing but there were some emerging new sopranos like Renata Scotto and Mirella Freni. The only time I risked of falling asleep was at a matinee of Parsifal. I loved the ouverture but I found the rest of the opera extremely boring. My mom encouraged me to go to all the performances, she also bought me a subscription for the season. If my grandmother was in town she would come along too and together we always had a good time.

One day during an intermission I noticed somebody looking at me and smiling. I was flattered that a guy so good looking and elegant was showing interest. I saw him again two weeks later at a concert with the pianist Nikita Magaloff. That time I smiled back and went to meet him personally.

He was about 6' tall, had beautiful blue eyes, dark brown hair, well shaven, cured hands and his voice was nice and deep, his name was Giacomo. He had a PhD in literature and was teaching in a famous Genova's high school. I was very fascinated by him and I accepted his invitation to go over his apartment after the concert. It was a cold and windy Sunday afternoon. I sat on the sofa while he was preparing some fruit drink. I was flattered, nervous and with some degree of anxiety. Giacomo asked me if I had ever heard the music of Karl Maria von Weber. When I shook my head he insisted that I hear two concerts for clarinet, then he gave me the drink and came sitting next to me.

We talked for at least a couple of hours. I was feeling very at ease with him like I had known him for years. The arguments varied from music to history and politics. Suddenly I looked at my watch and realized it was time for me to go. He tried to make me stay for dinner but I knew Concetta would not have appreciated that. So I wrote his phone number and left assuring him I would have called very soon.

Going home I was excited of such encounter thinking that if nothing physical had happened, sooner or later it would.

During that week I was so busy focusing on the 4 hours Math test coming up on Saturday morning that I didn't even have the time to go to the cinema. Saturday at lunch I was so relieved that I had passed the test that I decided to relax for the whole week end. My plan was simple: I told Concetta I had been invited to spend the night at some friend's house. I called Giacomo and asked if I could go over. I took a nice long bath, put on some casual clothes and went to his place.

Giacomo had prepared a nice dinner. The table was very well decorated and two candles were lit. He offered an aperitif and then we started eating some ravioli. The main course scaloppini al marsala with a nicoise salad. Remembering my "sweet tooth" he served some profitterol with vanilla cream. We sat at the table for another hour smoking cigarettes before he proposed to sit on the sofa and listen to some music. I told him about my family, the boarding schools, Lavarone, my friends and the trips I had made. He was a good listener and he knew what to say with a perfect timing. I was fascinated, but the subject "sex" was not coming up so I was wondering if the guy was just interested in friendship or something more.

It was getting late and he noticed I was looking at my watch. He asked me if I had a set time to get home but I told him that my parents were abroad and there was nobody there so I could be as late as I wanted. Finally he reached my hand and with the excuse of looking at my palm he started caressing it and finally gave me a long hug.

My lips were searching his, my blood was boiling, my hearth was beating fast when he started kissing me holding my head in his hands.

We rushed to the bedroom where he started undressing me very slowly exploring each part of my naked body. I was trying to do the same with him but in a goofy way since I did not have much experience in that particular case. My mind was thinking about sins, my parents, Silvio who was probably looking at me then, Wilma and Bruno asking if I had lost my mind and so on. But the pleasure of him kissing me all over, licking my private parts, sucking and touching my body with those soft hands was just irresistible.

He had a beautiful penis, larger than what I had imagined. I was playing with it and putting it against mine. I do not know how long we went on making love, probably a couple of hours. I did not want him to stop and I knew he was very much enjoying himself playing with me. At a certain point he turned me upside down and started rimming my ass. Nobody had ever done that to me. I felt weird but it was feeling so good that I didn't try to stop him. All of a sudden he penetrated me. The pain was extremely strong and even though I tried to get away he kept me tight pounding me. After the first minute the pain turned in a pleasure that I had never experienced before and when I came it was an explosion of pleasure. We fell asleep in each other arms and slept until noon.

I was feeling embarrassed for what had happened but before I could say something he pushed me into the shower and under the warm water he started making love to me again. When I went home I did my schoolwork and I went to bed early thinking about Giacomo and masturbated before falling asleep.

During the following days I was feeling strange like if everybody knew what had happened Saturday night. I even called Giacomo asking him not to tell anyone. He laughed and reassured me, but he wanted to know when I was going over to see him again.

I kept a low profile for a few days but then there I was at the cinema looking for some encounters again. It seemed nothing else was on my mind but that.

This time the school was going well even because we were mainly studying in details what was studied during the previous years. I had some problems with the teacher of English but nothing I couldn't keep under control.

During Easter I decided to go visit my sister in Milano and explore that city that was never appealing to me, probably because it doesn't have the sea.

I went by train, took the bus, arrived at Wilma's house in the early afternoon. I met some of Bruno's friends and we all had dinner at his parents. The next day I went to the downtown area to explore. Even though I had been to Milano before, this was the first time I was there by myself. Nice stores and buildings but the atmosphere of the old Genova just wasn't there.

I walked to the park where there were many people taking sun and looking after the children. Around the little lake there was a public toilet and I had to go inside to see if something was going on. There were only two old men, so ugly that I didn't want to remain there one second more.

In the mall I saw several groups of guys walking around that were visibly gay. Noticing that one kept looking in my direction I took the courage to go ask him how they were meeting guys in Milano. He smiled and told me they had cinemas, bars, discos and different cruising areas but he would not recommend those because they were mostly for hustlers. I got a city map and he pointed out some of the most popular spots.

During that week in the big city I ended up not meeting anyone but I mostly hanged around Bruno's nephews who were about my age.

I was back at home and back in school for the last term. This time I knew I was going to pass on all the subjects and I was relieved because during the final 5th year Math was not going to be in the program.

In May I started going to the beach across the street to take sun and mingle with Roberto and my other friends. I also started taking tennis lessons and I still was going to the pool to swim with the team. I was building up some muscles and I think I gained 4 or 5 pounds!

The school ended on the first week of June and I was ready to go with Wilma and Alberto, my nephew, to Torre del Mare when my dad called and asked me to go to Lavarone to make sure a crew of people was working on the house. They were redoing the floors, the garage, one bathroom and the kitchen. I agreed and there I was, all by myself, eating at the Cervo and sleeping in the house. My usual friends were not arriving before the 2nd week in July and the only people in the village were the natives.

In the morning I was having breakfast, then I would ride my Vespa to the lake where I would rent a boat and row until lunchtime. Then I would go back home making sure they were working and to check the progress. After dinner there was nothing else to do but mingle with the locals.

On evening after I had got back from dinner there was a big thunderstorm and the power failed. I was on the 3rd floor in my room changing clothes to go out with some friends. I lit a candle with some kitchen matches and walked down the stairs to the living room. The rain had stopped but the power was still off, so I extinguished the candle, left in the middle of the dining table and walked out locking the front door. The house is isolated but there is a private little road going to the main square, about ¼ of a mile. We went to a local disco and we basically closed the place down around midnight. When I got back home the power was back, the candle was always in the middle of the table but it was broken in half. The box of matches was open and they were lying on the table in a half circle. This house had been built by my grandfather who had died in Venezia one year before I was born. On its site there was nothing but forest and to my knowledge nobody had ever died in it. Scared to death I went up to my room, locked the door, opened the shutters to be able to see the stars and tried to go to sleep. The next morning I called my sister and told her what had happened but she did not have an explanation for it.

Another strange thing happened for three times in a row: every other morning around 6, the sanitation was coming to collect the trash so I had to put the container out in the evening. Three times the container was already out and I did not move it at all.

Once more I heard someone knocking on the door of the basement, it was during the afternoon when I was the only person in the house.

I was glad to see my parents, my grandmother and Concetta arriving. All the works had been done and the house was back to normal, or at least I thought so.

Alberto was growing fast and all the attention was concentrated on him. Besides the usual friends of my mom coming for tea every afternoon, now there were my sister's friends coming to visit with their offspring. I was trying to stay out as much as possible organizing long walks with my friends and treasure hunts.

Due to the many long rainy days during that Summer somebody got the idea of turning my garage in a private dance club. We started decorating it with soft lights, murals, different colors and a small bar area. The night of the grand opening it was a success. In those days the music equipment was modest and the noise did not disturb the people upstairs. If some couples wanted to be alone they could wonder outside in the woods. A few guys from other groups showed up and we welcomed them with a modest cover charge. Soon the basement became a popular alternative spot to the Ruota.

Even that pleasant Summer was coming to an end and there I was back in Genova getting ready for my 5th and hopefully last year of high school. There were fewer books to buy and the class had reduced to 16 people. The atmosphere was more relaxed and the teachers were more courteous than ever. We were coming to that age when we were not kids anymore and we were supposed to act like young responsible men.

Most of my friends had a girlfriend and there was none eligible for me (not that I was looking for one). The big goal now was my 18th birthday on February the 3rd, the day that I could finally get a driver's license and be independent. Dad had promised me to give me his old car to become an experienced driver and I could not wait. Every now and then I was driving that car out of the garage, go around the block and parking it. Once I hit the side of the garage wall with the front right fender causing a small but visible damage. I did not say anything but the next day I asked my dad to give me a lift to school because it was raining. He did not notice the damage, took me to school and went to his office located in the downtown area. I had it all figured out in my mind: he would park in the usual public parking lot, lock the car and walk to the office, hopefully without noticing the damage because it was on the passenger side. I still was kind of nervous.

That evening he arrived home later than usual and he told us what had happened: "I got back to the car and from a distance I noticed that there was something wrong with the fender. After a close check I called the attendant who apologized for what had happened assuming that another customer had hit the car. He filled out a complaint for the parking lot insurance company and the damage will be paid in full"

I couldn't be more thrilled…everything went exactly the way I was hoping it would! I never told anybody the truth to this very day.

At school the guys in the lower classes were looking at us like if we were gods. Some were timidly approaching us to find out about professors, schedules and subjects. Some were even looking for protection against bullies. We had to act like those that knew it all. My grandmother was coming to spend Christmas with my parents and I was getting ready to go to Lavarone for the usual ski fun. I invited a schoolmate to join me, a really cute one, and he accepted. Roberto had his 18th birthday in October and his parents gave him a brand new Mini Minor, therefore we were going to ride with him to the mountains.

We have never been early risers and that morning we left around 11. After Milano we stopped for lunch and we arrived in Lavarone around 4pm. Roberto had booked a room at the Cervo, we went to my house that had previously been heated and the water had been turned on. Wilma, Bruno, little Alberto and Concetta were arriving three days later.

Gianni, my schoolmate, fell in love with the place and the area and when he met all my friends he told me he was kind of jealous about me. I said that jealousy was a bad beast, we had been friends for the past five years, I was sorry not to have invited him before, but I was sure my friends would have liked him very much and he had to consider himself completely at home and he was welcome there anytime he wanted. We were sharing my room that had two twin beds. We both liked to stay up late and get up late so there was no conflict there. At dinner there was the usual big long table and we were still raising hell with the servers. Just as I had thought Gianni had an immediate success and I saw a few girls smiling at him. When we finally went to bed he was a very happy camper who couldn't wait to see the slopes and to ski among the newly acquired friends.

Those two weeks were some of the best I can remember. There was plenty of snow, the days were sunny and kind of warm, the lake was totally iced and a few times we went to skate. We had brought all the latest favorite records and the portable player had to get new batteries on a daily basis.

Gianni was definitely not gay but we got so close that we started sharing our most intimate feelings and finally I told him everything about me. He was not shocked, on the contrary, one of his best friend was gay and he wanted me to meet him when we were going back to Genova.

That new year's eve we had the usual classic dinner topped by the Dom Perignon at midnight, then we went to the new disco in the village, the club 21, had a pizza around 5am at the Pom and went barhopping until sunrise. We all met at the Cervo for dinner after spending the whole day in bed and watching on TV the Vienna concert directed by Herbert von Karajan.

The night before leaving we all went to Trento to have dinner at a special restaurant, the Cantinota, still famous these days for Austrian food. The road was icy and really dangerous with a lot of curbs going from 1400 meters on the sea level to 200 meters with a mountain on one side and deep gorges on the other. The drivers seemed very confident going really fast. Thinking about that night I still wonder how we did not get killed in a fatal accident.

The holiday was almost over and we were on the way back. In the car we were listening to "bandiera gialla" the top of the pop. One of the most popular songs was "Good Vibrations" by the Beach Boys; on the Italian chart it was "29 Settembre" by the Equipe 84. Gianni was extremely enthusiast and asked me if he could come again in Summer to see what the place looked liked.

Roberto was thinking about living Genova the following year to go to study at the university of Bologna (city where Anna was living) because he had in mind to become an attorney. (Bologna is the 2nd oldest university in Italy, the 1st being the one of Camerino).

The last two days were spent to take care of the homework, and we were back to school ready for the final two terms.

Michele, one of ours schoolmates, did not show up. Everybody was worried because not coming to school for over 15 days without a very good reason could cost him the entire year, but he was not reachable. A few weeks later we all got an envelope with tickets for a theater: Michele had become a pop singer and was inviting us to his 1st concert. His songs were played by the radio and he was on TV many times, but after five or six years his popularity decreased and these days only a few people remember him.

During the second half of January I started going to driving school, not that I needed to, but dad insisted. The written test was tricky but really easy. Before the road test I had to take something to calm me down otherwise I would have seemed too nervous to the instructor. A few days after my 18th birthday I got my license and I celebrated that with some close friends. The "Simca Montlery" that my father gave me was a medium sized car, quite big in those days, but very comfortable and strong like a tank. I remember my dad giving me the keys and saying: "this is like an arm in your hands, do not exceed in speeding and remember that a car does not only require gas to run". That was a moment of absolute power in my life. Now I could come and go as I pleased and I could even decide to leave town with friends and go spend week ends anywhere.

The second school term was coming to an end with the 10 days Easter holiday and we were sitting at the Tonitto bar trying to decide what to do. Roberto came up with the crazy idea to drive to Paris for a couple of days. Two hours later four of us had packed a few clothes and were ready to go. We left around midnight and entered Paris in time for breakfast at ten o'clock.

That was a fun week end with just the four of us: Roberto, Gianni, Ruggero and me. We decided to look for a cheap hotel in the Latin Quarter, Saint Germain des Pres, the oldest part of town across the river, very colorful inhabited by artists, prostitutes and transvestites. I started showing the city to my friends who were very impressed by its beauty and the friendly atmosphere (friendly because we all spoke French and the Parisians are usually not friendly to those that don't).

2006

After a nice dinner in a typical restaurant, they were dying to go to see the famous shows at the Lido and the Folies Bergeres. Gianni suggested that I could go to a gay club and meet them later. They knew me just too well than force me to go see some striptease. I was on my own, got on the subway and went directly to Faubourg St. Honore' where I had heard there was a famous sauna. The place was huge, old and decadent. I went to a locker room, got undressed, put a towel around my waist and I started venture around. It was Saturday night but it did not seem crowded. The sauna was very hot and too lighted, the pool area had a couple of sorry individuals, nothing to look at, the resting room was filled with little beds but the steam room was quite full. I ventured in and I sat in a spot that seemed isolated. Soon enough there were a couple of guys that were touching me. The only problem was the steam and the weak light that did not enable me to see those guys properly in the face. I had to get away from one because I felt he had a potbelly, the other was slim and fit too so we started fooling around. It was really hot in there and we were sweating too much to be comfortable. Finally I succeeded to get him out of there and look him in the eyes. He had been living in Paris for 5 years but escaped from Tibet after the Chinese invasion. He was handsome, intelligent and had some oriental deep brown eyes. The time was flying and I had to meet my friends by the Pont Neuf. I asked him if he wanted to come with me or if there was anyway we could meet again the next day. From the time I was nine, always having been fascinated by the orient and its people, I had sympathized a lot for the Tibetans that were invaded, decimated and forced to fled to India. My religious ideas had always been very close to the Buddhist than to the Christians. Tenzin, that was his name, gave me his telephone number and told me to call him after lunch. I was very anxious to get back with him.

It was almost two when I met my friends. They were enthusiastic about the French women, so liberal and sexy. We all went to a bistro for a quick supper and finally to bed to sleep until noon. I gave everybody a treat taking them for lunch at the Bigorneaux, a very good restaurant by the old market place. Around 2pm I called Tenzin and we made arrangements to meet at the café de Rose, a semi-gay place in St. Germain. While my friends went sightseeing, we had a long and interesting conversation about Tibet, India, Buddha, the lamas and Milarepa, the lama that introduced Buddhism in Tibet. I had my mind made up to visit that country very soon, maybe after high school. That evening Tenzin joined us for dinner but I went over his apartment to spend the night. A new lifelong friendship had started.

On Monday morning we were leaving Paris for the long drive back home. I guess everybody had a great time. It was one of those crazy things that make life enjoyable and remains in our memory forever.

That was a good training for my driving. I was getting more confident every day. We got in Genova after dinner having stopped to eat before the Italian border in a place where there were many truckers eating. (In Europe that's a synonymous of good food: they are on the road all the time and they know where the good food is served, even if the restaurant doesn't look that nice).

We spent the rest of the holiday playing cards, going to the cinema, relaxing, playing tennis and I had to resume my training with the swim team. The last school term was just around the corner and we were confident everything would have gone smooth.

Nothing much exciting happened except for a quick visit of Alan who was arriving from New York and was going to join his dad in Cairo.

We had a long talk, almost the whole night, and I told him about my idea of going to India when the school was over. I would have loved to go to visit Tibet, but the Chinese authorities were not releasing visas. Alan and I had many thoughts in common and he welcomed the idea with enthusiasm. He couldn't promise anything but I knew he was going to do all in his power to join me. He had met a girl in Germany that he liked and they had been dating for over a year, her name was Gisela, she would become one of my best friends in the years to come.

The last two months were filled with interrogations and simulated examinations. The teachers for the final tests were coming from different schools to make sure there was an absolute impartiality with the final judgments. The tension was very high because everybody had to concentrate on hundred different things and recall those lost during the five years: the most insignificant note taken years before could be helpful during the orals and also during the written tests. I was spending many hours with Gianni and other schoolmates asking and answering all the questions that would cross our mind. I must say that our teachers were the best, with the exception of the English one…

The final week was kind of fun. There were parties, talks, discussions, debates. Now we had a ten days break before the written tests, everybody recommended us to relax, eat well and get a lot of rest. The weather was beautiful and as it usually happens at the beginning of June, the temperature was rising into the upper 80's and in Italy only a few private schools were air-conditioned and the wide opened windows didn't help much especially if one is wearing suit and tie.

All tests would last 4 hours. The first was Italian. We were given the choice of one of three proposed titles for a composition about art, a recent event or the influence in history of a special personage. I picked the one about art, it took me about 1 hour to fill up a couple of pages and I was out of there.

The second day there was Math: we had to demonstrate a theorem that I had done before with Gianni and Roberto. I couldn't believe my luck! Gianni and I looked at each other and smiled. We were out of there in less than one hour.

The third day it was Astronomy and Navigation. We could use the nautical charts but it was rather complicated. The heat was intolerable, everybody was sweating (in those days those antiperspirants had not been invented). It took us the whole 4 hours and probably 3 people on 15 finished the test. Leaving the class we started comparing our efforts but it seemed everybody got a different solution.

The fourth day was the composition in English on any subject of our choice. I invented a trip to Australia giving details of places and people that I met. I guess she must have been happy because at the oral she asked me more about what I had seen and done and she was satisfied in just five minutes of conversation.

Now that the big part had been done we could relax and go to the beach until the following week. The orals were starting on Monday with Italian and History, Tuesday with Math, Wednesday with Astronomy and Navigation and <dulcis in fundo> Thursday with English.

That weekend I went with Gianni to Torre del Mare. He fell in love with the place while I met a very cute young man, Antonio, who was from Genova and was visiting some relatives in Spotorno, a village nearby. I relaxed with Antonio for the whole night and the next day, Gianni relaxed with a girl he met on the beach. I'm not a real fan of fish but on that Saturday night in Noli we had one of the better grill mixes. Sunday afternoon we were on the way back to Genova not really worried about the Italian test.

Ms. Foco, sitting next to her colleague from a different school, was very nice and extremely professional. They had liked my composition and they asked me a few questions about the Renaissance and the influence of the Vatican during the 16th century. They dismissed me with a smile and while leaving I heard the other professor complimenting with her for her incredible teaching skills.

The next day Ms. Munna said she was surprised about my test. As I had foreseen I did not answer correctly to all the questions they asked me, but due to the fact that my vote in the written test was quite high, the average came up sufficient and they made the effort to let me know that before they let me go.

Wednesday I had to prove to the two teachers that I knew enough about Astronomy and Navigation in spite of the written test that was not sufficient. Apparently only five students had completed it correctly.

Thursday there was the final English conversation that was a success.

Now it was the time to wait for a full week before going to school and look at the results that would be hanging from the wall by the dean office: Promosso meant "passed" Respinto meant "repeat the year". Closed to the names there would be the average vote obtained during the two weeks. I knew mine would not be one of the highest because of Math and Astronomy.

Finally, on the 21st of June 1964, I had completed high school and passed with the average vote of 7. I was happy, my mom, Wilma, Bruno and Concetta were too, my dad said that he was expecting at least an 8.

I went for one week to the sea and then up to Lavarone to enjoy my newly acquired freedom form school. Except for Luigi that had graduated the year before, all my friends had passed the big test. Now we were encouraged to party all Summer long.

But I was thinking about India so right after august the 15th I called Alan and told him I wanted to leave and start with Pune. He was in Frankfurt at that time and apparently was living in the same house with Gisela. Three days later they both arrived in Lavarone and we started to draw our plan.

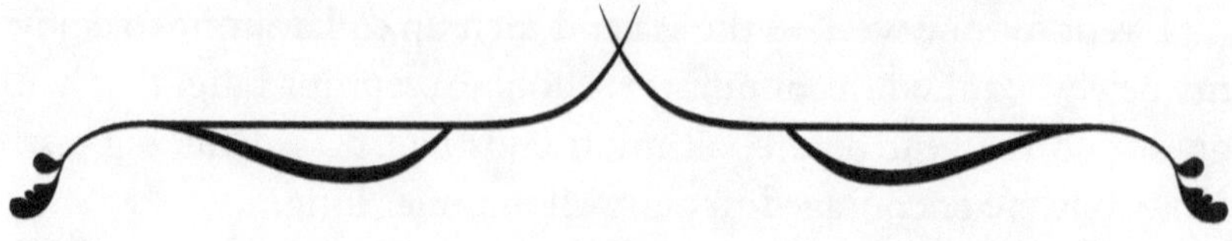

Chapter 6

India (Aryavarta)

My parents were absolutely opposed to this trip but after evaluating different pros and cons and after talking with Alan and Gisela, seeing that they had their "head on the shoulders" as we say in Italy when a person is OK, they agreed to let me go.

During the early 60's there was a new movement that had started in England, the hippies, or the children of the flowers, guys dressed with very colorful clothes and wearing very long hair. The Beatles and the Rolling Stones were the most popular groups in the world and their songs were beautiful. My idea of going to India had nothing to do with that. I felt I belonged there. I had my own theory of reincarnation when I was nine, had my own idea of the divinity, believed that I was part of the divine and that I had always existed and always will be under different forms and in different parts of the universe. I knew I had to go to Pune to meet somebody who would show me the way and would teach me more than I had imagined during my short life. Alan, Gisela and I were sharing more or less the same believes and we had endless debates about life and philosophy.

The preparations started with a list of vaccinations we had to get. At the end we had a stack of medical documents to keep with our passport. My mother insisted that we fly Swissair because that was the only airline she trusted. The flight was long and the plane was one of those new jets called Coronado, supposed to be more silent and stable than the older equipped with propellers.

Credit cards were not an option in those days so we had to carry travelers cheques. Bruno gave us three money belts as a gift, something that I would use for many years to come.

To communicate with our families was going to be the biggest problem because in India there were few phones and the lines did not work well at all. It could take hours to get a bad connection.

We decided to leave with a very little luggage, just the necessary, as we would have bought most of the stuff there. My dad gave me the address of a friend in Bombay to contact in case of need.

The day of departure was just a couple of weeks away when I decided to go see the Passalacqua and say goodbye. He gave me a big lump of money and recommended to have a good time. Even my grandmother and Bruno did the same. Among the three of us we had more than enough. We got on the train to the airport of Zurich, Kloten, on the 20th of October of 1964 and boarded the plane just before noon. The adventure had begun!

We flew to Teheran where we had a little over one hour to walk around the airport, and back on board for the final flight to New Delhi where we arrived early in the morning. Nobody had slept on board even though the seats were more comfortable than those on modern jets. The passport check took a couple of hours and finally we were in a cab going to a specific hotel near the town center. The city appeared to be huge, wide roads, large squares, a lot of traffic mostly of bicycles, motorcycles, a few cars, buses and people walking everywhere. We got quickly accustomed to see cows wondering everywhere. We passed by a huge open market on a square where everybody had merchandise, food, animals, spices and arts for sale. When we got to the Samrat hotel it was lunchtime but we jumped into bed and were off for the rest of the day.

The city actually consists of two parts. Old Delhi that was the capital of Mughal India and New Delhi, the imperial city created as the capital of India by the British. The harmonious blend of the historical and cultural past and trend-setting innovations of today make New Delhi an amazing contemporary mega city of the world.

The next morning we had a nice continental breakfast and we were on the way to explore the city. We would walk as much as we could, eat wherever, look for bargain clothes to buy and get a cab back to the hotel when we were tired.

We had to see the Indian Gate, a 42 meters high arch that was raised as a memorial to soldiers who laid down their lives in the 2nd world war. It has emerged as the icon of Delhi and by far the most important landmark.

The Jantar Mantar, a unique structure designed by the astronomer maharaja Jai Singh the 2nd of Jaipur, as an astronomical observatory.

The Red Fort, a magnificent monument built by emperor Shah Jahan. The appellative "red" comes from the red sandstone used in the construction.

The Qutab Minar, was the tallest tower in India standing at over 72 meters.

We had been warned by the hotel manager not to wear jewelry, to carry little cash, not to change dollars with rupees on the streets and not to give change, candies, cigarettes or other items to anybody on the streets.

We picked up a nice looking restaurant for lunch and drank only bottled water. The tandoori cooking was, in our opinion, the best. The smell of curry was everywhere and we quickly got used to it.

We reached a big market where we started browsing and it was there that we decided to change our European clothes with something more Indian so that we could blend in better and not feel embarrassed with people looking at us all the time.

From my point of view some Indians, probably those belonging the lower ranks, were very handsome, nice cut faces, high jaws, very black hair and piercing black eyes. The people with lighter skin were kind of chubby and their skin did not appear too nice. Some of the younger women were beautiful but it looked like in their later years they were loosing their shape and also some of their beautiful white teeth.

We were walking by the main police station when the sight of a building caught our eyes. It was the Sisgunj Gurudwara commemorating the site of the 9th guru of the Sikhs, Teg Bahadur's martyrdom's. The guru was be-headed by Aurangzeb in 1675. The building had been extended during the centuries but they had done a good job as it was almost impossible to tell the additions apart from the original structure.

Happy but exhausted we had dinner at the hotel and were soon in bed thinking about the next day.

To visit the National Museum located in Janpath it was a must. This museum has a large collection of items from the 2nd and 1st century B.C. A separate section is dedicated to the Harrapa (Indus valley civilization).

The Chandini Chowk, the main market, was definitely the place where we spent more time in that city. We also found a tailor that cut the material we chose and made some shirts and jackets while we were shopping. It was unbelievable how cheap everything was.

We had to decide how to reach Pune. The train or the bus was our only possible option but, considering the fact that most of the roads were not paved, we decided for the first choice.

A cab left us in front of a station where we tried to understand when and if there was a train. The station was loaded with people, some were traveling, some where just there trying to sell anything to make a living. It was then that we noticed not many people were wearing a watch.

Finally we were told where to go to wait for the train that was arriving from Rampur heading to Jaipur, it was on track 3, my lucky number! Of course nobody knew when the train was arriving but that didn't seem to worry anybody. Some were praying, children were playing, an old man was redoing his turban and another was cleaning his feet near a small fountain. The wait went beyond three hours but the surprise was when the train arrived: there were people sitting ton top of the wagons!

We finally managed to get on board and find three seats close together. Another full hour went by before the train decided to move and even then it moved at an extremely slow speed. It was rather hot and the wind blowing through the open windows was helping us not to breath that marasmus of smells of curry and sweat that everybody seemed saturated with.

We don't even recall how many times we stopped. It was helpful to get some food and some bottle sealed beverages that looked like Coke, but didn't taste like it. We agreed to stop in Jaipur because the prospective of staying on that (or another) train for days was not the ultimate experience.

Jaipur, the capital of Rajasthan, it's also known as "the pink city" from the color of the building in the old town center. It sits on a dry lakebed surrounded by barren hills surmounted by forts and crenellated walls. This buzzing metropolis is certainly a place of wild contrasts and feast for the eyes. All though Jaipur has retained its strong Rajputana flavor tempered by several influences - the Munghal being the most prominent. From the colorful fountains of life to the sublime Birla Temple, from the architectural delights of the City Palace to the most serene Jal Mahal.

The Johari Bazaar was, of course, the main point of attraction for us. I have always been fascinated with flea markets from the Porte de Clignancourt in Paris, to Portobello in London, O'bei O'bei in Milano, Porta Portese in Roma…but these market were most interesting exhibiting artifacts I had never seen before.

1970

We went to visit the Albert Hall Museum where they had models of yogis in various positions.

I would recommend a visit to the Hawa Mahal, known as the palace of the winds. From there the ladies of the court could look out at festive processions without jeopardizing their modest exclusion.

We were trying to reach Pune so we went once again to the train station to try to find out when we could leave. There was a train in 30 minutes. We went to collect our luggage, were back at the station but the train didn't show up until 5 hours later.

The voyage to Bombay was one of the longest extenuating I had in my whole life: it lasted almost four days with numerous stops to eat and sleep because nothing was available on the train.

When we finally arrived we crawled in a cab and asked to take us to a decent hotel, he deposited us in front of the Leela Kempinski, not too far from the airport. It wasn't exactly the best location but it served the purpose for us to rest, eat and take long soaking baths. Our goal was to reach Pune that was only another 170 kms away and this time we decided to try the bus. We didn't do any sight seeing in Bombay saving it for better days.

The trip to Pune took another full day. Along the road there were people walking, many bicycles and some guys sitting in circle practicing some kind of yoga. Their clothes were more colorful than we had seen before and we knew they were hippies coming from different parts of the world to meet their gurus. The road was climbing on pleasant hills and at a certain point we passed through Lonavala, a charming resort at over 600 meters on sea level, after that came Khandala and finally Pune. We took two rooms at the Saras hotel close to the stadium, rested for the whole night and had a beautiful breakfast with a bunch of fruits all native to the area. The hotel manager recommended the Amrapali restaurant.

The climate was not bad at all. During the day we were reaching the 20 C and at night it would go down to 4-5 C but we had bought some very warm and cheap cashmere sweaters for that.

The influence of Bhagwan Rajneesh was felt trough out the city and his admirers were everywhere, probably arriving there by the hundreds every month.

I was certainly not attracted by the hippy kind and the fact that a lot of drugs were commonly used everywhere was bothering us. People were sleeping on the streets using dirty covers and the unpleasant smell of marijuana was filling the air.

The natives were used to see these "guests" around, and their main intent was to get as much money as they could out of them.

The close crematory ground in Pune, especially gruesome at night, is considered highly attractive by the yogi: "he who would find the Deathless Essence must not be dismayed by a few unadorned skulls".

On the 3rd day in the early afternoon we were making our purchases in the bazaar. We pushed our way trough the colorful medley of housewives, guides, priests, simply clad widows, dignified Brahmins, and ubiquitous holy bulls. As Gisela, Alan and I moved on, I turned my head to survey a narrow, inconspicuous line. A Christlike man in the ocher robes of a swami stood motionless at the end of the lane. Instantly and anciently familiar he seemed; for a trice my gaze fed hungrily. Then doubt assailed me.

"you are confusing this wondering monk with someone known to you" I thought. After ten minutes I felt heavy numbness in my feet. They were unable to carry me farther. With some difficulty I turned around and my feet regained normality. I faced the opposite direction and again the peculiar weight oppressed me.

Alan and Gisela were probably feeling the same way: the monk was magnetically drawing us to him! We looked at each other all thinking the same thing: "are we crazy"? We reached the narrow line. Our quick glance revealed the quiet monk steadily gazing in our direction. A few more steps and we were at his feet!

His face was one that I had seen in many visions. Those halcyon eyes, in a leonine head with pointed beard and flowing locks, had often peered through the gloom of my nocturnal reveries, holding a promise that I had not fully understood. Was this the same feeling going through our minds?

"You have come to me!" said the monk with his voice tremulous with joy. "How many years I have waited for you!"

We stood silent. Words seemed the rankest superfluities. Eloquence flowed in soundless chant from the heart of master to disciples. We were sensing that our guru knew the truth and would lead us to it. The obscuration of our lives disappeared in a fragile dawn of prenatal memories. Dramatic time! Past, present and future are its cycling scenes. Our hands in his, our guru took us to his residence in Pune.

Tall, erect, about fifty-five, he was active and vigorous as a young man. His dark eyes were large, handsome with plumb wisdom. Slightly curly hair softened a face of striking power. Strength mingled subtly with gentleness.

As we made our way to the stone balcony of the house overlooking a pond, he said affectionately :"I shall give you my hermitage and all I possess" "I give you my unconditional love" "Ordinary love is selfish, its roots are in the dark, a mix of desires and satisfactions. Divine love is without conditions, without boundary, without change. The flux of the human heart is gone forever at the transfixing touch of pure love" he added humbly, "if ever you find me falling from a state of God-realization, please promise to put my head on your lap and help me to bring me back to the Cosmic Beloved we all worship"

He rose in that semi-darkness and guided us to an inner room. As we ate mangoes and sweetmeats with almonds he wove into his conversation an intimate knowledge of our natures. We were awestruck at the grandeur of his wisdom, very well blended with an innate humility.

We had not made references to our lives; everything seemed superfluous.

He smiled and told us to meet him in the afternoon outside the ashram. In saying so he gave us a page with a script and we left. There were a few sentences written in Sanskrit that we couldn't read. Sanskrit is the elder sister of all Indo-European tongues. Its alphabetical script is called "Devanagari"; literally "divine abode". "Who knows my grammar knows God!" Panini, great philosopher of ancient India, paid that tribute to the mathematical and psychological perfection of Sanskrit. He who would track language to its liar must indeed end as omniscient.

Deeply shaken by this encounter we went to bed and spent sleepless hours thinking about what the next day would bring us.

During breakfast everybody was silent but we couldn't wait to meet Dayananda.

We went to the ashram and waited. There was a nice crowd of people, mostly foreigners, some talking, some singing, some chanting mantras. At three o' clock sharp our guru showed up, touched our hands, then invited us to sit in a circle on the grass. He looked up in the sky, down to the earth and straight in our eyes. His voice sounded nice and firm and in a perfect English he told us to join hands. He started chanting a simple one word mantra, then he stood silent for a few minutes. We figured out he was looking at our auras and feeling our vibes.

He said that we came a long way to know the truth, but the truth could be found within us. Words were not necessary to communicate, we could do that with our minds since we were all speaking the same language. Some people were not as lucky and they had to learn different languages to understand each other. Rivers of words were spent by humans but in the majority of the cases that was not necessarily lead to concrete conclusions. Most results were only apparent and even if it seemed things would take the right course they would change in the space of a heart- beat.

He said goodbye and told us to be there the next day.

His words could sound sibylline but they made sense to us.

We went around to hear and see what other groups were doing and detected that some guys where there to learn, some just because they were in a state of confusion. Many were talking about drugs because they wanted to reach a state of perfection through them.

That night we stayed up and talked until dawn. We knew exactly what Dayananda was expecting us to do…but…were we ready to do it? And what about our families, friends, our lives! When we finally went to sleep we had not reached a final decision.

When we got up we placed three intercontinental calls to talk to our families and that turned out to be an adventure that took all day. When we finally got through the communication was so bad that we could hardly talk. The lucky one was Gisela so Alan and I talked to her parents asking them to call ours and tell them everything was fine. At that point it seemed impossible to explain by phone what was going on. The important thing was to let them know that we were all right since we couldn't go into deeper details. We were trying to decide what to do: follow our instinct and get to know our guru better or go on with our trip and move on to Goa. We decided to spend another week in Pune. Looking back to our experience if I had been alone I would have probably stayed there and learn more from the teachings of Dayananda. That would have changed my life completely. Being with friends and knowing that they were not ready to do so was a big deterrent. We went to the ashram every day. We got annoyed with some people that were insisting in using drugs and wanted us to join them. Most elements of the crowd were getting on our nerves. At that point I realized that I didn't have sex with anyone since we left Europe and as long as I was involved in philosophical discussions I had not even missed it!

Much to our guru's regret we left Pune on a beautiful morning to head back to Bombay and from there, with some luck, down the coast to Goa.

We crossed many small towns on the ocean by bus. During those five days we slept in the worst hotels and sat among the most incredible and smelly people and animals. We found out that the best food we could eat was in the local markets but we had to be careful with the drinks: only sealed soda bottles.

Finally Goa appeared to us from the bus just before sunset. We got off and walked to the beach across the street and jumped in the water in our underwear. It was so refreshing to do that after hours passed on that dirty bus! It was then that we noticed some people looking at us with an amused expression on their faces. Of course we didn't care and basked in the shallow water.

Not too far from that beach we could see a market and that's where we went carrying our bags. We bought a bunch of fresh fruits and I gorged myself on tomatoes, my favorite vegetable.

It was time to go look for a hotel so we stopped a taxi and asked the driver to take us to a good one. That was the first good night of sleep in a week! And finally in a clean room with a private bath!

The next day we tried to call our families to let them know we arrived safely in Goa that would be our residence for at least a couple of months.

Having been a Portuguese colony until 1961, the town was filled with Christian temples of interesting architecture, some built in the fifteen hundred. We were more interested in the Hindu and Buddhist buildings.

The idea was to spend a few weeks at the beach and we started with asking our cab driver if he knew of some accommodation available in a good location. Thirty minutes later we were introduced to a nice old British lady that had spent there almost her entire life. She showed us a little house, fully furnished, overlooking a nice, clean and quiet beach: the price was right and we moved in the same day. The rental agreement included cleaning service and some kind of pest control. Soon enough we befriended a fisherman and his family that were living next door and it was agreed that one of his daughters would cook for us.

It was a cool brake from the usual habits and eating at home we could have a better variety of food then going to the restaurants all the time. The house had 2 bedrooms, 1 bath, a small kitchen and a spacious living room. The nicest area was a wide terrace with some rattan furniture and a curtain to repair from the strong sun. The view of the sunset was absolutely stunning.

I do not usually eat fish and I'm very bothered by the fish bones that, no matter what, always end up in my mouth. I must say that Deyanira always took care of that and during those 3 months I never had that problem.

We adapted well to the life in Goa and joined a very serious Yoga class. Our master was a follower of the Dalai Lama who had escaped from Lhasa in 1959.

By then we had found the way to communicate regularly with our families in Italy through a telephone office downtown. We became very friendly with the employee so that every time there was a communication he would send for us in a matter of minutes. That's the way that I met Nizar whom was called "the messenger".

Nizar was 32 years old, 5'9" tall, the skin was not too dark thus denoting some mixed blood from two different casts. His hair was black and curly, beautifully designed lips and his eyes were dark and deep.

At this point Alan and Gisela were involved to the point that nothing and nobody would distract their attention. I started staring at Nizar the first time I saw him and I thought I noticed he did not mind that at all. It was a couple of weeks later that, during a call, Gisela noticed that he was looking at me with some light in his eyes and she gave me the hint that he was probably more interested in me than what I had thought. That seemed a good occasion to invite him for dinner and the fact that he promptly accepted was a confirmation that Gisela was right.

It was Alan who helped both of us to "break the ice". After dinner we spent most of the night walking on the beach, like two old friends that had a lot to catch up, talking about our lives, in a way so similar, yet so different for living in two different continents. Our ideas, aspirations, dreams, were basically very similar. His family was very well off before the British invaded the country and his father had died living him a heritage of good principles and some old books about the Buddhism.

We sat on the warm sand, looked at the very dark blue sky covered with stars, and for the first time our hands touched. That was a sensation I will never forget. It was like an electric shot went through my body. The funny thing is that at that point I still wasn't sure if Nizar was thinking about me in the same way I was thinking about him. For the very first time in my life I decided to take the situation in my hands and kissed him. His lips were moist and soft and to my pleasant surprise he started kissing me again and again. I thought I was touching Heaven with a finger and I wanted to pinch myself to make sure I wasn't dreaming.

We called the night and I went home to dream about my newly found Indian guy.

The days that followed would be remembered as some of the most wonderful in my life. I had many crushes on people before, but I had never experienced such powerful interest for one person in particular. I was thinking about him constantly, talking to him in my mind and for the first time around people I was acting like myself, without fear to show my intimate thoughts. Not being ashamed of using inflections in my voice that I would never dare using around friends and family.

Nizar and I spend more time together feeling a mutual attraction, mental and physical, to which we resisted for another week or so. He was going to be off work for 4 days and came to spend them at our house. The first time we made love was like heaven on earth. He was so sweet, great kisser, perfect touch and had the power of driving the body to a total relaxation.

We started doing everything together and sometimes I would go around with him while he was working. We visited all the surrounding areas including some ancient temples covered by the vegetation that had been forgotten for centuries. My biggest fears in India were close encounters with spiders and snakes. Nizar told me how to avoid them and I kept those advices for the rest of my life.

Our visa was coming to an end and we were enjoying the last week in Goa living every hour to the fullest. I knew I had to leave my beloved but in my hearth I believed I could come back soon and spend my life with him. The last night was spent outside looking at the stars, hand in hand, hoping the sun would never raise. When the light erased the last shadows of the night and our good driver came to pick us up to take us to Bombay it was like some big tie had broken. There were no words that could express all our sorrow.

Alan and Gisela did their best to cheer me up during the long drive. The next day we were sitting on the plane thinking about all the wonderful things we had seen, the beautiful people we had met and all the spiritual teachings that would have imprinted our future way to look at earthly things.

The flight was long and boring. We arrived in Zurich before noon and my parents were at Kloten airport to pick us up. Nobody had slept on the plane, the jet lag did the rest.

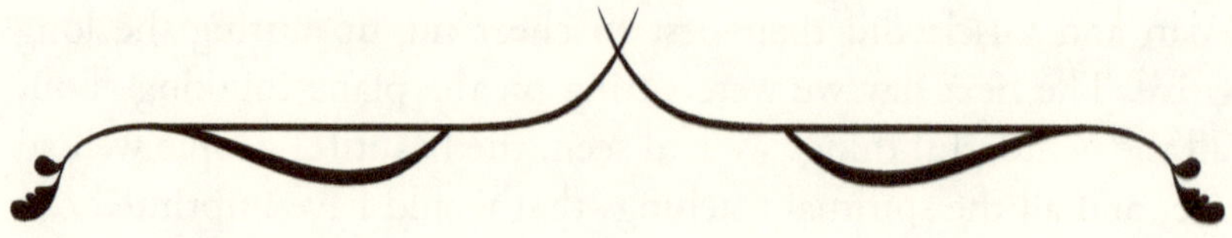

Chapter 7

Germany

1969

It took me about two weeks to get back to the normal routine of the European way of life. India seemed like a distant wonderful dream. My parents and friends were constantly asking about the experience but all I was doing was giving them a pile of photographs to look at. I did not feel like talking with them and I certainly was not in a good mood thinking about that world so different and about the people I had met. Nizar was at the center of my thoughts and I thought I could die for sorrow.

Of course time is supposed to cure everything, so I put into practice some teachings and with the help of some long distance calls to Alan my mind could work better and see things in the right light. I also succeeded in calling Nizar to make sure he was doing all right and when he told me not to worry I was very happy.

There was one problem coming up: my military duty.

Since I went to maritime high school I would have to join the Italian navy and that meant to be away from home for the next two years. My father had been a hero during the second world war and had a high rank. All the present admirals and also the minister of defense had been his navy mates. Unfortunately he was determined not to move a finger to help me out of the situation because he believed that every young man had to perform a military service: that was good for his life and it would help to grow up like a real man. Useless to say that my mother had an opposite view on the matter, so I was not really surprised when they both came up with a compromise.

My father told me that I could have skipped the service if I wanted to go abroad for a certain number of years, ten to be exact. His favorite shipyard was in Wegesack, the port of Bremen, in Germany. The general manager would have let me work there (to do a favor to my dad) and I could have rented a small apartment owned by a nice old widow of an engineer of the shipyard.

I had been to Wegesack many times and I loved Bremen. It didn't take me long to decide what I wanted to do and at the end of September I packed my things and left with dad.

The trip took two days. We met Frau Rutschmann, I looked at the small apartment and settled in. Now it was time to go to the office and meet the colleagues I would work with. Since I had never worked before I was a bit nervous. The people were very nice, they all knew my parents and had a great respect for my father. My duty was to work with the archive: piles of invoices and documents to put in order of date and in files! For that I would get paid 400 DM per month and, of course, my dad would pay for food and rent.

I was all set. We found a nice green Volkswagen beetle and I was on my own.

The bad thing was that I had to be at work by eight, so I had to get up at seven (something that I really hated to do). On the way to the office I was stopping at a Bakerei to have breakfast with some hot coco, freshly baked bread, butter and honey or jam. At 12 we would break for lunch and by five pm we were off for the day. My landlady was preparing for me a good dinner and then I would go out to the disco. There were no gay bars in Wegesack, but Bremen was just 16 kms away.

During the week- nights I had found some cruising areas in town, around the river Weser, but on Friday and Saturday nights I was off to Bremen and my favorite spots were a cute bar called Bei Hans and a disco called the Olympia. At the bar I could chat with a lot of different people. It was like being in a living room with comfortable leather chairs and coffee tables. The juke box was operated by the patrons and most of the songs were British and American. The Stones with songs like "let's spend the night together" and "Ruby Tuesday" were very popular. Some German songs were nice too if they didn't sound like military marches.

I was more interested in talking to some mature men even though there were some nice looking young guys there. There were different kind of conversations going on, sometimes sexual but most of the time about politics, religion, history, music, opera and life experiences. Soon enough I knew most people in the bar and I became very popular. I was looking forward to those interesting talks. Until I was 14-15 years old I always refrained from commenting when older people were chatting, but now I was ready to take the challenge and express my point of view on different matters. Every week end I was learning something or I was trying to convince some that not everything was all black or all white.

I had a preference for some nice looking men in their forties. In those days most people were slim and if there was something I could not take was a potbelly. I often ended up going home with somebody and I must admit I was seldom disappointed.

In Wegesack my cruising was somewhat successful but nothing to be excited about. Every now and then I would meet some nice looking guy but it was only a one time deal and would never see them around again. There were some guys close to my age walking around but non of them would attract my attention in spite of the fact that the young "bell 'Antonio" in Genova had blackmailed me just a few years before.

I did meet a nice girl in a disco while dancing the hottest song by the Monkeys "I'm a believer". I took her to my apartment and we had some fun, but she was too inhibited compared to the guys.

In Germany it was much easier to keep in touch with my parents and all my friends. The telephone system had improved a lot since the fifties and long waits were not necessary anymore to make a long distance call.

Alan was now living in Paris sharing an apartment with a nice Australian doctor to be and Gisela had decided to go to Oxford to study psychology.

At my office the work became routine interrupted by the many coffee breaks that everybody had. My colleagues were very nice but very gossipy about people working in other departments. A large number of workers in the shipyard were from Turkey but they wouldn't mingle with the locals and that was mutual.

At the office I had met some guys my age that were already making a living working various jobs. Many nights we would go out for dinner and to a bar or a disco. Girls were the primary things on their mind but there were many other arguments. Furthermore they were starting a little band and they were most interested in some Italian songs of which I knew the words and I could translate them into German.

I never told a soul about my preferences and they never asked. I do not think that knowing about me would have made any difference. People in the northern countries have always been much more open and well disposed about all kind of "human failings" (like somebody closed to the catholic church liked to call them). With my two friends we went several times to a nudist camp just outside Wegesack and we always had a great time.

1966 was coming to an end and I had 8 days vacation coming up between Christmas and New Year. I called Alan and decided to go spend that time in Paris, city that I considered my second home.

I drove on the autobahn at a very high speed and it took me only a few hours to reach Paris. I got a very warm welcome by Alan who informed I had the choice of sleeping on the sofa or to share the bed with him. I choose the last one, of course.

Paris back then was really ready for the holiday season! It was called "la ville lumiere" for a good reason: all the trees in the Champs Elisees had millions of lights and the decorations were stunning. I forgot about driving and was riding the very fast subway. In a matter of minutes I could go from one side of town to the other re-visiting all the familiar places. Alan and I walked a lot around Saint Germain des Pres, Montmartre, Pigalle and from the Etoile to the tour Eiffel. We loved dining in the bistros and looking at the art work displayed by the numerous starving artists. Life never stopped there; to walk around at 4o'colck in the afternoon or 4 o'clock in the morning was basically the same. It was interesting to go by the Halles to see how the food supplies were poring in from the countryside.

We also toured some new gay clubs and we met some really cool people. We did spend Christmas eve at home but we did not miss the midnight mass at Notre Dame. For the night of the 31st we booked a table "chez Madame Artur", the most famous transvestite club in Montmartre, just a few hundred feet away from the "Moulin Rouge". Gerard, the Australian roommate, joined us with his girlfriend and we all had a blast.

I talked to Alan about my prospective of staying abroad for 10 years in order to avoid the Italian military service and I expressed my doubts that I could stay away from home for such a long time. That was a very tough decision to take considering that if something had happened to my family I would have been stuck abroad. Before going back to Germany we did pay a visit to the flea market at the "Porte de Clignancourt" where I bought some new clothes according to the fashion of the time (mini pulls where the big things) and I also bought some records of Michel Polnareff, Gilbert Becaud, Charles Aznavour and, of course, Edith Piaf.

Driving back to Wegesack was not as pleasant since I was leaving my good friend and I was going back to the usual routine.

The work at the office was rather boring. Working in the archive did not lead to anything interesting. But at least I was making plenty of pocket money to enjoy every week end the way I wanted.

Hamburg has always been a fun city and was only 150 kms. away. I checked the gay hotels and clubs with the help of the bartender of Bei Hans and on a Friday afternoon was on the autobahn again. This time I was on my own in a city that was considered very sinful and the Ripperbahn, or the San Pauli amusement area was to be discovered.

The hotel was fortunately nice and clean and close to all the places I wanted to hit. I started with a gay restaurant and soon enough two guys sitting at the table next to mine invited me to join them. After dinner they offered to show me around. Before I take advantage of any situation I have to study the people carefully. Observe how they talk, if they make mistakes in the grammar, how they smile, if they are up to something no good and check every little detail that could make me wonder if they are up to no good or if I can trust them in general. A lot of this I learned it in India under the teachings of Dayananda and also my beloved Nizar. I can usually tell if their scope is just purely sex, if they have in mind to take advantage of a certain situation, or if they are just motivated by an interest to know somebody and take it from there. They seemed OK guys. Had lived together for 8 years, had respectable jobs, they were not into drugs and I knew that their ultimate goal was to get in my pants for a three way. Both of them were good looking and I decided that I would play the game.

We started with a gay bar filled with loud people. I got many looks and I looked a lot myself. I was drinking some plain apfelsaft (apple juice) while they were drinking beer. Then we went to a disco that was very popular. It was very cold outside but it was just too hot inside. They kept drinking beer and I was starting to wonder if by the time we were going home they would still be fit for some good sex or just to drank to pass out. To my surprise after 2am they started drinking soda and they sobered up. Around 3 we decided we had enough and they asked me if I wanted to go to their apartment to crush. I accepted pretending I was too sleepy to go to the hotel.

They were living in a nice penthouse overlooking a modern part of town. We had something to eat and then they started touching my legs and kissing me. It took at least thirty minutes to undress each other and crawl into their big bed. Their mouth and tongues were all over my body and the excitement was so high that I came very soon. They kept working on me for at least another two hours and finally, exhausted, after we all came another two times, we fell asleep.

We walked up around noon and one of them prepared some good German meal. After lunch we repeated the action of the night before.

I got back to the hotel and went to take a nap. Walked up around dinner time and decided to go have a drink in a bar nearby. It was still early and the place was not crowded. Saturday night people tend to go out late. While the bartender was serving me the usual apple juice I noticed he had very nice eyes, a great smile, slim fit body and he was staring at me. I started a conversation and after a short while we were like old buddies. I learned he was getting off at midnight and I could read in his eyes he wanted me to be there at the change of the shift. I went to have dinner and returned around 11. At this time the bar was much more crowded and he begged me to be patient and to wait for him even because he was too busy to keep me company. That hour seemed long. Several guys started a conversation but I was cutting them short. I had my eyes on the bartender and at that point nobody around compared to him. When the juke box started playing a few songs that I had selected he finally finished his shift and proposed to get out of there to unwind. We went to a different bar, much more quiet, where he had a couple of beers and we chatted in a very relaxed atmosphere. This bar was not gay but he started kissing me indifferent to the people that were around us. My face was red for the shame and my penis was getting harder by the seconds. I felt like everybody was looking at us. He reassured me and said that nobody would care, but to make me feel more comfortable, he asked me to follow him home. We got in a cab and after a few minutes ride we were going up the stairs of a three story condo. His apartment was small, clean and well furnished. His parents lived in Holland and he left home when he had turned 18 to live in the big city. Worked several jobs until he became a bartender for that gay club where he had been for 12 years. His goal was to save enough money to buy the place from the owner that was going to retire soon.

He was a very happy individual, always smiling and joking about everything. In bed he was sexy and hot, just the way I had expected him to be.

That was my wild weekend in Hamburg: I had paid two nights in a hotel just to leave my suitcase there. But I had some good memories to cherish in my mind. It wasn't all just about sex but to get close to some human beings that were for brief moments part of my life.

I worked and rested for the following week but Friday I was looking forward to going to Bremen for the weekend. The days are very short in January and I remember walking just before sunset around town when I saw a guy on the other side of the street in the company of a girl. He was as tall as me, about the same age, black hair, very blue eyes and so good looking like I had never seen one in Germany. I wished he was gay but I knew that was only a dream.

My big surprise came the very next afternoon when walking into Bei Hans I saw him standing at the bar talking with an older guy. I could not believe my eyes. His manner was very masculine and even somebody with a trained eye could be mistaken. I had to go close and try to meet him. His name was Dieter, he was 19 and was a freshman at the university. We started chatting about different subjects and I formed the idea that he would not be an easy target. He liked older guys, like I did, because they had more experience and they were "more men" as he put it. He was intrigued by the fact that I was Italian, had gone to school in France and Germany, and I had lived in India. Buddhism was the key to his mind and so I started introducing him to that philosophy. After a few hours we decided to go have dinner together, just to return to the club for the rest of the evening. Around 11 to my surprise he invited me to go to the toilet with him where he started hugging and kissing. We also masturbated each other in a few minutes which is something I had never done in a bar.

We were still sitting there after midnight when the members of a very famous British band came into the bar. They were having concerts at the Stadthalle (civic center) and they had rented a villa in the outskirts of Bremen. Their leader offered a drink to all the people in the bar and then they invited everybody to a party over their house. Dieter and I decided not to miss the occasion.

There was a large house in the middle of a park guarded by their body guards. We were a total of 36 between guys and girls. The living room was huge with plenty of sofas and a thick fluffy carpet on the floor. Drinks were flowing and very soon they started cutting Marlboro cigarettes to mix the tobacco with hashish. Moreover they were putting some drops of LSD on sugar cubes. Dieter had never taken any drug and so did I. We were looking at all these people getting high and were worried that the police would have come in to put a stop and take us all to jail. In a matter of minutes everybody was naked and having all kind of sex on the floor and on the sofas. The lights were dimmed but it was possible to see clearly what was going on in every corner of the room. The orgy went on until around 6am when finally the tiredness had won the last resistance of the players. We had got very excited but remained on our spot and had fun without mingling with the rest. The leader of the group, a guy beloved by many girls, did not have a nice body and had indiscriminate sex with males and females. All the rumors that were circulating about him appeared to be true.

We got up around noon. The living room was a battlefield. Some girls went to buy food. We all had some chicken and chips and finally left that "sinful" mansion glad that the police had not come to interrupt that interesting experience.

I kept seeing Dieter on and off. Ha was very handsome and even fun to be around but not the kind of toy I would get attached to.

The days were passing slowly, the week ends were over in no time, my job was not exciting and I was seriously taking into consideration the idea of returning to Italy and get it over with the military service. I talked to my parents and they agreed that was probably the best decision. After that I could have done whatever for the rest of my life.

We were at the end of February, it was pretty cold and the sun seldom shined. I packed my stuff, said goodbye to my colleagues, friends and bartenders. Frau Rutschmann was very sorry to see me go. My sister had been one of her tenants a few years earlier and she considered us like a part of her family.

I was once more on the autobahn heading south to sunny Italy.

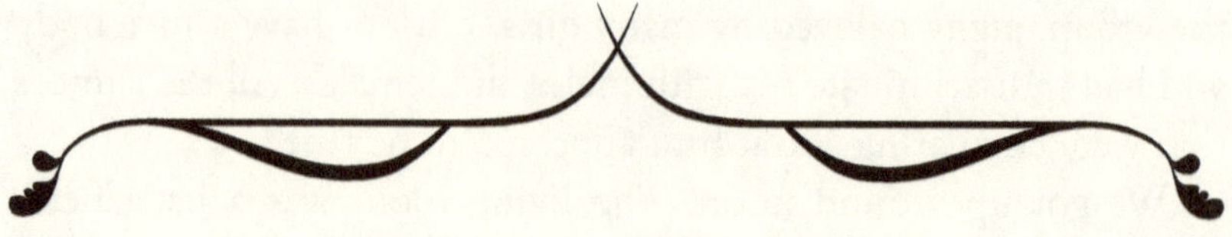

Chapter 8

In the Navy

At home not much had changed. My parents were in Hong Kong and Concetta was as usual running the show. It was good to eat her good food, to be close to all my things and to see my old friends. I had to organize a party and get them all together.

Two days after I was home I got in the mail the "famous postcard" from the government for my medical examination. I was not looking forward to that and I hated Italy and it's mandatory military service with passion.

Since my childhood I could never hear as well from my right ear as I could from the left one. I knew the military were strict about fitness and health, so I figured that it would be reasonable to inform them in advance of this problem. They scheduled a visit at the ear doctor and there I went hoping I could be invalidated out. The doctor came in, looked inside my ears with a flashlight and without saying a word plugged in an instrument that looked like a diapason. While he was approaching my right ear my instinct made me move my head in the other direction thinking he was going to give me some electric shot. That was probably my big mistake because the "luminary" decided there was nothing wrong with my ears and that I was faking it.

My departure date was April the 20th and the boot camp was in La Spezia, just a 1 hour and 45 minutes drive east of Genova.

My parents had come back from China and dad had to deal with a ship in Napoli. Together with the Passalacqua (the couple that did not have children) we decided to go to Napoli for a couple of weeks. My father could keep an eye on the work in the shipyard and we could go visit that city that, for some reason, had a certain appeal to me.

We left Genova and headed south east with two cars. We spent the night in Tuscany and the next day we were having lunch just south of Roma, in Viterbo. This trip will be well remembered in my life for the fabulous food we had in some of the best restaurants listed in the famous Michelin guide.

Napoli was the most chaotic city I had visited in Italy, not comparable to an Indian town…but pretty close. It was kind of dirty everywhere and at night big rats were contending some left over food on the side walks with fat cats that had no intention of hunting the rats. The traffic was heavy and we all came to the conclusion that people would constantly keep a finger on the horn after starting the car. Also at night it was so noisy. The traffic lights had colored paper over the light bulbs but the red signal did not stop the cars, it was just slowing them down to accelerate if the intersection was free. During the two weeks we spent there we did not witness a single accident.

I liked it there, it was like discovering a city similar to Genova and yet so different with a very nice and friendly population. One has to be very careful walking around there keeping the wallet in a front pocket and a hand on it to make sure it's not "somehow" gone. I started exploring the old town on foot and in the big flea market I was offered a big variety or merchandise: from packs of American chewing gums to…a real gun caliber 7,65. The police were around but they didn't seem to care much about what was going on. Around 1pm we were meeting for lunch, and then back to my discovery of the city until dinner time. The hotel was conveniently located in the downtown area. It was at night that I was cruising around in all the places where good boys would not go. Since I had no idea about the location of gay bars, I had to shift to parks and cheap cinemas. There was a cinema under the Galleria Umberto (the covered mall) where I found my hunting ground. The fact that people were constantly moving around was the sign that something was going on. It was clear that nobody had gone there to watch the movie.

Very soon I knew how everything was working. The ticket taker would make sure nobody was bothered while "playing" in the restroom area. Of course he had to get a small donation in exchange.

I had discarded several guys that did not appeal to me but I was attracted by this guy my age with brown light hair and gorgeous green eyes. I seldom take the first step but in that case I did and moved close to him. By moving a few inches at the time or, better, sliding the back on the wall, I was now grazing the left side of his body. A few minutes went by and nothing happened when suddenly I felt the palm of his hand touching mine. We started kissing and hugging among the curtains covering the back wall. He asked me if I had a place to go to and when I told him I was staying in a hotel, he went to the ticket taker and asked him if he knew some place around there where they were renting rooms by the hour.

We left the cinema and a few minutes later he was ringing the bell of an old building. We had to go up three flights and a guy came to open the door. Stefano (that was his name) gave him the money for the room and we were alone.

We had a lot of fun for about an hour, undressing each other, discovering the body, touching, feeling, kissing, hugging. He was just too beautiful to look at. The problem was that we were both used to go with older guys that knew what to do and suddenly we came to a point that neither one had any idea. Neither he nor me had ever performed oral sex and we were not going to experiment that night. We decided that a mutual masturbation would have been fair. I always blamed myself for not keeping in touch with Stefano. People are like milestones in our life: you remember some and forget about many.

Back in my hotel room I did masturbate again thinking about him.

With my mother and our friends we wanted to go visit Pompei but we learned it was closed because the guardians were on strike. We went to see Ercolano instead.

The Campanian coast was beautiful, the temperature mild, all the plants in bloom.

We didn't go as south as Amalfi but we ate in almost all the restaurant from Napoli to Sorrento. I must admit that even the fish was good, tasty and without bones as they were assuring me.

During that week Napoli suffered the loss of one of the most talented Italian actors: Toto'. Almost one million people participated to his funeral.

I went on board of my father's ship to see the works in progress. It looked like there was enough for another 20 days or so. One guy from the crew told me he had been in the navy 30 years before and commented: "after I got out of the service time has been flying" these words I will remember as long as I live.

The last night in Napoli before the departure was spent dining at the Don Chisciotte, probably the best in town. When we left the restaurant I decided to go back to the hotel on foot and started walking near the fence that runs along the maritime port. In a distance I noticed a small group of guys chatting and smoking cigarettes and when I got nearby I could clearly see that they didn't pose any threat because they were all gay and some really effeminate. We stared at each other and exchanged a few words. One in the bunch was particularly interesting to talk to and we started a long conversation about sex and sexual preferences. I told him about my adventure with Stefano and he couldn't help it to laugh at me but he offered to teach me how to do oral sex if I would follow him to his apartment. So I did. The whole thing was quite exciting. He was not handsome but very interesting and he had a fit body disguised under his clothes. He told me to make sure that the other guy was clean (in Europe we are not circumcised and some guys can smell if they don't wash themselves thoroughly). We got comfortable in his bed and he started to perform a blowjob to be remembered as the best I had so far. Suddenly he stopped and invited me to do the same. I was very reluctant to put his penis in my mouth but forced myself to do it. It only lasted a couple of seconds. The feeling I was getting was strange and very different than sucking on a thumb. It took me at least an hour to get used to it, being careful not to touch it with my teeth or to close my mouth too much. I still wasn't sure if I liked it or not and it was at that point that he suggested the very classic "69". I had to admit I was quickly changing my mind on the matter and I could see what was the pleasure I missed out.

He wanted to ejaculate in my mouth but I absolutely refused to do that, on the contrary he took all my load and I guess he swallowed it since I didn't see him spitting it out. I had learned something new that I thought I would have never ever done in my life.

The trip back to Genova was very festive and took 3 days because of some stops in Siena and Lucca, cities that I had never visited before.

With a few days left to my departure I wanted to spend some time with my friends and take my car to La Spezia since it was mandatory to ride the train from Genova.

The night before I partied with all my friends until dawn. The train was leaving at 2pm and the ride was only 90 minutes along the Ligurian Riviera through many tunnels. We went to the station and I got on board thinking that my life was ending that day. There were many other "soldiers to be" talking loud and probably excited to start that new adventure and the compartment was filled with smoke. The train ticket was kindly offered by the ministry of the navy.

Now I had a plan: I was told by a doctor. Who was a friend of mine that they would take a physical upon arrival at the barracks. I had to eat half a pound of butter before the X ray and that would temporarily enlarge my stomach and consequently they would send me back for not being fit.

I had the butter in my suitcase, ready to use. Little I knew that as soon as we entered the gate all our suitcases were taken and locked in a room while we had to stand in line to take the X ray!

Now that my last change had gone down the drain there was nothing else to do but apply to those hated rules of the military.

We were assigned a bed in a dormitory that we had to share with 20 people. They told us how the bed had to be undone every morning, they assigned one locker each to put our civilian clothes and personal effects that under no circumstance could be used for the next three months.

The reveille was at 6,30am. We had 30 minutes to wash and shave, breakfast was at 7 and consisted in some bread with milk and coffee. Alignment was at 7,30 sharp when they called the roll.

I knew they were going to shave our heads so I had come prepared and my hair was less than one inch short. Many had very long hair and some were crying while the barbers were totally removing it.

We had to clean floors, mop them, polish brass plates, march for hours while they were forming the platoons and go to classes to learn about military ranks, different type of warships, duties and discipline. At 1pm we would have 1 hour break for lunch and then back to work until 5pm.

For the first 15 days we could not leave the barracks for any reason.

It was a big rectangular building with an inside court that could accommodate 20 platoons for marching and parades. All around there was a covered area with different shops, amusement arcades, a bar and some kind of eatery. These premises were managed by civilians who were making a lot of money thanks to our forced support.

The second morning we had to go to a specific office where they were dispensing two working uniforms, two dark blue uniforms for the winter, two white for the summer, two pairs of shoes, one pair of boots, socks, T-shirts and some "fancy" boxer underwear that I would have never worn even if they had paid me to. Useless to say that all these clothes were too big, too long and too large. But there was a tailor in the premises that could take care of that for a reasonable sum that I could afford but many could not.

I was kind of desperate thinking that I had to spend the next 730 days of my life in that environment. Looking around I didn't see anybody worthy to talk to and they all looked very ugly to me, with the same clothes, silly white hats and bold. My mother was very concerned and she was calling me every evening. From the tone of her voice I knew she had complaint with my father a lot for sending me there. I knew he thought that was a duty owed to the country and the people to which every good citizen had an obligation. To me it was just a big portion of my life taken away.

The 15 days finally passed and for the first time we were ready to go out to discover that city wearing our brand new blue uniforms. We could go out from 5pm to 10pm almost every day, if not on duty. At 10,30 the lights were turned off, and everybody had to be in bed. When leaving the barracks we had to show a condom because the officer wanted to make sure we didn't have unprotected sex with the local prostitutes. Condoms were given out free.

So we went out the gate. Wearing that uniform made me feel really bad because I thought that all the people on the street were staring at me. When I walked around Via del Prione, in the downtown area, some prostitutes started calling me and offering their services. Some also said they smelled the naphthalene from our uniforms, meaning we had been in storage for a fortnight.

First of all I went to see a friend of my father who had a company for the manufacturing of ship parts. He was supposed to give me pocket money that my dad would reimburse. The monthly salary from the navy was enough to get me just one pack of cigarettes a day!

Finally I could go to a regular restaurant, eat well, buy food to put in my locker and, the most important thing: drive my car.

When one is serving in the military usually does not have much money to spend, that set me in a very good position. I could pay somebody else to take my place on duties I did not want to perform. I have always been a night guy but I hated to wake up early in the morning.

There were at least 500 soldiers in the barracks and none of them seemed to appeal to my taste for men. Some officers were cute but it was in my best interest not to fool around them. The Italians are not really interested in sexual behavior but a sissy guy was always attracting attention and bad comments from the others. There was a cute but nelly guy in our platoon and he was probably at the end of the rope. One morning during the third week there was some commotion in the barracks: he went to the shower's area and hang himself. I was really sorry to hear that things like that could happen in a so called civil society.

We started some stupid test that would decide what kind of work we were going to do in the navy. On purpose I answered without even looking at the questions. The comic thing is that I got assigned to the electro-mechanic department when it was obvious that I did not understand anything about the subject. The very bad news was that the class was going to last three months and it was held in Taranto, SE of Roma.

I finally got to know a couple of guys from Genova and we started going out together. Wearing the uniform was not really nice but there was no other way otherwise we would incur in some disciplinary punishment. My friends were kind of penniless but I had a car and that was a plus. Since we could not take off for more than 14 hours on a Sunday, providing we were not on duty, we decided to make a few "escapes" home. We would leave the barracks, go to my car, drive out of the city limits, wear civilian clothes and head to Genova. The trip by car would take less than two hours driving really fast (the highway had not been built then). The surprise of my mother and Concetta was great when they saw me arriving with my friends! They were going to spend those few hours at home and we would meet after dinner to return to La Spezia.

This went on every time we had a chance to do it. We were always in fear to be caught leaving the district. Fortunately there was no speed limit to respect otherwise we would have got in trouble with the police.

The three of us harmonized pretty well. They did not have any school title but they had common sense and they were street smart. I never told them about my sexual preferences but I was sure that wouldn't have changed anything.

In the meantime I had found out that there was an old theater used as a cinema, near the train station, that was also frequented by gays and I started going there from time to time to search for quick sexual satisfaction. I did meet some guy who invited me to his house and with a lot of circumspection I went several times. He told me there was also a park near the arsenal where people were cruising but to be on alert because the military police was raiding the place on foot.

At his house I also met other guys that were into military. That way I didn't have to risk going to unsafe public places. At my age I was hornier than ever.

With that side of my secret life covered I was a bit more relaxed and could spend more energies concentrating in different directions.

The big incognita was the final destination after that stupid class in Taranto. As my dad was telling me in the military they send people from the north to the south of the country and vice-versa. I wanted to stay as close home as possible. La Spezia is not an ugly town to live in but I wouldn't imagine what it would have been like to live in Sicily.

The end of the boot camp period was approaching with July. I decided it was time to pay a visit to the petty officer who was keeping our military files. When I met him I told him that my mother had a hearth condition and in case my destination was far away I had to prepare her in advance to the news. When he asked my last name I noticed he was thinking and finally he asked me if my dad had been an officer during the war. I nodded and he smiled: he had been a sailor on the same submarine and had admired my father who earned a bronze medal in action (this medal thing was news to me). He told me my destination was going to be Messina

(Sicily) but, since I was the son of his ex commander, he was going to change that with a port of my choice! Genova was out of the question because there were only five sailors there, all volunteers, working for the Oceanographic Institute of the Navy, but in La Spezia there was the possibility of working on a frigate that was seldom leaving the arsenal. I couldn't be happier. My dad did not want to move a finger to help me, and here there was this chief that would! I decided I would never tell a soul but just let everybody think that it was due to my good fortune.

Relieved, I invited my two buddies for dinner and we went to party in a straight disco.

The day of the swearing arrived and all the families of the sailors were invited for the ceremony. All aligned in the big court, after the "long" speech of the commander in chief, we had to lift our right arm and say "lo giuro" (I swear). Most guys, including myself, said "l'ho duro". It sounded very similar but it meant "I got a hard on".

Three hundred white hats (we were now wearing the white summer uniform) went up in the air and most people remained in the barracks to have lunch. I snob them all by going with my friends the Europa, my favorite restaurant.

Before leaving for Taranto everybody got a two days permit and (wow!) a free train ticket to go visit our families. My parents were in the mountains in Lavarone so I spent those two days relaxing at home alone, went to the beach, met a cute guy and had a good time.

The return to duty was sad. During the drive nobody was in a talkative mood. Pippo was going to Roma to be the chauffeur of some admiral and Ruggero was going to Gela, in Sicily, on board of a mine-sweeper.

With all the guys in our platoon we organized a last dinner in a trattoria close to the barracks. By the time dinner was over most of them were drunk on wine. Some accidents occurred that night: the guys that was sleeping above me got sick and vomited all over and some condoms filled with water had been placed under mattresses causing to flood the guy below. When the whole room was finally immersed in silence some started to masturbate following a rhythm given by someone that remained disguised in the darkness.

Since that was our last day in that barracks we were allowed to sleep one hour longer!

In the morning we all packed our military bag and aligned in the courtyard to collect the train tickets and the military papers to give to our new commander. While we were leaving to go to the train station we saw the new recruits arriving. I felt sorry for them.

Finally I went on the train and I sneaked out the other way to reach my car and drive to Taranto. I was not supposed to do that but I had no alternative. I went to the house of my dad's friends, changed in civilian clothes, and hit the road. I had plenty of time: the train was going to take at least 14 hours, driving it wouldn't take me more than 8. I could arrive in Taranto, check in a hotel, find a suitable parking place, put on that damn uniform and be at the military base on time to report for duty. That was my first time to that southern region of Italy and I thought I was going to be among troglodytes.

The interstate was nice and smooth. I stopped a couple of times and arrived ahead of schedule.

I spent sometimes going around the city to learn where everything was, then I found a motel not too far from the gate of the base. I noticed there was a huge parking lot that was probably used by the military personnel and that's where I decided to park my mini.

I waited until the last minutes to make my entry. The base is still called "Capo San Vito", It is located about 5 miles south of the city and it's composed by several barracks, one military school, some recreational buildings, an infirmary, a cinema, several little guard houses scattered around the bay and a brig. The rooms for the officers were near the main gate. The whole complex occupies at least 400 acres.

I had to go through the documents check with the captain who told me where to go and had me escorted by a sailor. It was a nice hot summer afternoon and the atmosphere was kind of relaxing.

The dormitory was nicer than the one at boot camp and there was room for 15 soldiers all on one single bed. The same rules applied here.

Having a diploma I got my first stripe after three months, but that didn't mean much because I could not command anybody, not even those recruits that were just starting.

After I put my stuff in the locker I went to explore the base. I sat on the beach looking at the sea and thinking about my friends enjoying their freedom and vacationing in Lavarone. I thought about Nizar, Alan, Gisela and the nice time we had spent in India. Everything seemed so far away like it had happened a century before.

At seven I went to have my first dinner. As I had figured out the food was kind of bad.

The very next morning we were entertained by a very ugly officer who was in charge of the class. If I ever thought of a subject more hated and odd, that was it! But who cared, I was not going to study it and what were they going to do to me? make me repeat the class?

We were obliged to take notes and pretend to pay attention to the teacher. Some were really getting into it. I was just waiting for the lesson to end and go to have lunch. This time I got smarter and went to the shop to get the food I wanted; to hell with the overcooked pasta with a lousy sauce and a steak that was as hard as the sole of a shoe. The fruit was the only thing I would take.

Like in La Spezia, my dad had some old supplier in Taranto and he had arranged for me to get the money that I needed through him. I went to visit his office on the very next day and came out with my money belt filled with banknotes. I started exploring the city and I liked the old port with old buildings, nice shops and some elegant restaurants.

Before leaving the base a short warrant officer was checking us out making sure everybody had clean hands, short hair, shaved beard and…the condom. Then for five minutes he would tell us to be careful with the prostitutes because they could carry venereal diseases. Moreover he was telling us not to go to certain places that were frequented by homosexuals. How nice: he was providing us with a list of those places!

I did not mingle much with the other guys but somehow they noticed that I was never on the bus to go to the city and they all wanted to be my friends. My mini minor by law could not accommodate more than three passenger therefore I was giving my preference to those that were nicer looking and better behaved. The problem was to get rid of them once in town so I got several excuses ready and I would pick them up on the way back to the base. Never than less one night they involved me in going with them to see a prostitute. I had not been with one since I was 16 in Genova, but I played along.

It happened in the old side of town in a small squalid apartment. We were taking shifts and the rate was 1500 lire each for 15 minutes. She was not what I considered my type: long brown hair, ugly teeth, too much make up and a very bright and red lipstick. Anyway I went into the room, had to wash my penis and she started working on me. She really did not turn me up in any way. She thought it was my first time, took the money and we pretended we were having an orgasm. After that they were all hungry and decided for a cheap pizza.

The next day they were still talking about it and recommending the girl to others.

It was during a hot sunny afternoon that going back to my dormitory for a quick shower my eyes met with those of a sailor I had never seen before. He was probably the most beautiful guy I had seen around there. His features were masculine yet gentle, his manners were natural, he looked very intelligent and his eyes were dark and penetrating like those of Nizar. It was like we had met in a previous life. There was almost no need to speak because we knew what we were going to say. Incidentally he was from Genova and we found out we had many things in common including the passion for esoteric studies.

Ettore and I became the best of friends. I didn't have to tell him about me being gay (by the way that's a word that was not at all in use in those day to classify homosexuals) because he already knew that and didn't bother him at all. We started going out together, I would buy him dinner because his parents could not afford to send him money and I was treating him like a brother.

During our free time we were discussing Buddhism and oriental philosophies and it looked like he knew much more than me. He is the one that introduced me to authors like Shure, Gourdjeff, Rene' Guenon and Rudolph Steiner. I was most grateful to life for this encounter that happened during one of my worse time in my life. I knew that with him I could go a long way without getting depressed about the remaining 20 months.

We started wearing a tiny golden star inside our hats: one for every month that was gone. Until the end of the class at the beginning of October there was no chance of getting a leave but we left the district a couple of times to explore Bari during its famous "Levant Fair" and to go to "Castel del Monte", an octagonal castle built by Federico the 2nd in the 13th century as a hunting lodge.

One day they gave all some shots against different illnesses and most of us got fever. I had to be recovered in the infirmary where I spend two days. The nurse in charge, a guy named Ricky, was very gay and did not make a mystery about it. Soldiers are usually very straight acting and they all swear they hate gays and would not even touch one. Well, those two nights I witness something that I would remember for the rest of my life. After the light was turned off at 10pm, the dear Ricky started the round and got fucked by 15 of the guys in the room (he had to skip me because I told him I couldn't stand him) then he went to bed probably to dream about more naked guys. The next day not one word was said by anyone, but after 10,30 the scene was repeated. I guess when a "so called" guy is straight but horny he doesn't really care if he sleeps with a girl or another guy. Just the fact that he can get an erection with another guy makes him at least bisexual. This matter would be disputed several times in the future with different hustlers who pretended to be totally straight.

In 1967 the fashion had called for pants that were larger at the bottom, now it was changing into a more normal tube form. I had to do something with my uniforms and learned that there was a specific tailor in town that was famous for military alterations. I went there to see what he could do and to make sure he wouldn't take forever to do it. He was one of those nice looking fit middle aged man with something very sexy about him. He asked me to try the uniforms on in the back of his laboratory and while I was getting undressed he pulled up my penis and gave me one of the best blowjob I had in my life. I wanted more so I went to see him every time I was horny and did not feel like going to the usual cinemas. Useless to say that he did not charge me a lira for his work and my uniforms looked really good. I just wondered if most soldiers had been treated the same way but would never admit it.

The class was a disaster and the ugly officer hated me for not participating in a more active way. Ettore was going to a different class that had to do with modern arms. I knew his final destination was going to be in a different city under different duties and I was really sorry about it. More than likely he would be going to Roma to the Ministry of the Navy. This damn officer, who's last name was Schembri, had an ugly grin on his left cheek, like if he was enjoying seeing other people suffer. He had told me several time that I would be sent to Sicily and had me worried so much that I almost believed him. I still had not said anything to my mother and she was really afraid that I would be sent to the deep south. I was mad at myself not to have stayed in Germany, but it was too late now to recriminate.

The final tests were coming. I was answering to all the questions without even reading them, just crossing out whatever. I scored 87 on 100 and ended up to be one of the best over 60. That was so fucking funny! Me: electrician!!! But now it was on my record!

Mr. Schembri was not pleased when he gave the results and red my name. He had also to read the final destinations and when he said my name his voice was angry: La Spezia, frigate "Centauro". I had made it and even without my father's "push".

It had been a long very hot summer with a draught to remember, but finally it was over and I could leave Taranto and hopefully did not have to go back to that "San Vito" ever again.

An interesting affair happened just two nights before my departure. I was on guard with some other guys at the main gate between 8pm and midnight when a high rank commander came to tell us to follow him to his car parked a few feet away on the road. In his car there was a cute guy who looked about 25 years old. The commander ordered us to open the passenger door and to intimate to his "friend" to step out. While we were following his order telling him: "get out of the car of the officer", the guy shouted: "he may be an officer but just a while ago he gave me a blow job"! Nobody commented and a couple of minutes later the captain went through the gate while we were saluting him. The very next day the story had already circulated all over the base.

I got the order to leave and board the Centauro that was due to arrive in Taranto and stay for one week docked in the military port. The big problem was my car: how could I take it to La Spezia if I was going to be on board? Ettore was going to leave for Roma so I kindly asked him to drive it there and use it until I could get a permit and go to rescue it. He was very happy to do this sacrifice. I knew I could trust him 100%.

Around 9pm on August 28 1966 I was on the pear waiting for the arrival of the frigate. There was a sailor communicating with the ship through a lantern. They were going to dock with the stern. Suddenly the all the lights on board went on for a few seconds and I saw the sailor dumping the lantern and running towards the land. For some bizarre reason the ship kept coming towards the wooden dock and hit it before it came to a complete stop. It took them more than one hour to complete the maneuvers and to lower the ladder and finally I could get on board.

It was a ship built in 1957 that had undergone some modernization. 106 meters long, 30 meters wide, equipped with three double cannons, two double machine guns, two shooters for anti submarine bombs and two triple missiles shooters. Nothing really impressive to look at.

I had got my second stripe at the end of the class and was due to become a sergeant by the end of October. They assigned me to a cabin with three berths on each side. There were no port-holes and when the lights were turned off a red night light would be on for the whole night. The beds were not really comfortable and not much wider than my body. The ventilation system was poor and the only air circulating was from the open door.

After an almost sleepless night we got up, had breakfast and had the pleasant surprise to learn that one of the propellers had been damaged during the docking. The obvious result was that we had to go to a shipyard for repairs and remain in that port for a couple of weeks. All the ammunitions had to be disembarked and that operation alone took two days.

I was introduced by my new officer, Mr. Forleo, to my new fellow soldiers of the artillery department. When he asked me where I wanted to work I had to tell him that I did not know anything about electricity and arms, but I knew how to run an office, type letters, keep files and do administrative work. Sgt. Mele was the secretary but he was due to leave the service in one month: what better occasion than learn from him all the duties and take his place! I could work in a nice office together with my officer who was a very nice looking guy in his mid thirties.

The life on board was much more relaxed than at the base. The wake was still early but breakfast was better and soon enough I would have become a sergeant and I would eat at the more selected table.

There was a little band on the ship and its leader was Aldo, a guy with an impressive knowledge of music and with a pretty good voice. His hometown: Udine. We became very good friends and still are after all these years. Even though he is married I always wondered about his sexual preferences.

Then there was Alfio, a very sissy sailor, who couldn't wait to go out every time he had a chance to sleep with different prostitutes… go figure.

Some of the guys were very cute, especially those from Napoli. Others were nice but I did not fancy them because of their very strong southern Italian accent. Then there were the volunteers. Some were in the navy for three years, some for five. They were the worst kind: very military minded and strict on the rules. After I became a sergeant they were the targets of my disciplinary reports.

The two weeks finally passed and we had to embark the ammunitions again. We left the port to escort a mini submarine to the Adriatic sea and, finally, we headed back to La Spezia. In the meantime Ettore had gone to Roma and was expressing his gratitude for letting him drive my car.

Being on a small ship, the waves in the open sea were making it rocking and rolling. We crossed the Messina narrows during a nice afternoon and arrived at destination several hours later cruising at a speed of 16 knots per hour.

The commander in chief was never among the crew, the second in command, Mr. Accame, was very cordial with everybody and it was rumored he had got his rank thanks to the influence of an admiral uncle of his.

It was nice to see the arsenal of La Spezia after months spent in Puglia. We docked between another frigate, the Margottini, and the Vesuvio, a supply ship. First we hit the broadside of the first, then the broadside of the second, and the one of the first again: Mr. Accame was a really expert officer!

I couldn't wait to land, eat at my favorite restaurant and see the people that I had met during boot camp, but I had to wait until the next afternoon.

During those two weeks I had become very well acquainted with my officer who promised to give me three days off to go to Genova and see my family.

The very first place I went to was the cinema close to the train station where I got picked up by somebody and I spent a couple of hours at his home. Then I went to the Europa restaurant and on the way back I went through the barracks to see if there were some people I knew. It was always sad to go back to duty after a few hours spent on a limited freedom. I called Ettore to tell him that I would have been in Genova for three days and to my surprise he said he was going there too and then they were going to transfer him to La Spezia for the rest of his term. That was really wonderful news. He could drive up, and we could have gone together to Genova in my car. That solved one more problem.

Those three days spent at home meant a dive in a past that seemed far away. Mother and Concetta were happy to see me, I could rest in bed till late, have good food, see my friends and wear civilian clothes. My haircut gave me away for being in the military. The trip back to the military district was more painful than usual as on my mind was the thought of many more long months to go.

I started keeping a diary and for the opening page I designed a calendar with all the days in the service: 730 little squares divided in months and weeks. That seemed the obvious thing to do but if I think back it was also a way to make the time go more slowly than ever.

The former secretary left the navy and I was now the only one allowed to stay in the office while the other guys were cleaning and working on the arms. It was my duty to schedule shifts, prepare permits, inform Mr. Forleo about the performance and behavior of the 3rd and 4th detachment. I was feeling do important when I got the stripes for sergeant that I went to a stationer's shop and had a stamp made with my name and rank. Outside the arsenal there was a huge parking lot and that's where I was leaving my car. Once in a while I would write my name on some specific guard, just to be equal and avoid comments from the others. My duty was done by 5pm and I could leave the ship and not come back until midnight, except when I was getting a special permit called "TST" (meaning "end of theater shows"). With that in my pocket I could go back on board at any reasonable time after 12.

The life on the ship was really boring, a waste of time and of my life too. We had to wear some ugly working uniforms and that really stupid hat (I hate hats). There were a few guys that I would talk to, otherwise I was not giving any confidence. I had noticed some cuties and sometimes I would go to take a shower just to see what was going on in there. Being all in our late teens and early twenty our testosterone was playing a big role in our lives. It was rumored that to keep the sexual drive low they were putting bromide in our food. If they did it certainly did not serve the purpose because everybody was hyper and sex was on our minds. It was during one of those showers that I started noticing what was going on. Some guys were smiling to others while touching their private parts. They would then disappear in the bathrooms and take another shower to clean themselves from the "debris". It appeared that a large number of them were acting this way, even those that would seem absolutely positively straight. I thought that was way too risky to do on the ship but I started to befriend those that I would fancy more.

I asked monetary help to my mom claiming I needed a place to get away from the military life and she started paying the rent of a small one bedroom apartment in the old side of town. One by one all my fellow soldiers that I liked came to see the place, eat there, rest, change clothes, shower or soak in the bathtub. Sometimes we were organizing some parties with girls they had met in local discos, a couple of times some came with a prostitute. I always liked girls for sex only so it did not embarrass me the least to be in bed with one or more guys and girls at the same time. I never told Ettore about the small flat but I knew that he was guessing what was going on. For him I have always been like an open book and I never used some way to block my thoughts to him.

The days and weeks were passing by slowly. I was always glad to add one of the small stars on my hat at the end of every month.

I had noticed that most of the times I was getting off the ship there was a luxury car parked across from mine with an older guy sitting at the driver side. He would follow me and come to dine at the same Europa restaurant, sitting at a table not too far from mine. The guy was not what I would consider "good looking" but I was curious to find out what he was up to. One night he finally waved to me and I went to introduce myself and joined him for dinner. He was a very well known producer of a foreign radio station that most of the young people would listen in the car. He told me he wanted to know me for a long time and that we should get to know each other for a good long lasting "friendship". He lived in Monte Carlo most of the time but his work took him to drive all over the Ligurian Riviera. He had a villa in Montreux where he was spending his vacation with his mother. The situation was intriguing even though I was not sexually attracted to him. It took me a couple of months to convince him that there couldn't ever be that kind of relationship between us.

In La Spezia there were a lot of rainy days, that's why it has always been called the "pissoir of Northern Italy". I always like the rain, especially in the long cold nights, being in my room, crawling in bed with someone nice. That was not really possible on board but I would go to my apartment, invite somebody over for a quiet dinner, and watch movies. By watching Concetta working in the kitchen I had developed a certain interest for cooking. That was like a relaxing hobby. I experimented on different dishes and was getting better all the time. My other pastime was reading books that Ettore would find for me from some Rosicrucian library that only he knew. All those months spent in India and the discussions with my guru had helped me a lot to understand the meanings of the esoteric books I was into. Strange enough I could not find a single soul on the ship that would share those kind of interests, but, as Ettore was saying, their moment of truth in life had not appeared at the horizon yet.

The days were getting longer and the temperature was rising and while I concluded my first year in the service my chief was getting ready to be transferred to another ship with a higher rank. Mr. Romano would take his place. Even my vacation was coming up: I would get 2 full weeks plus two days for the trip wherever. I asked and obtained to take it in July so that I could spend it in the mountains of Lavarone together with my old friends. Aldo and I left on the same day. I drove him to Verona where he got on the train to go to Udine, his hometown. During the drive we were listening to songs of Lucio Battisti, the most famous music writer in Italy.

My arrival in Lavarone was festive. I wore my uniform until I got home. Being a place way high above sea level, the natives were puzzled for seeing a navy sergeant. I found all my friends and we partied all night long. They were all asking me about the life in the navy but I didn't want to tell them too much about it. I wanted to erase it from my mind for those two weeks. My father told me he was puzzled when he heard that I was sent so close to home. I never told him how I got that destination. He kept saying that it was not the navy he had come to know during his service and seemed kind of disappointed. He was also more disappointed when I told him that it was a waste of time and that I did not and would not learn anything good from it: I hated it so much and my mom was giving me support in that.

I got worried about my grandmother not feeling too well because of her high blood pressure. The mountain height was not suitable for an 82 year old lady and she was forbidden by the doctor to drink espresso coffee which she liked very much. Even Concetta was getting older and they had a local woman helping her during the work around the house.

Those two weeks passed in a hearth beat. As a sexual break I did go to Trento one night, with an excuse to my friends, where I met some nice guys in the park in front of the station. I did go home with a cute guy who's mother was out of town and we had some real fun together. I saw him again a few times and we're still friends these days.

Before I had to leave to go back on duty I pointed out to my father that my car was getting old and had passed the 100.000 Kms. Since I had such good written record from my officer about the work I was performing on board, he promised he would do something about it for Christmas, just a few months away. That made me very happy because I already had in mind the type of vehicle I wanted so bad.

I arrived in Verona just a few minutes before Aldo's train was entering the station. He was very happy to see me and during the drive we talked about the things we had done during our brief vacation. He was tan, I was not because, for some odd reason, I was never able to get tan in the mountains, not even when I was going to take sun by the lake.

Before entering in the district of La Spezia we had to stop in a parking lot and put on that hated uniform. That night I did not sleep well since I had to get adjusted to that uncomfortable bed again. In the morning it all went back to business as usual but I was already thinking about my next permit.

Somehow the rumor that I had an apartment in town had spread to several people that became very friendly with me. Some wanted it to spend a few hours with their girlfriends, others to use it as a place to change clothes, others just to go to sleep for a few hours on a comfortable bed. I had to be careful and select the people that I would let them use it. I certainly did not want some officers to know about it.

The problem exploded one night. I was out until almost 3am with the usual TST permit signed by my officer. Of course I didn't go to any theater but I had found a guy, a postal worker, and I had spent too many hours at his apartment having sex. When I got back to the arsenal a stupid chief asked for my documents and looked at the TST permit. At that point he started saying that I could not stay out that late and questioned the validity of the signature of Mr. Romano. Since the note was signed by an officer, I did not let him have it and went back on board. The next day the captain called me and I had to tell him the whole story. Of course I did not mention the guy but I did say that I had met some foreign girl and that I spent some extra time with her. For the next six months all the TST permits were revoked in the whole district and nobody ever knew it had been my fault. Mr. Romano told me not to worry about it, after all, the captain, who knew my father, was not going to take any action against me.

You should know that in those days gay military were tolerated but the more flamboyant were not welcome on ships and in the barracks. Just 30 Kms. North of La Spezia there is a small town called Aulla, site of a big ammunition depot. That was also the place where those soldiers were sent. Useless to say that also Ricky, the nurse that got fucked by all those guys in the infirmary of San Vito, had been sent there. It was funny to see them coming to La Spezia during their free time, in small groups, acting like drag queens in military uniforms. Some were also carrying a handbag with god knows what (maybe lipsticks, mascara and make up). They were certainly not keeping a low profile even when passing by other sailors. Fortunately we never saw them venturing inside the arsenal. I'm sure the chiefs would have stopped them at the gate.

The summer was basically over and the days were getting shorter. With Aldo and Ettore we went to the beach for the last time to get some tan (the water was too cold to swim), then I offered a dinner at the usual restaurant. Ettore had to go back earlier because he was on duty, Aldo joined some friends that were passing by and I remained alone and horny. So I started walking at the edge of the park and I noticed that some guys were cruising along the little trails inside. Pushed by my curiosity I ventured inside the park. It was dark, but I could see very well who was around and what they were looking like. One of the guys started following me from a distance when, all of a sudden, the military police went by driving a jeep. I knew they saw me but they were on the road and could not come to get me unless they had stopped the car and chase me on foot. With my hearth beating fast I started running in the opposite direction, then went in the middle of some bushes, and when I saw they were trying to get around the park to get me on the other side, I changed direction again. The whole running around lasted at least 5 long minutes but I managed to escape on a lateral street and gain the main street where I sat at the table of a bar to drink some juice. I didn't even want to think about the consequences. I joined some sailors that were going back on board and quietly we entered the gate of the arsenal. That park was permanently erased from my mind for as long as I was in the service.

Another surprise was waiting for me on the ship: we were going to leave La Spezia to join some American and Turkish ships on the Ionio sea for some electronic war. The mission was top secret and we could not communicate with our families for the whole voyage.

We left at 4am with all the lights off and a few hours later we were met by a submarine and another frigate commanded by that same officer who had the hustler in his car near the gate of San Vito. When we were about 100 miles West of Napoli we were joined by some American ships. We arrived in the "war" zone late at night and we were supposed to spot some Turkish smaller ships. I had my shift from 10pm till 2am and had to stand on the main deck looking in some powerful binoculars. There was no moon and it was pitch black, but I got lucky and spotted not 1 but 3 different ships. The alarm was given and the electronic war started: something to do with radars and equipment to disturb the radar. That was all in the hands of the COC, a special unit in charge with the communications.

The "battle" went on for three days and three nights. During my breaks I would go to sleep or to read in my office where nobody would dare to disturb me with the exception of a cute Neapolitan guy, Antonio, who knocked at the door and with a stupid excuse managed to have a mutual session of masturbation.

As silently as we had left we arrived at the arsenal during the night and in this case the captain managed to dock the ship without incidents and in a very short time.

We had distinguished ourselves during the battle. The ship gained a medal and I had some honors for spotting more ships than anybody else! that really made me feel good… (I really didn't give a damn). But I got a whole 5 days off and went home to relax.

This time I did not wait until the last minute to drive back but I went to spend two full days in the apartment I was renting. I had always liked the sergeant who was sleeping above my bed and I knew that he was interested in me. I went to the bar where he used to hang around during his free time and sure enough he came by and started chatting with me. With the excuse of having dinner together I asked if he would care for some spaghetti with pesto sauce that I had brought from home. He was surprised to know I had a place to stay and accepted my invitation without preambles. After dinner we had some dessert and watched some TV relaxing on the sofa. Our hands casually touched and finally we were embraced, kissing, licking and sucking for several hours. The same happened the next night.

Once back on the Centauro we never talked about it again, but I remember this episode like something very special. I know that now he is married and has two kids.

The second Christmas was approaching and before some of us were sent home for a brief permit the news came that we had to sail to Genova for the ceremony of the consignment of the new frigate helicopter carrier Carabiniere.

It took us only 5 hours to leave the arsenal, go to the main port of Genova but it took us 2 hours to dock our ship between the Carabiniere and the Caio Duilio, the second admiral ship of our navy, a destroyer missiles carrier. First we hit the destroyer, then we hit the new frigate, finally we hit the pier!

I had a special permit to leave the ship and go home for the night and so did Aldo who was my guest for the night.

While we were sleeping in a comfortable bed a team of sailors was repairing the damaged sides of the three ships. They had to look good by 10am when the bishop was coming on board with the admiral in command of the high Tirrenian Sea.

It was a boring and long ceremony but it was finally over and everybody had a meal good enough to impress all those high rank personalities.

We re-entered the arsenal that night.

During the 8 days vacation for the holiday I went to Lavarone to ski and the very last day during a descent I lost control and almost broke my right wrist. This time I went back to La Spezia by train with my arm on a sling. My old car had been traded with a new Alfa Romeo that my father had bought me as a Christmas present and it was sitting in the garage waiting for the new tags.

When I got on board I found Mr. Romano on duty at the stern. He ordered me to go to the military hospital to have my arm checked, so, in the morning, I did.

The doctor was an old officer who remembered being on duty on the same submarine my father commanded during the war! What a coincidence! He noticed there was no broken bone but he managed to cast my arm in a way that, once out of the district, I could take the cast out and keep it out for the next month, until I had to put it back on, go back to him, have it cat off, and spend another 15 days at home recovering.

That very afternoon I was riding the train in the opposite direction. My parents were on some long trip, Concetta was in Milano helping my sister with her 5 year old son, and I had the whole house at my disposal.

The tags had arrived and I started showing off my new red car.

During that month without worries one night I met some guys in a very cruisy spot before the Brignole train station. Some would park there and walk around, others would drive up and down the street that was crossing the park looking for somebody to pick up and take home. I befriended a small group circled around an older guy named Piero. He was not too handsome but had some magnetic eyes that were capturing the imagination of the younger guys. I slept with him a couple of times and he told me about this beautiful guy my age that had been his lover for a couple of years. I finally met Enio and we instantly felt there was a certain bond between us. He was just one week older than me, same sign, and we knew that been both Aquarians made us special friends. His father was the manager of the major theaters in town, the Duse and the Politeama Genovese. Enio actually had appeared in some plays with famous stage actors. His mother was Austrian so she had a strong German accent when speaking Italian. His parents had known about Enio being gay since he was a little boy but did not have any problem with that. He was tall, blonde with curly hair, had green eyes and a great smile. The voice was pleasant and his interests matched mine but he was more creative and could do many artistic things. He had an interest in young men and his friend at the time was a very cute 18 years old.

We became best of friends and would share many things in the years to come.

With Enio my interests took a different course. I started going to see plays, got more interested in the classic Italian authors, met a bunch of actors , went to reversals and to long midnight dinners with them. I liked the way they were discussing about politics, art, history and I took an active part in their talks.

That was a very interesting month and a half for me, my horizon had widened and I felt I grew a lot. But of course it went fast and I was once more on board of that stupid vessel.

We were always docked at the same spot, but something new was going to happen: the ship had to undergo some modern transformation and that was going to happen in may 1969. My term would have ended on April the 20th. The commander in chief decided to go in the open sea and shoot all the ammunitions on board for exercising, avoiding the disembarkation of the same that would have taken a couple of days. The site was the open sea between Tuscany and Sardinia. For the occasion the admiral would be on board.

We left at night (of course) and went first South to the Elba island, then West. At about 200 nautical miles from Cagliari, at 2pm, they gave the order to shoot with the cannons, the machineguns, the races and also the anti-submarine bombs. I was locked in my office but the tremors were so strong that books and files were falling all over. I decided to go to the main deck and started looking around smelling the acre scent of the gun powder. Suddenly I noticed a red tracing light on the larboard, then a second and a third one. I asked the captain if he knew what that meant. He jumped on the binocular and started screaming to cease the fire. The headphones were not working properly and the fire went on for another minute or so but it seemed an eternity. A messenger was sent to the COC and finally the only noise was the one of the engine and of the blowing wind.

What had happened was that the COC did not inform the ships of the merchant marine sailing in that area that we were going to shoot. We almost hit an oil tanker and a fishing boat with 12 people on board. The admiral was furious. It could have been a disaster to remember. Moreover the weather changed and our light frigate started rocking and rolling. It was only a force 4 sea, but it was enough for us to reach the closest port of Cagliari, the second largest city in Sardinia. We were docked there for a couple of days so I had the change to go on shore and visit that city. I didn't think much of it and the wind was very strong. Sardinia is famous for its lobsters and I decided to invite Aldo for dinner and we went to the best restaurant in town. That was the first and the last time in my life that I tried to eat lobster: I did not like it a bit.

The weather was getting better so we moved to the North and reached the port of La Maddalena, one of the largest naval bases in Italy. Next to it there is Palau, site of a famous base for the American Navy.

The wind there was so strong that while the ship was docked it was constantly leaning at an angle of 30 degrees. It was peculiar to be on board and walk like if we were on the leaning tower of Pisa. Also sleeping on the bed was kind of uncomfortable. On the other hand the island was nice, the village old and attractive and the natives very friendly (that's because the base was their major resource besides the economy based on fishing). Next to La Maddalena there is the island of Caprera with a famous boating and sailing school and the even more famous house where our national hero, Giuseppe Garibaldi, lived and died during his last years. He is the one that in 1861 conducted the expedition of the 1000 that from Marsala in Sicily remounted through Calabria, Basilicata,Campania and Lazio to Teano liberating Italy from the Borbone (ruling family of the kingdom of the Two Sicilies) and acclaimed Vittorio Emanuele the 2nd as the first king of Italy.

His figure in history has been acclaimed at times but also blamed because there are still people that nowadays would like to have the South separated from the North, considering the South and its inhabitants like North Africans. But every country has differences between the North and the South.

We had to stay one week docked with a very blue sky but the strongest wind, when finally the speed decreased and the ship had an almost straight angle. We shipped back to La Spezia where we arrived on a very early morning. I did not have to be on duty many times during the night, but if there is something I do not want to see is the sunrise. By going to bed at 4am we had to put a note on the bed in order to sleep until 8am instead of 6. Those four hours were not enough.

I had bought the 24th small golden star and my hat had an almost full circle of them on the inside. This was the best month of all because the new comers were cleaning our shoes, making our beds, do our laundry and serve us at the table. I never had to do that when I started because I was so nice to befriend the "granpas" (that's the way we called the guys at the end of the term) that nobody had ever asked me to "serve" them.

Those final days seemed so long. I had nightmares dreaming that everything was starting all over again. These kind of dreams would go on for several years after this long experience and they always seemed so real that waking up I was never really sure of not being there.

The eve of the 20th I invited all the 12 guys that were in my contingent to a memorable dinner. We took many photos, some got even drunk, but everybody was so happy that it is kind of difficult to describe. All I know that for me it was one of the best days in my life. I had learned nothing, I had lost two years, I did not think my homeland would deserve so much and I could not stand those volunteers, military minded, that were so much into commanding others.

That night the trumpeter played for us the "not in conformity with rules Silence" and that was awesome to know it was done just for us.

In the morning I rapidly collected my stuff, went on the bridge, stayed in line for the very last time, listened to the fairly long speech of the commander, and finally broke the lines and walked through the arsenal for the last time.

I gave a lift to a couple of guys that were also living in Genova, we exchanged address and phone numbers, and drove right home. Oh yes: we took off our uniform and wore our civilian clothes.

Before I left the ship one of the volunteers asked me some information about Portofino. He was planning to go there with another volunteer and they were wondering if I knew a cheap place to eat. That was my vendetta. I told them to go to the "Pitosforo" that had the best fish at the most reasonable cost. The prices were not listed on the menu and by all means that was and is the most expensive restaurant in the area. I learned from some friends on the ship that they went, ate, didn't have enough money to pay the bill and ended up helping in the kitchen. They are probably still looking for me somewhere.

Chapter 9

Out of the navy I had to recover the lost time. First of all I decided to take a vacation in Lavarone, all by myself, for at least a fortnight. So I packed a mix of light and winter clothes and I took with me a crate of yummy marzipan in the shape of different fruit that one of my father's employees had sent me from Sicily. There were 10 kgs and it took me less than one month to eat.

I arrived at the house in the early afternoon, unpacked, prepared my bed, open all the windows for some fresh air and went to the Cervo to make arrangements for my meals since I was not in to mood to cook at home.

The month of May is usually beautiful. The mornings and the nights are chilly but during the day it warms up to a pleasant dry 22C. There was not much to do in the village so I ended up mingling with the natives. After all I knew them all, we had practically grown up together.

In the morning I was having my delicious breakfast with fresh bread, local butter and honey and fresh milk. I was then going to the lake to rent a boat and get some exercise paddling for a couple of hours.

At lunch I was really hungry. The owner of the hotel, Daniela, has always been an excellent cook and she always prepared plenty of food.

In the afternoon I was taking long walks in the wood, carrying my portable record player, listening to all my favorite songs and munching on some marzipan. Sometime I would fall asleep on the soft grass surrounded only by the sound of the wind blowing through the leaves and the nice singing of the birds.

Ettore had given me some books. The more I was reading them and the more I was finding them interesting.

My dinners were always lighter than lunch.

The local would gather at the bar around 9pm and from there we would go to the couple of bars/discos open during that season. I was playing cool pretending to be interested in some girls that were usually working as waitresses or hotel maids. Several times I found out that they were quite interested in me and a couple of times I ended up sleeping with them. It was fun but I was afraid that from sex we were going to switch to dating or more. I didn't want any drama because for me it was just sex and no strings.

Silent were the nights with the sky covered with stars. The Milky Way was very visible like a huge mantle.

I rested, gained a couple of pounds, got a nice healthy skin color, and even reduced the number of cigarettes from one to half pack a day. I broke the monotony of the long silent nights with a few trips to Trento to see a few friends to chat, cruise, have sex and goof off in the park by the train station.

I finally decided to go back to Genova. My friends were finishing the school term, the days were getting warmer and it was time to hit the beach in Torre del Mare.

I asked and obtained from my mother to renew my wardrobe and I was set to go. My sister with her son and Concetta were already there.

My good old friend with the sport car had passed away after a massive hearth attack. So I found my other friends having a good time getting tan, listening to all the new songs of Petula Clark, Sandie Shaw, Charles Aznavour and other American singers. Around five we were going home to shower, change clothes, eat dinner and meet around nine in the small square to decide if we wanted to go to the mini golf, to a disco or to walk around in one of the villages nearby. Thousand of people were doing that until late night, eating ice creams, chatting and having a good time.

I invited Enio to spend a few days with me and he arrived driving an old beat up Fiat 600. The vehicle looked so bad that we were driving around with a big hammer: he would go behind a luxury car stopped at a red light, push on the breaks, stop just a couple of inches behind it while I would bang the hammer on any metal part of the 600 making the classic noise of a crush. The driver in front would hear the noise, see our car in the back, think that we had hit him, step out to check the damage (that was not there), while we were taking off because the red had changed into green.

All my friends enjoyed Enio's company. He knew how to treat everybody and with his light humor he was making us laugh.

One afternoon we took a quick trip to Varazze, just about 30 minutes drive, to see Ettore who had a job in a local hotel for the summer season.

A couple of nights I drove to Savona , the major city nearby, to check a cruisy cinema and the park by the port filled with some sorry old "queens". But I got lucky by meeting a cute young man while walking under the arcades of the main boulevard. He took me home all the way to Genova and drove me back to my car very early in the morning.

We spent the whole month of June at the sea and did a lot of water ski while my brother in law was enjoying his scuba diving.

During the week there were mainly housewives with little children running around the beach all day but on Friday afternoon until Sunday night or Monday morning all the husbands were arriving making it all look like a very festive place.

The big cleaning was done the day before the departure and the house would be empty until the beginning of September when we were going there to spend the last warm sunny days prior to the cold dark winter that I hated so much, a grey season without all the color and the smell of the plants in bloom.

In Lavarone it was like taking a step back into the past. The two years I could not spend with my usual friends had left their mark. Most all my friends had a girl or a boy friend and some were even planning a life together. Our thoughtlessness had gone to be replaced by the real problems that life poses at that stage. Some had started going to the university, others had gotten a job and could come there only during the week ends. There were some new kids on the block that had taken our place sitting around the bar after dinner to decide what to do for the rest of the night. They were way too young for us to mingle with. I seemed that most guys in our circle had calmed down and it was more difficult to organize walks, dinners and nights out.

Due to that situation I started going to Trento more than once a week. The train station park was the place to find casual sex with the most wide variety of people.

Suddenly I learned that Claudio, a cute employee of the post office, had met the wrong guy one night and was stabbed to death inside his apartment. He was only 34. I knew that sometimes it could be dangerous and we were always on the look out for possible murderers and hustlers.

In the middle of august my father decided to take us on a trip to Germany. He had a ship in Hamburg and we all rode in Bruno's car, one of those big Citroen that looked like an iron, very comfortable, fast and safe for those days when we had not even heard of seatbelts.

Knowing the taste of my sister and Bruno I stuck with them and ended up having a beautiful room in the best hotel in Hamburg. My mom and dad went to sleep in the ship owner quarter on the oil tanker that was docked in the port very close to the downtown area. I was eating with them but I was basically on my own for the rest of the time going to check all the gay clubs in town and spending most nights at the Ripperbahn, St. Pauli quarter, frequented by the "rough" people from the crews coming from all over the world. That was one of the busiest ports in the northern Europe together with Amsterdam and Antwerp.

I had my share of fun and I had my first encounters with some latino guys from south America. The best and most good looking were from Brazil. The bizarre episode happened when I met this guy from Panama who wanted to take me on board of the ship he was working…but that was the ship where my parents were staying. We ended up renting a room by the hour in a dingy hotel and I never explained him why I didn't want to go to his cabin.

1989

On the way back to Italy traveling at a very high speed on the autobahn we made a stop overnight in Zurich because my mother had to visit an ex schoolmate. I let them do the visit while I walked around the old part of town discovering that it was filled with gay clubs. A nice guy that befriended me in the Barfuesser took me home and we had sex in his bedroom with the walls covered by a huge picture of a Samoan beach.

Back in Lavarone I resumed the usual life thinking what I was going to do with my future.

My parents were definitely moving to Lugano Switzerland because my dad was fed up with the Italian taxes and with the frenetic city life. My mom, being Swiss, wanted to move there badly. At the beginning of September we went to check Lugano out and to look for a house to move in. It is a very pleasant town overlooking the homonym lake with a very medieval center surrounded by beautiful and extremely modern buildings and villas with luxuriant gardens. Many hills and high mountains in the near distance. Just 16 kms North of the Italian border and the city of Como and only 1 hour drive from Milano.

I had grown to like Genova but I had to admit that the prospective of living there by myself was not what I had in mind. Most of my friends had gotten a job, some were planning to marry and even Enio was busy helping his father with the management of the theaters. Ettore was somewhere in Central Italy and had met Angela, a girl that I didn't like too much because, deep in my thought, I had always thought him and I were going to share something together.

The prospective of living with my parents was not really interesting, besides Lugano could have been fun during the Summer and Spring but for the rest of the year there were tourists coming in only during the week ends to walk around the lake and to gamble at the casino.

So I started evaluating the option of going to a university and, perhaps, to study the subject that I liked most: History. The problem was: which university?

The answer came when I talked to my dear old friend Shazzy, ex schoolmate, who's father was in the same business of mine. He had got married and was working at Cunard in London to improve his English and to start his career in the merchant marine business. When I talked to my father about it he approved and started making a round of phone calls. He had many friends and also partners in London and one of the brokers had an office in the city in the very same Cunard building.

A few days later Mr. Halford sent him a detailed letter with the information about several universities in the United Kingdom. London was excluded due to the large number of Italians living or visiting there, but one emerged above all: Brighton on the coast of Sussex.

In those days it was quite difficult to visit England because there was no European Community and everybody had to get a visa, give a reason for entering the country, tell the authorities how much money they were carrying and get their passport stamped with the time that they were allowed to remain. For me there was no exception. So Mr. Halford had to write a letter saying that he was providing the money for my food and lodging. Moreover he had sent me the documents of the University of Sussex showing that I was a registered student, that all the taxes and the books had been paid for and that I was going to rent a small one-bedroom apartment from a Mrs. Cruttenden at the cost of Lst. 9.- per week.

England in 1969 had still the old currency of pounds, crowns, shillings and pence. Not very difficult to learn: 1 pound was divided in 20 shillings, 1 shilling was equal to 12 pence and 1 crown was equal to 2,5 shillings. Oh yes, I forgot the guinea that equaled 21 shilling and was used only in some fancy stores and restaurants.

My allowance was going to be 40,- Lst. per month and for that I had to open an account at the Barclay's Bank so that money could flow in from London if needed.

This was going to be quite an adventure. IU had never been to England. I could speak enough English to get by because I had studied it for five years at the Maritime High and I had some experience while I was living in India. But I knew that the accent and the pronunciation were totally different.

I prepared a couple of large suitcases with a ton of light and heavy clothes and a certain variety of shoes. I remember putting two umbrellas in the car since they warned me about the long lasting rainy days.

My parents had found a large apartment in Lugano and they were busy with the movers. I escaped just a few days before so that I didn't have to fool with it. I always hated carrying and moving stuff.

My sister who had lived in England and Scotland when she was a teenager gave me the last recommendations and I was finally heading North through the mountain passes to Basel and them towards Paris.

I did spend a couple of days at Alan's apartment and we had a pleasant time remembering the "Indian experience". I left Paris on the 19th of September and there I was in Dieppe waiting to put my car on the ferry with destination Folkestone.

The crossing of the channel was lasting four hours and the ship was loaded.

Everybody had to get in line with the passport and the documents to get the entry visa. Some were settled in a few minutes, others took much longer. When it was my turn he took all the time to go through each single document, asked me if I was going to drive, reminded me that they drive on the left side of the road, and told me that the maximum time I could stay in the country could not exceed six months. After that I would have to go to London to the immigration office where they would renew my visa for another six months.

It is odd to get off the ferry and start driving on the left, especially having a car with the steering wheel which is also on the left side. When I was passing another car I could see face to face the other driver and some of my visibility was shortened.

I realized I got used to it in a matter of hours. The speed limits were still in miles but I had a pretty good idea of how many kms. I could go. I didn't want to incur in any sanctions to begin with.

I headed to London where I was supposed to meet Mr. Halford and went to spend the night with my friends from Genova. They were living in Ealing Broadway, a quiet residential area served by the very efficient "Tube" or subway. They had a beautiful 3 months old baby girl that was born in London. I parked my car in a safe place and the next morning we went to The City by tube.

If the subway in Paris was busy, this one was extremely busy during the rush hours. I saw for the first time those people wearing dark suits, carrying an umbrella and with a funny bowler on their head, just as I had seen in movies and documentaries. Everybody looked busy running around from office to office.

In that labyrinth of streets and meadows I would have been lost if it wasn't for my friend. We arrived at the tall Cunard building and said goodbye while I was searching for my father's friend.

Mr. Halford was not there but there was his son that I had never met before. He was a nice and cute young man that was following his father's footsteps in brokerage. We went to the bank where I opened an account and I got my very first checkbook. Back to the office he called Mrs. Cruttenden who gave me directions to reach her house.

Brighton is just 90 miles south connected with a highway or with a fast train called the Brighton Bell.

The countryside was very green and pleasant. The hills reminded me of Umbria, a region in central Italy. A few houses became a multitude when I was approaching the suburbs of Brighton. I followed the directions carefully and I arrived in front of a cute two-story blue painted house among others just like it but of different colors. Fortunately the civic number on the front was very visible otherwise I could have rang somebody's else bell.

A short lady came to open the door and introduced herself as Mrs. Cruttenden: "but you can call me Terry", she said. I walked in the foyer and from there to a nice size living room where there was her husband sitting on a sofa and watching some soccer game. In a distance I could see the door of a bathroom wide open with their son and daughter playing in the full bathtub. Perry was five and Paula was eight years old.

Her husband, Eddie, got up and offered to help me get my luggage. My apartment was on the second floor, had a separate entrance from the backyard, and was composed of a small bedroom with a single bed, an armchair, a desk and a chair and a large armoire. The kitchen was tiny but functional. The bathroom had something missing: there was no "bidet". I soon learned that British do not use bidets but a lot of toilet paper.

I started unpacking and put everything away. The most important thing was my little stereo and about 200 records (45rpm) of my favorite songs. Now I was ready to meet the entire family.

We got acquainted over a cup of tea and some cookies. It was a little bit difficult at first to understand each other due to differences in the pronunciation. I finally understood that in the rent they had included breakfast, dinner, washing and ironing of my clothes. At the university there was a good cafeteria and if I wanted to eat on my own I could have used my kitchen. All that for 36 Lst per month! Little I knew that 1 Lst in those days was buying more than I ever thought.

To celebrate our meeting they invited me to go to the local pub after dinner where I did not fall in love with the beer, lager, but with the apple cider.

At the time I had switched cigarette brand to Muratti Ambassador and I was disappointed when I found out that was not a known brand in England. I tried several different packs and came to the conclusion that Marlboro red were possibly the best.

Terry gave me a map of the town and for the following two days I went to explore everything on foot.

We were on a hill overlooking the town, about three miles away from the center. A couple of miles South there was the beach that with Bormouth were the most famous in the country. Along the beach there was a double road called Marine Parade. Two long wooden piers stretched out to the sea and on one of them there was some interesting construction that I learned was the site of slot machines.

Queen Victoria used to spend some time in the Royal Pavilion, a building downtown that looked like an Indian palace and was entirely decorated with Chinese furniture, vases, paintings, embroidered silk, statues, carved wood and exquisite ivory pieces. The only English style room was the huge kitchen.

Some nice rectangular squares were everywhere in the old part of town with little meadows and in the relatively new side. Everything was clean, the locals were friendly, the traffic very ordered. There were a lot of young people walking around and sitting in the cafes. Being at a higher latitude I had expected a colder temperature but it was pleasant either during the day or at night.

To locate the university I had to drive my car because it was at about eight miles from the house. Mr. Halford had already contacted the secretary, Mrs. Lyons, who was very nice and gave me a tour of the campus. On October the 2nd I walked for the first time in the class and started meeting the dean, Mr. Graves, my history professor, Mrs. Richards, and some of the students that were from all over the world. I had never imagined that so many guys would be interested in a PHD in history!

There was Gisela from Zurich, Manfred from Vienna, Hans from Rotterdam, Yasser from Jordan, Ricardo from Mexico City, Mariefrancoise from Beauvais (North of Paris), Aldo from Roma, the only other Italian besides me, Olaf and his wife from Finland and last Zena and Michael from Addis Ababa, niece and nephew of his imperial highness the Negus of Ethiopia Haile' Selassie.

The opening speech of the dean was impressive and very sharp. He wanted that we all spoke English within the campus. No other language was allowed. The classes were starting at 10am and go on until 3pm with a one hour interruption for lunch, Monday through Thursday. Friday they were ending at noon.

During lunch I discovered that my new friends were all very simple and nice. We would become very close and have a lot of fun together. But not one single time I spoke to them in a language other than English. Zena and Michael were the only one that were often communicating in Aramaic.

The cutest guy was Ricardo and the prettiest girl was Mariefrancoise. Soon we would become a team and do many things together. Her and I were the only one that had a car with a foreign tag. With the exception of the Ethiopians who were driven everywhere by a chauffeur in a jaguar, everybody else was relaying on the local, very efficient, public transportation. Living in different areas, Mrs. Lyons had a net of landladies ready to host foreign students for reasonable rates. The only difference was that my flat was the exception that confirms the rule in England: it had central heating! We will see later what that meant.

I was slowly getting acquainted with British food. Porridge, eggs, bacon, grits, corn flakes, coffee or hot coco, toast butter and jam and some orange juice for breakfast and a very good abundant dinner with meat and veggies or some spaghetti with a rich homemade sauce that was so different but very good. For lunch I would rely on the cafeteria at the university and if I wanted to have something more substantial than sandwiches I had to drive to a pub where I could chose among meat pies and quiches. The cost of living was amazingly cheap for us. One pound could last up to three days buying cigarettes, food, candy and even newspapers. I could eat at a fancy Italian restaurant for less than 18 shillings. Also the famous Pickwick restaurant was cheap in comparison. I discovered Maynard's wine gums and I was eating them all day long buying them at the newsstand for a few pences.

The days were getting shorter but the temperature was still above average. Brighton sea has the benefit of the Gulf of Mexico warm stream that enables the growth of plants that otherwise would not live so far north.

The classes were very interesting and Mrs. Richards was an excellent professor. During the breaks she would have a cup of tea with us discussing various points of the subjects.

In the afternoon some of us would study together. After dinner, that was always early for my standards, we would go to the Egyptian café to chat and to some straight discos to have a good time. I needed to find out about the gay clubs and the cruisy spots in town so I went to hang around the public toilets by the station. I spotted a guy who was definitely gay and asked him what there was to do for fun in town. The New Curtain and the 42 clubs were the most popular. The first was open during the week ends only, the 42 was open every night after 8pm till 3am and it was located on the second floor of a building overlooking the beach. Both required a membership card that could be purchased for 2 Lst. and lasted one year.

I was not a drinker but I had to play along when going to the bars. The first thing the bartender was asking upon entering the place was: "what would you like to drink" and I needed to have the answer ready right away, so I was having a coke with a twist of lemon or a seven up. I tried the most popular gin&tonic and the big mugs of lager but the taste was not appealing. While I was sipping on my soda for one hour or so, the people close by already had 3 or 4 drinks.

The guys were more feminine to confirm my sister's hypothesis that most British guys were gay. Some straight women were always there, especially Betty. She liked to sleep with cute guys regardless of their sexual orientation and it was rumored she had most of them including a three way with the owners, Sydney and Roy.

The New Curtain club had a different kind of crowd. The doorman was always wearing a tuxedo and was greeting everybody like they were kings.

Here the crowd seemed more intellectual and there were more grown up then kids. The club was always packed but it was big enough and the music was not loud to the point that we had to scream to understand each other.

The first time I joined the club my attention was caught by a very refined man, well dressed, tall, good looking and always surrounded by some cute guys. He did notice me too and very soon somebody introduced us. He was Paul von Lobkovich, a German prince related to another friend of mine, Egon von Furstenberg (who years later would become a renowned stylist). Paul was also a Templar of Malta, or at least that's what he told me. He had a beautiful cottage in a fashionable area of Brighton where he used to give private parties with guys performing strip tease and sexually entertain his guests. On the whole, he was a very interesting person and he could converse about a wide variety of subjects.

I met an attorney visiting from Cheltenham (Wales) and we ended up in his room in a gay hotel he was staying. Until that point I did not know that several hotels and guest houses were totally gay and Brighton was a homosexual "Mecca" not only during the summer season but also during the weekends. Each hotel had small bars and living rooms where the guests could entertain their occasional friends and go to their bedrooms to have sex without any problem and under the delighted look of the owner. Not bad for a country that had an anti homosexual law still on their books from the times of queen Victoria!

One thing I had found out about the British: they were not that clean. Besides not having a bidet in their bathroom, they were not too keen on taking showers and some smelled. Even their white shirts had dirty collars but that seemed not to upset them at all.

In Europe men are usually not circumcised unless they are Moslems or Jewish. That means that if they do not wash their private parts, the smell is not really pleasant, at least it is not to me. From that point on I made sure that the person I was having sex with was clean or else I would decline.

With my luck my adopted family, the Cruttenden, were all very clean and took frequent showers. Terry was from Cornwall and Eddie was working for a window cleaning company. Rufus, a black I do not know what race big dog, was washed once a week. Thank God… because I do not like the smell of dogs!

Their TV was always on and I used to go downstairs to watch the news and some really funny shows on the BBC and the Anglia channels. I started loving the British humor of Danny la Rue, Benny Hill, Simon Dee and especially David Frost. The Saturday night show was delightful with singers like Cilla Black and Cliff Richard. The one I could not stand because I found so boring is a soap opera still going on these days called "Coronation Street". BBC did not have any commercial interruption but Anglia/ITV had several. That was the time Terry would go to the kitchen to prepare some coffee or tea and to roll a cigarette with a little metal box that I never learned to use.

She loved to cook and bake. I quickly got used to her cuisine and was eating whatever she was preparing. On a Sunday the main dish was roast beef in gravy with Yorkshire pudding and when she was serving the apple crumble with heavy cream that was to die for. The dairy products in England were absolutely the best. A pint of milk with the silver cap was just "pasteurized", one with a golden cap had the heavy cream on top and that was my favorite one. I believe that the yogurt was not comparable to any of the famous brands in the rest of Europe. I also discovered Cadbury chocolate and I was eating it often during the day. In spite of the fact that I was eating like a pig I never went over the 135 lbs. During the time I spent in the U.K. I reached that peek for the first and last time in my life.

I did not have a telephone in my flat so every time my parents were calling Paula or Perry were dispatched upstairs. My classmates were also calling after it started getting cold to come to study at my place because they did not have central heating and it was costing them one shilling for every hour they had the electric bars turned on to heat their room.

If the cost of living was extremely cheap for us, the cost of electricity was up to three times higher than in the rest of Europe. The electric heaters that I mentioned earlier were widely used across the United Kingdom. Most hotels and guest rooms had a niche covered by a curtain where those bars were "hiding". A meter was on the side and with 1 shilling everybody could enjoy some tepidity for about half an hour.

Mariefrancoise, Ricardo and I had become inseparable. She was living as "au pair" in the house of an old lady that needed someone to chat with and to do some light work around the house, he was renting a room at a lady who was a friend of Terry. Sometimes riding my car, sometimes Mariefrancoise, we became the target of all the traffic wardens in town because we used to park where ever, not really caring if the place was a parking spot or not. We never paid one single fine (each violation was 2 Lst.). After all we had foreign tags and we knew they would never get to us. After one year she beat me 27 to 22. The funny thing is that they were attached to the right door (the driver side in England) so sometimes we would find a couple stuck together, but that only if we had a passenger. We did stop giving a hard time to the wardens after we found a note saying: "we know you are foreigners and there is nothing we can do…but please refrain from parking here, these spaces are reserved for police and emergency vehicles".

The three of us decided to take advantage of the long weekends and to explore the country. The first time we left right after the class and headed west on the coast. The road was picturesque following the sea, sometimes over cliffs. Traffic was never heavy but those roundabouts, designed to slow the traffic down, every two miles or so, really got on our nerves.

The fist village is Chichester with the impressive castle of Arundel, home of the duke of Norfolk, cousin of the queen. We did pay a visit. Ricardo was taking pictures of everything and got me in the same habit so I bought myself a small Kodak camera and started shooting.

Proceeding west we encountered Bognor Regis, the ruins of a big Roman villa. While taking a guided tour I noticed that in the basement there was a round furnace with brick ducts going to different directions. "That was the way the Romans heated their houses. The furnace would produce the heath that would be running under the floor" the guide explained. At that point I could not retain myself and said: "See…the Romans were heating their houses two thousand years ago and yet the British are using these stupid electric bars that are warm in the front but leave you cold in the back"! The guide did no appreciate my comment from the look he gave me.

We went to sleep in a cute bed and breakfast in Bournemouth, the second most famous beach town on the coast. It was cute indeed, but from our stand point Brighton was much better.

It was decided that every time we could we would take a trip and so the following weekend we were on the road again to drive to Stonehenge.

The countryside in England is always stunning. So green all year round because of the frequent rain, nice hills, small quiet villages with 1000 years old houses, clean, neat, like the time had never passed. We spent the night in Winchester where we admired the beautiful cathedral and took some pictures of the statue of William the Conqueror, the ancestor of queen Elizabeth. Between this city and Stonehenge we saw some ruins of some abbey that was destroyed by fire in ancient times. Finally the stones emerged in a distance on the left side. A small parking lot was filled with tourists crossing over to wonder around this ancient temple. In those days it was still possible to walk around freely. It was sad to see that many graffiti were covering the rocks.

We never did drive all the way to Cornwall because in the following trip we headed north and east.

Back in Brighton everybody was getting ready for the holiday season. The town was getting dressed with colorful lights. Every shop, every department store and every house were displaying Christmas trees and candles. The temperature had dropped but it was still pleasant.

Talking to my parents it was decided that I would go home for a couple of weeks to spend a few days in Lugano and new year's eve in Lavarone with my old friends, my sister and her family. My father said that the road conditions were not really the best to travel and so it was decided that I would fly from London to Milano and he would pick me up at the Malpensa airport.

There was not much to do in Switzerland but to sleep, rest, take walks and go shopping. While walking downtown I discovered the park by the lake and it was there that I met some local gay people. This park was open all day and all night. There was always somebody cruising around, looking and smiling, asking for the time or to light a cigarette but those were excuses, just to get to know the person and to see if a hook up was possible. There was a tall skinny guy, very feminine, who was walking around wearing a long black fur coat. The locals called him "la mamma" (the mother). Then there were some cuties always in a group. It was possible to meet German, French and guys from other countries that were either working there in hotels or visiting for a few days. In the evening I had a good time with some of them while my parents thought I was spending time at a famous disco or at the Kursaal, the local casino.

My father kept a small office downtown. I managed to make a copy of the key and I used it sometimes when I found someone who did not have a place to go to play. I knew my dad was in bed by 10 and was using it only seldom in the morning. I remember an Arnold, a Dave, a Ugo. But best of all I met an Austrian journalist named Alex. He had been following me for a few minutes when I decided to talk to him. He was tall, slim, fit, blonde and was wearing a black leather outfit revealing some interesting features.

I invited him to go to the office and for a while we talked about different things. Then I started kissing him and suddenly he became very bossy telling me what to do and how to do it. Perhaps I was a bit scared at the beginning, but the more we had sex and the more I liked it. Possibly the most excitement I had in a long time.

Going to the mountains I enjoyed meeting my friends. They were all there. We went to ski every day until sunset and before heading home we were having some hot coco at the bar by the ski lift. During the night there we were going to the usual nights to dance and to the pizzeria to have an early morning snack.

By January 6th I was back in England telling the Cruttendens all about the Dolomites, my friends and showing them the pictures I had taken. They were very impressed considering that they had never been abroad.

The classes resumed and we were back to the same life.

The lessons were getting more and more interesting. With Mfrancoise and Ricardo we decided to take the first examination and asked Mr. Graves when it was the possible date. We studies really hard for a couple of weeks and passed with a very good vote, 28.

The ski had turned grey and all of a sudden we had a big snowstorm. It was not rare, but so much snow put a lot of businesses on hold for a couple of days. I did not have snow tires, the public transportation was not reliable, the university was cut off so we all walked around a lot looking at the kids building snowmen and hitting each other with snow balls.

Zena and Michael passed on an invitation for a party at the Ethiopian Embassy in London that was going to be at the end of January. Almost all of us decided to go by train and spend the night in a hotel near Victoria station. Tuxedo had to be worn for the occasion.

It was going to be fun! 9 of us left on Friday afternoon on the Brighton Belle. We arrived in London and walked to the hotel where we had booked the rooms for two nights. We went to dine at Mr. Pickwick's, after, we went to dance in a huge disco on Leicester Square.

On late Saturday morning we had brunch and some went to visit the Imperial War Museum, some the Victoria and Albert and the usual trio (us) went to see the paintings and drawings collection at Buckingham Palace. The flag was not on the pole, which meant the queen was at Windsor.

Around six we gathered at the hotel to take a shower, shave, and get prepared for the party that was starting at eight. A black limousine came to pick us up and we all crawled in. The embassy was in a very nice building, all the lights were on. Zena and Michael were received like royalty and we all followed them inside the foyer. Several personalities and also celebrities were coming in announced by a master of the ceremonies. I all seemed like a scene from the past. The ambassador and his wife were doing the honors but the most important guest had not arrived yet. Princess Margareth arrived in a white Rolls Royce and was greeted by a general applause. The party was officially starting.

An orchestra played the British national anthem first then the Ethiopian.

The waiters were offering drinks and in a large saloon there were several tables covered with British and Ethiopian specialties.

To my surprise Paul von Lobkovitz was among the guests so after the usual greetings he showed me around introducing me to dozens of people. He knew everybody.

While I was in the navy I had gone to see a movie directed by an Italian but with an all British cast. The leading actor was among the guests. He was very handsome and I had dreamed several times about sleeping with him. It didn't come to my surprise when Paul told me he was definitely gay. While the chats and dances were going on, I spent about one hour sitting on a sofa talking to him. I thought he would have been as fascinating as he was on the screen, but to my disappointment I found him rather silly and dull, trying to impress me beyond his possibilities. The sight of M.Francoise and Ricardo gave me the excuse to leave him while he was looking around for somebody else to chat with.

1967

It had been an interesting party but not the kind that we would have liked to participate often. Once or twice in a lifetime was enough.

We stayed until late, then some of us decided to call off the night and rode a cab back to the hotel.

Check out time was at 11am on Sunday and we finally made it waking up everybody on time. When I got home I crawled into bed and slept until it was time to get ready for the lesson. By the end of that week we were going to have our first examination and there was no time to spare.

We all passed with a 28 and that was a pretty good vote to begin with, also counting that it was not in our native language.

We decided to take another trip, this time going north. We left on an early Friday afternoon, crossing in Surrey, with destination Oxford. That was a longer trip than we had expected and arrived around 11pm. The next morning we walked around the town, visited the beautiful ancient buildings of the university, took many pictures and decided that we liked it a lot. After lunch we were back on the road to go to Stratford upon Avon. This small town was just like when Shakespeare was living there, very nice indeed. We got a room at the Swan Hotel and went to visit the house and the cathedral where the famous William was born and was baptized. It was quite cold and…you guessed it: the room did not have a central heating!

Behind a curtain Ricardo discovered the electric bars and a meter and we manage to stay warm until 3am…when we ran out of shillings. The three of us were sleeping in the same bed, fully dressed and covered all the way to our neck to be somewhat comfortable. From that time we decided to make sure hotels were fully heated before checking in. The total cost was 3 Lts plus 23 shillings in coins!

Sunday we headed to Cambridge but neither of us liked it as much as Oxford. In the afternoon we started driving south, skipping London, stopping in Greenwich, where we took a photo while stepping on the first meridian, and crossing into Kent through very pleasant country roads leading to Tunbridge Wells. From there we went through another winding road to Horsham where we arrived at sunset. It was getting dark real fast and we were hungry. There were no houses, nor farms around. Mfrancoise was studying the map when Ricardo noticed some lights on a side road. We stopped at what looked like a pub in the middle of nowhere. The light was coming from lanterns, there were no cars around, but some bicycles were parked near the door. We entered the place: the atmosphere was smoky, dark, some people sitting at the bar, other playing darts. Nobody seemed to pay attention to us. We sat at a table that had a couple of burning lights in the center, an old woman came to tell what there was to eat and we ordered some meat pies, cider and apple crumble for dessert. The food was excellent and the price was extremely cheap.

We left and arrived in Brighton late at night.

A couple of weeks later we were still praising the food of that pub, so we decided to go back there, this time during the day, to have lunch. We were driving on the same road and we were approximately in the same area but we could not find that place.

Going around in a circle we stopped at a little farm and asked the owners if they knew about a place to eat in the area. We were disappointed to hear that there was nothing around for miles. Could all of us be wrong and got on a different road? An old man that was sitting on a rocking chair said that there used to be a pub, just a couple of miles away, when he was young, but the place had burned down some 30 years before. He got in the car, gave the directions to the site and to our astonishment there it was, in ruins, plants growing from the basement, but located on the same spot, just near the main road, exactly the way we remembered it.

When we got back to Brighton and told Terry about this experience, she was not surprised at all, all she said was: "my friends, you had dinner in a ghost pub, it can happen in our countryside"!

Still these days we remember the event and cannot explain what happened that night and I assure you that, even if we grew up in the time of LSD, pot, the children of the flowers etc., we had never tried any drug.

Later on that week happened another episode that would mark my life.

One afternoon, taking a walk after class, I had to pee and went to a public bathroom located in the main square, near the Royal Pavilion. Not used to go to the urinal, I went to one of the closed in toilets where a small hole in the wall caught my attention. I peeked inside to discover that it went all the way across the wall to the next booth where there was somebody jerking off. Suddenly the other guy was looking straight in my eye, then he introduced a note in the hole asking me to meet him outside if I was interested. I waited for a couple of minutes, flushed the toilet and went to wash my hands while he was doing the same. He was really cute and at first glance he seemed quite intelligent, so we started a conversation. He was a dancer in the ballet of the Covent Garden in London but he was in Brighton for the weekend, staying in one of those nice gay guesthouses near the Marine Parade. We spent the whole afternoon in bed and when it was dinner time I invited him for dinner at a good Italian restaurant. After dinner I took him as a guest to the 42 Club and we spent the rest of the night in his room.

A few days later I started feeling some hitch in my penis and became convinced I had a hair stuck inside. I saw there was a little red spot but I could not find any other sign. The hitch was getting worse and there was some kind of fluid coming out. Not knowing what it could be I waited another couple of days to see if it would get better; instead some glands started to swallow in my pubic area. At that point I went to seek medical attention. After the doctor examined my genitals he told me those were the symptoms of gonorrhoea, a common venereal disease that would develop two or three days after the infection had occurred. He told me that if I knew the identity of the guy I had slept with it was my duty to report him in order to avoid the spreading of the infection. I was a good citizen and I had to comply. My punishment consisted in three painful shots of penicillin in my butt and no sexual contacts for at least two weeks.

My parents, and my father in particular, never ever talked about sex or venereal diseases probably because of the way they were brought up in a puritan society of the early and mid 1900's. My mom never said a word out of place and the only remark that I over heard from my dad, talking about her with his brother, was that she definitely was not interested in sex, probably for the kind of upbringing that was very common in some families of the upper class post Victorian society. That was a big mistake because when children learn from other children about this kind of matter the reality is always somewhat distorted or very vague.

I kept very quiet for the following three weeks and I never told a soul.

We were preparing for a second examination that went even better than the first and brought me a 29. The three of us were determined to burn the stages and to get our PHD in less than 3 years.

The Cruttenden family was very nice and supportive. Terry was preparing tea with cookies and cakes every time my friends were coming over to study. We had developed such a friendship that is still going on these days and I basically consider her like my British mother. As she told me she never had this kind of relationship with any student she had before.

The days were getting longer and the term was coming to an end. Most of my schoolmates were going home for the summer but we wanted to stay there longer and to visit other parts of the country.

We started going to the beach to get some tan and we also tried to get in the water but it was too cold for our taste.

The ground is not covered by sand but by pebbles that are not really comfortable to lie on. The east side of the beach, where Marine Parade is higher on the sea, is reserved for nude bathers that can be easily noticed from the cars above.

Ricardo was flying back to Mexico and he invited me to go. Mfrancoise was not really in good terms with her boyfriend, that we had never met, and she was going to drive home to spend some time with her sister who had a newborn son. I went on a trip to Scotland and to meet some distant relatives that were living in Newcastle. One of my father's aunts had married an English man and had a son and a daughter. George lived in Aberdeen with his wife, two sons and one daughter. They were all convinced Jehovah's witnesses and they thought the world was coming to an end by the end of the century.

They were very nice and welcomed me with great enthusiasm, especially Andrew, the older son who soon offered to show me around. He was five years older than me, tall, handsome, nice body and big eyes. I knew that there was something more there than just be nice to a distant cousin and show me around. The feeling was mutual. Soon we were having sex at the house of one of his friends who had respectfully gone shopping for the afternoon. Andrew claimed I was the first Italian he had slept with. He was feeling bad because, as he put it, it seemed we were committing incest. So we did commit incest another three times before my departure.

I drove all over to make a stop in Inverness and visit Loch Ness without seeing the monster. Glasgow was a very industrial city and did not particularly attract my attention. I tried to board a ship to the island of Man, home of the famous tailless cats and also land of witches but the sea was rough and I had to give it up. Manchester and Birmingham were too industrial but I enjoyed Coventry and its castle.

Back in Brighton I had to decide what to do for the rest of the vacation. All my friends had gone home, the town was filled with tourists and Londoners, but I didn't feel like driving all the way to Italy. So I decided to remain there, possibly meet new people, and prepare for another examination.

At the 42 Club Betty introduced me to an Italian guy named Antonio from Roma. We became good friends. He had been living there for a couple of years and he gossiped more than a servant. He had a couple of friends that had been living together for almost 15 years: Gino, from Mantova, butler of a Mr. Villiers, architect that had worked for the queen, and Eric, pastry chef at the best hotel in town where they usually have the political conventions. Gino liked older guys and Eric was 15 years older. They were living in a delightful house in the west side of town.

We became good friends and confidents. Gino invited me and other people to dinner at the house of Mr. Villiers who was living in London but was coming to Brighton to party with young guys, mostly hustlers, while Gino was cooking, serving, cleaning and making sure that nothing was missing. He was very well paid for his work and the house was a beautiful two story building in a totally round square with a common central park. The furniture, the paintings and all the art works were stunning and tastefully placed. Gino was an excellent cook and he also knew my landlord because his company was cleaning the windows of all those houses.

Our friendship became a solid one that would last for a lifetime. They were taking a vacation in Italy every year to visit Gino's son and to stay in a house they owned in Garda by the lake. Numerous times I was invited to dinner and often Eric was preparing desserts that looked great and tasted even better.

The new term was approaching soon and most of my classmates had returned to town. Soon enough we were back to the same old habits. Mfrancoise had broken up with her boyfriend and now I had the feeling that Ricardo would have liked to date her. They were both surprised when I announced that I was going to take my examination by the end of September.

Dining at the usual Italian restaurant I met a cute guy from Glasgow. We started dating for a while and it was also fun. I was not in love with him but I guess he thought that ours was a serious developing story. He started sending flowers to my flat and a few times he showed up with little presents like a pair of coffins, a lighter and some 45rpm records. The matter took a very uncomfortable turn when one afternoon a policeman came to my door to make inquiries about this guy. It seemed that he had stolen some merchandise and they were trying to track him down. I got very upset about the matter but didn't know how to get in touch with him. He called me a couple of days later from Eastbourne begging me to go there to rescue him because he was in distress and madly in love with me. In case I didn't want to go see him he was threatening to kill himself!

I hate this kind of drama and I didn't think at the time that the guy was serious enough to go ahead with his plan. Anyway I got in the car and got there a couple of hours later. He was staying at a friend and was crying desperately while telling me he did not want to lose me. I had to use all the diplomacy to calm him down and finally I brought up the fact about the police. He swore he had nothing to do with it and I could not find out anything more.

I asked him not to call or try to see me again but phone calls, letters, and even flowers kept coming for several weeks afterwards. Eventually I never heard from him again.

Back to normal, munching on my wine gums, drinking my cider, enjoying the clubs and my friends, I was having a good time and all the examinations were passed with very good votes.

The usual three of us started going to London more often. Carnaby Street was at its peak. The most in fashion clothes were sold there together with the most silly gadgets that we bought for fun but never really used. Always fond of opera we went several times to the Covent Garden and to Albert Hall enjoying concerts and ballets. The best artists were performing almost every day. Nureyeff was one of our favorite as well as Montserrat Cabaille', Placido Domingo, Renata Scotto. Also the theaters had good plays and musicals with many famous actors performing. It was not uncommon to see members of the royal family sitting in the audience, I recall seeing Charles and Ann several times also at a performance of Hair.

It was fun to go to Hyde Park corner on a Sunday to see people screaming their opinions to small crowds, or go to Portobello Road to browse around for something really out of the ordinary. It was the fashion of long overcoats and we could buy one for 5 Lst or less. Ricardo was very fashion conscious, he was buying only on Carnaby Street.

The road to and from London became so familiar that we could drive with our eyes shut. To slow down the traffic the authorities had placed some life size figurines of policemen strategically placed on both sides of the highway. Once the trick was discovered it bothered only the newcomers.

Now you should know that in England pubs were open a couple of hours during lunch, then they would re-open at 5pm until 11pm. Exceptionally they were closing at midnight on week ends. The big fun was coming after closing if somebody was organizing a party that could last until early morning. All they did at these parties was drinking and chatting, nothing really exciting was going on. The most popular drink was gin and tonic and eventually I had one every now and then. They did not drink in moderation so it was not uncommon to have to drive somebody home.

The parties organized by Paul were something else but fortunately he did not allow drugs of any kind. I don't know where he was recruiting all those cute guys, certainly not a single one was a hustler and several were just a pleasure to look at.

Gino had told me that his boss was coming to Brighton a few times a year with a group of cuties and he liked to use the whip and other gadgets when having their orgies. I couldn't picture such an old man doing things like that.

After I had contracted that venereal disease I was much more careful when I was sleeping with somebody. Still, the British were not that clean, so I was checking for crabs with some special powder I had bought in an Italian pharmacy. When I was somewhat suspicious I was using a condom. Furthermore I went to the library and I red all I could about STD. There was enough to be scared and I became convinced that the school should have played a role in teaching about sex starting from an early grade, after all I came out when I was very young.

For some weird reason I felt like changing and see if I could pick up a girl, something that I was not good at.

One night I was out with Zena and Michael when they introduced me to a girlfriend that was visiting from Birmingham. She was pretty, slim, my height and about my same age. Chatting at the pub I asked her out to a disco and she accepted. We slow danced for a couple of hours and then we went for a drive in the country. It was an interesting approach but I didn't know if I should start with holding her hand or kissing her. To my surprise she made the first move and we ended up in my bed at the flat. The preliminary was fun. I slowly undressed her and it looked like she couldn't wait to undress me. We kissed, hugged, licked. I was leading and with my experience I knew all the right and most sensitive spots to work on. She was moaning and almost screaming so I begged her to relax otherwise the people downstairs would have wondered what was going on. She became so horny that she "almost" lost any inhibition that most girls have when they are with a guy. I know she reached orgasm at least three times. At the end we jumped in the shower together, then we smoked a cigarette. At this point I was ready to take her back home but she fell asleep on my bed. I had never slept in the same bed with a girl for the whole night but it seemed not polite to wake her up and give her a ride home at 3am, therefore I tried to sleep too. When I walked up she had prepared some breakfast. Her idea was to eat and have another round of sex; my idea was to eat and run to the class since I was preparing for another examination. She asked me out for that night again but I had to make an excuse. It had been fun but I did not want to start a relationship, besides I did not want to go twice with the same girl: there was nothing to discover anymore.

This episode gave me some confidence for future hook ups and it also warned me to be careful interacting with the emotions of a woman who is not a nymphomaniac.

The other cousin of my father who was married to a dentist and lived in East Grinstead, just south of London, invited me for a weekend. Kent is very rural and green. The drive was pleasant even if I had to step out of the car for a couple of times to read the road signals for the right directions. Usually the print is very small and one cannot see it.

They lived in a nice clean cottage on a hill called "Killreymond". I had met her once in Italy but didn't know the rest of the family who turned out to be very nice. On the contrary of her brother they were not Jehovah's witnesses so I didn't have to hear about the end of the world and stuff. They showed me the village and we stopped at a little farm where they were producing butter, cheese, yogurt and honey: those were the very best products I had so far. I had to shop there again before I left to bring some home for myself and for Terry because I knew she would have appreciated it.

My aunt cooked typical English meals but she made a salad that I never had before with walnuts and apples that was delicious.

During the second world war she was with the Red Cross working with princess Margaret with whom she had kept in touch for all those years. She asked me if I would have liked to have tea with the queen in London because once a month there was such possibility for foreign aristocrats. I told her I would be delighted not only to meet the queen but also to go inside the royal palace.

A couple of weeks went by and I had forgotten about our talk when Paula came upstairs to tell me there was a call from Eileen, my aunt. She gave me a reserved telephone number of one of the secretary of the Foreign Office that I would have to call at 10am the next day. This lady asked me several personal questions and then she said I would receive a formal invitation by mail stating the day, time, place and dress code for the event. I knew then that this was not a joke. The Cruttendens were more excited than I was. Living there all their life they had never seen the queen in person.

It was going to be on a Friday afternoon. I was supposed to be at the south gate by 4 o' clock sharp, dressed in black, with the invitation card at hand and my passport. There were another twenty persons there but that did not diminish the importance of the event.

We were introduced in a small courtyard and through an old wooden door we entered Buckingham Palace. Some butler and a couple of waiters guided us through dark corridors to a nice size room with red draperies on the walls and rich decorated furniture. We were told to wait and speak softly. At 4,55pm another butler came in asking us to stand in a line. The queen came in at 5pm sharp, greeted everybody, shook our hands and asked a couple of questions like where were we coming from and what were we doing in England. Tea and cookies were served by several maids. At 5,30pm the queen took her leave and we were invited to follow the butler to the exit of the palace.

I remember that shaking the hand of the queen with a bow I noticed her skin was really beautiful. My regret was that no pictures were allowed. The next day in the small print of "The Times" there was the announcement under the coat of arms of the Windsors that these specific guests had tea with her majesty and my name was on the list.

To show my appreciation to my aunt I sent her a bunch of flowers.

By that time I had to get back to serious studying because we wanted to take another examination very soon.

It didn't seem like Ricardo was trying to date Mfrancoise and she was not pushing in that direction either. Everything had remained the same, we were always the best of friends and that situation suited me a lot better otherwise I would have felt like the one too many.

More trips were planned and more were done. We explored the whole south of England but we had never been to Canterbury and we had to read the famous "Tales" in high school. We were looking forward to those Friday afternoons because we loved to get in the car and leave. We were studying hard all week long determined to prepare as many examinations as possible. Our efforts paid off because we did graduate very much ahead of time thanks to our perseverance and also because we had a very good memory remembering lessons and content of the books.

I loved Brighton but I didn't like the routine in general and it was getting to that point. Each one of us started to work on the degree thesis. Mine was going to be about the pre-

Colombian civilizations of North and South America.

Zena and Michael had already left the class but they were still in Brighton. Zena was affected by epilepsy and it was rumored that Michael was taking drugs even though we had never seen him high.

My doctorate in history was an easy target to get. I gave Terry one month notice and spent those days partying and spending more money than usual. I also indulged myself to a massage parlor in London but was disappointed when I saw the masseur was a woman.

The night before my departure Gino and Eric had me and some close friends over for dinner.

To say goodbye is never an easy task. I was confident I would have returned to Brighton soon to visit and to re-catch those good old days.

Terry and Paula were almost crying while I was loading my car.

My two good friends came all the way to Folkestone. They were going to remain in Brighton for another couple of months. That would be the last time I saw Ricardo. I imagine he's happily married with kids living in Coyoacan, Mexico City.

While I was looking at the sea and the ship was slowly rolling out of the port my mind was going back to my first arrival in that large island. I had grown, had more experience than guys my age, and now I was ready to conquer the world.

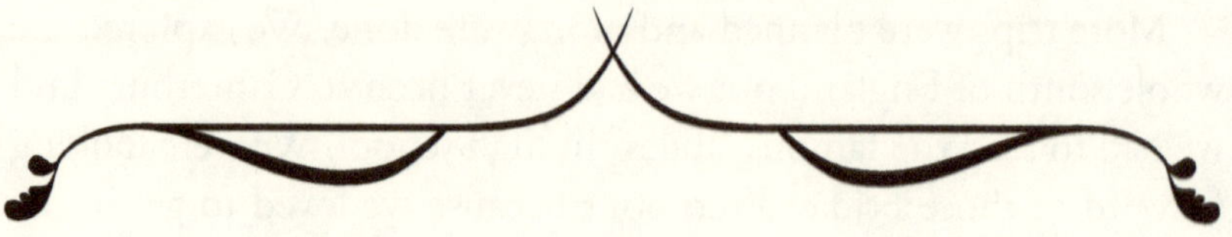

Chapter 10

Milano

I took my time to go south and cross France. Stopped in Paris at Alan for a few days, then in Lyon just to get a glance of the city. I crossed into Switzerland and stopped in Geneve to see my cousin Philippe, then with a last drive I arrived in Lugano planning to relax and enjoy Concetta cuisine.

It was march 1972 and the city was slowly waking up from a cold winter. Being on a lake the plants could benefit from it so well that before spring everything was already blooming.

My parents were renting a large apartment while their house was being built. My mother was very particular. She looked at many properties until my dad became convinced the only way to please her was to have it built the way she wanted it.

Some tourists were already arriving and the hotels gradually re-opened. It was quite festive to walk around. Not to waste any time I started going back to the old habit of the park. Almost every night I met someone interesting to take to my dad's office or to go to their hotel room.

Bruno, my brother in law, had opened a new office dealing with import/export of chemical products and that was not surprising since he had a PHD in chemistry. He came over for lunch on a Sunday with my sister and the little brat nephew of mine. Chatting at the table he asked me about my future plans. I had none at that time. He offered me a job as some kind of customer service in the office because the mother company was German and had branches all over Europe and also in the USA. The only foreign language he could speak was French, on the other hand I was fluent in three.

This prospective was interesting enough and the salary was very desirable for a starter.

His family owned a five story apartment building in Milano with two small penthouses and one was free.

I decided to check it out so on Monday I was on my way to Milano. The apartment was located on the top floor and consisted in a small living room with a corner kitchen, a bathroom and a bedroom with a wide balcony overlooking the street. It needed some work and of course furniture. My sister took me to the basement that was loaded with all kind of furniture that had been discarded by them and their relatives. There was enough to fill three flats. We recuperated a nice antique table, four chairs, a big bed with a night stand and a small desk that would serve as entertainment center. For linens, pottery, dishes, silverware, towels etc. my mother gave me all the necessary and even more because I had to travel twice to Lugano to get all the stuff.

The idea to start a job was tempting but scary at the same time. It was a jump in the unknown and I did not know if I was capable of doing real work of any kind.

I went shopping for serious clothes and on the 2nd of May I was walking (it was only half a mile away) to the office.

Dr. Mora was the manager. He was tall, good-looking, curly hair and in his mid fifties. Carla was the secretary, a red headed lady in her early thirties, fluent in English and with some knowledge of French. She was nice. We became good friends right away (and we still are).

During the first week I was learning a lot. Carla had a great experience from her previous job. She was the secretary of one of the greatest Italian manager of ENI, the Italian oil company, who had died in a very suspicious plane crush.

With her help and her complicity we formed a good working team. Dr. Mora was often out of the office to visit customers, Bruno was coming in sometimes to sign documents and take care of the financial part of the company.

For lunch we would call the bar down the road and a few minutes later a cute waiter was delivering food and beverages.

Very soon I was understanding the purpose of the company, learn by hearth the names of our foreign correspondents, talk to them on the phone and take notes of all the information and questions that had to be reported to Dr. Mora. Carla was taking care of typing offers, letters, filing, telex and other minor tasks. Occasionally I was sent out to personally deliver some important documents. It really was a light work and I was getting paid 200.000 Lire a month (about 250$) net.

I was getting acquainted with the city. I had to be at the office at 9am but I certainly didn't go to bed until 1 or 2am.

I discovered a gay bar very close to my flat called Petit Paris owned by Alfonso and Mario. This was some kind of intellectual club where people were going to talk about various arguments or just to play cards. Once in a while there was an exhibit of a famous painter with the presence of some famous Italian celebrities from the cinema or from the sport.

Some characters were cute, some were old and ugly, but most of them were nice and friendly and not pushy. With the excuse of the permanent art exhibit there were all kind of people coming in to check it out.

One night there were two of the most feminine older guys playing cards when a cute young man came in to ask some directions. One of them acted in a very straight manner but, apparently, gave the guy some wrong information. At this point his partner started blaming "her", talking in a feminine way, saying "she" was out of "her" mind and the guy better follow "her" directions. At that point the man was gone while everybody was laughing like crazy.

Another place that I checked out was the famous cinema "Rosa", very cruisy all day long. With 200 Lire I could go in, watch a movie, meet a cutie and consume there or take him home.

Compared to Genova the possibilities were overwhelming.

The Petit Paris was my favorite club for the wide variety of people that I could meet and also because it was in a walking distance from my flat.

One night I met this guy named Carlo who was the administration manager of a company manufacturing machines for the polishing of metals. I was not physically attracted to him and after that was cleared we became good friends. He was always talking about one of his employees nicknamed Milo and he was praising him so much that I really wanted to meet him. One night he arrived at the bar with him and it was love at first sight. Milo was my age, dark hair and eyes, very cute and also very intelligent. He was extremely well dressed and he smelled good. The secret was in a cologne called "Brut" and his suits were hand made by a guy that eventually became also my tailor in Milano, Mr. Colombo.

With Milo we hit it on immediately also if there was no sex between us. I was happy to be around him, to do things together and to have long conversations about various subjects and many aspects of life. He had a very good taste and he could pick up most anything that looked good but that had a reasonable price.

When I invited him over for dinner on the first date, he looked at my flat and gave me some good advices to make it nicer. He also helped me to put up the wallpaper and to change all the light fixtures. Like me, he was attracted by older guys. Apparently there was this mysterious man that he was seeing on a regular basis. Deep inside I was jealous but I never said anything.

By that time my colleague had figured out that I was gay. She has always been an "amateur" psychologist and even now she still things that being gay is a choice. During our free time at work she would bring up the subject to see if I was going to change my mind. When I introduced her to Milo she thought she had more ground for her theory.

In Milano I was slowly getting close to some people that eventually became close friends, a bond that still goes on.

One morning in June Mr. Mora called me and asked if I wanted to go to spend a month in Germany to work for the mother company. I thought that was a wonderful idea and told him to make all the necessary arrangements. I had already met some of the people when they were coming to Italy on business.

Carla was not happy to remain alone at the office for over a month. Dr. Mora had a bad temper and sometimes he was difficult to get along with him.

I packed a large suitcase, went to spend the week end at my parents, and on a sunny Monday morning I drove through Switzerland to cross into Germany by Basel. Before the border I stopped for a quick lunch and I met a guy that was heading to Amsterdam, hitch-hiking. I didn't see any harm in giving him a lift, after all driving all alone was kind of boring. It was after we went through custom that he told me, with a big smile, he had a box of hashish camouflaged as crayons by "Caran d'Ache". I would have left him on the autobahn but since the damage was already done I kept driving.

I had to stop for the night and chose the city of Heidelberg. I asked the guy if he wanted me to leave him on the road or spend the night in the hotel and go on the next morning. He chose to stay.

Since my company was paying we went to a nice hotel and checked in. I had never been in Heidelberg, which is a very nice old university town. We walked around and while we were chatting I found out that my occasional friend was intelligent, clever, well mannered and not really a pothead as his behaving in the car let me believe. He was going to Holland to see a girl he had met during the summer on the beach of Rimini where he lived with his father who was a lawyer. I suggested we could eat at the Ratskeller, one of my favorite restaurants in Germany. After dinner we went bar hopping and ended up in a small disco frequented by a lot of students. He had one beer too many so I had to call a taxi to get back to the hotel. We tried to go to sleep but he kept playing with my foot and at that point I had enough and started touching him. Surprise, surprise…he started hugging and kissing and we had sex for a couple of hours. Finally, exhausted, we went to sleep. When we got up and went to have breakfast it was like nothing had happened. I tried to bring up the subject to let him know that I had enjoyed it a lot, but he pretended he did not remember what had happened because he was buzzed. He got off the car in Koeln not to be seen ever again.

To go to my destination there was another hour drive through the beautiful Ruhr, original site of the famous Neanderthal men. It is a very busy area with several big industries like Bayer and Weba. The villa of Krupp (the steel magnate famous during the second world war for the "Big Bertha") was just a few miles away in Ketwig, near Solingen, the birthplace of German swords and knives.

Muelheim an den Ruhr was my final destination: a nice old village on the bank of the river Ruhr, located between the cities of Essen and Duisburg.

It was easy to find the hotel. My company was just two kilometers away. The very next morning I reported for duty and I finally saw the faces of the people I had talked to on the phone so many times. Fraulein Beutler was the secretary of the CEO. She welcomed me and she told me to rely on her for anything I needed. My job was pretty much the same as in Milano but here I had to deal with their American sister company in New York and Houston.

That evening I went to explore the village. There were a few bars and they were not very crowded. Nothing gay, not even the small park by the river. The only solution was to get in the car and drive to Duisburg. Once there I adopted the usual system and went to check out the train station. In the newsstand I saw something that attracted my attention and that I had never seen before: a gay magazine called "DU + ICH". That was something like "The Advocate" but the photos were very explicit. Fortunately I didn't have to cruise the public toilets because the magazine had an insert with all the gay bars and activities of that city, Dusseldorf and Essen, all in a close driving distance. The most popular bar was half way between the station and the hospital, the disco was just a couple of blocks further. I checked the bar first. I love the music and to dance but to get to know people the bars are best and less noisy.

The crowd was pleasant. The owner was a woman who must have been a beauty when she was younger. Later I learned she was a man who had the operation done in Casablanca. I would have never guessed so because they had removed even the Adam's apple under her chin. The doctor had really done a great job!

The bartenders were extremely nice introducing all the new comers to the usual customers. I found myself at ease and everybody was friendly and not going straight to sexual innuendoes. For my first night I was jolly satisfied. I had met a bunch of people in a foreign town, befriended the owner of the bar and the bartenders, located the two clubs that I was interested in, but I got back at 3am. At the office they were starting at 8.

The next morning I called my dear friend Marie Francoise who was working in Koeln for Dynamite Nobel. She was surprised and happy to know I was so close and we made arrangements to see each other during the weekend.

She was renting a cute flat in a nice area of town and she had bought a Volkswagen Beetle. We hugged and kissed and started speaking in English like we used to do in Brighton. At that point I reminded her that Mr. Graves was not around to fine us for speaking a different language and I proposed to speak French. She was very surprised because she did not guess that I could. All that time and I had never said one single word in French!

I cooked dinner and we went out for a walk remembering the old good time in England. She had not heard from Ricardo after he had gone back to Mexico so I showed her a letter that he had sent me just a few days earlier. We sent him a postcard with greetings. That was the last known address we had and neither of us had ever heard from him again.

That was a pleasant Saturday with so many things to remember. I headed back to Mulheim early on Sunday afternoon saying that I had to do some work but instead I was going to check out the bar in Duisburg during the day.

There were more people than I had imagined probably because with the thought of Monday morning going to work nobody wanted to be late. I had my Martini, not knowing what else to drink, when I got approached by a very nice looking guy in his early thirties. He was a plumber, married with kids, there looking to get laid. The problem was that he did not have a place to go and I could not take anyone to my room. We ended up in his car, with the windows steamed. I was kind of nervous but, as he explained, it was perfectly legal if nobody could see inside the car. It was fun and I regretted that was the only time I saw him.

Back at the office Carla was calling my daily to give me a report of what was going on in Milano and about the different moods Dr. Mora was in. She was missing me a lot and couldn't wait to have me back. I was missing her too but it was just too fascinating being abroad for a while.

In Koeln I found the Blaupunkt stereo for the car that I always wanted. The old 45 rpm vinyl records were by the obsolete and the cassettes had replaced them. I had a wide collection of at least 600 records with all my favorite songs, classic music and opera included, and I had started slowly replacing them. This was taking some time because it was difficult to find exactly the same music in French, Italian, German and English/American. One cassette was replacing at least 12 records and I could skip any song just pushing a button. The stereo had a great sound and the Dolby system was taking away the hissing noise.

With Marie Francoise we decided to go spend the following weekend in Amsterdam, just a couple of hours drive to the West.

We stopped in Nyimwegen, just across the Dutch border, for lunch. By paying in Marks and getting the change back in Gouldens they made a mistake and not only we didn't pay the meal but we also got 20 extra Gouldens. Not my fault, I did not notice it until we were already on the way to Harlem.

In Amsterdam we found only one double bedroom. After checking in we went walking around the canals looking for a characteristic place to have dinner.

There was a strange atmosphere that night. During the trip we had listened to the Bee Gees and the Platters and one of our favorite song happened to be "Only You".

After dinner, sitting on a bench over a bridge, M. Francoise told me that she was in love with me and she considered "Only You" to be "our" song! I was overwhelmed and also kind of happy. I liked her a lot but I had never thought that we could be lovers. Never than less I did not want to disappoint her and I played along.

That night we slept together for the first time and I could feel she was very happy. The next day we walked around Amsterdam to see the museums of the most famous painters. After dinner we went looking for a disco to dance. There was one called "Napoleon" that looked promising from the outside, even the music was good because we could hear it on the street. I opened the door to let Mfrancoise walk in first but the door slammed in my face. One minute later she came out to explain that was a lesbian disco and men were not allowed in. We finally found one opened to everybody but the guys were more numerous than the girls.

On Sunday morning the sun was shining so we decided to go to the beach to try to get some tan. When we got there it was around 11am, the sky was the color of lead, there was a cold wind blowing and many people swimming in those frigid waters. We headed back to Koln.

The following weekend we had planned to go visit the famous villa of the Krupp. This is a large square building , very German, with too much wooden interior, kind of heavy baroque style. Not too far there is a river with small sailing boats, and nearby a barn with horses. We spent the afternoon riding in the countryside. Back to her flat I cooked dinner and we slept together again. That was kind of a record for me: twice with the same girl! By Sunday afternoon I had enough and I was aiming to go back to Mulheim. That night I had in mind to check out a club in Essen, just about half an hour drive to the east. I had some difficulty in finding the place because it was hiding in the basement of an apartment building. It was kind of dark, nicely furnished and not many people around due to the fact that the next day was a working one. I was sipping a drink when my attention was caught by this gorgeous guy, a bit older than me, same height, well built, black hair and one of the most beautiful faces I had ever seen. Apparently he had noticed my looks and came towards me with a big smile. He told me he was from Poland but Germany was his adopted homeland. He was an architect and had a studio in downtown Essen. After a few kisses he invited me to go to his place. There was a full moon, the living room was very shady, but I could see the bright smile on his face. He had some records of opera and started singing along with the voice of a tenor, strong and firm. I was so taken that I couldn't resist and started kissing him all over. We were slowly undressing each other to discover each part of the body. His was very well toned with a broad chest, small waist, smooth skin, fleshy lips, but when I finally took his underwear off he did not have an erection and his penis was no longer than the one of a two year old baby. I couldn't believe that such a gorgeous guy could be that way. Of course I pretended not to pay any attention to this minor aspect, on the contrary I enjoyed every minute of it. He reached orgasm without an erection for three times! I felt so sorry for the guy but if I had lived there I would have probably loved to date him.

1972

Back to reality my love story with M.Francoise was becoming more serious that I thought. I had to go back to Italy at the end of august and she decided to take a few days off, drive with me to Lavarone, then fly back to Koln from Milano.

My 45 days in Mulheim were coming to an end. I had enjoying being there and to be frank the idea of going back to the same routine now that fall was coming did not appeal to me.

We made arrangements for the trip back. I went to pick her up on a late afternoon and we headed south east to Austria to get to Italy through the Brenner Pass. We traveled all night long and arrived in Lavarone early in the morning just when Concetta was getting up to prepare breakfast.

My sister, who knew about our arrival, had taken down the pictures from the walls around the staircase replacing them with some awful ones to give the impression we were simple country people. My mother had not seen that and she made a big fuzz about it (we were constantly playing jokes and she took everything seriously).

We spent a couple of relaxing days in the mountains and she met all my best friends who were surprised to see me so intimate with a girl. We drove to Milano where she stayed for another couple of days to see the city and to shop around, and then it was time to say goodbye. The idea was to spend Christmas together in Lugano and to go ski for a couple of weeks.

Back to the office Carla was so happy to see me that she spent hours telling me all the things that had happened during my absence.

There was a new movie premiering in Italy, "Brother Sun sister Moon" by Zeffirelli, a director that has always been among my favorite together with Ken Russel and Stanley Kubrik. With Carla and her boyfriend Pino we went to see it one night during the first week of September. That movie signed my life for months to come.

It was all about the life of saint Francis of Assisi. The way Zeffirelli portrait him was somewhat on the romantic side but the principles of Francis life appealed to me. I went to a specific library and bought a couple of books to know more about what really happened when he formed his order. I think it took me a couple of days to read them both and I became so inflamed that I had to check everything in person. Quickly I gave up my job (against the advice of everybody that was around me), got in the car and headed to Assisi where I took a room in some ancient hotel. I was imagining the place 600 years before. Not much had changed except for the vehicles, the lights and the paved roads. The first place I went to visit was the "Porziuncola" the abandoned chapel that he started restoring when he came out of his illness. It is pretty little church with a tiny bell tower but it is not surrounded by the beautiful blooming fields of Umbria. During the Renaissance the architect Bramante enclosed it in a huge basilica called S.ta Maria degli Angeli. Very impressive but not really in the spirit of the Saint.

The second visit was paid to the Convento of San Damiano, the first founded by him and his followers. I forgot to say that one of the first guys to join his order was one of my ancestors back in 1231. Now, I knew all about the rules of the order, and I knew the monks could not touch money or wear more than it was necessary to protect their body form the cold. Therefore before taking the guided tour of the monastery I had got some bread that I kept in my pocket. The monk was very well dressed and was also wearing socks and regular shoes instead of the more typical sandals. At the end of the tour he received several tips from the people around me but all I gave him was a pound of bread. He almost refused it and that made me quite angry but I kept quiet.

On my quest for following Francis steps I ended up in "La Verna", the last monastery he founded. The intention was not to build anything permanent. The cell he was sleeping in was inside a cave of the rock and the bed was made of straw. La Verna is a stunning place. I arrived early one afternoon and checked in the guest room. This was on the right side of the big construction, close to the souvenirs shop and 100 meters from the small cemetery.

There were at least forty monks and most of them were in seclusion. During the centuries they had amassed such a wealth through donations form sympathizers and members of the third

Franciscan order. The largest ceramics of "Della Robbia" are kept under the gallery leading to all the different chapels the last of which is on the very place where Francis got the stigmata. Each chapel was granting two to four years indulgency for a stop and a pray. The one of the stigmata was granting a perpetual forgiveness to any pilgrim. I was thinking how Martin Luther would have felt walking through that place.

It was the donation of a nobleman to the saint that made the building of the monastery possible. The birthplace of Michelangelo, Caprese, is just a few kilometers away. I was the only guest but during the day there were numerous buses and cars coming to visit the place, take pictures and buy silly souvenirs. The monks had a little bus at their disposal to go to the closest city, Poppi, to watch movies or to do god knows what.

The guest rooms were austere. A large corridor had ancient portraits of serious priors hanging on the high walls. The room was bare, simple, just an armoire, a big bed with a night table and a chair. The rest of the wing had a living room with a TV set and a large dining room next to the kitchen.

The food served was the same that the monks were eating: a first course of pasta for lunch and soup for dinner, a second course consisting of meat or fish with veggies, seasonal fruits and coffee. In the morning they were serving tea or milk and coffee with bread, butter and preserve. The total cost for the full board and lodging was around 18$ per day.

I spent three nice days walking around in the forest listening to the birds singing on the trees and to the noise of some water flowing in a stream. Some monks were working in a big orchard from sunrise to sundown.

One afternoon I took a trip to visit another famous monastery nearby called Camaldoli. This was in a very secluded mountain hill, founded by San Romualdo in 1012, composed of 20 cells, a very baroque church and a small house for the doorman. All surrounded by a rectangular wall. A place meant for solitude and meditation that underwent numerous transformations. Their only contact with the outside world is an ancient pharmacy where they sell homeopathic medicines made from the herbs they collect in the woods.

When I got back to La Verna I found out I was not the only guest. There was a German car and its plate was unmistakably from Hamburg. Next to my table for dinner there were a couple of guys that I could immediately label as gay.

To be courteous I answered their many questions and I know that they had figured out that I was gay too. We watched some TV and when we called the night they openly said they would have liked for me to join them in their room to have some fun.

I was on this trip driven by some emotional mystic impulse. Sex was totally out of my mind. I was outraged that those guys could feel that way in such a "holy" place! The next morning I had packed and left heading south to Roma.

The mountain road to the capital was pleasant and with very little traffic. I went through several small medieval villages perched on the hilltops. I did stop in Fiuggi, site of the famous spring of freshwater so good for the liver, famous from the Roman times and preferred by royalties and popes. When traveling in Italy I had learned that the best places to eat were those where truckers would stop. That always worked. There was not a big menu but the food was always excellent.

In Roma I went to stay at Luigi's house, my friend who had the house in Lavarone. His parents were extremely happy to see me but disappointed that I was going to stay there for three days only. I told them about my experience and how disappointed I was to see that the old spirit that had moved Francis was not to be found again. Who knows, maybe I would have joined the fraternity otherwise. I always considered his mother like an aunt and she was more a confidant for me than my mother. Marisa was used to play cards with her friends every afternoon and they involved me in a game of poker that lasted four hours. By the end I had won more money that I had spent during the whole trip! I left Roma heading back to Milano not knowing what I was going to do next, but I was not worried about it at all.

My friends at the Petit Paris welcomed my return. It was late September. The leaves were changing colors but the days were warm and pleasant. I decided to go to Venezia to see my house and visit those friends that had such a great part in my childhood.

The city during fall was just stunning. I say "was" because nowadays there are so many tourists all year round that one cannot really enjoy it.

I made the usual round to see my relatives. Some of my ex schoolmates were still there. It was fun to go down "memory lane" and find out what happened to everybody. Unfortunately one had died falling through the glass roof of a green house when he was only 17.

Venezia has never been a gay hot spot with the exception of the nude beach of the "Alberoni" at the very end of Lido. At night people used to walk around St. Mark Square and up and down the "Riva degli Schiavoni" by the bridge of Sighs. Later at night there were only those that were looking for something more than walking.

So there I was, hanging around by the main square, on that early morning on the 7th of October 1972.

There was this guy chasing me and he was so insistent that I finally stopped and talked to him. He was not attractive and way too feminine for my taste. Anyway I was never rude and besides he could give me some good leads on where to go to find a better cruising spot.

He was trying his best to invite me over to his house, when I saw somebody standing by one of those little fountains that tourists use to wash their hands or to get a quick drink. He looked about my age, taller, nice built and with a very pretty face.

When I asked the annoying guy if he knew who that was, he answered saying that was a Swiss hustler and I'd better leave him alone. Needless to say I didn't pay attention to him and walked right by the guy asking him first in German, then in French where he was from. He was American, in the U.S. Air Force, stationed in the military base of Aviano, just a couple of hours far from Venezia. When we started chatting the other guy realized there was no hope for him and left.

This casual encounter was going to change my entire life.

He introduced himself as Tom from Memphis Tennessee. He had been in Italy for about two years after spending another two years in S. Korea. Soon enough we discovered we had many interests in common including the love for animals and nature. He invited me to spend the night in the room he was renting in a pensione, so through alleys and bridges we went there. I was impressed by how he knew his way around. The city can be a maze for someone not living there.

We spent the night holding hands and talked until dawn. At seven I had to leave the room but I didn't want to leave him so I invited him to go to Lavarone because he had never visited the Dolomites. Much to my surprise he accepted but before he had to go back to Aviano to get some warmer clothes. He said he would be back around 3,30pm and we would meet at the train station.

We parted while I was thinking I would never see him again but I was proven wrong when the train from Pordenone arrived and I saw him walking on the platform.

I was so happy as I had not felt in a long time. We walked from the station to the Piazzale Roma where my car was parked and we headed to the mountains.

I didn't mean to impress him with my driving but I could tell he was somewhat concerned about the high speed and the way I was boarding those sharp curbs. In those days there were no seat belts and he was holding himself to the seat. I reduced the speed and I saw him getting more relaxed.

We arrived just before sundown to discover that we were not going to be alone. My father's car was parked in front of the house and his friend (or mistress) Teresina was preparing the bed in the master bedroom.

I made the introductions while she was explaining that they were just driving through. They went to have dinner at the Cervo while we went to the Antico. Before going to bed we went for a walk in the deserted streets while the temperature was dropping to almost freezing.

In the morning Teresina had prepared a nice rich breakfast, then they said goodbye and left. With Tom we went hiking up some trail in the wood to the Belem (my secret place) a terrace overlooking the Caldonazzo and the Levico lakes one thousand feet below. In the horizon the majestic snowy tops of the Brenta group were reaching the clouds. That was a scenery Tom would never forget.

We tried the local cuisine which is a mixture of Italian and Austrian. After lunch, I found out that Luigi had arrived for the weekend so we spent a nice quiet evening together while he was trying to tell Tom, in a bad English, about his trip to Finland on a C5A military plane of the American A/F when he was in the Italian Alpines (mountains soldiers).

We got up early the next morning since Tom had to be in Aviano by 3pm and I wanted him to see the spectacular view of the Dolomites.

When we arrived by the base and there was just the time to say goodbye he reached his wallet and gave me twenty dollars for the gas. I resolutely refused it but before leaving I asked him a phone number to get in touch with him.

My return to Lugano was kind of sad. All alone in the car I was pretending Tom was still there and we were chatting. There were so many things I wanted to tell him. We did not sleep together yet I had never felt that way before, not even with Nizar in India.

Back at home I was moody and trying to avoid any kind of conversation. I didn't know if I wanted to call Tom or not and I was dying to know how he was feeling. Finally three days later I went downtown to the post office and I called the number and the extension he had given me. To my surprise he answered the phone and we talked for a few minutes, enough to know when he was going to be off duty again.

I went to my bank to get some money, then, with an excuse, two days later, I left to go on a trip, officially to Genova to see Ettore and Enio. My destination was obviously Aviano.

This time I checked in a hotel just a couple of blocks from the base. I didn't want to call Tom again, but I knew he was getting off duty around 3pm so I walked down the street from where I could see the quarter he was living in.

Destiny works in some mysterious way sometimes. He was looking out of the window when he saw me, he got out in the yard and called my name. He had never thought he would see me again.

We went walking around the town to stop for dinner at "Tony's" a bar where they were serving some kind of American food. That was the first time I ate a burger and I must say it was delicious. The next morning he came to my hotel and we went on a drive around Pordenone and to the coast. I was introducing him to the Italian music and to my favorite singers like Patty Pravo, Ornella Vanoni and Mina. That night we parked the car in front of one of the most famous Palladian villa, Vendramin Corner, while listening to the music, holding hands and looking at the stars.

I told him Tom I would be there the following week when he had his days off and by then I knew he believed me.

Driving back to Lugano my mind was going back to the nice and happy hours we had spent together. I couldn't wait to go back and to show him more places. It was like I could be myself without pretending.

My parents didn't really question my coming and going but they could sense something was going on. I was watching TV, going to bed at a decent time, going downtown to make my phone calls so that I would not provoke embarrassing questions since I was speaking in English.

I had to let go my flat in Milano and I also got rid of the furniture I had bought. Things come and go and I was never much attached to them because I didn't have the time to. There were just some items that were given to me as presents that I was keeping in my room and that I would never sell or give away.

Another week went by. I went to withdraw some money and told my parents I was going to Milano. A few hours later I was back in Aviano.

I had been in the USA and Canada when I was six years old with my parents for a couple of weeks. Aviano reminded me of a small American town in some way. There were many Americans driving big cars with the tag AFI, the police cars had the lights on the roof like I had seen in New York City, some of the houses were built in the same style too. Tom told me that many retired air force officers had retired in the area.

He showed me the military airport and he told me about his duties driving a large vehicle inside the base. There were some huge planes on the ground. He had traveled on one of them going from the USA to Seoul and then to Italy. Thank God he had not been sent to Viet Nam or we may have never met.

I had to show him Udine because it is a beautiful town rich of history. When there we went to visit my dear friend Aldo who was on the Centauro with me who was very glad to see me and to meet my friend. While we were drinking some wine he offered us a cigarette and Tom took it. That was the first and the only time he ever smoked.

Driving back to the base he told me that his time in the military was coming to an end and he needed to leave at the beginning of November for New York to get all the discharge papers and go back home to Memphis. These were devastating news for me. It meant our story was coming to an end but I didn't want to accept that. We agreed on the idea that I would go to Aviano to pick him up, drive him to Milano, spend a last day together, and take him to the Malpensa airport to board the TWA 707 to New York.

The sad days arrived quickly! I was on the way to the base with thousands of thoughts on my mind. I wanted the time to slow down but I knew it was going to be gone fast. What was so captivating about this so far "sexless" relationship? I didn't have an answer but I knew I didn't want it to end so soon.

When I arrived in Aviano I had the courage to walk inside the base by showing my "ex" military ID from the Italian Navy. I walked around the BX and I even talked to some American guys that were playing pool. Then I got on the phone and I told Tom I was there. We loaded his big military bag on the car and he was carrying a small suitcase with the military record. We headed to the highway crossing for the last time Roveredo and Pordenone. We arrived in Milano in the afternoon and got a room at the Hotel Tripoli.

After dinner we headed back to the hotel and we spent the night holding hands while the hours were going by fast.

It is not describable what went through our minds while we were driving those forty kilometers to the airport. I parked the car, helped him to carry the heavy bag to the check in, had a quick breakfast and kissed him goodbye. While he was walking to the passport check and disappeared behind the boarding gate I felt like something had snapped inside. I didn't go back to the car but I went to the observation deck and waited for the plane to take off.

After the last passenger was on board and the door closed, while the plane was taxing to the speedway I was praying for everything to go smooth. When the large plane took off and disappeared in the sky I was crying like a baby careless about the people that were around me.

With tears in my eyes I went back to my car and I drove back to Lugano where I arrived in time for a lunch that I would not eat because my stomach was closed.

My parents did not understand what was going on and, of course, I never explained to them why my mood had suddenly changed. There had never been much dialogue with them, but I got on the phone with Enio and Ettore just to hear some friendly voices and get some comfort.

The following days were probably the worst in my life. I knew Tom had arrived in New York, I knew he had to spend a few days there to get his honorable discharge after the four years in the Air Force, I knew he was going to Memphis to rejoin his family… but

I didn't have any way to get in touch with him and to know if he was feeling all right.

I was falling in a deep depression, getting up late, eating very little, sitting on the sofa to watch TV without even paying attention to what I was watching. It was late November, the temperature was already too frigid for my taste, the short days and the cloudy sky were all elements that didn't help. One full week passed before I had the courage to go to the post office downtown and tried to call the number where Tom was supposed to be in Memphis. Somebody answered but didn't know where Tom was at that time, just that he had called from New York and that he should have arrived home soon. At least I knew that he was well and that was some comfort to me.

Another week went by in the same way. I called one more time but I didn't want to be too insistent in order not to arise some suspicion by his family, so I asked a girlfriend of mine to call and to ask if and when he was going to be back. Still no news.

I wrote a letter but at the last minute I decided not to send it in case it went to the wrong hands.

One morning I walked up quite early, the weather was awful, it was raining and also foggy, I had enough of waiting for some news and I took a drastic decision. I packed a suitcase, had breakfast and told my mother I was going to visit Anna in Bologna. Of course she tried to convince me not to go or, at least, to wait after lunch. But I didn't pay any attention: I loaded the car, went to the bank to get a considerable amount of money, and headed to the Malpensa airport.

I parked the car and went to the TWA ticket counter. I was lucky: I was just under 25 years and they had a special ticket to New York that lasted two months and it was only 250.00 $. They checked my visa on the passport and there I was, boarding the 12o'clock flight to Kennedy Airport.

We left on time. The 707 was not full. The weather was really bad. Crossing the Alps the turbulence was bad enough that we had to remain seated with the safety belts on. For technical reasons we had to land in London where the flight was delayed for two hours. Finally we crossed the Atlantic while I was smoking like a chimney and they were showing the movie "Treasure island".

On board the lady seated in front of me was at her very first flight and I had to reassure her about the safety of the plane. My worries were about my parents: what if they had called Anna and found out that I was not in Bologna? How would my mom take the news?

We finally arrived around 4pm and went through the immigration office. I was wearing a beard at the time and I suppose that didn't help, especially when the officer asked me where I was going to stay in town. Of course I had not booked a hotel and did not have any idea about where I was going to spend the night. I spent two hours at some FBI office when I finally had the idea to call the YMCA and see if they had a room. Finally around 7pm I got on the bus to Manhattan and checked in at the Sloane House on 38th Street. With the six hours difference it was already 3am when I finally went to bed and tried to get some sleep.

That was my first time in New York city by myself. Being a bigger city than London or New Deli didn't bother me at all. I got up quite early considering there are six hours difference with Italy and I went to have a rich breakfast in a diner nearby. My concern was the cash that I was carrying around in my money belt, so I went to the American Express and I changed most of it in traveler's checks.

My father had a correspondent office in Manhattan and I had met once its manager in Genova. I walked to the high rise on Park Avenue and asked the receptionist to see Mr. Stinnes. Luckily he remembered who I was, and he was also pleased to see me. I asked him if I could send a telex to my father to inform him of my where about, then he invited me for lunch.

Now my goal was to go to Memphis and try to get in touch with Tom. The cheapest way was to ride the famous Greyhound bus.

I spent all day walking around. My attention was mainly taken by 42nd Street with all the sparkling lights, the sex shops and the electronic stores selling everything at very cheap prices compared to Europe.

Port Authority was just a couple of blocks west of Fifth Avenue. There I checked on the departure time and I bought the one-way ticket.

Now that my parents had been informed I could relax and enjoy the big apple for another day. I explored Broadway, Central Park, the famous Met and everything seemed so big, especially the cars.

I made one last attempt to call Tom but all I got was "We don't know where he is but we are expecting him home any day"

With the thought that I may or may not see him again, I spent the night exploring Manhattan and ventured in the famous Greenwich Village. There were a lot of gays around, even some holding hands. I was fascinated by a bookstore that had small booths with porno videos. I noticed that some had more than one guy hanging inside and even though my curiosity was tempting me to join, I resisted that impulse and carried on. I got to the YMCA very late at night and I spent most of the time turning around in the bed without falling asleep.

After a rich breakfast I went to deposit my suitcase at the bus station and I kept walking around the streets looking at the shops that were displaying all kind of goods also due to the approaching of the holiday season. Most of the stuff that interested me had prices lower than in Europe. I could have bought several items but I resisted thinking that I had to save the money for unforeseen events. My decision proved to be the wise one.

At 4pm I was boarding the Greyhound to Memphis. The seat was comfortable, the bus was not full, the crowd was mixed and seemed clean since there was no bad smell except for the smoke of cigarettes. We left Manhattan through a tunnel that emerged in New Jersey. The day was cold and the tall buildings were projecting their long shadows on the ground from a sun that was slowly disappearing below the western horizon. The industrial area crossed by the turnpike was quite ugly. Some oil refineries of Getty were the major attraction. Slowly everything was in the dark with the exception of the vehicles that were sending beams of lights in both directions. We made several stops in some rural areas, villages and even big towns. I tried to sleep but the seat was not so comfortable after all so I tried to stretch across two seats.

It seemed like the interstate was never going to end. In the late morning we stopped in Nashville where I saw something that looked like a Greek temple. I had something to eat and then back on board for the last segment across Tennessee. In Germany, France and England they always decorate for Christmas but what I was seeing here was beyond belief. Every house had colored lights, candles in the windows, shining trees, dears and Santa were everywhere, even on the roofs! It was a feast for the eyes, or so I thought back then. Our bus was always in the fast lane but we were passed by huge long trucks: it was like looking at moving walls.

We arrived in Memphis around 3pm and I got in a cab to reach the YMCA that was located in the downtown area. Fortunately they had rooms available at a very reasonable price. I crawled in bed and went to sleep for the rest of the day and night.

In the morning I called Tom's home to leave a message so that in case of his arrival he would know how to get in touch with me. I went to have a rich breakfast and to get a map of the city. The best way to visit was to go on foot. The whole downtown area is quite extended but it was very easy to get around. I had seen pictures of some streets and buildings in a geography book and it was easy to recognize some places, especially the bridge on the Mississippi river crossing into Arkansas. Near the YMCA, on Monroe, I found a bookstore with some boots with porno videos like I had seen on 42nd Street in Manhattan. My curiosity drove me in. There were only a few guys hanging around but obviously I caught the attention of a black man who promptly introduced himself and after chatting with me for a while he asked if I would have been interested in performing sexual acts in front of a camera with another guy for a compensation of 500 $! Of course I declined and left the place in a hurry.

Back at the hotel I met some other guys that were permanent residents and we spent the rest of the evening chatting and playing cards. Some of them had never met a European before and they were very interested.

I was surprised the temperature was rather high for the time of the season but, two days later, when I got up and looked outside the window, the streets were very shiny and it looked like there was a strong northerly wind. The surprise came when I ventured outside: the temperature was in the teens and the shine I had seen was a thin layer of ice covering everything, even the trees. The sidewalks were very slippery and some shop owners were breaking the ice with shovels. Fortunately I was wearing gloves but my ears were freezing so much that I could only walk for a few minutes and enter in some convenience store to warm up with some hot drink. It was near Jackson Avenue that I found a big record store where I bought the music cassette of our favorite song: the love theme from Romeo and Juliet of Zeffirelli composed by Nino Rota. Too bad I didn't have the equipment to listen to it.

The days were passing slowly and still no call from Tom. I didn't call his aunt anymore because I did not want to arise suspicions, but I had spent almost all my money and I had to find some solution. One of the guys from the Y advised me to go to an office called Manpower, so I did. The employee was very nice and did not really object to the fact that I was not American and I didn't have a working permit. He made a few calls and found me a temporary job as a secretary in some company but…I would need to shave the beard in order to be hired. The salary was around 3$ per hour.

It was December 18. I went back to the Y, gave the news to my friends, when the lady at the front desk called me and gave me a note: Tom was back in town, he had called and was waiting for me to call him at his brother's house. I was in seventh Heaven. I was shaking dialing the number and my happiness was even greater when I heard his voice from the other hand. I called my parents and told them that I would be home for the 23rd in time for Christmas and also in view that Mariefrancoise was arriving from Paris to spend the holiday with me.

Now that Tom was becoming a reality again my business in Memphis was coming to an end. The purpose of my trip was to see him once more and to make sure that the bond that had started in Venezia would go on for the rest of our lives. Sure he would stay in the USA but I would come see him many times in the future. The developments of our story would prove I was wrong.

He came to the Y and was very surprised to see me there. The first thing he asked me to do was to check out and be a guest at his brother's house where he was staying. It was my duty to call the guy at Manpower to decline the job offer and we headed to meet Stan and his wife who was expecting a baby. This was my first time in an American home and I did not know what were the habits of true American people. Dinner time came and went when finally Tom's sister in law prepared some quick meal and we ate in front of the TV.

The next day Tom and I went downtown where he bought two tickets for a show at the Auditorium held by one of his favorite singer: Judy Collins. Then Tom decided to check in at the Holiday Inn, the original one in Memphis. Back then I didn't know that there were hotel chains all over the U.S. The room was much more comfortable than the one at the Y and the price even for those days was only 7$ per night.

We went to see the performance and I had to admit that I became a fan of Judy Collins even if I had never heard about her before.

The next day we were invited by Tom's aunt for dinner. They were living in a big house in the middle of several acres of land not too far from downtown and on both sides of the river. I met Tom's cousins. They were all very nice and asked me a lot of questions about Italy and Europe in general.

That very night was the first time that Tom and I made love.

I told him that now that I had seen he was all right I could get on the plane and fly back to Italy but with my great surprise he told me that after giving many thoughts he was ready to come back with me. I could not believe my ears and I was sure that was the best thing that could happen to me.

He had quite a bit of money saved while he was in the military and got two one way tickets to New York and, for him, to Milano. We left Memphis on the early afternoon of December 22nd on an American Airline flight with a stop over in Cincinnati Ohio. The plane was overbooked and we ended up in first class. Unfortunately there was a delay and we missed the connection at Kennedy with the TWA, so we were forced to spend the night at the Intercontinental Hotel by the airport. The Boeing 707 was not leaving until 6pm on the next day but there was nothing else to do than waiting for the departure hanging around the cute TWA terminal that had a huge moving Santa in the middle of the hall. IT was a cold rainy night when we finally went on board and we left the American soil.

I never really liked to fly all night because I cannot sleep on those uncomfortable seats. But the fact that I was not alone was a good reason to enjoy the trip. When we arrived in the morning I spent my last money rescuing the car from the expensive parking lot at the Malpensa airport. There was snow on the ground and I had to change a tire because it got flat during the time I had spent abroad.

It took us about 40 minutes to drive to Lugano and while we were pulling in the driveway my father was arriving with Mariefrancoise that he had just picked up at the train station.

Chapter 11

England

The introductions were made: Tom - Mariefrancoise - mother and father - Tom. My parents did not ask me any of the usual questions that in a normal family they would have asked to a son who had disappeared for 20 days to go to Bologna and instead had gone to another continent. My mom said that when my dad called her to tell her where I was, she said: "Oh good, I was worried because it was rainy and there was a thick fog, but if he's all right in New York, that's just fine". On my side I was not surprised at all about her reaction. As far as my boy friend goes he had a very nice welcome and felt at ease immediately because my parents treated him like another son.

The only one that was a bit puzzled by the whole story was my girlfriend who did not quite understand Tom's presence and why I had spent most of December in the U.S.

So we spent Christmas with my parents and the inevitable Teresina, my father's mistress. Concetta was also there preparing the usual best dinner. On December 26th we were in the car on the way to Lavarone to meet with my sister, Bruno and my nephew who was then nine years old. Mariefrancoise already knew most of my friends. Tom was welcomed just like everybody else. There was enough snow to ski and during the night we were having the usual good time bar and disco hopping. It was fashionable to have a pizza before retiring home to go to bed, but by that time it was already 2 or 3 am. I guess my girlfriend understood then what was going on between Tom and me, but she did not really question it until the day she went back to Paris. We would remain good friends.

We welcomed 1973 with a big party at the Hotel Cimone and we didn't go to bed until late morning. Another 4 days and Lavarone would have been totally empty of tourists except for the children of the various schools that were going there for the so called "white week".

Driving back to Switzerland we were all tired and not really talkative.

Back at home we spent another couple of days going sight seeing around the lake and then it was time to take Mariefrancoise to the train station and kiss her goodbye.

Tom had to take care of his finances and solved the problem by transferring his money from City Bank to our local UBS with the help of my father. My mother was spending hours to chat with him and it clearly appeared that she was very fond of him. I knew they would get along well having in common the passion for plants and animals. In the meantime he was doing his best to learn Italian words and pronunciation.

At that point I was faced with a new problem: I was very happy to be together with someone I loved, but his future in Europe was uncertain. Being American Tom did not need a visa to stay in the country but he could not even attempt to get a job.

After January I started thinking that the best way for building a future together was to move to an English speaking country. The U.S. were out of the question, but Great Britain could become the perfect place. I had a couple of friends in London that had told me several times they would help me to get a place and they had good connection for an eventual job. After discussing the matter Tom and I decided to pack and cross France with destination Calais.

We left on a cold sunny morning and crossed the San Bernardino pass covered in snow. The same evening we were sleeping in Lyon and the next day we were in the beautiful Paris where we stopped for a couple of days. Being my favorite city I took pride and joy to show it to Tom. We checked in a hotel in Montmartre and went walking around. It didn't seem the case to call my ex girlfriend for obvious reasons.

Crossing the countryside on the way to the ferry we had breakfast in Beauvais, a small town famous because during the construction of the gothic cathedrals they had in mind to build the biggest in the world. The result can still be seen: The front of the church is massive but the rest of the building is not there because they ran out of money.

That afternoon we crossed the channel and at the immigration office we managed to get a six-month temporary visa to stay in England (that was thanks to the cash that we were carrying with us).

I could tell Tom was glad to be in the country where his ancestors were coming from. We arrived in London in the late afternoon and headed to Notting Hill to the house of Roy, a British friend of mine that I had met in Milano years before. He was a doctor who had many connections and had promised to try to get us a job. Him and his lover hosted us for the night in their guest room: that was a night to remember! The bed was just a mattress on the floor. The floor was not leveled. The window did not have any curtain. The outside temperature was just a few degrees lower than inside. That was not the best approach I would have wished for Tom in a city like London!

The next days it appeared clear enough that Roy did not have all the connections he claimed he did. Determined not to spend another night in that room, we decided that it would be best for us to drive to Brighton, a less expensive town, where at least I had some good friends.

The times had changed since I was a student there. The U.K. had adopted the decimal system and the shillings had disappeared. Now 1 Lst. was divided in 100 pences and the guinea was no more. The prices had more than doubled in just one year. The economy of the country was in bad shape because the imports were at 70%. The commonwealth that had sustained the empire for more than a century had basically ceased to exist. Even the price of dairy had risen. People were unhappy, blaming the government and some were also blaming the queen and the whole royal family.

I quickly found out that one pound was not lasting long and several were needed in one day. We took a room in one of those gay guesthouses near the waterfront and opened an account at Barclay's Bank.

Terry, my ex "British mother" was happy to see me again and to meet Tom. She had rented the apartment to a student from Holland for a fee that was three times the one I was paying. Gino and Eric were also very happy to see me and when we manifested the intention of living in Brighton they offered us to rent a room in their house. It would be cheaper, convenient, comfortable, and it would help them out with the expenses of the utilities. That seemed a very good idea and one week later we moved into the house.

The goal now was to get a job in order to save Tom's money. Terry's mother was managing a candy store near the pier owned by a Mr. Lewington. She managed to get us an interview with him to see if we could work in his factory just a few miles west of Brighton. We did have a nice chat with him and he seemed well disposed to offer us a position, but the matter of the visa came up and at that point he did not want to risk and declined.

Not discouraged, we started looking in the newspaper starting a long sequel of calls and short trips to find out that the problem was always the same: no working permit. Actually the employers seemed more keen to give me a job than to Tom, I guessed because I was European.

In the meantime we were driving around the south of England because I hat to show Tom all the wonderful places, villages, castles, I had visited with Mariefrancoise and Ricardo. So, while we were looking for a job, we started traveling in the south discovering some small villages that even I had never been before. In East Grinstead we visited my father's cousin and her mother, the Jehovah fanatic, who gave us a book in which they had predicted the end of the world for the end of the century. At least we had another 27 years to go… One of the town we visited was the famous Tunbridge Wells except there was not much to see there and we ended up going to watch the just released movie "Cabaret". Heaver castle, the home of Ann Bolen, was also one of our favorite site but we didn't like the fact that it had been remodeled and updated by the Astor family. Even Canterbury was fascinating thinking about the famous tales resembling so much those of the Decameron by Boccaccio.

The accommodation with Gino and Eric was perfect. We had our room with a double bed upstairs, our bathroom, use of the kitchen and a comfortable living room. Gino was still working for Mr. Villiers and Eric was still the pastry chef at the Metropole. The 42 Club was still hopping but a new club, the Manhattan, had taken the place of the old New Curtain Club.

Tom was not a bar person and I respected that. He was more of a home buddy, interested in reading books and watching programs on TV about animals, art, history and the famous British comedy. He was not a night person like me. I had to get around, see people, go to the clubs, socialize. These differences were slowly merging but our life in common was certainly not touched by that. There was this special bond that neither one wanted to end even though we both knew it would be extremely difficult to live together in Europe. It would be like walking on broken glass and watch for each one of our steps all the way. I knew that, he knew that too, but we both refused to acknowledge it.

The idea of kissing him goodbye and take separate ways was really scaring me.

In the meantime the time was passing by and we were spending more than we had foreseen. Our sexual life was basically non existing and since that was not really the foundation of our relationship, I started looking for some easy one stand in the places were I knew I could find satisfaction. That meant going out after dinner and coming back late at night when everybody was already asleep.

Finally one morning on the daily paper I saw and ad that looked promising: some laundry company was looking for a washing machine operator. An easy job, I thought, and the salary was 20 Lst a month, just what we needed to get by. I called, got the interview and the job. The working time was not the best from 7am till 4pm Monday through Friday. I had to get up at 6. The first day went by smoothly because I had to learn my duties. The second day was a bit harder. By the end of the week I was kind of tired and also bored with it, but it was payday and that gave me some interest to go on. The work consisted in loading the machine with several bags of dirty uniforms, wash them, unload them in a basket and put them in a drier. I do not recall how many loads in one day but I remember they were heavy. By the end of the second week I had enough, got my paycheck, and told my boss that was it. When I went back home even Tom agreed that was not a job for me. It was the end of march, during those three months all we had made were some miserable 40 Lst and while we had spent almost 2000. It was perhaps time to take a drastic decision going back to Lugano to stay with my parents.

At that point I was determined not to part from Tom no matter what. I needed him and I knew he needed me even more. The thought of him going back to the U.S. was just worrying me to death. I knew that if I really wanted something to happen I could obtain it, but England was not the right place.

We spent one last week traveling around, visiting castles, abbeys, battlegrounds and the interesting town of Bath. Gino and Eric were not happy to see us leaving but they understood the motives. We packed and left Brighton on a beautiful and warm day of March. After crossing the channel with very quiet sea we headed to Paris where we spent the night in a cute small hotel in Saint Germain des Pres.

Always avoiding the usual highways we drove towards the Swiss border when, suddenly, the pedal of the accelerator went flat to the floor of the car because the cable had broken. We were on a mountain road but fortunately there was a service station nearby and in a couple of hours the cable was replaced and we could resume our trip. We arrived in Lugano late at night just before my mother was going to bed.

Chapter 12

Milano

Relaxing at home was always pleasant. We did not have to worry about cooking, preparing the table, washing, cleaning, dusting and do all those things that the daily routine requests. My father had moved his office downtown and he was gone most of the day. Even though there were only three ships to manage he couldn't remain still at home. My sister was coming to visit often with my nephew who was then 10 years old.

Switzerland had now adopted the PAL system and we had one of the first color TV. In Italy they were still on black and white because the government had not made up its mind about going with PAL or SECAM (eventually they would chose PAL to please the Americans).

After spending Easter with the whole family I realized that we couldn't stay in Lugano forever and one morning, point blanc, I went to buy the Milano newspaper and started looking for a job. After reading all the ads I pin pointed one, called, made an appointment for an interview on the very next day and told my dad I was going to get that job. He started laughing and said: "yes, they were just waiting for you!"

I was at the office just before 10am, well dressed, shaved, short hair, manicured and wearing some Canoe. The lady in charge called me in and I gave her a copy of my very short resume. Besides my phd in history, the work in the Italian navy and a few months spent in my brother in law's office I did not have much experience… but…I could speak four languages, all fluent. This was the Italian association of all the electric companies. The manager was an engineer and the president was the owner of a big factory of appliances. The secretary, Dr. Negri, was basically in charge.

The interview lasted about one hour during which we covered several points of interest for the association. I probably did not have all the qualifications required but…I spoke five languages and that was enough for her to give me a three months trial period. The salary to start was going to be around 300 $ per 14 months to be increased if my performances were going to meet the requirements. My job consisted in translations of circular letters to all the affiliated companies and the preparation of the various congresses that would take place in Milano, Roma and in other European cities. All the directions were coming directly from Dr. Negri and had to be typed by her two secretaries. My desk was between those two. I was supposed to start on the following Monday.

I drove back to Lugano and at dinner I gave the news to my parents that were kind of shocked to hear I had got a job so fast and on one call only.

Now we had to decide what Tom was going to do while I was working in Milano, staying at one of my sister's apartments during the week and spending the weekends at home. It was agreed that Tom would stay in Lugano and help my father at the office. My parents had not asked me yet why Tom was staying in Europe and not go back to the USA. I was sure that the question was never going to arise.

So I started working for ANIE: my first job without relatives around in the office and with some responsibilities that did not worry me at all. My ex colleague Carla was still working for my brother in law and was ready to help me in anyway possible since she had a big experience in that field.

There was a young guy working on the second floor that was a real flamboyant queen who reminded me of Ricky from the navy. One of the secretary was al older woman always working hard and gossiping during her coffee breaks. The other was Agnese, a lesbian, who did not talk a lot, but the few times she did everything was making sense. I couldn't stand the boy but with her we were getting along just fine.

My day was starting at 9am, lunch break was at 1pm, then back to the office from 2 till 6. There was a very convenient rotisserie at the corner and the food was excellent. For dinner I was cooking myself with some advices from Concetta that was always handy and ready to help. Every evening I was calling Tom to make sure he was all right and to tell him that I was missing him a lot. But I was also working on that so that we could be together again in the big city.

This routine went on for about one month when suddenly the Dr. called me to her office to tell me that they had decided to hire me permanently because they were very satisfied with the work I was doing. Even my salary was going to be increased, not by much, but it was a good beginning.

One block away from the office, in the same street where our good friend Marta was living in a luxury apartment, there was a high rise residence called Daniel's Palace. It was not the most economical place to live in, but it was nice, clean, centrally located (just 1 mile away from the Piazza del Duomo (the main square in Milano). I asked if they had a one bedroom available and they told me that one was coming available at the end of that month for 80 $ cleaning service included. That night I called Tom and told him that we were going to be re-united again.

My mom was a good help in providing us with pots, pans, dishes, covers and everything that was needed to make our life comfortable. During the week ends we would still go to Lugano to relax, wash clothes and watch the color TV that was becoming a mania by that time.

Our life started again on the 8th floor of Daniel's Palace. Tom started to become familiar with the city and the transit system. My sister, who owned a small fashion company, was giving him some secretarial work at her office and she was also trying to find him some real job through her numerous friends. We knew it was not going to be easy because he did not have a working permit, but we were confident that there was a chance.

It was during the time we were staying at the residence that I started noticing some peculiarities about Tom that I had not notice before. I knew he was shy, but it seemed he was scared to face people, especially if we were together. He would not walk next to me but he was always a couple of steps behind and when there was to meet somebody we would disappear from sight. I attributed that to the fact that being in a foreign country where he did not speak the language and with the fear that he could be considered a clandestine, was making him very nervous. Actually I was afraid that some immigration officer could find him and send him back to the US. We had to be on the alert. The fact that we were going back and forth to Switzerland was actually helping because every time he was crossing the Italian border he had six whole months to stay. Even the residence could not have been the safest place to stay because all the guests had to be registered like in a hotel, so I started looking around for an apartment to rent.

I went to a rental agency because the housing situation in Milano was the worse at that time. Rents were very high or not available at all. The penthouse at my sister's was fine for one person but too small for two. The agency gave me a few addresses and on the third try I found a one-bedroom apartment on the second floor of a building located near one of the largest hospitals in town, the Niguarda.

In all we stayed at Daniel's for three months. Even though it was nice to live in the downtown area, it was very difficult to find a valid parking spot for my car.

We moved into the new apartment that was already furnished with some outdated furniture that did not match our taste. At least the rent was low, there was a parking spot upfront and several in the court protected by a locked iron gate next to our bedroom window. Via Taormina was a not so quiet short street connecting a small square to an important boulevard leading south to the center of Milano and north to the freeway to Como/Switzerland, the ideal to go home during the weekends. On the other side of our street there was a relatively new building of the so-called "popular housing". Next door there was a warehouse so from the early morning trucks were going in and out.

It was decided that Tom would have to learn some Italian to get by, so he started going to a class at the Dante Alighieri School near the central station. I went on with my duties while my work was becoming even more interesting that I had expected. We were then working on a congress that was going to take place at the Hilton in Roma by the end of May. That was actually a good opportunity for Tom to see the capital since he had never been south of Firenze.

I obtained the permit from my boss to drive my car to Roma. There I had my room booked for one week but Tom would have stayed in a less expensive hotel like the YMCA close to the Termini train station. On the way back I would have taken an extra day off to go through some Umbria and Toscana itinerary that I wanted Tom to visit.

Everything worked fine. The congress lasted four days every morning for 4 hours. Lunch was a must and then I was free until the next day. Tom and I went to visit all the monuments worth to see and after the third day I managed to sneak him in my room at the Hilton where he could be more comfortable.

In those days they were shooting in Roma some scenes from a movie on the Bible. Burt Lancaster was staying in a suite next to mine and I saw him several times in the elevator and in the dining room during breakfast. One evening I even saw standing next to me, in the shopping gallery, one of my favorite Italian singers, Massimo Ranieri. In person he was even cuter than on TV.

Fortunately we had great weather for the whole month, so when we left Rome we had all the time to take scenic routes and to stop in some remote villages that are usually unknown to foreign tourists but they have many centuries of history as well.

That was a nice break. My boss was happy about the results of the meeting and she was looking forward to the next one that was going to be in Bruxelles just before the summer.

Back at home life resumed as usual with the novelty that my sister needed some help at her office and Tom had to go work for her part time. He was happy to do something and I was glad he was occupied during the day.

My dad had given us a small black and white TV and that's what the Italian RAI was showing. The Swiss TV had all its programs in color so it became imperative to buy the new appliance in Lugano. Since there was the problem of custom I had my father coming just across the border with the TV, pretending it was for his house in Lavarone, and I picked it up from him. That doesn't seem much these days, but back then the color TV was becoming a very hot item to have, like the flat panel TV these days.

I started going to the Petit Paris again, playing cards with the usual and new friends there, going dancing at the Nuova Idea on Friday and Saturday nights, and going to the newly discovered cinema Alce that had taken the place of the old Rosa as a cruising spot. Tom was doing well with the Italian and was not sociable enough to mingle with my friends. He was rather staying home watching TV, or, at least, that's what I thought.

The boulevard leading to the hospital had some fields where local retired people were cultivating orchards. The area had many trees and bushes and during the night it was a heaven for gay guys cruising because they could walk around in the trails and hide in the shacks. It was a kind of last resort place for people of all ages but even a dangerous place because of some gangs going around harassing and beating. I had found out about it because I had seen some movement while driving nearby and I guess Tom noticed that too.

I was very much in love with him but that was beyond physical/ Sex has always been an important part of my life and after dinner, with an excuse or another, I was always going to the Alce or to the "bastioni" where we would park the car and walk around chatting with a bunch of guys. While at the Alce it was possible to "consume" in the restrooms or in the dark alleys upstairs, at bastioni people would meet, chat and, eventually, go home with somebody for a better and more private encounter. There were also other cinemas that were notorious for cruising, but many places were in the open, especially in the park of Milano or around squares that had "vespasiani" or public toilets. The police knew about these sites but they rarely intervened because it was not something obvious that was performed in front of strangers.

My work was going great and my boss was very happy about my performance. With Agnese we had become good friends and she was one of the few persons which whom I could talk freely about anything. Nobody could stand the other guy who was not only a flamboyant queen but also very arrogant and outspoken.

At the club I was seeing Milo and Carlo. We were playing cards together and also go to some concerts, plays and cinemas. One of my favorite singers became Ornella Vanoni and we rarely missed her performances. My cassette collection was getting bigger and my stereo equipment was becoming more sophisticated due to the new models that were built and that I was buying in Switzerland where the prices were lower on the electronics.

Carlo was pushing for me to have an interview with Miss Mirella, the owner of the company he was working for. They were looking for someone who could speak languages and who could take care of the export department. The position was going to be more interesting than the one I had, involved more traveling and the salary was much higher. At the end of the summer I finally agreed and set up the appointment.

I did not tell anybody about this idea. My family was very happy that I was doing so well at the association that they would have probably tried to discourage me to change. On the other hand I knew that with my parents backing me up even if I went wrong the problem would have been minimal. I went to SILLEM one morning in September and chatted with the owner for about one full hour. The office was nice, clean, with a lot of light. There was a secretary, Mrs. Elvira, four salesmen all around my age and the secretary of Mr. Gudino, the manager of the department, Miss Laura. Downstairs there was the chief of personnel, Carlo, Milo and Lorenzo in the accountant dept. and Miss Mirella's sister. The other side of the building had at least 25 workers manufacturing medium and large machines for the polishing of metals like pots, pans and silverware. My duty would have been to take care of the foreign customers, take them out to lunch, dinner, shopping, sightseeing, translate our offers, take care of different fairs that could take place all over the world and arrange for the shipments of the machines and parts to the various final destinations.

She asked me what I would want as a salary and at that point I said that 500$ net, for 14 months would induce me to accept that position. That was considerably more than what I was making but she accepted right away leaving me with the task of giving my month notice to the Dr. Negri. I was not looking forward to that! I hated to disappoint somebody who believed in me and in the work I was doing.

Of course I asked Carla and Agnese how I could handle this delicate matter and from both came basically the same answer that can be reassumed as follows: "employers are usually doing what is best for them and the company, but I had to look forward to my future and grow through experiences of this kind. If I thought that this step was going to improve my career, I should have moved on".

Agnese helped me to write the letter of resignation that I put in an envelope placed on the desk of Miss Negri. The following morning, as I had foreseen, she sent for me and she told me how disappointing it was to let me go after, of course, my month notice. During that period she treated me with respect but at a distance to make sure I understood I was not the privileged guy there that she had considered me.

A small chapter of my life had ended and a new, may be more exciting one, was starting.

My family took the news with nonchalance. After a short brake of four days, there I was, getting familiar with the company, the departments and all my new co-workers. The office of Miss Mirella was just at the end of the hallway and I could sense she liked me just as much as I liked her.

Elisa, the girl that was leaving, spent a couple of weeks explaining in details all the duties involved in shipping from ordering the suitable crates to contacting the many shipping companies in order to obtain the best rates either by air, truck or sea. Moreover we spent time at the banks where the export documents were prepared and at the custom, introducing me to the officers I would have to deal with to handle everything as smooth as possible. It was a rather complicated and bureaucratic process but nothing really difficult to understand. Laura also knew quite a bit and she was very supportive with advices. The one that was working non stop and was probably under paid for her job was Mrs. Elvira, a widow, with a son working downstairs in the accounting dept. who was also gay, friend of Carlo, and frequenting the same Petit Paris. The other guy working there was Lorenzo, a very handsome blonde young man, pupil of Carlo, but apparently very straight.

I started liking my new job and very soon I got to know the peculiarities of Mr. Gudino who could change his mind about everything several times a day driving Elvira crazy.

He is the one that would launch the ideas of having exhibitions in different countries but, since he did not speak any language, I was called innumerable times to his office to write letters or to talk on the phone with our different agents and customers all over the world. The only other person who was speaking English was Laura and she was handling the British market.

Almost every week there were customers arriving in Milano from all over. I had to go pick them up at the airport, book their hotel, take them to some of the best restaurants for which I had an authorized signature, and sometimes take them shopping at Gucci, Valextra, Ferragamo, Versace, Armani and other famous boutiques in the Via Montenapoleone (the Rodeo Drive of Milano).

Using my car for these duties was out of the question since it had two doors so I was assigned a more convenient sedan that I could take home and use sometimes also during the week ends.

Tom had completed a three months Italian class and could now understand most of it and form longer sentences. The novelty came from one of my sister's friends, an engineer, who was going to open a new factory in Monza to manufacture door mats made out of plastic. That was a good occasion to get a job and Tom was hired but without a working permit and with a fixed "under the table" salary of 350$. That was a good news because at least he would be occupied during the day. The bad thing was that he had to ride on the bus for half an hour each way, be there by 8am and not make it home before 6pm, Saturday mornings included. My fear was that he did not have documents other than the passport and, of course, he couldn't carry it in his pocket going around in Milano. I convinced him to carry his military driver license so "just in case" he could show he was still in the AFI.

My job was getting better and busier. There were some slow weeks that I had to spend at the office, but foreign customers were arriving with short notice. The busiest month was going to be July because the whole company would shut down for the month of August for the summer vacation. With both salaries combined we had more money to spend on food, furniture, trips and clothes. It became an obsession for me to renew my wardrobe. My sister could supply very good material at a cheap price and Milo's tailor could make some perfect cut pants and jackets for a reasonable price. Also some shirts were tailor made. During the following two years I owned at least two tuxedos and 38 suits good for each season. Tom had also a wide number of clothes including many leather overcoats he had bought in Aviano and Venezia. Too bad he's three inches taller than me otherwise we could share.

In the few first months I became very familiar with shipping companies, custom, rates, banks and documents. Even going around town was easier knowing all the backstreets to use when the traffic was blocking the main ones. Entertaining the customers made me know more about the museums, the churches, the private collections like the "Poldi-Pezzoli" and the surrounding areas in the countryside like the Abbey of Chiaravalle. Memorable was one visit to the church of Sant'Ambrogio with a couple of newly wed from Buenos Ayres. After we visited the roman apse, we descended in the crypt where there are the mummified bodies of Sant'Ambrogio, the holy patron and first bishop of the city, and San Gervaso. There was an old lady praying on her knees in front of the glass sheath. While I started telling them with a low voice whom the two bodies belonged to, before I could mention the 2nd one, the wife of the customer said: "He was the wife of the bishop"! The old lady, horrified, signed herself for three times, gave us a dirty look and left in a hurry. We all started laughing and fortunately there was nobody else around.

Another time I had to take out to dinner a really cute customer from Barcelona. After eating he asked me to take him to a cinema where they were showing porno movies because in those days, Spain still ruled by Gen. Franco, they were forbidden in his country. So, there I was, this cutie sitting next to me with a hard on, and me pretending to be just interested in the idiotic plot on the screen.

During all my years living abroad, meeting a wide variety of people, I had learned to figure out very quickly how everybody was. I knew when I could make up jokes, when it was not the case, to talk about politics, history, religion, philosophy or other things concerning current matters like the approaching royal wedding of Charles and Diana. The only subject I would not discuss because I hated it with passion was sport, football in particular.

Tom was taking pride in his new job and he would also prove what kind of a hard worker he was. Several mornings, when it was still dark and very cold or even foggy, I was driving him to Monza and sometimes I was also picking him up in the evening. Even though I had to get up quite early to be at the office before 9am, I was still going out every night and would not go back home until after midnight. The bar, the disco, newly met friends and cruising were my regular hang out places. During some week ends instead of driving to see my parents I was going to Genova to visit Ettore or to spend some interesting time with Enio and my other friends. Enio had met a girl, Marina, and they had rented a strange apartment/loft in the old section of town. His girlfriend was not really the cleanest person in the world so I had to make excuses not to stay in the room that they had reserved for me. a few times I was checking in some cheap hotels where it was easy to pick up some stranger to spend the night with. Of course I was never wearing jewelry or carrying more money than I needed to be on the safe side in case of dangerous encounters.

Tom was definitely not a social animal and was spending his free time watching TV or reading. His Italian was getting better even though we kept speaking English all the time. Unfortunately the fear that he could be caught as an illegal immigrant was making me very nervous and he was sensing that. We had the first of a long serial of fights during which I was hoping he would collect his stuff and go back to the USA, but in my hearth I was afraid that he would do so and we would loose each other. I would have given part of my life to solve this huge problem. He was never answering the phone unless he was absolutely sure that I was calling making the phone ring twice before each call. When the weather started getting nicer and warmer we were driving around in the country to visit old cities, villages and our favorite spots: castles.

I recall a trip to Torino to visit the famous Egyptian museum, to the Valli Valdesi were the protestant movement started in Italy in the 17th century, to the Val d'Aosta where we visited the magnificent and perfectly preserved castle of Fenis, the lake Maggiore with the San Carlone statue and the beautiful islands owned by the Borromeo family, and Grazzano Visconti, a tourist attraction built at the beginning of the 20th century as an exact reproduction of a village from the 12th century.

During these trips we had to avoid restaurants and busy hotels because Tom was not feeling at ease among strangers. So I would have to go to buy food that it would be consumed in isolated places or in the car. The whole peculiar habit was badly tolerated by me and it was cause of more fights. In the end the apology was the rule and we would spend the night cuddling in bed.

It was during a rainy Saturday afternoon in the spring of 1974 that we both decided to go to check out a spa where I had heard people were cruising. The place was not very crowded but a nice looking guy tried to approach Tom in the pool area. Tom probably did not respond very well to the attentions and the guy turned to me. I was really overwhelmed and attracted to him. We started talking and ended up exchanging telephone numbers. His name was Franck, he was a French living in Milano with his ex lover and he was working in the fashion industry.

As usual I thought I would have never heard from him again, but only two days later he phoned to invite me over his apartment for dinner.

I had found someone who was intelligent, good looking, pleasant to be with and, even better, a guy who liked to make love instead of just having sex. He was sharing an apartment with his ex lover, Antonio, whom I had met before in another sauna. Apparently Antonio was even more a slut than me.

I started dating Franck and he somehow managed to invite Tom over for dinner, but that was the only time. In the meantime I had discovered that when Tom was going out for a walk at night he was going to cruise in the area by the hospital. This information came from a friend of mine, Gino, who was going there every night. I was not happy to hear that, as a matter of fact I was very worried that something bad might happen to him since he was on foot and could easily be stopped by the police or by gay bashers.

With Franck I met a lot of new friends and I was introduced to a whole new kind of pastime. During the week ends, if the weather was nice, we were going to the park of Ticino river, some 30 Kms. west of town, to spend the entire day basking in the sun and swimming in clear ponds not too far from the main river bank. The place was stunning and even more stunning was the fact that everybody was walking around naked. So on a typical Sunday we would get up around 10, prepare some food, meet at Franck's house and drive to a certain spot to park the cars. Tom would come too but instead of walking with us to our usual spot, he would go to some secluded area and meet us again at sunset.

Dinner was usually at Franck's place but Tom had to be taken home because he did not intend to mingle with us. Part of the group were Antonio, Emilio, Franco (a longtime lost friend from a town near Lavarone) and the "Old Fox", an older guy who was a painter always waiting for his rich uncle to kick the bucket. An estimated 150 people, mostly guys, were walking around the area and more or less they were all very friendly and stopping over for drinks, chit chats or to play cards. Moreover the sun was providing a wonderful tan all over our bodies. The only problems were the mosquitoes that would attack at dusk.

Franck was a very good cook and I was still experimenting remembering some recipes of Concetta. Soon enough it became a habit to have dinners at each other's apartment every Saturday night. I was getting better too and was modifying some dishes according to my taste with really good results. In other words we were trying to impress each other with elaborate dishes. I must recognize Franck was always the best.

Just a few feet from my apartment there was an open market every Saturday morning. The food was fresh, cheaper and better than most grocery stores. Our orientation on meat was for chicken, turkey and pork trying to avoid red meat. Our diet was becoming more varied including a lot of veggies, fruits, cheeses and eggs, and, of course, always desserts before the fruit. Some of the products that we did not find in Milano, were bought by my parents at the fabulous Migros in Lugano, a supermarket with all kind of Swiss goodies including chocolate and candies that have always found plenty of room in my life.

During April of 1974 my boss told me we had to prepare for a fair that was going to take place in Paris and that lasted 12 days. This was a great news. My favorite city again. I called Mariefrancoise (who in the meantime had given up on me and was dating some guy named Michel) and Alan who was still living there with his fiancée. Everything was carefully prepared in advance and we finally flew to Paris. I was always afraid to leave Tom at home by himself and asked my sister to keep an eye on him in case he needed something.

It was so nice to fly first class and stay in luxury hotels. That was the idea of my boss who would not settle for less also to give the impression of "opulence" to eventual customers. My duties were light but, since he did not speak French, I had to spend all the time at the stand and deal with all kind of questions from potential customers or from many curious people. But after 5pm I was free to go and to do whatever I wanted. Those were two weeks to remember, not only because I was close to my ex girlfriend but also because I spent some time with Alan, my old friend, remembering the year we had spent in India with Gisela.

At the cinema Dal Verme in Milano I had met a French guy who owned a gay club in Paris gay district of Rue St. Anne. He was glad to see me again and gave me a tour of all the new clubs including those with a dark room where everything was happening.

One night I went to one of this alone and, being a Monday, there were not too many people. I just got a drink when I saw an extremely handsome guy coming in. It was like a mirage, one of those unreachable "prey" that remains in everybody's dreams. A little while later I was looking around for him but I assumed he had left, so, just in case, I walked behind the curtain and ventured in the dark room. It was not as dark as I thought it would be. I could distinguish persons, walls and some furniture, but to my astonishment there was my "prey" all naked and surrounded by a bunch of guys touching him all over. I remained in a distance enjoying my sight. He did not only have a face like Alan Delon, but his body was perfect, like the one of a Greek god. I went closer and closer and started touching him too while my blood was almost boiling for lust. To my surprise he interacted with me kissing and slowly taking my clothes off and pushing everybody else out of the way. I still could not believe what was happening to me but enjoyed every second of it until the final orgasm put an end to the action and we got dressed while other guys were trying to delay this operation.

Seldom losing contact with reality I had put my wallet inside one of my sock just in case somebody was trying to go through my pockets.

I called a cab and called the night regretting not to be able to get the name and the phone number of that fabulous partner.

Another evening I went to an old sauna in Faubourg St. Honore', probably the oldest in Paris. The place was big and the Turkish baths were very hot and foggy with a smell of eucalyptus. I could hardly see who was around me but I was feeling several hands touching me. Of course I had to touch back making sure the body was fit and without a potbelly, so I came across a guy that seemed all right, but I had to drag him close to the light. He turned out to be oriental from Tibet. We played around and then we went to a bistro to have dinner.

Mr. Gudino had no idea nor he ever asked me where I was spending my free time. Luckily most of the personnel were speaking Italian so that I did not have to be around all the time.

The day we had to return to Milano came fast but I was glad to see Tom and Franck that I had missed very much. Soon it was back to the same routine waiting for the Summer break. Those months of June and July were some of the hottest. Several week ends we went to Torre del Mare but some we spent on the Ticino river coming home late at night covered by blisters caused by the hungry mosquitoes.

Not to spend the whole month of August in Lavarone, while Franck was going to Saint Tropez at his father's villa, we decided to take a trip to Yugoslavia and check the beaches on the other side of the Adriatic Sea. We left on a late morning and driving slowly through back roads we arrived in Trieste at dusk and we checked at the Jolly Hotel. The next day we ventured across the border into Tito's domain. It was obvious that was a socialist country from the way the buildings looked, the people's clothes, the Russian made cars and the whole atmosphere. The problem arose when we started looking for a hotel: they were all fully booked. Finally late at night we found a place where they were renting small caravans for an almost reasonable price. In a farm nearby I bought some food and fresh milk. I love tomatoes and so far those were absolutely the best I ever had.

Not to repeat the same mistake the next day we went back to Italy and chose a city, Gorizia, nice but certainly not blessed by the presence of thousand of tourists. That was our spot for the following week with a beach by a river to relax and take sun during the day. The old castle overlooking the town was also very appreciated by us.

The following three weeks were spent in Lavarone eating the good food of Concetta and enjoying my old friends.

Back to work the echo of everybody's vacation had not even gone when my boss got the idea to participate to a fair in Moscow to be held in October. I had to find all the connections, hotel, plain tickets, fix the dates and make sure the Italian chamber of commerce would give us all the necessary support. The factory started manufacturing five machines that had to be sent by truck and assembled by our technicians at least one week prior to our departure. Needless to say that most things went wrong due to the Russian bureaucracy so that we lost the morning of the grand opening.

I was kind of excited to go not only to see the Kremlin but also to check out the local guys that from many documentaries watched on TV seemed quite nice.

The flight on an Aeroflot's Tupolev was kind of scary. The plane was vibrating constantly, the service was poor and the food was terrible.

Upon arrival we had to wait on board for another hour and it took us three to go through custom and passport check. Finally we were on a "socialized" cab on the way to the capital. The roads, called "prospectives" were wide and the traffic was almost non-existent. Many people were walking and more were on bicycles. The hotel Krasnapolski was a big old building that would have probably impressed tourists during the time of the czars. Even checking in took us a long time. The carpets were worn out, the furniture antiquated, the bed kind of hard, no TV, but there was a radio that was always in the on position and could not be turned off. Fortunately the volume could be turned down to zero. Some ugly and fat women had a desk outside the elevator on each floor and without saying a work they would hand us the correct key to our rooms. They could also supply towels, soap and some sandpaper that was intended to be toilet paper. We had brought some from Italy.

The only people allowed in the hotel were foreigners. A few prostitutes were hanging around the lobby and the bar area but they were doing that at their own risk because the police could arrest them at any time.

Even though the subway system is supposed to be the best, most efficient and clean in the world, my boss would only go by taxi but cabs were serving several customers at the same time, like a mini bus with frequent stops. Eventually he got used to that, but not before bitching for days.

After taking care of the stand at the fair, letting our technicians setting up the five machines, providing a lunch and dinner for everybody and let Mr. Gudino finally go to bed, I finally ventured out of the hotel to explore the city. But there was not much to explore. The large boulevards were empty at night, the Red Square was patrolled by some armed guards. The temperature was kind of freezing. The whole scenario made me go back to the hotel and see if something was going on in the lobby and the bar area, but there was nothing besides some prostitutes and some strange people that I believed were from the KGB. I already figured it out that I would not have fun for the whole two weeks.

We did manage to visit some of the Kremlin and the thumb of Lenin. I missed the Bolshoi where they were performing "Swan Lake" because apparently there was no way to get tickets sold out for months.

The fair did fine, we sold the machines as my boss had hoped and he got a large order that would keep the factory busy for months to come.

I must say that Moscow did not appeal to me at all. It seemed like being in the suburbs of Milano and the only impressive sites could be visited in a couple of days.

Leaving the country was a nightmare. We could not carry even one single Russian coin. They searched our suitcases and spent one hour examining the portable projector case and videos. Finally we boarded the plane hoping that it would take us back safely to civilization.

Miss Mirella was so happy about the Russian success that the whole commercial department got a bonus in the paycheck.

Even 1974 was coming to a close and I liked living in Milano and being close to all the places, my family, my friends and Tom who had managed to work very hard in that factory. Watching "Baretta" on TV we got the idea of having a parrot pet thinking it would be nice to teach him to talk. We were going to settle for a Cacatua but they all seemed too large for a small apartment like ours. Near the Piazza del Duomo they had a variety of Loros and when one flew on my shoulder and said "ciao Loreto" I bought it. He was one year old, green, yellow fronted, with all kind of colors under the wings. We took him home without thinking that he would need a big cage or a tripod to stand on. The first night we used a chair but the next day I went to look for something more suitable and I got home with a stand, cups and toys... but I couldn't see Loreto. A whistle directed my attention to the top of the curtain and there he was, hanging upside down with no intention of flying down.

At the store they had told us to feed him seeds, rice, fruits, veggies and an egg once in a while so we made sure his cup was always full and changed the water every day. Sometimes he would take his food and throw it on the floor or put his beak in the water cup and shower his body. We loved him very much but some screams were extremely loud. At night it was just enough to cover him to make him sleep until morning.

The only thing we did not take into consideration was that during the day there was nobody at home and Loreto was probably getting bored and scream at the top of his lungs. Some neighbors asked me if we were nursing a child.

During the Christmas holiday we went to Lugano and introduced Loreto to my mother who fell in love with him first sight. She always loved pets and even had a monkey while I was in the navy. The solution was obvious, she was going to take care of him so that he wouldn't stay all alone in Milano. I had to ask and obtain a passport for the bird to the Swiss authority for the animal control in order to carry him across the border.

With Franck we spent new year's eve in Lavarone together with my sister's family and Concetta who, apparently, did not approve Franck and I sleeping in the same room. There was plenty of snow, all my friends were there, we had a blast skiing and partying. Concetta almost caught us taking a bath together in the tub. I guess that was part of the excitement.

Back to a new start with 1975. Everything was great except the fact that Tom was still illegal and could be expelled anytime.

My job was quite satisfying. I was meeting people from all over the world. Getting prepared for the big fair of Milano coming up in April, booking several hotel rooms for our agents and customers, running to the airport to welcome them, taking them shopping and so on. Some of the fancy stores knew me by then and were offering some commissions on whatever my clients would buy. I never took advantage of this opportunity considering it unethical and tacky.

One of the sales representatives, Roberto, was very cute and very straight and always talking about his sexual encounters. Carlo told me he had dreamed about him but there was nothing to do and I should get over it. This was a challenge that I could not let go. Roberto had two girls that he was seeing periodically, Bianca and Ornella. I knew he loved the sea and I started talking about my house in Torre del Mare. The weather was very nice that March and warm enough for him to propose a week end with his two girlfriends. Everything was arranged and we left on a Friday afternoon for the sexual adventure.

The girls were nice, cute and had great bodies, just the way I like them. We had dinner in Savona and then we were at the beach house. To break the ice we had a drink and started playing strip poker in the living room. Pretty soon everybody was naked and we spent the rest of the night in the master bedroom having sex on the same bed. I had accomplished my wish to see Roberto naked and to even touch his body (by mistake, in the dark) several times. He was well endowed as Carlo and I thought. The rest of the weekend was pleasant and we managed to get some tan on the terrace because it was too breezy on the beach. When I went to the office on Monday morning I had something exciting to tell Carlo who was in return biting his nails and Milo who could not believe it.

This episode proves my theory that a good result can be obtained when strongly wanted.

The fair opened and I was busy at the stand answering all the technical questions that very curious people were asking. During my breaks I was going to check other pavilions with artifacts from all over the world. I have always collected items that are unusual and that catch my attention and my home was gradually getting crowded with them. Not only I was enjoying the sight of them but they were also the talk of my friends. Part of my collection was in my room at my parents house because I have always been afraid that somebody could break into my apartment and steel them.

Also my wardrobe by then had reached a considerable amount of clothes for every season. I had to wear suit and tie almost every day and I made sure I was never wearing the same cloths twice in one month. My shirts were tailor made too. Casual wear was only when I was going to the mountains or to the sea.

We were missing Loreto who was getting along very well with my mother. I guess my dad did not appreciate the loud screams, but he was working at his office most of the time. Once in a while, when my parents were going on a trip, we were going to Lugano to get the parrot and take him back to Milano.

With the beginning of the warm season we resumed spending the week ends at the Ticino river. By then there was a small group of 7 - 8 people some coupled and some single. We would meet at Franck's flat and drive almost to Vigevano. From there we would walk through the forest, cross a few streams, and reach our customized place by a fresh water pond. Franck, Emilio and Enzo were preparing lunch, the pasta was cooking on the fire and the meat was roasting through an elaborate watermill manufactured by Franck. After lunch we were playing cards, sunbathing in the nude, drinking soda and pure water from a source nearby.

Many friends were coming by to join us or to chat about the usual different subjects from politics to sex or to ask advices about where to go on vacation during August (the month when all the business close down in Italy).

Sometimes we would wear our bathing suit and we would go for a long walk on the myriad of little trails. In the shades the mosquitoes were really bad but they were nothing compared to the horseflies that could be very painful. The most reckless guys were going cruising in the forest looking for sexual encounters. When they were coming back we could always tell by the blisters that were covering their bodies.

The sunset was always something to enjoy on the river. With the first shadows of dusk we were walking back to the cars and drive to somebody's home to have dinner, chat, or to watch a movie on TV.

It was during some of those walks that I met Massimo, a cute guy my age, that was always walking around naked and was wearing a nice smile every time our paths crossed. Soon we became good friends and he joined our group. By then the sexual attraction between Franck and me had almost died and Massimo and I started dating in the city during the week.

My concern was always for Tom who was working too much in a very noisy environment and had not got even a small raise. I wanted something better for him but without a working permit there was absolutely no hope. We also thought about emigrating to

Australia because they were looking for immigrants. Through the Consulate they were offering a free voyage by ship, a secure job, a place to stay and the minimum permanence required was two years. We applied and they accepted my request but rejected Tom's. Of course I declined.

The work at Sillem was fine but it was a dead end and I started reading the classified section of the Corriere della Sera, the main Milanese newspaper. There was just one ad that caught my attention because it didn't mention the kind of work but the knowledge of a fluid English language was specifically requested. That was the month of May . I called and scheduled an appointment for an interview.

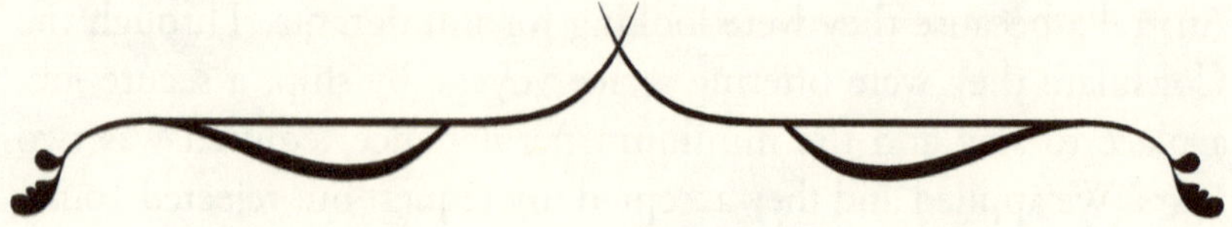

Chapter 13

Milano - Emery Air Freight

With an excuse I took half a day off and went to check out the company that had placed the ad in the paper. It was an American airfreight forwarder, a carrier, that I had never heard before.

Mrs. Testa, the secretary, told me they were looking for salesmen. As soon as I heard that I said I was not a salesman and I was not interested in going to sell anything door to door. It took her a few minutes to convince me to go ahead and meet Mr. Bowman, the manager, because it was not the kind of work I had guessed but something very different and also very well paid. Reluctantly I agreed and walked into a very nice, well furnished office and introduced myself. English, of course, was not a problem. Bill was a nice courteous American guy just a few years older than me who loved Italy and had been living in Milano for the past ten years. I had the impressions that he was "family" but I was not sure 100%.

They were looking for somebody with absolutely no experience in sales. The company was a leader in shipping and receiving with the advantage of having their own cargo planes, their very competitive rates and an excellent service targeting some of the most important firms in the world. As he put it: "the Rolls Royce service of the airfreight worldwide". They were providing for a formation class, a starting salary of 700 $ net a month for 14 months, 28 working days paid vacation a year, a company car for me to use even for personal use, all expenses paid, a raise every year, bonuses in company stocks and plane tickets with a 75% discount twice a year with any IATA airline.

The offer was extremely tempting. The trial period was for three months before being confirmed for the job.

I left his office with a turmoil in my mind. I knew I was probably not able to face potential customers trying to sell…a service, something not tangible. But on the other hand I did not see any reason to turn it down and try. After all there were always my parents ready to help me out in case of failure.

I decided to think about it but in my head I was also wondering if I had made a good impression and if I was getting another chance to interview with the district manager who was the one to make the final decision to hire me.

Three days went by and I wasn't even thinking about this job when the phone rang and Mrs. Testa asked me to have a second interview before the end of the week. At this point I called my sister and Bruno and asked their opinion.

I went back to Emery and met with the big shot from Bruxelles. Apparently he was impressed by my entry, my presence, my clothes, my personality and my English. We chatted for less than half an hour and he asked me how long before I could join the company.

At home that night I discussed the matter with Tom and I told him I was going to take the challenge. The most difficult task was then to tell Miss Mirella that I was going to quit Sillem and give her the usual month notice. She was not very happy, but she called her secretary and had an ad placed in the paper to find my substitute.

That month went slow and fast. One week after my resignation a new employee, Antonio, started working at my desk while I was informing him of his duties, showing all the files, touring the factory and introducing him to all his new colleagues.

I collected my last salary and the check with the liquidation that was equal to 3 monthly salaries. On my way to the bank I was having serious doubts about my future. I called Massimo and we went to my favorite restaurant to relax and to talk about this big event in my life. He encouraged me. We decided to make a trip to Venezia during the week end to get away.

That was a fun trip. I remember every minute of the time spent walking around the "calli" the S. Mark Square, the visit to my native house in Lido, my relatives, the dinner at the "Taverna dei Dogi" the Fenice theater and two nights of passionate love during which my right eye got squirted by some sperm: that was the most painful experience and the most red eye for the whole next day!

Monday morning I was ready to start my new job.

My colleagues were all around my age. All very professional and dedicated to their duties. During the lunch break some were going home but most were switching from the pizzeria to the trattoria nearby making it more pleasant to get together and chat. The topic was, of course, work.

On the third day Bill called me and gave me the key to my new 124 FIAT. I was not expecting to get the car so soon. Now I had two cars but Tom was not driving in Milano so I put mine in my sister's yard and started using the company car for everything.

The other sales lady, Nicky, was coming back from a trip to Australia where she had some joint sales calls with our colleagues there. When we met that was "love at first sight" and I knew that we would be a good working team.

After spending a few days in each department to learn all the procedures of shipping and receiving, I was on a flight to Bruxelles for the actual class held at the Holiday Inn by Ivan. There were five new salesmen from different countries and for five days we had to go through the various stages of the selling skills, a program elaborated by Rank Xerox and considered to be the most efficient and up to date. Every evening Ivan would take us to a different restaurant and the last day we had a fabulous dinner at the "Auberge aux Princes" where the chef had been the cook of king Baldwin for years.

I managed to escape one of those dinners because I met a nice guy at the sauna of the hotel who invited me to his flat to eat and to spend the night, otherwise Bruxelles was a rather boring city.

The class was concluded very satisfactorily. We did not get a grade but we could tell that Ivan was happy about the outcome. Now it was up to us to demonstrate in the months to come that he was right to put his trust in us.

The flight back was kind of bouncy and now I was really worried that something would have gone wrong. I followed Bill's advices and Nicky was such a great help that I would never forget. We divided the areas so that she would keep the center and the south of Milano and I would get the north. My regions would be Liguria, Veneto and northern Lombardia. The pleasant aspect was getting to know the existing customers. Making at least six calls a day and spending Friday afternoons at the office preparing for the next weeks appointments. The paperwork was not very annoying and was easily done. Multiple offers were prepared by Gabriella, our secretary, who was very skilled and didn't need many explanations. The customer service was supplying us many leads and sometimes even scheduling appointments with new prospects. Enrico was in charge with that and I was really amazed by the way he was using EMCON, the Emery computer system.

My entire life was taking a different direction while I was getting involved in my new job and finding more interest in American things. I was now chatting with American colleagues on a daily basis. All my messages were signed "Danny" and that gave me some proud even because I liked that sound better than the Italian name. The office had supplied a portable videocassette made to show our customers how the company was operating and I recall taking it to Lugano to proudly show it to my parents. Tom was also very happy for me to the point that we invited Bill over for dinner one night.

Going around the city every day I stopped one morning at the medical office to have a blood test made for venereal diseases. I didn't think anything was wrong with me, but I never had one done since my days in Brighton.

When, one week later, I went to get the results, I was puzzled to hear the news: I had syphilis!

When I got home I told Tom and asked him to get a blood test too, not because we had sex or anything, but to make sure he was all right. Unfortunately his test came also back positive. During the treatment abstinence was a must. We had to go to the clinic every other day to get a shot of 1.200.000 units of penicillin each and sometimes it was kind of painful. After that we had to wait for one whole month and get another round of shots.

Of course we had no idea on how we contracted the disease, it could have been anywhere and at anytime. The certain thing was that we had no visible sign of it on the skin or the genitals. Sometimes we did not have time to go to the ambulatory so I became skilled enough to mix the liquid and the powder myself and to inject Tom and me. The key was to make sure I didn't hit any vein because that could be very dangerous. So I had to insert the needle, see if blood was coming out, then inject the medicine.

Being so sexually active the abstinence was driving me nuts. Franck told me he had it a few years back, got the same treatment, but the sign would show forever in the blood. Antonio had it too and probably had transmitted it to Franck when they were lovers.

My mood had lightly changed even though I was not thinking too much about it.

It was during that time that my European supervisor decided I had to fly to New York to visit the import manager of one of our most important customers. I was on my last month of shots and I had to bring the phials with me.

I left on the usual TWA flight and I got a warm welcome by my counterpart at Kennedy airport. Flying first class meant to be able to sleep on the 747. I was going to stay one week but I could not bring any syringe for fear that some custom agent could find them and think I was into heavy drugs. Once in Manhattan I started going around in Greenwich Village and I asked some gay guy if there was a VD clinic. There I explained my case to the nurse and finally I could get the shot by an expert.

It was hard to be in abstinence in Milano, but it was even harder in New York City! Of course several occasions were lost.

The trip was successful because I managed to keep the customer and on top of that I got a couple of routing orders from two different prospects that were receiving goods on a weekly basis. At that point, together with my American colleague, we decided to have a fancy dinner at the Del Monico restaurant charging it to the company.

I spent some time shopping around buying Rayban sunglasses and some electronic gadgets that had not reach Italy. In those days the stores to shop were all located on 42nd Street and near 11th Avenue at the Triestino and the Romano.

Back to Milano on the night flight my life resumed as usual with the get together on the week ends and the dinners.

For the recipes I was calling Concetta who was giving me some good tips on how to cook meats and poultry. I also tried to make potatoes dumplings but after a couple of failures I found a bread shop that was selling them already made and they were just like those made at home. Obviously I always said I made them from scratch.

I really liked my job. It was not stressing, I had plenty of time to do all the things that a working person has to do during the "off" hours. I had seen the way my foreign colleagues were working and this idea started forming in my mind: Emery could eventually transfer me to the U.S.A. If they could provide me with a working visa I could have moved with Tom and the fear of him getting caught by the immigration officers would have gone, besides he would have been in his own country, among his people and even his fears would have gone away.

This became some important goal in my life and when I talked to Tom about it he started laughing and said that with all the restrictions there were I could have never achieved it. Of course that increased my desire for succeeding and I started inquiring my Italian boss and the European regional manager if such a move had ever happened in the past. The answer was neither positive nor negative but I got right the fact that it was not really impossible.

I had got Tom a subscription on National Geographic that was delivered every month. He has always been a great reader and I was getting all the information about the most important cities in the world, their people, the places to see and all the information one would need to visit them. I was growing this interest for the US and I started to plan a trip for the summer. Thanks to my 75% discount tickets I could visit multiple places in one month spending very little money. August was approaching and Tom could spend that month in Lavarone with my family.

In the meantime we kept going to Ticino to bask in the sun and have fun. While Tom was disappearing in the woods we were having a god time eating, drinking, playing cards and cruising in secluded trails hunted by the numerous mosquitoes and by those terrible horseflies. After sunset we would walk back to our cars where Tom was showing up at the set time like a Swiss clock. I was always happy to see him because I was worried dead that something bad could happen to him.

I spent the whole month of July to plan my trip. I could use any major IATA airline twice a year with my discount and my mother insisted that I fly Swissair. New York was going to be my first landing place, then Orlando to visit Disney World that had just opened. An old friend of mine from the boarding school in Paris had moved to the United States with his mother, a widow, who had married somebody from Pasadena. Tony, that was his name, had joined the US Navy and was based in a small Florida coastal town, Pensacola. The West coast was also a must. In 28 days I could see quite a bit.

I left on a beautiful morning from Zurich with a light suitcase and 1200 $ stuffed in my money belt. Upon my arrival in New York I checked in at the YMCA on 38th St. and from there I started my adventure.

Chapter 14

Trip to the USA

With all the recommendations of Tom on where to go and what to see I left on a beautiful morning on a flight to Zurich. In those days it was very important for me to leave from a different country because of the monetary restrictions in Italy that did not allow to leave the country with more than $ 1000 per year. My father cousin was meeting me at the Kloten airport, with plenty of cash to stuck in my money belt. Everything went as planned and I was on my way to New York where I arrived around 2,30 pm.

Knowing my way around the terminal and the immigration office I was sitting on the bus to Manhattan, then standing in line to check in at the YMCA Sloan House on 38th Street.

Besides the six hours difference I took a quick shower, changed clothes and went to walk around in the Greenwich Village looking for cool places. Everything was interesting and I noticed many gay guys looking at me. I thought my Italian clothes where attracting their attention but I had to change my mind when, while having a drink at Uncle Charlie's downtown some guys started talking to me: to my great surprise they found me attractive! Something that I had never ever been told before! They asked me to go to have dinner with them and so we went to the Trilogy, a restaurant on Christopher Street. The food was "interesting" the price was reasonable…what was left to do…we ended up at the "Bookstore" where they had an arcade in the basement with porno gay movies.

Even though I was tired and in jetlag we all had some fun in the boots. When I got back to the YMCA I had to take a shower and went right to sleep for the next 11 hours.

After a rich lunch I started walking to the Central Park area. It was kind of warm but not too humid. I went to the National Gallery and zoomed through the whole museum in a couple of hours. The Guggenheim was just across the street but I decided to walk around the park and observe all the different people, some walking, some jogging, others visibly cruising. I stopped by a large pool where there were some guys playing with different models of boats. I went through a little zoo and then I walked to an elevated area with some big rocks that immediately I recognized like a gay section. It was nice, a little stream nearby, some guys walking, some taking sun on a field and some chatting while sitting on some benches. I also sat and a few minutes later a guy started talking to me. He was nice and I started a conversation. I learned all about that place and even about what was going on at night. Quite scary, I had to admit. He strongly advised to leave before sunset. We walked towards 59th and 5th when a tall slim lady who was wearing a beige raincoat took my attention. Long blondish hair, dark sunglasses and she had two dogs on a leash. I always regretted not having a camera with me that day because, as somebody told me, that was Greta Garbo, one of my favorite movie stars.

I left my newly acquired friend and walked back to the YMCA where, in the shower, I met Allen, a guy from Denver who was there with his boyfriend but he was obviously looking for some fun on the side. He was a model for a cologne in fashion at that time, Royal Copenhagen. We spent some time in my room and we exchanged addresses and phone numbers. I thought he was gorgeous. This trip to the USA was really going to be promising and that was only the beginning.

Exploring Manhattan I really liked it because of the variety of races, places, architecture and easy way to get around, mostly on foot. It was nothing like London, more live and colorful.

It was time to get on to Florida and I boarded the plane to Orlando, a flight to remember. Eastern was the official Airline to Disneyworld and Mickey Mouse was on all their napkins. On the way to Orlando there was a stop over in Tampa. The last segment was only 18 minutes but a summer thunderstorm could not be avoided. The plane got hit by a lightening and the lights were out for at least twenty seconds. Some people were screaming but it all was forgotten when we landed.

Going out of the terminal it was like walking inside a sauna: we were in the deep south!

I caught a taxi. The Holiday Inn I had booked was located downtown but it was very different from Manhattan: nobody walking around and nowhere to go on foot from the hotel. It was only 9,30 at night and I was not really in the mood to watch TV and go to sleep. Across the street I saw that there was something going on, so I lighted a cigarette and went to investigate. I was right, there was a small arcade with booths and porno movies. A decent looking guy was trying to get the attention of a really cute one inside a booth with the door half open. When the cute guy saw me he suddenly changed direction and started following me. I was not really in the mood to do something there while I had a room at my disposal across the street, so I started chatting with Ronald, that was his name, and I invited him over. We spent a couple of unforgettable hours and I finally could go to bed and relax.

Early in the morning, after a large breakfast, a special minibus stopped at the Inn and thirty minutes later I was at Epcot to see for real the globe and the other wonders I had read on the National Geographic. I didn't know then that that was the first of several visits to that site in the years to come. The next day I visited the Magic Kingdom and I had a lot of fun in the haunted house and the space mountain, the best roller coaster I had ever been. It also rained some while I was in line but it was almost a blessing because of the heath I was not used to.

From Orlando I boarded a Greyhound bus with destination Pensacola but when it arrived in Tallahassee late at night, I decided

I had enough of the bus for that day and stopped over for the night in the capital city. I got off in the downtown area, near a post office. Nobody was around and I had no idea on where I would have spent the night since there was no sign of a hotel. Fortunately a guy who stopped to check his P.O. box helped me out and gave me a ride to a motel. He was, you guessed it, gay! And we did spend some time together.

The next day, after another five hours ride, I finally arrived in Pensacola where I rented a car and started driving around to look for a hotel. My plan was to stay there at least one week to enjoy the beach and see my old friend.

American cities are so different from the Europeans where most hotels are located downtown. I could not find anything because all the lights were misleading: theaters, shops, fast food etc. but one big light was on top of a tall building and it read "San Carlos Hotel". The place looked kind of fancy: marble, stain glass, drapery, mirrors and a large foyer. The price was really cheap, only 65 $ for a room for one week. I checked in.

I had gained one hour from the east coast. After dark I had to go walking around to check the area. Nothing much on the streets but in the ground floor of the hotel there was a lounge called Fiesta and yes, it was gay, very similar to the Bei Hans, the bar I used to go in Bremen. I tried to drink a beer but the taste did not agree with my mouth, then I tried a screwdriver but Vodka was not pleasant either. Finally I switched to ginger ale and that was something I could easily drink. There were some characters in the bar that I met almost immediately: Margie, a black lady who used to come in around 5pm walking with a stick, Hendrick, a very distinguished Dutch man who was working in a department store, Geno who was a cab driver, a woman on a wheelchair, the bartender and Jack, an older doctor from one of the richest families in town. I befriended everybody from the first time we met even if I didn't fancy anybody sexually. Every now and then there were some cute guys coming in for a drink or two and it was really easy to start a decent conversation that would lead somewhere either to sexual encounters or just some exchange of ideas. One of these guys was Bill but he was much younger than average.

The day after my arrival I surprised my friend by calling his house after so many years of silence. He asked me where I was staying and came to pick me up to introduce me to his wife and his two children. He also told me that my choice in the hotel was not the best because the San Carlos had become a pole of attraction for hookers and homosexuals. But at that point I had already paid for one week and I could not back up. Not that I wanted after I heard all those comments!

My friend had a beautiful house in the west side of town with an indoor heated pool. His wife, much older than him and at her second marriage, was originally from Napoli. She cooked some spaghetti and promised to take me to the beach the next day.

We left around 2pm and fifteen minutes later we crossed the toll bridge leading to the main beach. She drove to the east and we stopped in a secluded area after the sign "National Seashore". We had to cross a couple of dunes of sugar white sand covered by seaweeds and the Gulf of Mexico appeared to my eyes for the first time in all it's splendor. Dark sunglasses must be worn at all time because the reflection of the sun on the sand is equal to the same on snow, extremely bright. Almost thirty miles of uncontaminated beaches with very few people, no tar, not trash, silky feeling, breezy and with the water much warmer than the Mediterranean Sea: it was like discovering Heaven!

When she noticed I was wearing an Italian bathing suit she told me I should buy the more castigated American one otherwise people would think I was gay. I found that excessive but I did follow her advice only because I found the swimming trunk more sexy.

That night I ventured to the Red Garter, the most famous gay club in town, just a couple of blocks from the hotel. The place was really nice and quite crowded with plenty of room to sit and dance. Guys and girls formed a mixed happy crowd like I was not used to see in Europe. Before midnight they cleared the dance floor and some drag queens started a funny show mocking some American celebrities. Around 2am, closing time, many people were already drunk and were on the main street, Palafox, waiting for a cab to take them home in order to avoid DUI tickets.

Back at the hotel I slowly went up the main staircase leading to the second floor where my room was located when I noticed a couple of guys sitting on a sofa. One was exceptionally cute, the other was nothing special and he was staring at me. Curious to see what was going on I entered my room slowly and left the door cracked. Not even two minutes went by that someone was knocking at the door. It happened to be the "nothing special guy" but, before I had time to be disappointed, he told me his friend was shy and didn't have the courage to approach me. He finally came in and we spent one of the most memorable nights of my life. The following night I went to bed thinking about him but I had not seen him around and I fell asleep kind of disappointed. A little after three he knocked at my door and we spent a few hours together. All I knew about him was his name, Jim. I regret we never exchanged addresses and phone numbers because that was the last time I ever saw him.

There was another bar in town called "The quiet village" frequented by some older guys. The place was nice but inside the air conditioning was kept on a very low setting therefore it was very chilly. I went there from time to time to check the crowd but never approached anybody interesting and never really stayed for more than a drink.

My week went so fast that I decided to stay for another three days to enjoy the beach. For lunch I was eating in some fast food nearby but at night I was treating myself to different restaurants downtown. It was very easy to drive around and I also became acquainted with Cordova Mall that offered a big variety of shops. On the beach I was enjoying watching the big birds like cranes and pelicans that apparently had no fears of humans and the funny sandpipers running up and down catching small shells. There were many crabs as white as the sand. The fish was abundant from very small to medium including some barracudas and some beautiful stingrays. In the distance dolphins were frequently seen swimming in groups. Even the few people walking on the beach were very friendly, something that I was slowly getting used to because in Europe nobody usually chats with strangers.

I got to the airport, returned the rental car, and I was on the flight to San Diego with a stop over in Phoenix gaining an extra two hours on the central time. I rented a Lincoln Continental and I spent the afternoon driving around that large city.

The military YMCA seemed a very promising place to get a room and there I was, in the middle of downtown, surrounded by a bunch of marines and navy guys. If the one in Manhattan was so cruisy I was wondering what was this one like. Unfortunately I was not going to be so lucky because it seemed more straight than usual, but at least the room was really cheap.

Balboa Park, one of the most famous zoos in the world, was the reason for my visit there. With my small camera I started taking pictures of animals and places that I knew Tom wanted to see. I also got him a subscription to the monthly magazine that supplied all the information about the animals, new arrivals, births etc.

The last afternoon I spent in San Diego I found a gay bar in a walking distance from the YMCA and there I bought my first gay guide to the USA, the Bob Damron's. Now I knew I could find what I was looking for during my long evening hours. I guess I was kind of desperate for sex because I located a bathhouse, the Vulcan, and I drove there not really knowing what to expect. I had fantasized about a place like that but did not know that it existed. I was asked for an ID, was given a towel and a pair of slippers and the key to a locker. I got naked and put the towel around my waist, then I started checking the strange place. There was an outdoor pool, a Jacuzzi, a shower area, a steam room, a sauna. Upstairs there was a large room with a disco ball hanging in the center and reflecting beams of light all over. In the hallways there were dozens of doors, some open, some locked, each one revealing a small bed, a night table and enough room for two people. A few guys were laying on beds totally naked or just lightly covered. The crowd was young and mostly military. A loud music could be heard all over the building.

I was just getting used to the unusual place when a cute Hawaiian guy encouraged me to walk inside his cubicle and started chatting with me. That was fast and the conclusion was obvious.

The next day, after I had lunch, I started driving north towards Laguna Beach. The speed limit was 55mph but it looked like I was the only one going so slow therefore I increased to 60-65 staying in the left lane. Suddenly a van that had passed me on the right started skidding and ended upside down in the median. Fortunately I had foreseen what was going to happen so that I had just the time to avoid a fatal crush. I decided then that the car I was driving was much too heavy to be driven at a speed higher than 55mph because the breaks were not responding as well as those of a European car.

It was almost 6pm when I arrived in Laguna Beach where, according to the guide, there was a gay motel on the beach. It was very easy to spot the "Boom Boom Room" probably one of the oldest gay establishments on the West Coast. I got a nice room on the second floor overlooking the Pacific, took a shower and walked to the beach to test the water: it was freezing! I quickly gave up the swim and walked around the very nice town filled with art galleries, restaurants, beautiful houses and colorful stores. That could have been my ideal living area if the water of the ocean would have been warmer.

Back to the motel the lights were on and the bar downstairs was getting crowded with some interesting people. The counter was made of glass covering a big and long aquarium. I did not talk to anybody except for the bar tender but I enjoyed sitting back and relax and observe the guys dancing.

I left Laguna Beach in the late morning and I arrived in Los Angeles during the first afternoon. I drove around Venice, Bel Air, Santa Monica and finally Hollywood. I could not believe how long was Sunset Boulevard.

Los Angeles did not really impress me, so I proceeded north and I stopped in Santa Barbara for the night. There was a motel on the guide with a note that the gay section was only on the fifth floor. I asked for a room on the fifth floor.

The night was quiet. Some noise was coming from the room next door. Spying from under the door I finally saw my neighbor saying goodbye to another guy. Neither one was attractive so that made me decide to turn off the TV and go to sleep.

The drive to San Francisco the next day was something to remember. The "Camino Real" is almost like driving on the Cote d'Azur in France: cliffs, winding road, small beaches, houses hanging over the ocean. One famous actress, Kim Novak, had her house there.

The drive was pleasant and so was the temperature during that august afternoon. While I was approaching San Francisco the temperature had dropped significantly and there was some patchy fog . Now I could see with my own eyes if the city deserved all the enthusiastic descriptions of my parents.

It was quite easy to find the hotel (picked up from the guide). It was the ex Majestic, just reopened as totally gay under the new name "Brothel". My room was on the 4th floor and as I understood I had been lucky to find one because on the following night there was the "grand opening" with over 500 guests. A gymnasium with hot tub, sauna and steam room were also available in the basement while a large dining room was located next to the foyer.

San Francisco was the new merging "Mecca" for gays from the U.S. and from all over the world. The Castro was the center of this merging group and it all started when a gay activist, Harvey Milk, became elected on the board of supervisor co-operating with George Moscone, the mayor.

For those of you that would like to know more about that "glorious" period, the "coming out of the closet", the first gay parades, Anita Bryant, the proposition 9 and the assassination of Harvey Milk and George Moscone, I would suggest to watch the award winning documentary "The times of Harvey Milk", narrated by Harvey Firestein.

Walking around in the city felt like being in a very different atmosphere, something that was already gone in the early eighties. The guys looked all alike with short military haircut and the majority was wearing moustache. It was like being in Manhattan with a lot of hills but not as dirty. In the Castro during the day there was a campaign going on against Anita Bryant and her coming to town. Some guys were handing out pins and buttons with slogans anti her visit. As I understood even the mayor had advised her not to show up. Gays could be seen all over and that seemed not disturbing the natives.

As long as I was walking in the sun it was pleasant but I was really getting chilly when I was in the shades so I entered a big department store and bought a light jacket. I must have walked for several miles up and down the hills admiring the panorama from the Golden Gate Bridge to the view of the Alcatraz from the blooming Lombard Street, then down to the palace of fine arts and back to the beginning of Market at the foot of the Bay Bridge. When I got back to the Brothel it was about 5pm and the crowd invited for the grand opening had started poring in. I went up to my room, took a shower and changed getting ready to go downstairs where the action was. The room across from mine had the door open and a very cute guy was standing there smoking a cigarette. Our eyes met, a smile, and we started to talk. His name was Jim, he was about my age, very nice eyes, Greek American who was living in New York City and was visiting San Francisco for the first time. We forgot the party and went out to a restaurant that he knew called Burton. Jim had a PHD in psychiatry and was a counselor for students in high school. We had many things in common and the more we talked the more we liked each other. We got back to the hotel while the party was at its peak. We mingled in the crowd to find out that most of those guys were nice, talkative, intelligent and some also very cute. The Champagne was flowing and most people were more buzzed than they should be. There were smaller groups of lesbians that could not be missed because of their masculinity. Probably more than 500 people showed up, not counting those that had gone around the floors looking for some possible temporary relationships with the guests. We enjoyed the party for a couple of hours but then we retired in Jim's room for a one on one private party that was definitely more enjoyable.

The next day we went to explore the Red Pines forest where we could admire those ancient and very tall trees by walking on a preset trail. The next stop was Sausalito where we had a romantic dinner at a restaurant overlooking the bay and the city.

Jim was just out of a relationship with Dairo, a guy from Colombia who had become an American citizen and was a computer programmer in New York. I exchanged some information with Dairo and promised to visit him during my next trip to the big apple.

The last day in San Francisco was dedicated to shopping and to the visit at the planetarium where, at 5pm, they were showing the famous laser show. Several hundred people were in line waiting to be admitted, many were smoking some pot, including Jimmy, in order to enjoy the show in a happier state of mind. I declined the offer and I must say that I enjoyed myself very much.

My flight was a very long one with a two hours stop over at JFK and then the usual overnight to Milano. This was one of the rare times that I was sitting next to a beautiful Hawaiian girl, Dani Jean, in the smoking section. That was the beginning of a sincere long friendship.

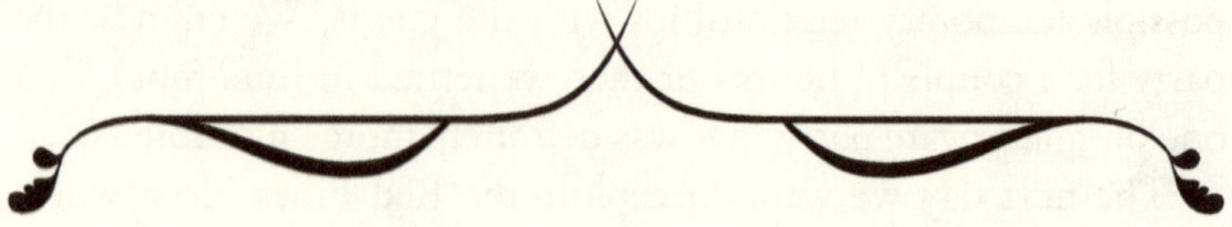

Chapter 15

Milano - Giorgio

I was back in Milano with a few days of vacation left before going back to work.

The flight in the company of Dani Jean had been most pleasant. She was going to visit her brother who was in the American Army in Vicenza. I gave her all the information about the country and the places she had to see.

At home Tom was waiting for me with hundred of questions about my trip. The photos that I took were quickly developed and printed including one of the okapi, very rare African antelope, from the San Diego zoo.

I must admit I was very excited and I wanted to go back every time I had a chance to do so. In the meantime I decided that I had to do something about my body and I started looking around for a gym. Sitting in the car all day and at the office was not helping.

Somehow an ex colleague of mine from Sillem told me that near my residence there was an ex body builder who had a private gym. I met him one afternoon in between calls and he agreed to train me for a couple of weeks so that I could understand how to use the machines and what muscles they were working on. The monthly rate was really reasonable. He gave me a key and I started the very next day. He had made the machines himself and they certainly served the purpose. Quickly I learned how to use them correctly and I coped with some inevitable body pain during the first week.

Due to my working schedule I could always stop there either in the morning or in the afternoon every other day as he recommended. I knew it would take at least six months to get in a decent shape.

This gym was kind of special, the owner was not there all the time and the members had a key to get in. This was very suitable because I could work out at any time in accordance with my sales calls. The exercises would take a little bit over one hour. Soon I had to buy my shirts and jacket a size larger because my shoulders were getting broader.

The lease of my company car had expired and I was given a choice of different models to replace the FIAT. I really liked a Renault and I was glad to make the switch. Our European manager, Ivan, gave the other interesting news to us. There was going to be a contest among all the sales representatives: the one that would have obtain more cargo import from the USA during the next three months would have won a two weeks trip to the U.S., in cities of his choice, to make joint sales calls, with all expenses paid and $ 1000 in pocket money. Needless to say I had to win.

There were some possible customers that I was keeping "in storage" for hard times. Usually I would get at least 4 or 5 routing orders per week. In this case I was competing against 65 colleagues scattered all over Europe, a very hard task, especially against the British that were particularly favorite. So I started putting more effort in my job, increased the sales calls, checked all the airway bills from different competitors, befriended custom agents and visited some prospects that were almost impossible to gain because had been using competitors for years. I also exploited some very important friends of my brother in law that had business with North American companies.

The number of routing orders increased to 15-20 a week. Gabriella was kept busy and my boss was really pleased and also amazed. The big bang happened when I made a courtesy call to one of my favorite customers and he gave me a lead. It was a new merging company that had just opened the office in the middle of my working zone. A so-called A+ customer. He gave us some 200 shipments per month!

I still didn't know how the others were performing but I was quite sure to be ahead of most.

In the meantime I still lived my life as usual, going to see my friends, having the Saturday dinners, visiting my parents, going to ski in Lavarone and to the opera when there was something worthy to be seen at La Scala.

Tom was still working hard at the factory and it was under contentious debate that he gave up his job and rest at home. I know the machines were extremely noisy and I was concerned about his hearing. Besides I was making plenty of money for the both of us and every time we were going to Lugano my parents were giving us plenty of food to stock our pantry for weeks.

My obsession with clothes had come to a rest. I had then over thirty suits for all seasons and many were signed by Armani and Versace, but most of all I liked an emerging designer, Missoni, who was mixing colors with an unbelievable skill. Through my sister I was able to buy signed clothes for a fraction of the price in the stores.

On Saturday morning, if I was in Milano, I was going shopping at the district market. We were always oriented to fresh veggies, fruits, white meats and fresh cheeses. Every time I would think of something different I was calling Concetta to have advices on the best way to cook and prepare. If the weekend was cold and rainy I could spend hours in the kitchen. At night it was always visiting with friends, theater, opera and, often, cruising at the most popular cinema, the Alce.

The end of the contest was getting near and by then I had used almost all the cartouches I had in storage for "difficult times". Mrs. Testa told me confidentially that I was ahead but the confirmation came a couple of weeks later from the big boss in Bruxelles, Yvan. At that point I had one month to decide where I wanted to go for two weeks and to coordinate the sales calls with my colleagues. The month I chose was April. I started calling my new friends, Jim in New York, Allen in Denver and Faron, a nice straight guy that I had met in Los Angeles. They all were surprised to hear from me and glad that I could see them again. Everything was going to be paid for by the company and it was understood that I had to stay in first class hotels. Of course the less money I would spend on food and lodging the more I could spend on me. The closer the day of my departure, the higher the friction between Tom and me. I learned years later that was due to his fear that something bad could happen to me during the trip. In return I was always afraid that something bad could happen to him while I was so far away, so I was asking my sister to keep an eye on him.

The day came when I parked the company car at the Malpensa airport and boarded the TWA flight in business class to New York. The booked hotel was the Sheraton.

I arrived at the usual time in Manhattan, it took me thirty minutes to check in (!) and I was on my way to meet Dairo, Jim's ex, who was living on 14th St. and 6th Ave., at the edge of the village. He was a very nice guy from Colombia who had become American a few years back. His next-door neighbor was a cute Peruvian guy who had a green card and was trying to become a citizen. Dairo's apartment was small but tastefully furnished. We went to dinner in a small restaurant in the village. We were not sexually attracted by each other but we became very good friends. Incidentally our birthday was just a couple of days apart.

In the morning I had the very nice surprise to have breakfast next to a very popular Italian singer, Little Tony, who was in Manhattan for a concert.

My counterpart arrived at 8,30 sharp and we started the sales calls for the day. Working in the city he was not driving a company car but he was getting an allowance for a new pair of shoes every three months. I found that funny.

A base of our weekly consolidation had been for years some fabrics imported by a famous American company located in Long Island City. Somehow I had the inspiration of saying: "why don't we visit the traffic manager and see if we can regain that business". So we did, we took him to lunch, and he signed eight routing orders for his Florence suppliers. That made my day and also crowned the purpose of my trip. Now I could really relax and not worry even if the rest of my calls would remain unproductive.

The next stop was going to be Detroit. On the plane I was sitting next to Beth, a nice girl that was in love with Italy and with the Italian men. We made arrangement to meet for dinner. That was one of the very few times that I ate in a Japanese restaurant where the show performed by the chef at the table was great, the food was too raw for my taste but the ambiance was really beautiful. After dinner she was probably expecting more but with the pretext that I had to meet my colleague early in the morning, I cut short and went to bed. Steven came to pick me up at 8,30 and we went to visit the first customer. Honestly I did not like the city except for the downtown area that had a reconstruction of the old Detroit with shops and alleys, a kind of an old living museum. We had lunch on top of a high rise building from where we could see Aberdeen, the island zoo, and Canada on the other side.

In the late afternoon I was sitting on a plane with destination Minneapolis where my counterpart welcomed me. The twin cities were kind of interesting to visit, very close together and very modern. One thing that caught my attention was the plethora of evacuation routes due to the harsh winter weather. The downtown was nice and clean, car free, but with very few people walking around. I already knew it would be impossible to relay on the Bob Damron guide to find a gay club, my colleague was old and very interested in chatting about work before, during and after dinner. The next day was very much the same. We stopped for a few minutes at the edge of one of the many lakes just outside the city and it's there where I learned that thousand of almost invisible mosquitoes populate the area. I was glad to be back on the plane that would have taken me to Denver.

Years before Dynasty Denver was not the big city that has became. It was nice, not too busy, and easy to get around. I rented a car and started exploring and looking for a hotel. Once I got checked in I called Allen who came shortly and, as I expected, he gave a warm sexual welcome. There was the whole weekend to spend together. He was living close to downtown in an old house that he was sharing with his ex lover. There was a large aquarium with two piranhas and candles, hundreds of candles everywhere. We had dinner and then off to the city to check out the gay clubs.

The next day I took my time to explore the outskirts and by chance I visited the thumb of Buffalo Bill and his wife. In the evening I went to dinner in a very nice typical American restaurant and then I went in search of the local bathhouse called "Ballpark". It was not too far from downtown and the door did not bear any sign. I rang the bell and I was lucky as it was the right one. Inside there was the usual check in point, the locker room, a nice common area with a cafeteria, the corridors with all the rooms, a big shower area, a porno TV room, sauna, Turkish baths and a huge Jacuzzi divided by a rocky grotto with a waterfall in the back wall. This was probably the nicest bathhouse I have ever seen.

I had started my collection of books of matches and there they had a very cute one, half the regular size, with blank lines to write name and number of the occasional friend. By then I thought that having casual sex with different guys covered only with a towel at the waist was the sexiest thing that could happen to me. Plenty of times to look, chose, spend some time in the intimacy of the private cubicle and go to take a nice shower afterwards. In Italy these places were not available and we just were hearing rumors that there was something like that in Amsterdam.

On Sunday afternoon Allen and his friend surprised me with a ticket to see the performance of "A chorus line" by the original Broadway cast.

I left Denver with the promise to visit again and was on my way to Los Angeles where I arrived in the early afternoon and checked in the Marriott close to the airport. The sales manager of Emery came to pick me up and took me to eat in Santa Monica and he gave me the schedule for the next two days. On Tuesday morning I was in the car with two colleagues to visit prospects that had a lot of shipments to and from Italy. While we were waiting in the lobby of a big company I noticed that a lamp was moving: we just had a mild earthquake! But nobody seemed to care.

The two sales reps were about my age and one was really attractive, like a GQ model. He told me point blanc that during his free time he was doing some porno video for a company called Falcon, admitting he was bisexual but had a preference for guys. I did not disclose myself but I showed that sexual preferences were strictly up to the individual and that in Europe we did not make a big deal about it. Of course I was wishing he would come to my room in the middle of the night to know him better, but it did not happen.

After work I got a glimpse of a typical unwind meeting: all the sales reps would gather for a few drinks in the bar of a Ramada Inn to write their reports and to discuss the losses and gains of the day. After an early dinner, or what I considered to be early since it was only 7pm, I was left at my hotel with no car and away from any happening place in town. I cruised the lobby, the bar area and ended up watching TV in my room.

The next day we got stuck in traffic on one of the freeways so I got a real taste of what they meant when they were talking about that problem. At 5PM they left me at the airport and it was only when I arrived in San Francisco that I found out I forgot my camera in my colleague's car. Don, the sales manager that came to pick me up at the terminal, was so kind to call the Los Angeles office and have my camera shipped overnight to my hotel. He also insisted in giving me a company car so that I would not be stranded at the hotel.

The last two days were busy but I had some time to get around and see again those places I liked so much. A visit to the local Club Bath was necessary. By Friday night I had checked in at the Casa Loma, a gay hotel near the Castro, where I befriended John who was visiting from Philadelphia and we spent some really nice time together. One night in Manhattan, the last shopping, and I was arriving in Milano on Monday morning ready to resume my work and my usual life. On the whole the trip had been a success for the business gained and for my enjoyment.

It was one night on the following week that I decided to go to the Argentina, a cruisy cinema that everybody considered better than the Alce for quality of people. It was quite empty and I don't even recall the title of the movie they were showing. I sat behind a guy that looked cute but that didn't mean he could have been gay. Nothing happened for a while but I noticed that his right arm was resting on the top of the nearby seat. It took me more than ten minutes to lift my leg in the way that it would touch his elbow. He didn't move, but after a while I felt more pressure on my knee. Finally he turned his face and looked at me with a big smile. Encouraged I got up and went to sit next to him. His name was Giorgio, he was from Udine, living in a residence not too far from my apartment and his job was in the same field as mine. He was in charge with the big exhibits around the world for a company that did it all, air, ocean and trucks. He did not have a car and was getting around with cabs.

We "clicked" from the time we met and I offered him a lift to his residence where I ended up spending three hours. I got home around 4am but I was so excited that I did not fall asleep and I took Tom to Monza before meeting my boss at the office.

Giorgio was extremely fond of art, especially opera, ballet and classical music. His small apartment was filled with tapes featuring old and new recordings, books, magazines, marquis, records and cassettes. Six feet tall, intelligent, smart, good-looking, great smile, he had all the qualities that a guy can wish. We spent hours and hours talking about Callas, Montserrat Cabaille, Tebaldi and many others I had only heard about from my mother who could have been a soprano if her parents had let her (but in her days that was not something a lady would do).

Sex was great too, he was a good kisser and he had a very nice body.

Emery was opening the office in Roma and Nicki and I had to go there for one week to help the new sales rep to establish his portfolio. We were scheduled to leave in the afternoon but Giorgio had found out that I had a bicycle so he convinced me to go out for a ride early in the morning. The city and its surroundings are very flat but we went as far as Monza, about 15 Kms away. When we got back I had time to take a shower, eat, and join Nicki on the other side of town. I was leading in my car and she was following. We stopped once for gas and to exchange audiocassettes, but in less than five hours we were in the eternal city. The next morning Bill arrived with Yvan, the regional manager, and we went to see the new office at the Fiumicino airport. After lunch we were on the road to go visit our first customer.

I always had a great time in Roma but in this instance we were staying at a Holiday Inn a little bit distant from the city. Never than less, in the pool area, I managed to get hooked up by a Canadian steward who had reddish hair and a very fit body.

The rest of the week went smoothly and we had a remarkable success in establishing good business for the new sales representative.

Back in Milano there was another surprise: Bill had been fired and suddenly replaced by the accountant manager. Nicki was outraged. In the months to come that proved to be a good move, in a way, because the new manager was less invasive than Bill and was not really interfering with the sales department leaving us more time to mind our personal business. Nicki left the company a couple of months later to go to work with Bill in another international trucking company. I was now the oldest sales guy at Emery with the task of finding a replacement for a lady that had been extremely prolific. I decided to take over her customers and to introduce Mauro to mine.

At this point my territory included the North side of Milano, Torino, Como, Brescia, the whole Veneto regions and Liguria. The lease with Avis ended and I was getting the choice of a new car. I chose a white Renault 18, nice, big, comfortable and sporty.

Giorgio was traveling a lot. In July he had to be in Guayaquil and at the beginning of September he had another big fair in Pecking. We were spending a lot of time together whenever there was a chance, talking about opera, listening to rare recordings. My collection of audiocassettes tripled in those days. He had an incredible collection of autographs, photographs of famous people, and tons of newspapers and magazines extracts with critics to movies, singers, authors etc.

He was not too social with my other friends because, apparently, didn't have much in common with them. During his frequent long business trips I was always enjoying their company with dinners, movies and social games. There was also a new addition to the company, Rosa, a nice girl that was renting the apartment next to Franck who, in the meantime, had a new boyfriend named Matteo.

Sometimes during the weekend I was going to Genova to visit Enio or Ettore. Enio had opened a framing shop in the historic center and was now living together with Marina, a girl our age who I did not fancy too much because of her involvement with drugs. My fear was that Enio would experiment in something that I always avoided. Time would prove me right. Marina remained pregnant and Igor was born.

Ettore was involved with Giulia, a girl he had been dating since the days of the military service, and was planning to get married in June. Of course I was going to be the best man.

Ettore and I had both joined the Freemasonry because of our interest in the esoteric aspect of life. Twice a month I was going to my lodge and those nights became quite important in my life. I was surrounded by people with my same interests, discussing about symbolism, cabala, life in general. My tailor made me a black suit just for the meetings, as those were very informal. After the closing of the session with several brothers we would go to some restaurant for a very late night supper.

My father had been a freemason for several decades and was then a member in the Lugano lodge. Frequently I was participating to their Sunday lunches and even Ettore and his wife were joining us from Genova.

The summer vacation was approaching. Tom had now quit his work, with my great happiness. I hated to see him leaving early in the morning and coming back late in the evening. He could rest at home and do his favorite pastime: reading books. For a change of scene I would take him to Torre del Mare, Lugano and Lavarone and leave him there for one or more weeks. In this way I was basically free to come and go without feeling guilty for arriving too late at night or to spend too much time with my friends. Not being a very social person, he was enjoying the situation. The only time I convinced him to come along for a weekend at the sea was once with Carla and her fiancée.

For August I had planned my usual trip to New York and Pensacola. This time I was going to stay in the village with Dairo for a few days, and then off to the sea.

Dairo, Jim's ex boyfriend, was a very nice guy, originally from Colombia, had been living in Manhattan for 15 years in the same apartment building on 14th Street where one member of the merging group "The village people" had an apartment. Dairo's next-door neighbor was a cutie from Peru. Unfortunately nothing sexually developed because at that time he was seeing someone special. Between Dairo and me there was only friendship being of the same sign and our birthday was only one day apart.

Jimmy was fun to be around, always smiling and ready to party. He took me to the "Men's country", a huge bathhouse five story high with something for every taste. We spent a nice week together and then I flew to Pensacola where I arrived in a warm sunny day. This time I rented a two door Lincoln Continental and checked in the usual San Carlos Hotel.

The downtown area had a new lifting. The main street, Palafox, had new sidewalks and lights. The Red Garter was always packed and the gay beach was nice as usual. At the Fiesta lounge I found the same old people and I also learned that Geno, the cab driver, had been shot and mugged and remained semi paralyzed in a wheel chair.

The fifteen days that I spent in Pensacola were very pleasant. I was very tan in a couple of days, enjoying a lot of popularity at the clubs, meeting new friends, especially Bill, a cute blonde young guy who was a military brat and was crazy for military guys. With him we went several times to the NAS, naval air station, where his father was a recruiting officer and where we could go to the military beach and meet a lot of marines. I must say that they were all nice and also sexy. In Italy I certainly never got all the attention that I was getting there. Most people seemed too nice making me wander if they were all gay.

With Bill started a story that would go on for years. We were both attracted by each other but at the same time we were dating other persons and this didn't bother either him or me. He took me to the Red Carpet, the oldest lesbian club in town that still exists today. Not much there that could interest me, but every now and then there was some cute guy popping by with the idea of having an adventure with a girl and, eventually, end up in bed with another man.

In the ground floor of the hotel there were several shops, one of that was owned by a couple of good-looking guys, both body builders. They had a small suite on the third floor. One rainy afternoon we started chatting in the lobby and, casually, we ended up in their bedroom for fun. I had never been in the middle fucking a guy while the other was fucking me. They had smoked pot and since I could not stand that smell one offered me some poppers, a substance that was giving a high rush for a few minutes. Three ways could work or not, but that was one of the few times that was really enjoyable.

One city I had not visited yet was New Orleans, just 200 miles west. One afternoon I got in the car and I started driving on I-10 keeping in mind I couldn't go over the speed limit of 55 mph. It was really a boring drive and I had to stop to get a cup of weak American coffee. When I finally arrived at destination I drove around downtown looking for the YMCA where I was always sure I could have a good time.

The city did not catch my imagination. Sure the French quarter was nice and very crowded but big crowds were not really my piece of cake. I returned to my room early enough to catch a guy taking a shower with a hard on, and the night was secured: we slept together.

The next day I was on my way back to the Florida Panhandle and couldn't wait to go back to that pleasant routine.

I got in touch with the agent for Emery who gave me a warm welcome and introduced me to many local people. He was also a freemason and he agreed to take me to the Masonic lodge and to the Turkish looking Hadj temple, headquarter of the Shriners. That was the second time that I had to exhibit my Masonic passport after the time I visited the grand lodge of Belgium in Bruxelles.

I went for some shopping at the Cordova mall and with much regret I was ready to leave Pensacola knowing that nothing and nobody could prevent me to go back the following year.

Back in Lavarone for a few days, very happy to see Tom, we were in Milano resuming the usual life.

Giorgio was leaving for China for a big fair that was taking place in Peking. I took him to the airport and was very sad to see him going. When I got back from Malpensa I learned that my sister had to be operated by the famous doctor Veronesi because they had found a lymph node in her right breast. Even if it didn't show that was devastating news for me. I tend always to imagine the worse. My parents were not informed about this matter, my mother would have freaked out and there was no reason to make her apprehensive.

The sister of my brother in law was a MD and she assisted to the operation that, apparently, went well without the need of a mastectomy. Wilma was slowly recovering at the clinic when finally my parents were informed and rushed to visit her. Dr. Veronesi said that if the cancer did not reoccur in the next seven years the problem was to be considered solved. Of course some chemotherapy was needed.

One month got by when my sister called me early one morning to announce the death of my beloved grandmother who had passed away after years of confinement to a specialized clinic for elder people with motion problems. She had broken her hip walking in Milano and had never fully recovered.

Winter was approaching when another bad news hit: my first teacher and her twin sister had suddenly died in Venezia!

I had never felt so much pain all at once. Nobody close to me had died before, except my father's mother that was not to close to me anyway. It was not the fact that people died that got me, but how it was happening. The more a person was suffering physical and mental pain, the more the matter was affecting my state of mind. For days I was remembering all the time spent together, the funny things and I always thought that remembering them would take them a step closer to the light in the other world. But maybe they were already reborn somewhere else to start a new life as new human beings.

Giorgio came back from China very happy for the successful fair and with many pictures taken from the window of his hotel during the funeral of Mao Tse Tung who had died on September 9th 1976. To take pictures was forbidden in those days in that very communist country.

We started going to La Scala to see ballets, opera and to concerts at the Conservatorio. It was amazing to meet all the artists he knew and to chat with them over dinner in fancy restaurants. It was like going back in time when I was going around with Enio and the stage actors in Genova.

My life was getting too busy. Work was not absorbing me too much, but I had the gym three times a week, the Masonic lodge twice a month, my dinner parties with Franck, Matteo, Rosa and the other guys, my social life with Giorgio, my parents to visit and some weekends with different friends to ski or to the beach. The only time I was really rushing for work was on Friday afternoon when I had to spend several hours at the office reviewing the visit reports of my silly colleague and to plan for the week ahead.

My days were going fast and at night I did not go to bed before one or two a.m.

To break the monotony of my visits in the local area I was scheduling calls to prospects or existing customers far from home that would take me to different cities for three or four days at the time. Those were my escapades that I needed to break the routine that I always hated. Basically I had friends scattered all over and I was managing to see them every now and then for dinner remembering the old days. Mostly straight people or even friends of my family. It was when I was on my own, later at night, that my real life was taking me to cruisy places, looking for some casual adventure that I liked so much.

One time driving to Trieste after dinner I had to stop at a gas station to fill up the tank. There was a nice looking trucker from Hungary who was wearing a coverall with the zipper down to his navel. We looked at each other and when back on the highway I let him pass me he blinked his stoplights and pulled in a rest area. International trucks have a small bed in the cabin and that's where we spent a couple of relaxing hours in lust.

Another time I was in Treviso, a nice city near Venezia, and I had dinner with some friends. Since I didn't know of any gay clubs around, I walked to the gardens by the train station, sat on a bench and started smoking a cigarette. Shortly after a nice looking man, very well dressed, came and sat next to me and with the excuse of asking me to light his smoke he started a conversation. Half an hour later I still didn't know where he was leading so I asked him if he was married. He was a widow and had a 23-year-old son who was…death and mute. Then he told me that I seemed a nice guy and asked my sexual preferences. It was at that point that he told me his son was gay, could not easily communicate with other people, and suggested that I should meet him. I took the challenge and followed him to his house. Meeting the guy was peculiar, we were communicating in writing. He was intelligent and handsome with very long eyelashes, black hair and blue eyes. His father, with an excuse, left us alone and we ended up in the boy's room where I spent the night. I knew that some people is strange but I had to tell this story to my friends in Milano because it was one of the most interesting that ever happened to me.

Giorgio on the other hand was not a saint either. He liked cute guys that were interested in the arts and I know he was sleeping with them every time he had a chance. He used to call them "pinocchietti" that means little Pinocchio. They liked to have his attention but for a reason or another they were never around for more than a week or two.

At the Alce I had Met Antonello, a cute talented painter. We talked so much about the United States that, somehow I convinced him to come with me during the Christmas holiday. He did not speak one word of English but that didn't bother me, I figured out I could translate for him anytime. We got TWA tickets and we left one morning with destination New York. The weather was nice but the temperature was freezing. After spending a couple of days walking in Manhattan and introducing him to my friends, we flew to Washington DC to visit Arlington, the museums, the capital monument and the White House. There was no snow but they had a snowmaking machine in the yard with some kids skiing. After dinner at the restaurant of the DC Eagle we managed to find a gay bar in a residential area where we befriended some local guys. Nothing came out of that except I started getting annoyed because Antonello was asking me to translate each and every word people were saying. After the bar we went o a squalid bathhouse downtown where I found somebody to have sex with and he did not. I realized back in the hotel that my companion was kind of jealous and was trying to have sex with me when I did not want to.

The trip went on to Fort Lauderdale and Miami to explore the beach, Monkey Jungle, Parrott Jungle and the oceanographic museum. Our hotel was right downtown, not really the safest area to be and the most difficult to find a parking spot. The Club Bath was also on our list. Located in Coral Gables it was a very nice place but too cold for the pool and the outside garden. That winter was one of the worse that hit North America that year.

The intention to spend a few days in Key West failed because we ran out of time and had to go back to Milano where he had some important customer to see on a set date. His suitcase ended up in Madrid by mistake. After I helped out at the airport that was the last time I saw him. I know that he is happily married with kids and lives in the country.

Tom was always happy to have me back safe and couldn't wait to see the pictures from the trip. I had one taken at Parrott Jungle with 5 big are on my head and my arms.

Giorgio was out of the country again and before leaving he told me he had asked the company to transfer him to London. I was happy for him because I knew he wanted to get away from Milano, but I was also sad because I was enjoying his company. I thought that it would take time before they actually transferred him and I did not think about it too much. I was also asking to be transferred to an American office and my regional manager was reassuring me that when and if a position would be available he would do the best to help. In the meantime months were passing by with no word about it.

One night at the usual Alce I started chatting with a guy named Rino and we ended up in his apartment in a very popular side of town. He was nice, bright, cute, small frame body yet one inch taller than me. He was working for the government at a Lotto office. His main interest was astrology. Rino knew everything about signs and also how to calculate the ascendant and to make a horoscope. It was one week later that I invited him over for a dinner at Franck's house so he could meet all my friends. Soon he became very popular and everybody was asking him information about the future, more as a joke than to take him seriously. It appeared that his predictions were slowly but inexorably coming through but he was very modest and was always talking about one of his friends that was really good with tarots and horoscopes, his name was Valerio, an employee of a bank during the day but a fortune teller after hours with his weekly program on one of the new private television stations that were starting in those years.

So one night we met at his favorite restaurant. He was tall, slim, very curly blondish hair and he had two magnetic eyes. His manners were very effeminate and that was one thing I didn't like about him. But he seemed nice and easy to talk with. I clearly understood that Rino had some admiration for Valerio and also the people that were sitting at his table did. But of course that could be because at the end of the meal he was the one picking up the tab.

We went to his studio that was filled with candles, gargoyles, incense, wands, crystal balls and anything one would expect to find in such places. I took a quick look at the books in the library but

I didn't see anything old or really worth. He wrote down my data and promised to prepare my horoscope free of charge. I told him I was member of an esoteric Masonic lodge and that seemed to polarize his interest.

With Rino we got into the habit of going out for a pizza or a fancy meal a couple of times a month.

My Roman friend Mario came for a visit and asked me to meet his new girlfriend, Fiorella, who was originally from Milano but was living in Roma due to her work as a flight attendant with Alitalia. Apparently Mario vas very jealous and he wanted me to keep an eye on her when she was in town. Flying overseas she was spending a couple of days in New York, Chicago and Miami and a couple in Milano, always staying at the Aerotel Executive near the Garibaldi train station.

Fiorella and I "clicked" right away. We would chat for hours, sometimes late into the night, about subjects of mutual interest. She could fly for free and I had 75% discount on virtually every IATA carrier. Christmas was approaching so what a better way to spend those holidays in New York. We met at the Sheraton on 7th Avenuc after she had arrived on Alitalia from Roma and I had arrived on TWA from Milano. I met some of her colleagues and we all watched the just released funny movie "Airplane".

The next day we went on a long walk in Manhattan and she showed me all the places she was usually stopping for coffee, pizza and books. She knew most of the owners that were originally from Italy. We had lunch in a nice restaurant that served her favorite vegetarian meals and we met with Dairo and Jimmie. Fiorella was impressed with Jimmie's eyes, very Greek. We both have this passion for expressive eyes.

On New Year's Eve at 6pm New York time I called Tom who was in Lugano with my parents to wish him a very happy new 1977 and then we celebrated midnight in Time Square with thousand of other people. On the 2nd of January we were flying back across the Atlantic to our different destinations. I was carrying a suitcase loaded with electronic gadgets and also a frozen huge London broil steak that I was planning to cook on my next dinner party with my friends. The steak was still frozen when I arrived home the next morning.

Life resumed as usual with the only difference that Rosa had now a boyfriend and she was expecting a baby. We were all going to be uncles.

Giorgio was always traveling abroad for work and I was missing his company. I did go to La Scala with Massimo and I remember seeing a great performance of Montserrat Cabaille singing different arias. At the end the stage was filled with roses thrown from the balconies.

The memories of Germany and Bremen where I had spent several months came back to haunt me so I decided to go spend a couple of days there. It was nice to be back in that atmosphere and to see that the mythical bar "Bei Hans" was still open and popular. Even though I checked in a gay hotel I did not meet anybody interesting. On the flight back to Milano Linate there was a very thick fog so the plane had to land in Genova and we had to go home on a bus.

The other short trip I took was with Fiorella to Paris for 4 days. We were guests of my ex girlfriend Mariefrancoise who was working for Lanvin and was now dating Michel who would become her husband the following year.

Mario and Fiorella had fallout and he was calling several times a day asking me to talk to her to see if there was a chance for reconciliation. She would not discuss the matter with me or anybody else. He was mad at me because he thought I didn't want to cooperate. That situation lead to a misunderstanding that lasted for 15 years. Paris was always beautiful as ever and we did enjoy our stay.

Back in Milano there was the countess Marta who was now thinking about moving to the States. Her wedding was falling apart because her husband was involved with his secretary. Her son, same age as my nephew, and her daughter were also ready for a big change. The chosen city was San Antonio because she had some relatives living there and an uncle working for NASA. I was going to that area during my next vacation to visit the Alamo and to see the city where Ton had been in boot camp. It was going to be an exploration and then I would report to her my sensations.

This time I was leaving earlier, in July, since Giorgio gave me the news that in September he was going to move to London where he accepted to open the branch of another big Italian shipping company. Therefore we decided to go on a tour of Tuscany and Umbria in August.

The winter season passed slowly with the pleasant interruption of a quick trip to New York, just one week end to see my friends and to shop. It had been very cold but the cloudy, rainy and foggy days were now taken over by an extremely mild spring. The novelty was that Rino, taken by all the talks we had about the States, was thinking about coming with me in July. Everything was planned and he succeeded in getting a discounted plane ticket through some people he knew. Tom was going to take care of my parent's house in Lugano while I was gone and they were in the mountains.

It was his first time flying so everything was new to him. We arrived in the big apple, checked in at the YMCA and walked all over for three days. Rino did not speak a word of English so it was my duty to be courteous and translate everything. At least he was not as pedantic as Antonello.

The second city to visit was San Antonio. We did not rent a car there but checked in a hotel downtown in a walking distance from the Alamo and the river walk. The weather was nice, hot and quite humid but we really liked the city and its inhabitants. During a quick visit to a bathhouse we befriended an air force officer who took us to dinner in a typical Mexican restaurant, very hot spicy food I must say, and then to drive around town. The idea that Texas is not green is just a utopia because there were woods and green valleys all around. We saw the military base where Tom had started his short military career. We were well impressed and decided to give a favorable review to Marta.

Atlanta was the next stop where we were going to rent a car to drive to Pensacola to spend one week at the beach. The San Carlos Hotel had closed down much to my regret so my friend, the Emery agent, insisted for us to stay at his house and gave us the use of a big room with the annex bathroom. Bill was happy to meet another Italian guy and filled us up with what was going on now that the Fiesta lounge had closed and the Red Garter had burned down and moved to a newer location right across from Trader Jon, a famous museum/bar for the aviation. The owners of the coin shop were not together anymore. One of them, the older, had stabbed and killed his father and was now in jail for life. I could not believe I had slept with a killer!

Rino was having an incredible success among the gays at the clubs and also on the beach. Fortunately he had different taste than mine for men so our path did not cross overboard. Even for the translations I was eased up because somehow he could understand most of them and they could understand him.

One night at the Red Garter I met a cute guy who had been to the war in Viet Nam. We chatted for a while and then he invited me to go over his house. Rino was getting cruised but a younger guy with long hair so I explained to him the situation since I was the driver. Everything was arranged so the young guy would give Rino a lift home and I was free to follow my guy. He was living in an area of town I was not familiar with. The house was small and kind of shabby, but it was clean. Like the Austrian I had met in Lugano years before, this one was kind of rough, just the kind that once in a while I would enjoy but that I'm not really sure about where it would lead. He had obviously been smoking pot and he was wild for at least three hours before he stopped and almost fell asleep. I was ready to get dressed and go home when he jumped on me and told me I had to spend the whole night there. To make sure I had got the message he also showed me a gun that he was keeping under the mattress. I knew he had locked the front door when we got in the house so the only way out was a window in the kitchen. I had to wait for another couple of hours to make sure he was sound asleep. At 4,30 am I finally took my clothes and very slowly gained the window and got outside turning my head frequently to make sure he was not behind me. Once in my car I left immediately wondering around for several miles before I got to a familiar section of town and arrived home. It was sunrise, Rino was asleep but our host was watching the big TV in the living room. He gathered I had a sexual encounter with some girl over at the Seville Square and insisted in making me breakfast to recuperate my strength.

The beach in July was better than in August. Rino was amazed by the white sand, the dunes, the big birds flying and walking around and by the temperature of the water. While we were lying there taking sun we saw a black round shadow in the water. When we went closer we noticed thousands of small fish swimming together in a round circle of at least 20 feet in diameter while some bigger fish were eating them. This went on for hours and when we left to return home the circle was reduced to 4 or 5 feet.

Bill was studying to get the pilot license and insisted for us to fly over the bay with his instructor. After a visit to the military base and its outstanding museum, we took off on a little Cessna and enjoyed a perfect view of the gulf of Mexico, the city, the intercostals waterways and the small and big islands that extend from Perdido Key to Destin.

Rino was really enthusiastic about this vacation and I was happy that he could experience it.

Left Pensacola we flew to Boston that was going to be the last stop before returning home. Not knowing where to go we started with checking in at the YMCA, two different single rooms. We decided not to rent a car and that was a wise decision because we were in a city where we could easily walk around. Nice boulevards, parks, buildings and the compound that more stole Rino's attention: the headquarter of the Scientologists!

We also visited a small museum with ancient Greek and Roman statues, nothing impressive, but cute. The old side of town was nice with its narrow streets, the small backyards and the lanterns. We spent hours browsing in the little artistic shops.

For the nightlife we consulted the Bob Damron's guide and started from a disco named buttons. There we met some guys that took us to a more popular spot that was gay only one night a week but to get in we had to wait on line. So, while we were there chatting and waiting for our turn, a guy came by, looked Rino in the eyes and invited him to follow. Luckily he could speak some French so I did not have to translate. I made sure he knew we were staying at the Y and told him to bring him back there when they were "done". They did not show up until lunchtime the next day. Rino was enthusiastic. This guy was living with his parents in a big house by the river. They had sex for a few hours and then they went to sleep with the lights on and the air conditioner set at the freezing temperature of 62F and only the sheets were on the bed, no covers. No wonder he caught a cold and his voice was messed up for the next 2 days.

I did not engage myself in any sex while in Boston but I saw very nice looking guys around and was committed of going back sometimes in the future by myself.

The flight back to Italy was pleasant with all the possible turbulence, just the way I like it as opposite to a very motionless flight.

My collection of photographs was growing so much that I was not satisfied with my little camera anymore so before leaving New York I bought some sophisticated equipment with telephoto and wide angular lenses. Following Fiorella's advice I had also switched to Sony brand for my Walkman. Many times when she was spending a couple of days in town we were going roller-skating near the piazza del Duomo listening to our favorite music.

The few remaining days before leaving with Giorgio on vacation went fast. I was busy catching up with all the sales leads at work, had to go pick Tom up in Lugano and take him to Lavarone.

Giorgio and I left in my company car on a nice afternoon without having a definite program. We drove south and stopped in Cortona, a very ancient Etruscan center. That first night was funny. Companies in Italy shut down for the whole month of august and 80% of the people go on vacation. We did not book any hotel and it happened that in Cortona there were no vacancies. We ended up sleeping in the big room of a convent of nuns and, before we turned the light off, two nuns came to check if we were all right, if we needed anything and to say a pray. Giorgio found that most hilarious.

Our drive took us to Volterra, San Giminiano and Prato at the outskirts of Firenze. Perugia was an obliged stop for the beauty, the history and the masterpieces, besides we had never been there before. The next day was not going to be a happy one because while we were at a railroad crossing waiting for the train to pass the radio announced the sudden death of Elvis Presley. We were both highly touched by the news.

Being so close to Montone we went to pay a short visit to Ettore and his wife and then we headed north towards Lido di Jesolo to visit Giorgio's family that I had yet to meet.

And the day came; his parents, his sister and her husband were there, welcoming us at a friendly table. I was treated just like an old friend and I don't think that they knew what was going on between Giorgio and me or maybe they knew but didn't care a bit as long as I was a nice person. They were all fond about music and we chatted for hours about opera and famous sopranos and tenors. Callas was always the most favorite but there was an emerging Bulgarian lady that had such a powerful voice to conquer many fans in the year to come, her name: Ghena Dimitrova.

Our small vacation was coming to an end. Leaving Jesolo they made me promise to go visit again in Udine, their hometown.

Giorgio and I made a stop in Lavarone to have lunch with my parents and then I drove him to Milano where he had to get ready to leave for London.

I was really sorry to see him going but I knew we would see each other again. His main office was in Firenze, La Scala was in Milano, and there were less than 2 hours flight.

Right after he left another bad news came from Paris and meant the end of an era: Maria Callas was dead at 57.

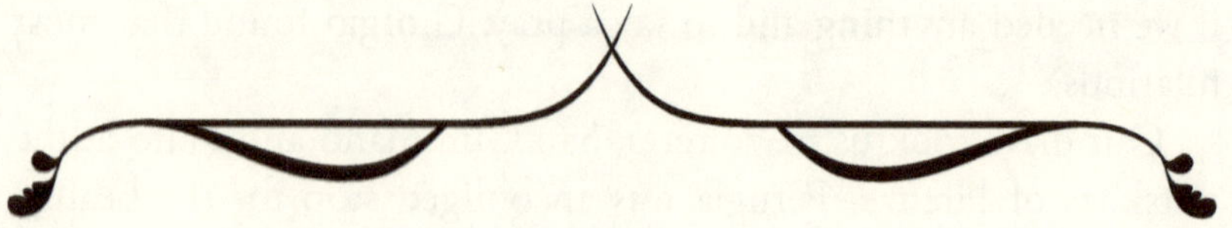

Chapter 16

Marika

My life was going on just as usual and I was always doing my best to keep in touch with all the people that I had met so far that had counted one way or another. When I was realizing there was no interest I would erase name and phone number from my agenda and also from my mind.

Friday afternoon, after I had done the schedule for the following week, I was getting on the phone and chat with a lot of people. Also my phone bill was ridiculously high because of the many calls I was making all over the world. But I was receiving calls as well all the time.

Just turned over thirty, I did not feel any different from when I was twenty. My appearance was always much younger than I really was and it was funny to get carted in the USA every time I was going to a club or when I was buying cigarettes.

I was in perfect health and after I started working out regularly even my back pain had stopped completely. There were just a couple of things I didn't like about myself: the shape of my nose and my teeth. For my nose I decided that after all it was not too important, but when a colleague of mine went to Rotterdam to get her teeth done for a reasonable sum of one million lire I decided to do the same.

The deal was simple: there was this dental company that in 3 days would remove the teeth and implant the new, all nice, white, perfect. I could see the result in Pina's mouth and I liked what I saw.

My parents were not too thrilled about the idea. I was fed up with going to the dentist all the time and pay a fortune. My teeth had too many fillings and I have always been eating tons of candies including hard liquorices. My parents had given me those teeth… they were going to pay for the operation!

So I took off to Rotterdam and I met the group of people at the hotel. One morning there was the total or partial extraction and the implant was going to be the next day. Everything was less painful than I had anticipated but to get used to chew regular food again and to talk properly were two different matters.

The night of my arrival I went out to dinner with Hans, my ex university Dutch friend who had come to study many time in my flat and was now a dedicated pastor in the protestant church. After he took me back to the hotel I managed to get in a cab and spend a few hours in a local bathhouse. Two days later I was sitting on the plane going back to

Milano with a sore mouth. For the following two weeks I had to blend all the food in milk and drink it because I was totally unable to chew. I remember going to Lavarone to ski for a weekend and on the way back stopping at a restaurant and having to drink a soup.

Slowly everything went better and the swelling in my mouth disappeared. Even the speech got better. To get used to chew I tried chewing gum, but resin teeth do not cope with that (until they invented freedent years later).

My dear friend Marta had left for the States with her son and daughter. Officially the trip was just to go on a vacation but they were going to explore and make a decision if they wanted to make the big move. She was quite intrigued by my favorable report on San Antonio.

They were gone for a whole month and not only visiting Texas. They came back with an extremely positive impression. She put her luxurious apartment on the market, sold it in a matter of days, packed and moved.

The kids were going to the last year of high school and then they were going to look around for a suitable university that turned out to be Notre Dame.

It was sad to see them leave. To obtain a residence in the U.S. she had to invest a large sum in any kind of business that would employ Americans. Money was no object. She bought a nice two-story home in a fashionable area of town, a condo with four units and two cars since her daughter couldn't drive at 15.

The way she did it was simple and fast. All my attempts to be transferred had been unsuccessful even working for an American company. I had to find the way to do it somehow. I promised Marta to go visit during the next summer vacation.

Nothing much happened in the rest of that bad 1977 with the exception that I had to go to Amsterdam for a sales staff meeting that lasted a whole week. Something to do with the new selling techniques that Emery had bought by Rank Xerox.

In December I was invited by Ettore and his wife to go spend Christmas and New Year's Eve on the Elba Island, the same where Napoleon had been kept prisoner for almost ten months from 1814 to 1815.

I went to Genova to pick them up in my car and we drove to Livorno to get on the ferry that in a couple of hours would take us to the small island. Being born and having lived in Italy for many years did not make me a good connoisseur of my country. I have never been south of Napoli on the west coast and south of Taranto on the east coast. Yet i had two aristocratic titles from two different villages in Sicily that basically belongued to my family since the 12th century. Anyway, back to Elba, Ettore and his wife had been there a few times before and had met some nice people, especially through the local masonic lodge. We were hosted by a newly wed couple and invited over for breakfast, lunch and dinner by different people. Fortunately it was not the tourist season so we were able to take our time to explore.

The last day of the year there was the usual big dinner that was starting around 9pm and drag until midnight with the opening of bottles of Champagne and a toast to the new year. A firework show was offered by the city of Portoferraio.

In the food market they were selling all the products of the island at very reasonable prices. I got some pure olive oil and a big bag of almonds that Ettore and his wife started munching on. That was the highlight of the trip: me wanted to save the almonds to take them home and cook some pastry with them and my friends wanting to eat them all! Still these days Ettore reminds me this story to tell me how stingy I was with my best friends.

Back to Milano and its routine my birthday was coming up quickly. Valerio told me that according to the place one is during his birthday the horoscope for the next year can change considerably, but i did not pay too much attention at that point because i was not in the mood to travel just for one day. All my friends prepared a surprise party and they gave me a beautiful present: a set of Thai bronze flatware. I had discovered a bread shop where they were making the best potatoes gnocchi in town, almost as good as Concetta's. I invited all my friends for dinner and offered them gnocchi with Gorgonzola pretending i had made them from scatch.

At work everything was going great, the business was constantly growing and my customers were quite satisfied of the service. We had never been a custom brokers because the consignees had their preferences. But sometimes it was necessary to suggest the name of a reliable company that could do the job and we had several that we could name, one of them was C&F with an office at the Malpensa airport and the administration in the city. For some reasons I had to go deliver some documents and I met the mistress of the owner, Marika, a pretty woman in her early thirties.

I can always tell if a guy might be interested in me or I can make one know that I'm interested in him. Surely I didn't do anything to let Marika know I was interested in her but I formed the impression that she was. The confirmation arrived when she started calling me at the office on Friday afternoon. The matter was flattering but I also had to be careful because I was dealing with her boyfriend on a weekly basis and, on top of that, they had a nine-year-old daughter.

I had soon become the talk of my friends. Rosa even told me that if I wanted to use her apartment I could. Matteo was teasing me saying that I was then more interested in a vagina. I could not take her to my apartment because Tom was there and certainly he would not have appreciated it. So I kept it vague for a few weeks. We went to the cinema, the theater and even to La Scala and I never laid a finger on her. It was funny during a scene of the movie "Being there" when Shirley McLaine is trying to sexually seduce Peter Sellers and he's just watching TV. Marika was trying to hold my hand while I was more interested in lighting a cigarette.

Finally I had to tell her that I was mostly gay and not really into women except for sex. She was not at all disappointed and insisted for seeing me. At that point she became part of our company and felt all right among us.

She started giving me presents that I did not want to accept. With the pretext that they were changing the bedroom furniture she insisted that I take this designer bed that they had paid 5000$ just a couple of years before or else they were going to call somebody to take it away.

The first time we finally did something was in Rosa apartment. She was almost living all the time with her boyfriend so she didn't mind. We all know how straight guys have sex with girls, they usually go right to the point and don't care if the girl has reached orgasm or not. Mr. C. was no exception. So when we started hugging, kissing and very slowly undressed each other she was hooked. I think she reached orgasm three times because I could feel it. For me that was the first and the last time. As I said girls are good for sex, but only once, maybe twice with the same, then it's off to another one with some long break in between.

We went on dating and at that point I made sure she could not expect anything else from me even though she insisted that time would tell. Her presents started bothering me and it was all more uncomfortable when I had to go visit some common customers with her boyfriend. The whole matter became even more complicated when at the usual Alce i met a cute guy named Dino who was living in a real farm near Monza. I started cutting with Marika to dedicate more time to Dino and she did not like that. But something bad happened. Mr. C., knwing that my parents were living in Switzerland and that i was going back and forth all the time, asked me if I could take some money, a considerable amount, to a specific Swiss bank. After careful consideration since it was illegal to take over one million lire out of Italy i had to refuse but I was suspecting something was going on with his company. So i informed my boss and with a quick investigation we found out that Mr. C. Had collected in advance all the import custom duty from his clients, he had not paid anything to the authorities and had left the country with something like 150.000$. Marika swore she did not know about this plan and apparently she got stranded with a girl to support and no job.

Strangely she kept living in her luxury apartment, her daughter was still going to a private school.

Soon after she got a new job and told me she had no idea where Mr. C. was. To this day his whereabout is still unknown.

Summer was approaching and I was planning for the next trip to the USA, by myself this time. Marta was now settled in San Antonio had had asked me to go visit. Tom did not have any suggestions about what I should see. We knew from the National Geographic that Atlanta was going through a big boom phase. So after I took Tom to Torre del Mare and from there, with my sister and nephew, they would all go to spend august in Lavarone, I left from Malpensa and flew to New York City welcomed at the airport by Jimmy. I spent a few days at Dairo's apartment and did all the usual shopping. Then I flew to Denver to visit Allen who in the meantime had a new boyfriend and had moved to a fashionable condo very close to the downtown area. They were both very nice and we had a great time, but no sex this time. On the weekend we went on a bicycle ride and ended up in a little park, filled with gay people, where I met a cute guy. The night before my departure I had to go to the bathhouse that I liked so much and I met some other cuties there. On the way back to the condo I saw three guys stealing a Porsche in a parking lot but I was too afraid to do something about it, they could have been armed.

Marta gave me a warm welcome at the airport. We drove home and went to collect her children from school. The area where she had bought the house was really nice and very green. Idefix, their Basengi dog, was a happy camper running wild in the backyard. There was a large common big pool filled with good-looking people from the neighborhood.

Having my Masonic passport with me I got in touch with the local Grand Lodge. I had never expected such a festive welcome! They came to pick me up in a limousine, gave me a tour of their temple and took me to a very elegant restaurant.

During those few months Marta had met a lot of important people, had given some memorable parties mentioned in the local newspapers and she was living the "Big" life. Being a Romanian aristocrat in the States she could make a big anti-communist campaign blaming Russia and Ceausescu, the president of Romania, for ruining her country. One of her aunts, a princess who was raising funds in the western world to fight communism, came to visit her and the media reported the occasion.

I enjoyed being with the kids but they were underage in the U.S. and we couldn't really go anywhere. At night, smoking like chimneys, we were playing chess and backgammon until 3 or 4 am. That was a week to remember.

The next destination was going to be Pensacola where I rented the usual big car upon arrival. The San Carlos was definitely closed down and the city was trying to convert it into some condo for elderly people. I went to stay again at the house of our Emery agent.

Two days later I was already very tan going to the military beach with Bill who had a new marine boyfriend. His parents had divorced but that didn't seem to bother him.

While I was in Pensacola a dear friend and customer of mine called to tell me he was coming to town for a few days with his fiancée. We met at the beach where we all agreed that was the best seaside in the continental U.S. I had to play straight until they left to drive to Atlanta.

It was one night at the new Red Garter that I started chatting with Philip, about my age and very handsome. He convinced me to follow him home, just out of town. So we went on I-10 and headed east. I realized that when Americans mean "near" it's quite a long drive. Forty miles later we finally left the interstate and after another few miles pulled into his driveway. That was another time that I arrived home around five and my host was again convinced I had found some girl at the Seville quarter.

Atlanta was going to be my next stop. When we landed I saw the airport on the right side of the aircraft but the plane kept going stopping at a totally new gate. To reach the rental car office it took me almost half an hour. I walked underground without realizing they had a shuttle connecting all the terminals. The new airport was the largest I had ever seen so far.

I drove downtown to look for a hotel and I found one near Peachtree St.

They were right: construction was going on everywhere in the city and now there were several more skyscrapers that made the 3 or 4 original disappear. My favorite was still the round one with the revolving restaurant on the top floor. The old porno shops that were numerous in the old part of town were slowly disappearing.

From the usual gay guide I spotted the club baths on 4th St. (still there today under the name Flex). So after exploring the city on the north/east side and visiting a cute small toy museum in the area now called Buckhead, I got a room at the bathhouse. It was a hot afternoon and there was not a cloud in the ski. After swimming in the pool and walking around to see what was going on some moaning guy caught my attention. It was in one of those common areas in the semi darkness with beds scattered all over. A big guy was fist fucking a short guy and this one was screaming and moaning for the pleasure, I suppose. That was too disgusting to witness so after a quick recognition I ended up watching TV in a lounge sitting next to this older and very handsome guy. We started a conversation and he told me he was a realtor, a very good profession in those days in Atlanta. He invited me over his house for dinner and then we went bar hopping to the fashionable Armory and original Library where he knew a lot of people. We ended up spending the night together and in the morning he served me a very all American breakfast.

Out of curiosity I asked him to show me some houses for sale in the Piedmont park area, which was considered to be midtown. The prices were extremely low compared to our European standards and I was really tempted to buy a three bedroom two baths offered for only 54.000$. For various reasons I didn't do it and at this time I very much regret that considering that my investment would have paid at least 5 time over.

That night I went to one of the bars we had visited the night before, right on Ponce de Leon: Mr.& Mrs. P where I started talking with a couple of elderly guys, one was Ron who had been the companion of the late Susan Hayward during her last 15 years of life. As he told me she was buried in Carrolton Georgia. I was not sure if Ron was telling me the truth or if he had made it up. After they left the only decent guy there was one that looked like a bodybuilder with really beautiful eyes and a killer smile. We went to his house where I spent the night. I had one more day left before leaving for San Francisco, the last stop before my return.

This time I did not rent a car since it was so easy to get around and the transportation system was working fine. I checked in at the Hyatt Regency that had a weird shape, full of plants and glass elevators. The city was in frenzy for the gay pride parade that was going to take place. People had arrived from all over the States. The Brothel Hotel where I had stayed before was no more but the Castro was hopping. I did not want to be in the middle of the parade but I got to watch it from a distance and I saw Harvey Milk in a convertible car. Slogans against Anita Bryant were repeated everywhere.

A visit to the local club bath concluded my visit and I was back on the plane for the long long flight home.

When I arrived at the airport in Milano around 9am I got in my car and started driving towards the highway I thought there was something wrong because the transmission was not shifting. Then I realized my car was not an automatic like those that I had been driving for the whole month in the States. I had it in first gear like I had set it on "drive".

It was always taking me a couple of weeks to adapt to the Italian way of life. On the other side of the pond everything was open 24/7, here at 7,30 pm everything was closed and the telephone system was not working properly.

Back to Lavarone to pick up Tom and everything was starting all over again waiting for more holidays.

2003

Milano was really getting on my nerves because of the traffic and the climate. I had most of my friends there and for this I was very grateful. Almost every weekend, if the weather was nice, we were organizing something at the sea or in the mountains. We would also go for long walks by the Ticino River in winter. I was seldom missing a Masonic meeting while Valerio, the fortuneteller, was pushing me to support his admission. I really thought he was way too flamboyant but then I introduced him to our secretary who filled up the application and after 4 months he was finally initiated in the apprentice status.

Two bad news characterized that 1978. On November 27 while several hundred members of a religious sect had committed a mass suicide, Dan White shot and killed the mayor of San Francisco George Moscone and one member of the board of supervisors for the city: Harvey Milk.

I closed the year flying to New York right after Christmas that I spent with Tom and my parents in Lugano. I stayed at Dairo's and we all went to celebrate New Year's Eve at the gay synagogue! That was interesting. After a couple of hours, bored, we were invited to a private party in Brooklyn but after midnight, when everybody was drinking like sponges, I left and went to check in at the club baths. It took me half an hour because of the line. Inside they had food and free drinks for the occasion. Everywhere they were playing "I will survive" from the just released album "Love tracks" of Gloria Gaynor. I knew then that it would become a "Classic" like "When a man loves a woman".

Anyway, I was wondering around when this gorgeous guy named Mark from New Jersey started cruising me. He was like a GQ model and I could not believe he was after me! That was a night to remember because we spent several hours together and when we left the baths we went to have breakfast together. I really didn't want to part but he had to go to work the next day and I was leaving on the 3rd. We did keep in touch for another couple of years but we never saw each other again.

Chapter 17

LONDON

It was during 1979 that I was beginning to realize how fast time goes by. Busy with work, Masonic lodge, keeping in touch with all my friends, organizing dinner parties, trips out of town during the week ends: it seemed like it was always Friday and always Monday! My sister was doing all right in spite of the chemotherapy she had to take. My parents were living in their nice Swiss home far from the Italian traffic and all the hassle of the re-current strikes that were bothering us. Concetta had finally retired in her home village near Venezia after spending almost 60 years of her life with my family.

Tom and my friends were the biggest joy of my life and yet I had this urge to meet new people, entertain, and to have new sexual experiences all the time.

Milano was beginning to get on my nerves because of the weather too cold in winter and too hot and humid in summer. I was ready for a change but I was too lazy too look around and evaluate other possibilities.

A dear friend of mine, a custom broker with whom Emery shared several customers, had just got the agency for a big American shipping company and was in need to hire somebody like me. He offered me a position with a higher salary than I was making, company car (smaller than the one I was driving) and a percentage on the business that I would gain. It was a big step and

I was checking this possibility talking with my friends and also with Valerio who could read the tarots cards so well. It came out that with this working contract I would have to pay taxes on my income, something that I definitely did not want to get involved with. Besides I knew that the service that Emery provided was excellent, so why would I switch to something I was not totally sure it would be successful. I decided not to take the job with a big disappointment of my friend.

Still checking the possibilities to be transferred to the U.S. with Emery I went on working trying to make it more pleasant and spending more time out of Milano as I could. I met even more people and wherever I was going I was spending the nights with different friends other than checking into expensive hotels. Eating well had always been a prerogative in my life so I was always spending more money on food than anything else.

Enio in Genova had got a son, Igor, from his girlfriend and the situation was slowly deteriorating because of their involvement with drugs. I was trying to make him change his lifestyle but it seemed I was hitting a brick wall. I knew he wanted out of that situation but apparently he was not strong enough to say "enough". They had got a loft in the old part of town, the bathroom did not have a shower or a bathtub and I was wondering how they could live in such poor sanitary conditions. At that point I kind of gave them up making sure he knew that in Milano he would have a place to stay if he ever wanted to leave Marina. I was enjoying spending time with Ettore and his wife and several times they were coming to Lugano to participate to some open functions at the beautiful local Masonic lodge.

My obsession with clothes was slowly decreasing and I had now the mania of complicated electronic wristwatches that I was buying in New York. With Fiorella we were going to the town center to roller-skate on the marble pavement under the arcades while listening to music played by sophisticated walkmans according to the fashion of the times. Tom was often spending time in Lugano, Torre del Mare and Lavarone enabling me to have friends over for dinners and also, sometimes, for tricks that I would meet at the cinema or at the very famous cruisy spot near the zoo. I met Canadians, Americans, many guys from various European countries and also a Japanese. At the Ticino river I met a gorgeous guy from Brazil who turned out to be one of the models used by Armani. He was renting a luxury apartment in Corso Venezia and had two other roommates from Long Island that were in the same business. We did party several times together and we started going to a famous restaurant in the area that was becoming very popular among the gays in Milano. Still there were no bathhouses opening in Italy while they were becoming renowned those in more liberal countries like France, Holland and Germany.

The novelty arrived in Milano with the inauguration of the One Way Club, a disco with a so-called "dark room" where everything was "happening" in a maze of cubicles adjacent to the dance floor. With Massimo we were going there at least once a week to dance and to look for different sexual emotions. If we wanted to have a fun time we were going to the Nuova Idea which still is the most pitiful disco in town with a variety of people ranging from transvestites to the older couple dancing cheek to cheek at the music of an old fashioned band. The other dance floor was for a younger crowd with very new releases of Donna Summer, Bee Gees and famous rock performers. During carnival the place was delirious because of the outrageous costumes and unbelievable people that were around.

During that summer I spent my last august at the San Carlos hotel in Pensacola because at the end of the year it closed down due to many restructuring problems that were needed. I guess the city was trying to get rid of this historical building once home to Wally Simpson and other celebrities.

2005

The usual customers had moved to the new Red Garter that was a very nice bar/disco with a cruisy poolroom and a small backyard. The new place in town was the Fancy Free in the Warrington area very well frequented by many Navy guys. Bill's parents had split up, his brother Ronnie had moved to New Orleans to take a job as a teacher and to live with his new boyfriend. Billy was just the usual mess dating, or at least trying to date, marines. He also had decided to join the Navy but he was dismissed after a few months for not openly disclosed reasons. Probably the fact that his dad was a recruiting officer had something to do with that.

The months were passing by fast and the enthusiasm for my work was diminishing because it was becoming routine. The new task force manager was now an English guy named Tony and he was coming often to Italy to supervise our sales calls and make sure we were following the scheme of the new professional selling skill. I still have several letters from him thanking for my outstanding performances and the results I was achieving.

Tony was also gay and he was getting transferred to the office in Los Angeles from London. When I started talking to him about the possibility of getting a position in the States he told me there were no chances because it would be impossible to obtain a working permit. If he could do it I didn't see any reason why I could not.

Giorgio was happily living in London and was constantly asking me to go visit him. Fortunately he was coming to Milano quite often and we would spend some time together. He was at that time very interested in the career of a merging soprano from Bulgaria that he had met in London. Through his friends in the field he was pushing for her to have an audition at the Covent Garden. Her name was Ghena Dimitrova.

It was at the beginning of 1980 when Nicki, my ex colleague, and another sales guy decided to open the Italian branch of the trucking company they had been working for as agents. They were very excited because of the high amount of goods exported to the U.K. The new office was not far from ours so I started going to see how they were doing and got to know more about road transport. Sometimes I would participate to their sales meetings giving us the opportunity to exchange leads.

My trips to the States were always more frequent and I liked Pensacola so much that for some reason I decided to spend Christmas there as a guest of my Masonic brother and agent who had in the meantime divorced from his wife.

That trip was not a very fun one. It was raining most of the time and the temperature was not as warm as I had expected. Still I managed to see my old friends from the Fiesta lounge and to meet some guys from El Paso. I remember that one night on my way home from the Red Garter two girls asked me if I would go on a three way. I accepted and we had a very strange and wild time together. It turned out they were a couple of lesbians into gay guys because, as they explained, they knew how to make love better than heterosexuals. They were both in the Navy.

During my stop over in New York I bought the usual gadgets including a very complicated electronic watch and a pair of sneakers that had not reached Europe yet. I improved also my camera buying a professional model.

Before leaving Kennedy Jimmy invited me to meet his brother who was working on the control tower. That was quite exciting looking at the planes from up there and then on the monitors while they were taxing. I was amazed to learn that the minimum amount of time to understand how to operate one position as a traffic controller varied from six months to two years. There was a lot of responsibility involved and the smallest mistake would resolve in a tragedy. That was one of the coldest winters on record. We had to board a bus to reach the plane and while we were on the bus some passengers thought we were already sitting on the plane and they were looking for the safety belts. That was funny!

Only when we became airborne and I started moving around the cabin I found out that the sister of my brother in law and her husband were sitting just three lines behind mine. That flight turned out not too boring as it usually was.

The whole year passed quickly while I was doing the usual things. Besides going to Lavarone to ski and to see my old friends Tom and I were spending some cold weekends in Lugano where I had met some new people in the downtown park and in the only gay club available. Most of my friends had married and were busy with their wives and children. The fact that I have always been a night person wasn't helping much because in the mountains after a certain hour there was nothing to do. So I would get in the car to drive to Trento to see what was going on in the park by the train station. Even there I had met some people with whom I would chat waiting for some cutie to come by.

One of the guys I had slept with a couple of years before had been stabbed to death by somebody he had met in a cinema. The murderer was never found and that was the topic of our talks during that month of September. Back in Milano we were still going to the Ticino River if the weather was nice until the end of October. Franck and Matteo were now a steady couple and they were remodeling their cute apartment just a few blocks from mine.

It was right before Christmas when Nicki invited me for dinner to tell me that their office was expanding and doing great and they were considering hiring a person to take care of their business in

England and to be a liaison with the mother company located near Birmingham.

I didn't say anything to anybody but I carefully asked Tom what he thought about living in London for a while. His response, as I had expected, was favorable.

Another two months went by without any new development until Nicki called me at the end of February to tell me that the company was ready to go ahead with the project and officially asked me if I was interested in filling that position.

I had to evaluate all the possibilities: I was going to leave a very secure job with very nice colleagues and to start a new life by myself in a city that I liked enough but not as much as Paris. The fact that Giorgio was living there was a big plus. Brighton was just at a couple of hours drive and there I really had a great time when I was going to the university. The good point was that Tom would have been in an English speaking country and probably would have "come out" of his shell and be more friendly with people.

To tell my parents about this opportunity was no big deal. I already knew that my mother would have encouraged it and my dad would not have said anything in particular.

In those years to find an apartment for rent in Milano was extremely difficult because of the government's restrictions. Most homeowners did not like to have set low rents and many flats were vacant. I took the decision to keep paying my rent and to keep my flat just in case something went wrong and we had to return to Milano. The other problem was Tom's visa. As American he could get a six months permit to live in the U.K. but then he could have some problems to get an extension. Moreover I had to give two months notice to Emery to allow them to find a replacement.

With all these things on my mind I spent a few week ends visiting friends and checking their opinions. Nobody wanted me to leave. Fiorella came up with the idea that we should marry (so her parents would stop bothering her) have a big wedding and split all the gifts and money!

The owner of the British trucking company came to Milano to meet me and to discuss my salary and lodging. We met on the day before my birthday and after a long talk I signed the contract. Now I had to write my resignation to Emery.

The conditions were extremely good. As most people know life in England was not as cheap as it was during my university years. One pound was the equivalent of 3000 lire and could not buy much. I was going to have a company car, all expenses paid, a flat in London and the net monthly salary of 2300 Lst. It was up to me to pay for the utilities. At the end of the year there would be a bonus in accordance with the good course of business. I was not going to have discounts on plane tickets but from London the cost of flights everywhere was much cheaper than from Italy.

I have always been reluctant to write a letter to resign and that time was no different. My boss was surprised and kind of upset even though he knew I had tried to get a position in the USA for years. Much to my surprise a couple of weeks later, he called me to his office and told me there was a vacancy for a salesman in Manhattan. There was no car allowance; the salary would have been competitive if compared with the American standard, two weeks paid vacation, no liquidation, no 75% discount on plane tickets! With a rent to pay in New York there was not much left and I had to decline the offer.

The last day at Emery was a Friday. I went to get pastries and Champagne for everybody and we had a little party. I was sad to leave the company and my 27 colleagues were sorry to see me go. Mrs. Testa gave me the last check together with the one of my liquidation, the equivalent of about 27.000$. There was more to come from the stock option the company was giving to all the sales staff but for that I had to wait six months.

The following Monday I started working for the Italian branch of BET with my friend and ex colleague Nicky. I knew enough about trucking service but I had a lot to learn, especially about rates and service.

Of course I had to give back the company car and use public transportation for the next two months.

In the meantime I needed to go back to Rotterdam to fix some of my teeth before moving to London. I decided to take advantage of a company truck that was going that way. The trucker was not a sexy guy at all but at least he was nice and could sustain a conversation. We left Milano on a Tuesday afternoon and headed for the tunnel of the Mont Blanc that we crossed in the evening. We stopped for the night in a big truck stop in France and the next morning, after a rich breakfast, we were on the way to Holland. My appointment was for Thursday morning at 8,30 but the truck left me at the border late on Wednesday night. On foot I crossed the border and I found a taxi that took me to a ferry that was leaving at 1am. Then I had to ride on a train to Amsterdam, wait another hour and finally board the train to Rotterdam. When I arrived at the dentist's office I was just 10 minutes early! I had not slept all night and I was kind of tired. At two I was done and back to the station to catch a train to Milano. I swore I would never do that again! I saved some money but it was not fun and my idea of finding some sexual adventure in the sleeping wagon did not work at all.

The time of my departure was approaching rapidly. It was the beginning of June when they finally gave the OK and they sent the telex with all the information about the flat the company had rented for me: it was going to be in Slough, just a few miles west of London and only three miles from Windsor castle. I remember reading the telex to Tom and trying to understand what they meant with "double glazed windows". The rent was 400 Lst. a month but that was not my concern. Nicky was going to fly with me to Birmingham and from there, after spending a couple of days as guests of the owner of the company to familiarize with the staff, she would have gone back to Milano and I would take possession of the company car and drive to my new residence. Tom was going to arrive a few days later by plane.

Upon our arrival in Birmingham they came to pick us up at the airport and after a 50 miles trip we arrived to a very nice village by the river Trent. The hotel was a very cute country house and our rooms were contiguous. We went for dinner in a very fancy restaurant and then for a chat at Mr. C.'s house. Back to the hotel Nicky and I spent another hour chatting in front of some homemade cider and somehow we ended in her room where happened what should have happened years before: we slept together. As I understood that was the first time she really experienced orgasm since her husband was definitely not a great lover and with him everything was over in a matter of minutes. I kind of felt embarrassed but in the end I was glad it happened because her emotional life had been dull for all those years. She said that was going to be our big secret and we swore not to mentioned it to anybody.

We spent almost all the next day talking about work, service, selling strategies and how we would communicate. In those days there were neither fax machines nor cellular phones. I got a medical card that would allow me to use the British medical care in case of need and a tax ID number, even though all taxes were going to be paid by the company. Josie was going to be my far away secretary and Mr. Grimes was going to send me the checks for my salary and all my expenses. They filled the trunk of my new car with paperwork, files and office equipment and while Nicky was flying back to Milano I was on the M1 driving south.

After a boring long drive I finally arrived in London in the early evening. I didn't want to search for the directions to go to Slough so I invited myself to spend the night at Giorgio's flat in Kensington, just a couple of blocks from King's Road. We were very happy to see each others and to chat about the recent events and also about work. After all now we were competitors.

We went to eat in his favorite restaurant and then we headed out to a couple of gay pubs.

Giorgio was very much involved with the opera, the ballet and classical music. He had met more artists in London than during all the years he had spent in Milano and Verona. I knew we were going to have a great time together and that was not in a sexual way.

In the morning he left for work while I was going to find out what my rented flat was like.

Slough was not that far away, just one of the first exits on the M 4 west. The town was small, nice, lots of green and parks. The flat was on the ground floor of a small two-story building with a little tiny front yard. There was one bedroom, a bathroom, a small living room and a very functional kitchen. The landlady welcomed me and she made me sign a detailed list of all the items in the flat. The furniture was certainly not in the best taste and the rest of the stuff was kind of cheap. I knew I was not going to renew the lease after the six months were over because I was sure I could find something more suitable for the same amount. After the company paid all the rent so I didn't have any ground to complain. I had some difficulties in setting up the telephone service and then I started realizing that plutocracy is not an Italian exclusivity.

It took me about one week to set everything my way and to learn my way around the area. Heathrow airport was just minutes away and Windsor castle just 3 miles south. I begged my sister to meet with Tom who had a list of items that I wanted to have shipped over. That included also the color TV, books, audiocassettes and a bunch of clothes. A truck would have delivered for me free of charge at the custom in Dover where I was going to pick them up. That was my first trip to the coast in years and my first visit to Canterbury.

Tom arrived the following week and I was glad to welcome him at the airport. Even if we don't always agree on everything and he is very stubborn I miss him a lot when he's far away. He found the flat "cute" and loved the countryside. I set up a corner of the living room as my office and started gathering all the information necessary to my work. I was going to be on the road a lot and needed detailed maps with the unbelievable myriad of streets in the city bearing the same names but one was "court", one "circle", one "lane", one "mew" and on and on. It was much more complicated than Paris.

The existing customers were in different areas but there were many potential customers to be targeted, so I started writing customer's cards and divided them by territory. I liked to do this preliminary work and have all the information together before calling the different traffic managers and arrange the actual meetings.

My color TV that I had shipped from Milano did not work in the UK because it had a different frequency (and I thought it was only a matter of plague!). I knew Tom would not survive without one so I rushed to the mall to buy one. While I was browsing I noticed that, despite the high value of the pound, prices of electronics and camera equipment were lower than those in Italy. I bought brand new stereo equipment and rushed home to install everything. The next move was to buy telephoto lens and a wide angle.

Tom arrived on schedule and he told me he had a good time on the plane chatting with an American girl who liked skyscrapers as much as he does. Hi liked the flat and we resumed our lives like we were doing in Milano but this time we had lots of new options.

My job was pleasant and easy. I was managing myself and reporting to the head office by phone almost on a daily basis. Josie, the secretary, was sending the offers to the traffic managers that I would contact in due time in order to get a trial shipment or the routing orders. It was mainly in import but somehow I managed to gain some traffic also in export. England has always been importing more goods being an isolated island and part of the commonwealth.

I was in urgent need to find a gym so I shopped around and joined a nice and clean one in the downtown area. The only problem was that to get a membership I had to be "assessed" and therefore I attended for one month to a fitness class and passed the examination. It was city owned and there was only a monthly paltry amount to pay.

I did not change my schedule from Milano. Every other day I was going there in the morning, around 9,30, and worked out for one hour. Then I was on the road to visit customers, usually about 5-6 calls a day. I had lunch on the road but usually I was back home by 4 or 5pm. The night I was cruising the cute small gay pub in Windsor or around the park downtown where I had noticed some action.

Summer was quickly coming to an end and being far north the leaves were changing color earlier. The British countryside was beautiful. We knew there was going to be a very long winter ahead but it didn't really bother us just because we were out of the Milanese routine.

My ex colleague Enrico, who had left Emery to join British Airways, was coming to London often to participate to different meetings. Usually he was staying in a hotel near Heathrow airport and very close to Slough. I had introduced him to Giorgio and all together we were going out for dinner and to the theater. Even Marie Françoise came to London on a business trip. She was now working for Lanvin in Paris and she was at the head of their buying office.

I started meeting different people especially friends of Giorgio working in the theaters. We went to several performances of ballets with Jacqueline Dupree, in a wheelchair, wife of the conductor Daniel Barenboim. Many benefits were held to raise money for muscular dystrophy research. Telly Savalas, Demis Roussos, Nana Mouskuri and other artists became part of my social life. We also met the ex king of Greece, Costantin, who was living in exile in London.

It was towards the end of 1980 when the husband of Gena Dimitrova, Giorgio, arrived by car from Germany and my friend Giorgio invited me to meet him for dinner. Although his last name was Stoykov, he was joking calling himself Mr. Dimitrova. He was an electronic engineer, very nice person, simple and extremely funny when he was telling jokes about the Russians. Being a Bulgarian he hated communism with passion and was not afraid of let everybody know. We became good friends and had long talks about art and politics. Gena finally arrived together with her secretary and pianist. Giorgio's mother had also arrived from Udine. We all met in the lobby of the Plaza and by then I knew that I had a newly found friend. She was very tastefully dressed and had a beautiful mink coat. Her manners were simple and her personality was outstanding. She was as tall as her husband. I could tell they were very much in love with each other. Married for several years they regretted not having children, so they had adopted a niece who was going to a university in Wien.

Gena had come to London because there was going to be a performance of Gioconda at the Barbican and the rehearsal was going to start on the following week. I was of course invited and I did not miss one. The cast was exceptional: Placido Domingo was Enzo, Barbara Conrad was Laura, Piero Cappuccilli (who had sang the same opera with Maria Callas at the Scala) was Barnaba. The conductor was Antonio Guadagno.

After the rehearsal we were all going to have a late dinner in different restaurants chatting like old friends, sometimes for hours. I knew that artists like to "live" at night and sleep late in the morning. No smoking was ever allowed around them. Placido's wife was part of the group and she was a very nice and intelligent lady. There was also another woman who was always joining us, some baroness Saidell, who was very fond of opera. Strange stories surrounded her life and people were questioning if she really was who she said she was.

That couples of weeks were intense. I did not get much sleep but I was very happy to be part of it. I have always some Italian bitter liquorice in my pocket and I remember being honored when Placido was asking me for some. I gave rides to the hotel to Cappuccilli and in the car he was telling me anecdotes concerning his long career. I remember seeing him in a performance of Gioconda at the Scala several years before with Callas and Irene Companeez.

The day of the performance came. That was going to be my first time at the Barbican. Wearing my tuxedo, also for a respect to the artists, the composer and the music, I found myself sitting in the very first row. The performance was stunning now that all the singers were singing with their full voice. The choir was so good that the audience asked and obtained an encore. Gena's voice was so powerful that could be heard over the orchestra and all the other singers.

The next day Giorgio gave me copies of the critics that he had meticulously collected from different newspapers: they were all very good.

Everybody had already left town except for Mr. Dimitrova who was going to drive to Germany to meet Gena in Berlin where she was scheduled to make a record for Deutsche Grammophon with the great Herbert von Karayan. Would I ever see her again?

Life resumed as usual as we were approaching the end of 1980. I was collecting some very important customers in the city and also in small towns in the south of England. The service that we were offering was good, but sometimes the operation office was making mistakes delaying or even loosing cargo in custom warehouses. The important thing was that it was not my fault. I was doing just fine and did not feel bad earning all that money.

At the gay bar in Windsor I had some eye contact with a guy my age that I thought was just gorgeous. He was wearing a sleeveless sweater, ha was about my age, a little bit taller, beautiful eyes and a killer smile. I started going there almost every night just to see if I could see him again and meet him. It was almost one month later when I saw him again, on a Saturday night. Our eyes met again and we both smiled at the same time. At that point there was no excuse but get closer and introduce us. His name was Paul, he was studying to become a lawyer and his hobby was singing.

We spent a couple of hours chatting and finally exchanged telephone numbers and the promise to get together during the week. He was sharing a flat with another gay couple in a village just a few miles away. I was, again, in seventh heaven! I wanted to meet him so bad and I had almost run out of hope to meet him.

Two days went by and I finally gave in and called him. He was rehearsing for a school production of Gilbert & Sullivan's Pirates of Pensance and he was insisting for me to go see the performance on that Saturday night. Of course that made me a very happy guy and I was sitting in the first row once again in an obscure little theater to applaud this new friend who by all means had a very good voice.

After The performance I invited him out to dinner and then we went over to his place where finally we made love for the first time and that was very nice.

We started seeing each other on a regular base and we also went out to the pub and to dance with his roommates.

My sister sent my nephew, then 17, to London because he was studying languages in high school and was in need to practice

English. I felt obliged to show him everything there was to see in the city. Of course he was not really interested in visiting museums and historical places. So he joined us a few times but he never questioned me why Paul was always around. Since he had heard so much about Terry, my ex landlady from Brighton, I took him there to meet her and to give him a tour of Kent and Sussex. He seemed to enjoy that very much. I also took him to meet my father's relatives living in Forest Row who had hosted my sister when she was studying in Aberdeen. Wilma was supposed to come to London for one week but unfortunately that never materialized.

I was noticing that Paul was acting differently when we were together and I was afraid that our friendship was developing in a big love affair. I liked him and sex was great but I did not want to commit myself to somebody else when I was living with Tom from whom I would never separate. I had to slowly let Paul go his way even though it hurt because I knew he was suffering a lot not understanding the real reason. After all these years I still think about him and I hope that the tragic events that followed in the years to come did not involve him. I'm referring to the AIDS crisis.

1980 was coming to an end. I had several choices to spend New Year's Eve and I decided to go to Brighton and stay in one of those cute gay guesthouses downtown. Giorgio was going to spend it in Udine with his family and Tom couldn't care less about partying. The weather was rather cold. I gathered a lot of food and drink supplies for Tom and left on an early afternoon to see if I could recapture the atmosphere of the times of the university.

For some reason I always liked those small gay hotels. A few times at the clubs I had met guys staying there and I had fun in several. It was so different from Italy because nobody would even question the fact that a guest was taking somebody to their room for a couple of hours or even for the whole night. That particular trip was a dive in the past, but it was a past that would not come back. Everything seemed dull. Except for a very few people that I knew I was all alone walking the streets and the lanes remembering moments, voices, faces that were not around. I did meet some people but nothing compared. The 42 club was still there with

Tony and Sidney running it. The New Curtain Club was gone and now the new club in town was the Manhattan.

I went to cruise at the end of Marine Parade, in the gardens, and there were a few old men there looking for casual sex to consume in the bushes with the fear that the police could catch them. I resolved to go to the newly opened bathhouse in Rottingdean and there I met Roger, a cute and really nice guy who had an Indian lover who was out of town.

On the 31st night I had dinner with Terry and some of her friends and then I went to dance swinging from the 42 to the Manhattan until dawn. I did not find anybody to spend the night with until I went back to the hotel where I found some "left over" sitting on the couch in front of a silent TV set.

Gino and Eric had invited me for a late lunch and at their table I saw people I had not seen in years.

January was a very cold month with snow, rain and fog. The most funny thing was that one-day the weather was so bad that on the news the reporter said: "The sea is rough, all the ships are in the ports, the airports are closed…the continent is cut off". No need to comment that sentence!

At the end of January I had to go to Milano for a business meeting. The night before my flight I had a strange dream: I waked up around 3,30 a.m. like I had felt an earthquake and the whole room was shaking. I had a bad feeling and somehow my thought went to Enio in Genova.

I arrived in Milano and went to check the condition of my apartment, then I drove to see my parents. My mother had always a different friend staying there, this time it was Rosita from Genova. It was her who gave me the bad news: Enio had hanged himself during the night of January 27th, the same day of his 33rd birthday. One of my best and dearest friends was no more. My waking up at precisely 3,30 a.m. was his way of saying goodbye. I knew his son Igor was going to miss him a lot but I didn't feel sorry for Marina who had pushed him to commit such a dramatic supreme act. I called his parents to give my condolences but I did not want to go to his funeral. Only his body was there, Enio was already somewhere else.

Nicki was glad to see me.

We had a couple of important meetings at the office and we went to visit some customers that were decision makers for goods going to England. Business was great because it had increased by a good 30%.

The day before my return to London I called all my friends and we all had a big dinner at the gay restaurant downtown. Rosa was the only one missing because she had a baby girl and was now living with her companion. Massimo promised to come visit me in the near future providing I would get a ticket for a musical he wanted to see.

Back in England I wanted to know some different people and I joined a club for singles called "Nixit". We would meet once a month in a different pub, drink, chat, get to know each other and eventually date. Of course it was a heterosexual club and the ages varied from 20 to 60, which didn't bother me a bit. So I became friend with Olga, a nice lady who was living with her cat and a canary in a flat by the Barbican. She wasn't sexually my type but she had a good sense of humor and we had some fun time together.

Another was living downtown, just a couple of blocks from Trafalgar Square. One day passing by her flat I rang the bell, she invited me in and offered some tea. It was one of those things with women; I could never succeed because I was not straight forward for my shyness I guess. That time she was sitting so close to me that I took the courage and started kissing and touching her. It worked! We did it on the sofa and it seemed she didn't have enough. That was the only time. I would never have sex with her again even if she tried hard to invite me over again.

The third lady I started dating was from Austria, married a British, divorced, about 30 years old. Her name was Inge.

She was a clever and intelligent girl and her flat was filled of interesting items, mostly of sexual pertinence. It was only during the third visit after I made some lasagne the Italian way that we relaxed on the sofa and she started to question my sexual orientation that, to prove her wrong, I jumped on her and went on fucking for a couple of hours. She finally admitted I made her happy and then she went to the store to buy some chocolate bars to regain strength to do it again. These kind of things were very flattering but I had to decline and took a rain check.

Nixit was fun for a while because it allowed me to meet different people, mostly lonely people. There were mostly women and the few men were all heterosexual and absolutely out of any sexual temptation.

Giorgio and I resumed going to the musicals, the operas and the ballets. Gena had sent us a copy of her German recordings and she invited us to go to the opening of the Arena in Verona during the summer season of 1982 with her singing Gioconda and Pavarotti as Enzo.

The winter was cold and seemed longer than usual. Fortunately I made a close encounter in one of those gay cinemas in Soho with a cute guy from Australia who was in London studying to become a doctor. We didn't have a place to go and it was too squalid to do something in the cinema, so we got a room in one of the many hotels in the area. That was my first time with an Aussie. We both had a very good time. Regrettably he was going to relocate in Newcastle in March. He is the one that told me for the very first time about a disease that was hitting the gay community in the USA. They did not have a name for it yet but it seemed it was affecting the cells of the immune system. It was the AIDS virus.

Jokes about the "gay" virus were spreading rapidly because people did not understand then what was causing it and how it spread around. But people were dying from it and apparently the science could not come out with a solution.

Most guys gave up the use of poppers thinking that was the cause. For sure we knew it had started in America. I remember going to a disco in Old Brompton Road, typical gay section of town, with an American friend of mine. Chatting with some guys they figured out my friend was from New York and at that point they refused to talk and left. Everything became anti American. Posters of bathhouses disappeared from the walls and all the imported gadgets and paraphernalia remained unsold in the pride stores.

Doctors gave lectures with an attendance never seen before. Very few people kept going on with their promiscuous lifestyle and even I started cutting down. It appeared that the important thing was not to touch saliva and semen in any way. Giorgio was well aware about the situation but he still was picking up cute guys right and left.

A friend of his from Udine had come to visit and it was his first time in England. Giorgio was just working too much and asked me to show him around. So I met Gianluigi, a nurse, and we started a friendship that is still going on in these days. He was in town for one week and I made sure he would see the countryside that is the best asset of the U.K. I also took him to Brighton and we stayed in another cute gay hotel where people are so friendly. I learned he had met Giorgio at the hospital in Udine and assisted him during an appendix operation. He had got the idea that there could be some feeling and that was the reason of his trip. It turned out he was wrong. Giorgio was not going to fall in love very easily because he was too demanding on his partner. Gianluigi went back to Italy saddened by the outcome of his visit but happy to have found a new friend.

There was an area that I had never visited before so one-week end I took off for Wales. Cheltenham was a place I wanted to see and, if possible, visit a lawyer I had met in Brighton during my university years.

It was a small town and it was not difficult to trace my friend who was very surprised to see me. He hardly remembered meeting each other at the New Curtain Club. We went to have lunch in a typical pub in the country and somehow it came to my mind the episode that occurred in Torre del Mare when the witch wanted to teach us black magic. He drove to one of the oldest churches in the country and with the help of the pastor they started going through old registries. The research lasted almost one hour but we were all stunned to read that in the year of grace 1665 on such day Ruth Mc Callum was burned at the steak for witchcraft. That could not be the fruit of our imagination after all. I couldn't wait to tell my sister and nephew.

Back in London I got a call from my Aussie friend who had moved to Newcastle and wanted me to pay him a visit there. I had some relatives living in that area that I had not seen since the 50's in Genova. I gave the matter a consideration, but I didn't fell like driving because with the speed limits and all it would have taken forever. So on a Friday afternoon I got on the fast train and when I arrived I found my friend waiting at the station. We didn't go out that night but were awake until late making love in his room reserved for the hospital personnel. In the morning, after a rich continental breakfast, he gave me a tour of the city and its park. The evening was spent meeting my father's cousin and his wife at their house for dinner. I knew they were involved with the Jehovah's witnesses but I had no idea that they were trying to convert us during that short visit. We finally left with an excuse, went to sin in a gay pub, and retired for the night in his bed to sleep together. Regrettably that was the last time I ever saw him because I lost his phone number. On Sunday afternoon I boarded the train to go back to London and we were stranded in the middle of the country for more than three hours for lack of power. To arrive in the city after midnight it's really a tragedy: no public transportation is available except for cabs.

We were at the beginning of the sixth month of lease for the flat in Slough and I didn't want to renew it. With Tom we agreed that it was time to move to the city. Through some friends at the Masonic lodge I was going to I met a brother who had a flat for rent in Richmond on Thames. There was no need for references and the fact that the rent was going to be paid by my company was a more than sufficient guarantee. I went to check the place out. It was a spacious two-bedroom apartment on a split level right on Kew Road. From one of the bedroom's window we could see the little pagoda in the botanical garden. The asking price for me was just 50 Lst. more than the one in Slough. I couldn't let this opportunity go by without grasping it and I signed a lease for six months. There was absolutely no objection to my decision from my corporate office. My landlady came over with the list of items and we checked everything. There was just one cup missing because it had been broken and I had to pay 2 Lst. to have it replaced.

At this point the gym I was going to became too far and I had to look around for another one. My American friend told me to check one in Kensington that it was rumored to be used by Lady Diana. These premises were much more upscale and the guys were less scraggly looking but not much cleaner because I saw them sweating a lot but a few were taking showers after working out.

Some nice evenings I was still going to the pub in Windsor and on the way back I would stop at the park in Slough just to see if I could get some. I met a really cute guy named Mark who was cheating on his girlfriend. We fooled around in the car and apparently he liked me so much that he confided he had this fantasy of having a three way. He was serious because a couple of weeks later he called me to ask if I could meet them at her house. As much as I wanted to I had to decline because I had a sore throat and was probably catching a cold or, even worse, the flu.

With the people of Nixit I was still in touch and going to their meetings. Living in town I started to explore different pubs and discos, even straight. One area that I found fascinating was the park of Hempstead Heath located on a hill. After dark there was a lot going on and it was not uncommon to see naked guys walking or even running around. I had some casual sex there but I was always very cautious whenever I was getting approached by somebody I could hardly see his face. The thought of meeting a Jack the ripper was always on my mind.

I had a sales call near Piccadilly Circus and when I was on my way out I saw a cute guy going inside a notoriously gay pub. It was after 5 and I went in just to see what kind of crowd was there. My prey was chatting with a couple of queens one of which started staring at me making me feel uncomfortable. I decided to be nice, smiled and went closer to their table, introduced myself and started answering to their numerous questions since they had gathered I was not British. The cute guy's name was Michael, he was working for an electronic company had had just moved to London from Liverpool. I called Tom to inform him I had a business dinner and invited Michael to an Indian restaurant. That was the beginning of a new relationship that would involve me for the remaining of my permanence in the country. Michael was a nice, sincere, intelligent and sexy guy. We spent several weekends together on the coast and he got so involved that he formed the idea that eventually we would live together. He knew that I was bound to Tom but somehow he thought that I would live him for good that I knew it was never going to happen.

The news on the AIDS virus was becoming more specific. It appeared that it was spreading rapidly and that soon Europeans would be at risk. It seemed the best way to have sex was to be safe in any way and to avoid any contact with body fluids. With Michael we got used to wear condoms but we were not sure that would help. After being infected with gonorrhea and syphilis I was checking my blood at least every six months. Even "herpes" that had been the fear of the 70's was now forgotten. The bad jokes about the gay virus did not make anybody laugh and the way people were having sex was slowly changing. News came that the big American chain of bathhouses "club baths" was closing down all over the States. Jimmy and Dairo told me the situation was not as dramatic as they pictured it, while some groups were blaming the government for testing some unknown virus to decimate the gay population. At that point it was "the gay disease" and it seemed that heterosexual people were immune to it. That was a fertile ground for the bigot American evangelists that would swear God was punishing us for our lascivious lifestyle. The media responded with more information and advices on how to protect us, and even the TV started to broadcast explicit announcements about risky sexual encounters. I know for sure that the gay community split: there were those that were sure that AIDS would never affect them and kept doing business as usual, those that became abstinent overnight, those that would masturbate in a group but without touching each other and the younger guys that were just "coming out" who didn't know any better and were tricked by guys that had nothing to loose to have any kind of sex. It was inevitable that with the modern means of fast traveling the disease was going to spread worldwide while the scientists were warning that life expectancy for somebody "HIV-positive" was reduced to a few months without any cure in sight. That was the end to an era.

Talking with Giorgio I knew he was quite preoccupied and I was sure he was taking all the possible precautions. He had recently made a long trip in the U.S. driving from coast to coast on vacation. At a certain point "poppers" was blamed for the epidemic. I had used it in the past, not too often, but I was kind of worried and I threw away the half empty bottle I still had.

Going to a disco on Old Brompton Rd. in London with my friend from New York we started chatting with some guys. As soon as they found out my friend was American they got worried and left. AIDS was still known as the "American disease"!

In the meantime my work was going great. Every two weeks I was getting my huge salary and I was going on shopping spree buying electronics and photo equipment. I was dedicating some weekends to taking pictures at Kew Gardens, Brighton and even the queen while she was in some parade.

With Giorgio we were never missing the premiere of an opera, ballet and musical. Often one or more members of the royal family were sitting in the audience. At a benefit foe the muscular dystrophy hosted by Jaqueline Dupres we went to dinner afterwards with Telly Savalas, Demis Roussos and the ex king of Greece, Constantin. Gena Dimitrova and her husband were coming often to London and it was always a pleasure to spend some time together. He was always telling jokes about the Russian regime.

2002

My landlord was also a Mason and he introduced me to his Masonic lodge. A few times I went to the Grand Lodge of England that was meeting for ritual dinners after the usual works. The Grand Master was the duke of Norfolk, cousin of the queen. Those rituals were very solemn, not at all like the more casual held in Italy. It was nice to wear the tuxedo so often.

With Michael everything was going great but I was not in love with him and there were days that I would not see him giving different excuses. I had found a parking lot on the north loop where there was some action and I would stop there every now and then just to have some occasional "safe" sex. In that case I would spend a quiet evening at home without the pressure of going to the gay pubs.

I have always been an admirer of Glenda Jackson who made such good movies like "Women in love" and "Sunday bloody Sunday" so it came like a pleasant surprise when I noticed that the local theater in Richmond had scheduled a play by Botho Strauss with Glenda in the leading role. I didn't like the play tat much but she was great. After the performance I went to one of the two gay clubs in the area and while I was chatting with a bodybuilder about a rich diet to make me gain a few pounds, Ms. Jackson came in for a drink! I resisted only a few minutes and then I had to end my chat with the guy to go and compliment her for her work and I was also bold enough to offer her a drink. She was really pleasant and I had the opportunity to spend a couple of quality hours with one of my favorite stars.

The winter was cold and snowy but the spring brought new life to the trees and all the plants were in bloom. With Tom we were going often to Kew Gardens across the street where I was taking many pictures using the telephoto and the wide angular lens. Brighton and sometimes Bormouth were my favorite spots during the weekends when I would drag Michael and stay in cute gay motels meeting other couples. At the beginning of June I had to go to Italy for work so I invited my Austrian friend from Nixit to join. It was supposed to be more a courtesy invitation but she decided to come so I had to "play" straight for the whole week. We stayed in my apartment in Milano and then we joined my sister and Bruno in Torre del Mare. I realized that the girl was acting more strange than usual and I gathered she wanted to have more sex with me. But twice was enough and I was not going for a third round. She ended up leaving two days before me and that was the last time that I saw and hears from her.

Summer brought the opening of the Wimbledon tennis contest and also a great heat that was unusually humid for London. This was the first time that I went to swim in the Channel and that I would go to Hide Park to take sun in my bathing suit. Giorgio was always too busy with his work and lately he had got involved with a cute young guy that he was calling "Pinocchietto". He was meeting most of his occasional friends at the theater because they were sharing the common passion for the opera and the arts. He was expecting the visit of a friend from Udine but he didn't have the time to entertain him during the week so he asked me if I could show him around. Gianluigi was a nice and cute nurse that had taken care of Giorgio while he was in the hospital for an appendix operation a couple of years back. We became really good friends and we still see each other once in a while or just chat on the phone frequently. Thanks to me he got to see the principal museums in London, some countryside with ancient castles and, of course, Brighton, where we had a brief sexual affair.

The month of August was approaching and with that the slow season for all the shipments coming and going to Italy. It was time to take my vacation. Tom was going to stay in London while I was going to fly to New York and Pensacola to enjoy the beach and see my friends. Tom's visa was also coming to an end at the end of October and I didn't know how we could renew it or if we could.

This was a shorter trip, just twenty days. The price of the ticket from the UK was exceptionally cheap considering this time I couldn't get any reduction. After spending a few days in the village at Dairo's apartment I went on to Florida to find out that my favorite hotel, the San Carlos, had been closed. My dear friend Tom insisted for me to stay at his house. This time I rented a fancy Lincoln Continental and I did the usual beach life. It was during this time that I started going to the gay beach. It was about 4 miles longer but I felt more at home with guys wearing the same bathing suits we wear in Europe. The nightlife was still hopping and the fear of AIDS didn't seem to be very strong. Everybody was just having sex as usual. Bill was happy to see me but he had become more of an alcoholic. I met some cute guys and Michael was soon forgotten.

When I got back to London I found out that one of my best customers had been lost thanks to the poor service that the home office had supplied. That was really infuriating since I had worked hard to get him. Thinking about the cold winter approaching I started forming the idea of going back to Italy for a while. Tom visa was not going to be renewed and he could certainly not remain in the country illegally. I talked it over with Nicki who agreed I could go back. The business had increased 70% while I was in the UK and they could be satisfied.

Going back home one afternoon I got stopped by the police because I was 8 miles over the speed limit on Kew Road. I was not in the mood to waist time and I told the cop to send the fine home once he would stop playing with the cute Japanese gadget that detected the speed. The notice that I had to appear in the Richmond court sometimes in September arrived to my flat a couple of weeks later!

That was the last drop. I called the owner of the company and told him I was resigning. He didn't want to accept it but I was firm about it, so I made the necessary arrangements to have my stuff shipped back to Milano.

I promised Michael that I would be back within a few weeks but I already knew that I was lying. I would never see him again.

I had to leave the company car at the head quarter in Stock on Trent, and on a hot hazy day at the end of august our British adventure ended on a plane to Malpensa.

My apartment was waiting for us but my landlord told me he could not renew the lease because he had to leave the flat he was renting. To find a place in those days in Milano was really difficult. Fortunately my sister was remodeling a unit on the forth floor of her building and she said I could have it for a reasonable rent. I had plenty of money not to worry about getting a job immediately so I spent a couple of months following the remodeling and buying appropriate furniture. I decided everything was going to be white: the walls, the high ceilings and all the furniture. I had also enough space to put to use the fancy bed that Marika had given me. I also had a wide terrace overlooking the street and in the city that was a very important asset and the envy of those that didn't have one. In summer it was possible to sit outside and also eat there.

The big move happened at the beginning of November when the days were shorter and really cold. In a corner of the kitchen there were some water and heating pipes exposed from floor to ceiling that I covered with hundred of cans of soda and beer adding some color to the white cabinets. It was odd but it looked "original" and people loved it.

We had a small house warming party and I got some nice presents like a new set of dishes, pots and various tools but my favorite was some bronze silverware that Franck, Matteo and Rosa gave me.

At that point I had to try to do something about my wish of going to the States. I got two tickets and flew to New York with Tom to explore our possibilities. Pensacola was my choice and also the place where I knew most people. Bill's father had a small car for sale and I decided to buy it because without transportation it would really be impossible to get around. I had several copies of my curriculum and I started looking around for some job in the field that I was most familiar with. My visa was good for six months. This was the first time that Tom was back in his homeland since 1972!

We stayed at a cheap motel in the west side of town. During the day I was going around to see if somebody wanted to give me a chance without a working permit. That was even harder than what I had imagined. My old friend who was also the agent for Emery introduced me to a Mr. Suggs who owned a selling point for the best vacuum cleaners money could buy, Kirby. He was impressed by my knowledge and decided to put me in his sales force. There was a small monthly salary plus a good commission for every vacuum cleaner sold. I decided to give it a try and went to look for an apartment to rent. Everything was considerably cheap. I found a nice place at the Rain tree apartment complex. Except for the kitchen the unit was, of course, unfurnished. So I went to rent some furniture and at the flea market I bought a color TV and all the necessary items that we needed. At night I was going to the usual clubs. The Red Garter had burned down but a new and much nicer had been open just a few blocks down the main street. The San Carlos Hotel had been definitely closed and its usual crowd had "moved" to the new bar. The Fancy Free was now the alternative place offering a bar, a disco and an annex restaurant.

The work was not exactly what I thought it would be. We were meeting early every morning, board a van, go to a specific area of town and try to give free demonstrations of the prodigious machine we wanted to sell. Most people didn't want to talk to us; some were interested just because they wanted a carpet cleaned for free. Those that wanted to buy it did not have the cash or enough credit to qualify. Seldom one of us was lucky enough to find the proper customer. During the first week I had not sold one single vacuum. The second week went better because I managed to sell one. After filling up all the papers, two days later our secretary explained that the customers didn't have enough good credit so the sale was voided.

After two months I had sold only five units and the commissions were not even enough to pay one-month rent. I started getting worried because I didn't see how we could make a living and the money that I had brought over was not going to be enough to sustain us for another couple of months. So I had to take the decision of giving up the thought of finding something in Pensacola. We lost the 400$ deposit for the apartment because the lease was for 6 months, returned the furniture to the rental place and on a sunny afternoon we started driving west to see our dear friend Martha in San Antonio.

Interstate 10 is a straight boring highway. Driving against sun it's one of the worse things to do because for at least two hours the sun is low on the windshield. We stopped in New Orleans, as I wanted to show that city to Tom, and the next day we were in Texas on the way to see Martha, where we arrived late in the afternoon.

That was a really warm welcome. We spent many hours chatting about our friends, us, our plans and remembering the jokes that we played in Milano. Tom knew the city well because he had been there in boot camp. He was at ease with Martha and her children since he had met them before.

Forgetting our problems we spent a couple of days going around in town. The surprise came on the third day when Martha, who was in the States on a year-to-year VIP visa, proposed Tom to marry her so she could get a green card. The idea was for them to marry and then they would get a divorce and she would marry me so that I could get a green card myself. I knew this wouldn't work and it was obvious that Tom would never agree to something like that. On her knees she was begging him to marry! The situation was not sustainable and we decided to leave the next day.

Trying to reconnect Tom with his family I drove through Texas, Arkansas and to Memphis. The city had changed a lot since we where there last. The main point of interest was Mud Island on the Mississippi river. Still Tom refused to go see his relatives. He only condescended to make a phone call and finally had a long conversation with his ant giving her all the information and his address in Milano. I must point out that in those days the caller ID was not an option therefore calling from a public phone in town or calling from Europe did not make any difference.

Leaving Memphis we headed towards the East coast. Tom was driving as we were approaching Washington when, suddenly, a tire blew up scaring the shit out of us.

We visited DC and headed up to Philadelphia and New York City. The money was almost running out and I didn't want to call my parents to ask for a wire transfer since I didn't want them to know about my failure.

The only possible and cheap place was the YMCA. While Tom was staying in to watch TV I started driving around looking for a travel agency to buy the one-way tickets to Milano and to find a place where I could sell my car.

In Queens I saw an agency and when I went to check on the flights I saw that the owner was looking at my car. He asked me what I was going to do with it if I was going back to Italy and when I told him it was for sale, he offered to buy it for his wife who was looking for the same two doors Lincoln Continental. I got the tickets plus another 1200$ for the car! Considering the fact that I had paid it 800 $ I was very satisfied. After all I bought it in Pensacola but I sold it in New York where everything was supposed to be more expensive.

Two days later we were on the TWA flight back to the old continent.

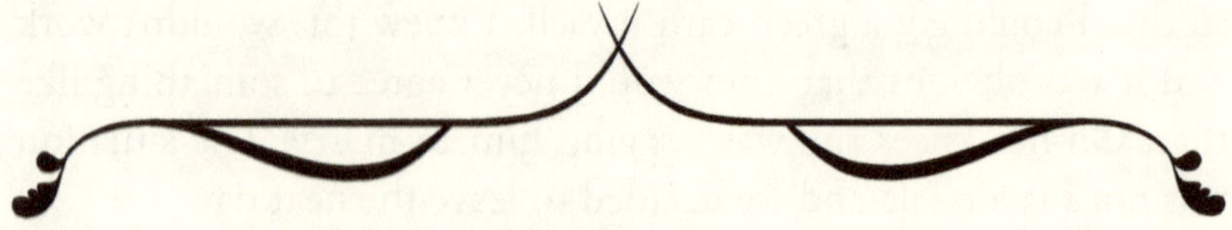

Chapter 18

Milano

At this point I had the task to look for a job in the same field. It seemed easy enough because of all the people I knew but I didn't want to ask around so I relayed on the newspaper. And there it was: a company affiliated to Alitalia handling domestic air and truck cargo was looking for an experienced sales manager for the north of Italy. I called, set an appointment and my curriculum plus good references did the rest: after the holidays spent partly in Lugano and in Lavarone skiing I started my new job with an excellent salary and a diesel company car. My new boss was a very easy person to get along with and was very confident that I would help keeping the existing customers and gain more.

With offices all over Italy and its islands we had a very efficient net of trucks and space booked on all the major Alitalia domestic flights. It was easy to establish a system like Emery with leads and follow-ups. The owner was in Roma but he was coming to see us often and was always open to new ideas that could improve the service. My work was totally autonomous and I had to spend very little time at the office enabling me to go to the gym, and do all the things that a normal 9 to 5 job would not allow.

A different group had bought Giorgio's ex company and he called me to ask if we had a job for Piera, his ex secretary. Incidentally we were looking for one and she joined bringing her valid experience. We became very good friends.

Tom had adapted to the new flat but he would never leave it I think because he didn't want to meet the neighbors walking up and down the stairs. I was taking him over to my parents' house in Lugano or up to Lavarone and leave him there for weeks at the time. That was giving me to opportunity to invite people over for dinner and also take home some tricks that occasionally I would meet at the usual cruisy spots or in some clubs. A guy that I was seeing often was a Canadian designer who had a beautiful body and could talk about many subjects of common interest. I was slowly changing and it wasn't just sex I was looking for but guys that had some brain and not only good looks.

My job took me also to Torino where I had a very nice female colleague. After making the usual sales calls I started going there in one of the first Italian bathhouses. The place was not as fancy as some of the American clubs but it was the beginning of the "liberalization" in the country. In Milano they had still to come, so for a quickie or just to find someone the One Way and the Stivale were the places that had a dark room where everything was going on.

I had joined a different gym, closer to the flat, very well equipped and frequented by nice people. My brother in law nephew was going there too. He was young, nice looking and smart and it was rumored to be gay. Living in the same building I was always hoping that one day he would ring my bell and…but it was happening only in my fantasy. Eventually he met a nice girl and started a family.

Giorgio was coming to Milano frequently for shopping and also for work. It was always a pleasure to see him and spend some quality time together. Ghena and her husband were also in town often due to her engagements at La Scala. This time she was reversing for "I Lombardi alla prima crociata" under the direction of Gabriele Lavia, a famous Italian actor. I went to several reversals and she gave me two tickets for the premiere. For the occasion I invited my sister who was very impressed and we were both sitting in the royal stall next to Vally Toscanini and other famous people. After the performance we walked to Ghena's dressing room and after she was through signing autographs and changing we all went to a restaurant for dinner.

A few weeks later with Massimo we went back to La Scala to see another memorable performance of Montserrat Cabaille'. After several "encore" they covered the stage with a rain of white roses.

With Rosa, Franck, Matteo and the other friends we were often going to see movies of a certain level like Pasolini, Fassbinder, Jodorowsky and others. It was always a pleasure to discuss the plot.

With Ettore and his wife we were often going to the meetings at the Lugano Lodge that were usually held on a Sunday morning. After the ritual work we were entertained by a fancy banquet.

Once in a while I was seeing Rino who was always working for the Lotto. One night, out to dinner with him, we noticed that Valerio (the astrologer, was sitting at a nearby table. We joined him and ended up in his studio chatting about horoscopes, tarot cards and magic. I told him I was a member of an esoteric Masonic Lodge and he said he always wanted to join the secret society but he needed somebody to introduce him. That was easy enough. I gave him the printed modules and introduced him to Pietro who was the general secretary for the Milano district. During the three months that was necessary for him to be admitted, we became quite good friends. He was working in a bank but after 5pm he was going to the studio to read tarots by appointment. For each reading he was charging 50.000 Lire, the equivalent of 30 $. He asked me to sit at the front desk, admit the people and collect the money. He offered me 10.000 Lire each. Sometimes he would see even 20 persons between 5 and 7,30 pm. I gladly accepted and my salary almost doubled. He had a program in a private TV on Sunday morning and I also started appearing with him on TV. Moreover he was writing a book about tarots and offered Tom the chance to gain some money designing the illustrations. Tom has always been a good draughtsman.

Valerio certainly didn't spare the money that he was making from this business on the side. The best restaurants in town, best hotels, and the Milano jet set were his usual hangouts. His initiation to the Masonic lodge occurred after almost four months and made him a very happy guy. Ettore did not really approve his admission but he was going to stand by and see how Valerio was going to act in that contest.

One evening while I was working at his studio he told me that a dear friend of his, a big shot at Alitalia, had offered him a free flight for two to any city in Europe. He wanted me to choose the city and to go with him on the trip. Still behind the iron curtain was Budapest that I always wanted to visit after hearing so much about it from my grandmother who had been there on her honeymoon. I figured that since Valerio didn't speak any language other than Italian, he wanted me to go along so I could translate, just as a regular friend.

We left on a Friday from Milano to Wien and then to Hungary. Over one hour to get out of the airport for the long socialist formalities, and we were in old Buda, just across from Pest on the other side of the Danube. The city was beautiful in his decadence. It seemed like Paris but with considerably less traffic, lights and people around. The evening was cold. We checked in at the Marriott and went walking around looking for the only gay bar in town.

It was easy and safe to walk. The people were very nice and courteous and if I may say so the men were very good looking. It was like being in Moscow but it seemed more liberal. The club was just a regular bar/coffee place with only men. A guard was standing by the door and was coming inside every now and then to make sure nobody was behaving in an intimate way. Everybody was polite. Two guys noticed we were foreigners and started chatting with us, or, better, with me, in German. For a while I was translating to Valerio almost everything that was said, but when they started with more personal questions I didn't find necessary to report everything that was said. Basically they told me about a very old hotel across the river where, in the basement, there were some kinds of Roman baths. They wanted us to check it out the next day.

Saturday morning we went to visit the cathedral to see the famous crown of Saint Stephan. In the oldest part of town there were several cute shops with typical artifacts but nothing that would really attract my attention. The Hilton was built on top of some ancient roman ruins and that we found to be very odd and out of place. For lunch we had to go eat at the "Apostoloc", the restaurant famous for the best "goulash" in the world. I must recognize that it really was.

Walking around we casually arrived in front of the Hotel Gellert, the one that those guys had mentioned. I asked Valerio if he was up for a visit to this famous bathhouse and he agreed to check it out. I think he was horny and he was thinking to have some fun there.

The place was stunning: we went to the male section that had several locker rooms, little stalls enclosed by curtains for massages, one large pool with cold water, one with warm water and one with hot water. Gorgeous mosaic was covering floors, walls and high vaulted ceilings and fountains and waterfalls were everywhere. To cover ourselves we had only a thin white cotton towel for the front part while the back was uncovered. As soon as the towel was getting wet it was obviously becoming transparent therefore useless to wear. Nobody was cruising but there was an obvious exchange of looks and I noticed also that many exchanged brief written notes. I saw the guys that we had met the night before and we started to chat again while taking a tour of the place. They told me that was just a meeting ground but that nobody would dare touching somebody or even trying to openly talking about sex. The notes were addresses and phone numbers. Everybody was connecting there for a more relaxed and private encounter at home. That's where they wanted me to go for a three way. They were handsome, tall and very nice, how could I lose such an adventure? The problem was to tell Valerio. He didn't mind but he didn't want to remain alone and insisted for coming to their apartment and wait there. As embarrassing that that could be we had to agree. So while we were having sex in their room, he was in the living room having a drink and waiting for me to be done. He was not in a good mood for the rest of that day but didn't say a word.

We spent Sunday morning visiting a silly museum and walking in the city. After lunch we went to the airport to catch the flight back to Milano.

During the rest of the month Valerio was acting strange. He didn't even show up at the Masonic meeting. But then he called me up because his friend had given him another two free tickets on Alitalia but this time the destination was going to be London. I didn't really want to go. It seemed that Valerio was after me sexually and he was definitely not my type. Tom suggested I should go so I could visit my friends there. We left on a Friday and the same evening we were dining with Giorgio and staying at the Grosvenor hotel near Piccadilly Circus.

I had arranged, at my expenses, to go to Brighton the next day. Gino prepared a rich lunch and Eric fixed a wide variety of desserts. Terry was very happy to see me and Roger showed me his new home Tudor style.

Everything went smooth until Sunday when I overheard Valerio telling Giorgio how much he had paid for the plane tickets. It was obvious that the big shot at Alitalia did not offer the trips to Budapest and London. This was just a move of Valerio to stay close to me as much as possible.

Back in Milano I told him I was quitting and asked him not to call me again. There was nothing I wanted to do with him sexually, we could be good friends (and Masonic brothers) but that was all.

The next two weeks went by and I did not get any phone call. Then he started calling Piera at my office. The warm season had started early and with the usual group we resumed our weekends at the river.

Probably mad because I wasn't calling him back, Valerio got all upset and started calling me at any time during the day and the night. I got so annoyed that I had to unplug the phone. Suddenly during a sunny Sunday afternoon I heard some noise coming from the street, like a car crash. Much to my surprise, looking out of the window, I saw Valerio driving his Alfa Romeo into the side of my company car parked by the sidewalk!

Tom tried to calm me down when he noticed how furious I was. I grabbed some cans of beans, the first ammunitions I could find, rushed outside the building and waited for Valerio to come back from around the block. After the third can he stopped his car, rolled down half way the driver's window and started to scream something. At that point I had grabbed the window, broke it, open the door and pulled the key out of the ignition. After forcing him out of the car pulling the new hair he had recently transplanted on his head, I obliged him to fill up and sign the papers of the insurance that determined he was fully responsible for the accident.

The whole sequence had lasted only a few minutes but it didn't go unnoticed by several of my neighbors. Fortunately I didn't give a damn about that.

It was the end of the "Valerio era". He didn't dare to show up at any Masonic meeting after that episode nor he called me again. I heard from Rino that he had manifested the idea of performing some bad magic ritual against me, which made me really laugh.

I was concentrating more on my job that was going so well that my boss gave me a big raise that compensated for the money I was not making on the side anymore.

My sister was going to spend the usual month of June in Torre del Mare and Tom went with her leaving me free ground at the apartment. That was a hot month and I knew July would even be hotter, but that's what I loved: windows open, breeze through, enjoying the terrace and having occasional friends met at the clubs or at the river. Something more had been discovered about AIDS and we knew we couldn't have sex without a condom. Poppers had been totally banned. Everybody was paying attention not to come in touch with any body fluid and that included the saliva. Kissing and oral sex were not considered safe and a great care was taken after each sexual encounter in cleaning and washing up. Some bad news was coming from the USA about people dying but it had not really hit Europe yet.

I was planning my trip to Pensacola, as usual, and this time I had to pay for the ticket in full since I didn't have any discount on the airlines.

Tom was going to spend July and August with my parents in Lavarone thus giving me a peace of mind because I didn't want him to be in the city all by himself. Milano is totally deserted during the month of August and 90% of the stores and restaurants are closed.

When I got to the airport I spent sometimes with my ex colleagues and they introduced me to the manager of TWA who upgraded my flight to business class. That was nice because I could arrive in New York all rested.

And so it happened, I arrived at Dairo's apartment around five, took a shower, and we went off to dinner with Jimmy and his new boyfriend Claudio.

I enjoyed those few days in Manhattan. Went shopping, explored new clubs, met some nice guys at Uncle Charlie's and walked all over.

The atmosphere was changed, the bathhouses had closed down, the Village was still festive but it seemed that everybody was more cautious.

They were shooting a gay movie with Al Pacino with scenes in the Mineshaft, a notorious club on Christopher Street. Some gays ruined the scenes by running naked in front of the cameras and that was in the news. The movie had a discreet success and it was titled "Cruising".

I flew to Pensacola where my old friend Tom hosted me and I started my beach life. Bill was living in Orlando with his temporary boyfriend but Jack was in town organizing weekends with different cuties on his condo in Perdido.

It was sad to see the big hotel San Carlos closed down. I started going to the gay beach that in those days was very nice and surrounded by high dunes. The people were so friendly there. On the way back to town I would stop at the Round Up for a drink and then to the new Red Garter for some fun.

One night I started chatting with this guy named Stephan and finally he invited me to go to his house. He was living out of town, east on I-10, and he asked me to follow him. He was driving a Jugo and his speed was not very high. We kept going and going for over half an hour. I was ready to turn around and leave him when he finally exited in Crestview: we had been driving for over 40 miles and at that point I realized that when an American was saying: "it's near" it could be quite a long way. But it was worth it. He was a nice handsome guy with a sculptured body. We had extremely safe sex. He told me his best friend had died of AIDS just a couple of months before. That was the first time that I heard that somebody in the area had been affected.

A couple of nights later at the Fancy Free I met two young twin brothers with red hair and we had a threesome in their apartment. That was another interesting experience. Until I came to the States I had not realized how many gay siblings there are around.

It's always a pleasure to go on vacation but time is always flying and it's time to go back home and to start the usual routine.

This time there was a surprise: Gena and her husband were going to stay in Milano for two months. She was going to be Turandot in the Zeffirelli's production for the opening of La Scala season. Placido Domingo was going to be the prince. With the exception of Piero Cappuccilli and Barbara Conrad, the singers were going to be together again. That also meant that Giorgio would come to Milano often.

Now that the "cyclone" Valerio was gone, and he also had dropped off the Masonic lodge, I had more time to dedicate to my friends and to the arts. With Franck, Matteo Rosa and Massimo we were going to see old good movies, to the theater to see funny comedies and also to see my favorite pop star Ornella Vanoni.

It was during a rehearsal that Giorgio told me his company wanted to open a branch in New York City and asked me if I still wanted to move to the States. He had mentioned my name to his boss who was also the owner who wanted to set up a meeting in Firenze at his headquarters.

Of course I said I would be very interested but a few weeks passed without hearing about the subject and I didn't want to push and solicit the issue.

Ten days before the big premiere at La Scala, Giorgio called me and asked if I could meet his boss in Firenze and so I did without telling Tom or my sister what I was going there for. That was a nice modern office with several employees and a big warehouse. They were very well introduced in the fashion industry handling cargo for Gucci, Benetton and other famous brands. Basically they needed an agent in the U.S. to store the shipments upon arrival, custom cleared them, re-label and ship them to the hundreds of different stores all over the country. To do that they needed an office with a person to coordinate everything and make sure that problems would not occur. The salary offered was very good: 4000$ per months net plus company car and all the expenses paid.

I was in seventh heaven! Yet it was a big step in my life. I was leaving a sure job in a country that I knew pretty well to go live in a huge city starting something that I was not sure it would last. Besides there was the issue of the working permit that I wanted the company to resolve.

The interview went very well and it was a point in my favor the fact that I was a freemason.

Back in Milano I had the task to give notice to my boss who had me in high consideration. Piera was the first to know and, of course, she advised me to go ahead and do it. She wrote the letter but I took it to Mr. Terragni so that I could explain in details the reasons for resigning.

I must say that he was very understanding but he asked me to remain for another month to find and train my substitute. That was the minimum I could do.

That month went fast. Ghena opened the season at La Scala with "Turandot". She gave me two tickets for the royal balcony and I was very glad to invite my sister who was also an opera fanatic. The day before I had the honor to be introduced to Zeffirelli by

Giorgio. Wearing my tuxedo we entered the grand hall surrounded by all the "crème" of Milano.

The stage was fabulous! The costumes were as close as possible to the original. Ghena's dress and hat were at least 30 pounds heavy and the lightings were just perfect. The performance was magnificent. Ghena and Placido gave the best as usual. The public was satisfied and the press gave a good review. During the intermission I met another soprano friend of Giorgio, soon to become very famous: Daniela Dessi', very nice and pretty young lady who was also an admirer of Ghena.

After the performance I took my sister through the backstage to Ghena's dressing room to greet her and to compliment for the astounding work.

Unfortunately the Italian TV did not record that performance, but that was done at a later date when the leading role with Domingo was taken over by Eva Marton.

I waited another few days and then I gave the news about my new job to Tom first and to my parents.

Tom has always been suspicious and scared by the "unknown" but he realized that it could be the only way to live together without the fear of being caught as an illegal visitor of Italy. My parents were kind of happy that I could finally fulfill my expectations to move to the USA. I decided to keep the apartment in Milano and pay the rent to my sister for as long as it would take for my position to be consolidated.

I started going back and forth to Firenze and the American consulate in order to get a working visa that would last for one year and that could be renewed for up to five times.

I met Mr. Locati, the person that would be responsible for the American traffic. Now it was a matter of finding a net of custom brokers and, most of all, an office in New York. He did not speak a word of English so I had to call several people and make appointments while they were getting the plane ticket and booking all the hotels for the business trip.

Through Giorgio I knew they quite excited to go ahead with the project of the New York office. Apparently there were some big customers that were waiting for that in order to give us their shipments bypassing their buying offices.

I kissed Tom goodbye on a Saturday morning to leave on the two weeks trip with Mr. Locati. We were going to meet at the airport in Roma and board the Pan American flight to Kennedy. The first appointment was scheduled on Monday thus leaving me time to see my friends in Manhattan. Mercurio was a rich company and was not going to spare money on anything. We were traveling in first class and the rooms were all booked in five stars hotels. Even I had got a lot of cash advance for the trip. What was most exciting was the fact that for the first time I was going to use my working visa.

We stayed at the Swisshotel and went to dine in the finest restaurants (Italian, of course) in the city. We met with several potential agents and the we decided that the one that could suit better our needs was Panda Air because of their facilities in Jamaica (around the airport area) and the big bonded warehouse. They would also rent us an office for a small monthly amount and let us use their telex machine and other equipment. Moreover I could eventually go around with their sales force to visit prospects with inbound from Italy since we would act as their Italian agent.

The second stop was going to be Seattle, a city that I did not know. There we had a meeting with another possible agent but the result was not really going to be successful. Seattle was nice, modern, kind of chilly and foggy in the mornings. I regretted I didn't have much time to explore it more especially on the gay side.

The next stop was going to be Miami and the flight was going to be a very long one from one end to the other of the country. Also the climate was going to be very different and for the occasion I had packed a couple of summer suits. We were staying at the Hyatt Regency downtown with some prostitutes at our steps. Mr. Locati was an easy person to get along with but he had some megalomaniac ideas and he knew how to spend a lot of money. I was glad he was keeping all the receipts because I did not want to give the impression that I was spending so much. I know he went to buy presents for his wife and daughter using company money.

Somehow I met some nice people at the nightclub of the hotel and I was invited to a party in a suite where everything was going. I kept out of the drug stuff that was circulating among those business people, but I managed to have some hot sex with a cute husband and wife. The following night after Mr. Locati went to bed I got a cab and went to the club baths on Coral Gable where I had some more hot fan with a latino guy.

The Miami stop was also successful since we made an agreement with a small custom broker owned by an extremely handsome Cuban guy who unfortunately was very straight and married to a pretty lady. New York was going to be the last stop to define the contract with Panda and to meet with a lady that was working for a competitor who could be possibly interested in joining our company. A personal friend of Mr. Conti had suggested her name. We called and invited Jeanne for dinner at Del Monico in the Wall Street area. There was no need for me to translate since she was born in Sicily and from the age of 15 she was living with her parents in Glendale Queens. She had gone to Colombia University to study I don't know what and she had been working in shipping and handling for almost 15 years.

1965

The impression she gave was really good. She knew how to handle all the office work, the documents, connect with the customers and well connected with the airline personnel. She came highly recommended but she had a managerial position at Ventana, the shipping company of FIAT. We offered a salary that was 5000 $ higher per year of what she was making but the job was more autonomous and more challenging than the one she had. It didn't take much to convince her to accept and to celebrate we went to have a cocktail at Trumpet, the nightclub of the Hyatt Regency over Grand Central Station.

She ordered a glass of Champagne but…she didn't drink it: she said she liked to look to see the bubbles going slowly to the top of the drink. I thought that was a little strange but kept my mental comments to myself. After all it was a 20 $ wasted drink.

Mr. Locati went on a shopping spree during the remaining couple of days. I didn't know what his salary was but it's certain he spent a big chunk of it in New York. I managed to sneak out one night and spend a few hours in a bathhouse close to the hotel. Before we left Jeanne took the task of finding me a suitable apartment in Queens and to carry on the preliminary to order a telephone line for the office and get the necessary supplies to get ready for business.

I took the occasion of flying to Amsterdam so that I could have my teeth replaced before the big move. Flying first class I could change the route anyway I wanted.

So my boss and I parted at the airport. I would see him in Firenze for a meeting on the following week.

That was one of the smoothest flights. I reclined my seat after dinner, asked the steward to wake me up for breakfast and fell into the arms of Morpheus. Unfortunately I was awakening just before landing so I skipped the rich morning meal.

I had made the appointment with my dentist in Rotterdam for the next morning so I decided to take a room at the Monocle, a cute hotel located in the very gay Kerkstraat, in a walking distance from everywhere. After a good rest and a big meal at a Chinese restaurant, I went barhopping among hundreds of people that were freely smoking marijuana everywhere. That smell was making me sick, so I decided to go to the famous Night and Day, a very nice and clean sauna where I met a cute dark headed Dutch guy and we spent the night together in my room. Two days later I was back in Milano where Tom was waiting to know all the details of my trip and about the arrangements that we had to do before leaving Italy. That was the first time that he heard my comments about Jeanne.

This was the second time that I was leaving my Italian friends and they had planned a big goodbye party. Those three weeks went fast. I got acquainted with the services Mercurio was offering to their customers working in their Milano office and sometimes in their headquarters in Firenze. My new colleagues were nice but I found that some were really not as skilled as they ought to be. I collected my first salary in Italian lire so I invited for dinner my sister's family and other relatives in a fancy restaurant. That was over twice the salary that I had been making at Rinaldi. Everybody had the idea that I would be gone for a year or so and then I would be back in Milano. Somehow I knew that was not going to happen. Nevertheless I kept renting my flat…just in case.

The ticket, another first class, was ready at the TWA counter for me but I had to buy one at my expenses for Tom. I got him a return ticket since it was cheaper than a one way.

Jeanne in the meantime had taken care of everything and she called to tell me there was a nice two bedroom flat, completely furnished, left by one of her Italian friends who was going home for good after working in New York for two years. She would come to pick us up at the airport to take us to our new residence.

Tom and I got separated upon arrival. Being an American citizen he didn't have to go through the long line of the immigration. It took me over one hour to join him at the custom area. We had brought three big suitcases with all kind of winter and mid season clothes. Winter was starting in a fortnight and it could be pretty harsh in the city.

Jeanne was expecting just me and she was surprised when Tom and I appeared together. I told her he was my American cousin who didn't want to go back to Memphis for a while. She had come with her best friend, another Italian girl who worked in the same field for a competitor. Her name was Marianne but immediately I nicknamed her "the monster" because of her not really pretty appearance.

We headed to Flushing in a very tall building overlooking La Guardia airport. The flat was on the ninth floor and had a stunning view. The subway station was just a five minutes walk. In less than half an hour I could be either in Manhattan or in Jamaica where the office was located. In the flat there was everything including sheets. As soon as the girls left I started calling my local friends to give them my phone number and to make arrangements to see them and celebrate. I spent the next day exploring the area and to find a rental car that my company was going to pay for.

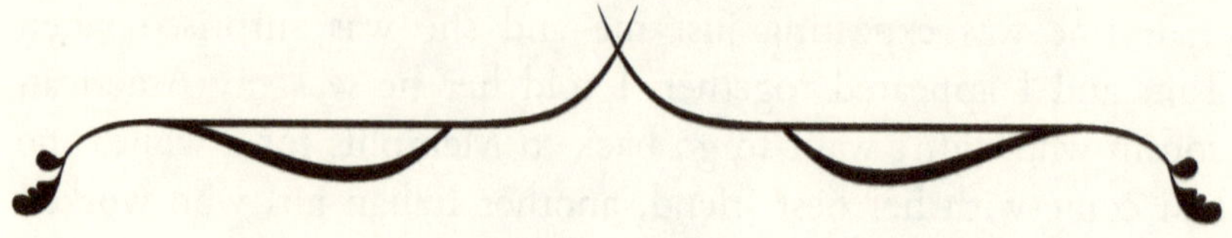

Chapter 19

QUEENS, NEW YORK

We were settled down on Kassena Boulevard. I started the usual routine office/home dealing with the heavy traffic of the Long Island Expressway. The manager of the building was pressing for me to sign a year leasing for the flat but she had raised the rent of 200$ more than the other guy was paying, and on top of that she wanted a security deposit for three months. I took time. I didn't want to pay all that money all at once, besides she did not inspire me too much. Marianne came out with the solution: her sister had a three story house in middle village and they had a basement composed of a huge living room/kitchen, a bedroom and a bathroom that they were never using. She was offering it to us for only 400$ per month, utilities included. Just two weeks after we had moved to Flushing, on a late night, with the help of some friends, we moved all the stuff to the basement and the next day I called the manager to tell her the flat was free. Middle village was also a nicer area, newer houses, there was a yard with squirrels, a big park nearby, less traffic, and just a couple of blocks away from the Silver Barn and the Lyon's grocery stores.

I had found a provisory car for rent, a Citation. Talking to the airfreight manager at Panda he said they had a deal with Avis, so I got a new Buick Le Sabre for a few dollars more per month. Jeanne was driving a big scary Ford, the Nova, which was everything but "new".

We had a small office at the Panda premises. Jeanne was there every day while I was going around visiting the existing and calling on potential customers. More and more I was getting familiar with the huge area covering the five boroughs. Every Friday I was at the office to coordinate the following week. To make things easier I had introduced the old Emery system of leads and customers profiles. During the first month we hit big with a huge shipment from Bologna for R.J. Reynolds making a big profit. The cargo started to pour in and the warehouses was working well in re-labeling the boxes and ship them to their final destinations. I befriended one of the salesmen, Vinnie, who was also gay. There was also a cute Spanish guy working as a custom broker who was very straight but also very gay friendly. Vinnie had been after him for months very unsuccessfully.

Jeanne was handling everything very professionally. Sometimes we would go to lunch together to a close by diner and it's there that by the talks she was making I gathered that she was not only very naive about life but also that she had some peculiar ideas going on in her brain. Her attitude started changing towards me after the first month, so I finally decided to ask her if something was wrong. The answer came on a quiet and rainy Friday afternoon: she wanted us to go out to dinner, dance and socialize more since she realized that between us it was just strictly business! I had started seeing my friends, Jimmy and Dairo, I was exploring all the gay bars and clubs that I didn't have time to visit during my short trips and I was sometimes driving around to see different areas of that huge metropolis. Astoria, for instance, was inhabited by Greeks, Jackson Heights by Latinos, Flushing by Indians and Columbia Heights had the headquarters of the Watch Tower (Jehovah's Witness). I discovered a small Ganesh temple. Also Tom was coming around to see the city from the car since he didn't want to mingle with people on the street or on the subway. Halloween was coming up and he said that if I would get him a mask he would ride the car in the Village during the parade! So we did and I think he had the time of his life. I also found a 24-hour gym not too far from the flat that I joined immediately.

In the mist of all of this Jeanne wanted to go out on a date! Somehow she had figured out that both Tom and I were single guys. She wanted to date me while Marianne could have Tom and maybe go out on a date all together!

To make her happy I invited her for dinner at the restaurant in the station in Forest Hill and then we went to dance in a straight club nearby. With caution I tried to explain that my life out of the office was spent with my longtime friends in the city and that I was really not interested in having a steady date. In the meantime she told me more about her life. She joined her family in the U.S. when she was 15. One of her brothers was a hairdresser and the other was a tile setter. Her parents were old, didn't speak a word of English, but they really didn't need to since the section of Queens, Glendale, had more people from Sicily than native Americans. Marianne was her best friend and confidant. Then she told me about her previous marriage. She was living and working in Miami some five years earlier when she met another Italian guy who was a maitre D and didn't have a working permit. After only one month they decided to get married. Jeanne wanted a big wedding but she didn't know anybody in town, so he invited his friends. The ceremony took place at city hall. His friends consisted of 19 guys and one girl. They had not slept together yet and she was still a virgin. Somehow he convinced her to add his name on her bank account. The routine that followed was not the way she had expected: she was working from 9 to 5; he was working from 4 to midnight. He would get home, jump in the shower, change clothes and leave her alone until 3 or 4 o'clock in the morning. After one month she demanded some attention. For all response he started sleeping on the sofa and a few days later he disappeared.

At her bank she found out that 17.000$ were missing from the account leaving her just a mere 100$. Her brother had to come to rescue her and that was the end of the marriage and the life in Miami.

After telling me this entire terrible story she asked me: "Do you think the guy was gay?"

She reported him to the immigration authorities but apparently he was never caught!

Having such a nice car Tom and I took the opportunity to go out in the country for short trips during the weekends. One of our favorites was to the end of Long Island exploring The Hampton and to the military Academy of West Point.

Through the Midtown tunnel it was easy to reach Manhattan in a few minutes if the traffic was not too heavy. It was also easy to park in the city after 6pm; otherwise the rates were extremely high.

I started going to a couple of clubs in Jackson Heights where people were nice and talkative. Close to our flat, right on Queens Blvd., there was "Breadstick" where I met several nice guys. Every Wednesday night they were showing "Dynasty" on the big screen and that was a "must see" because of the gay characters in the show.

Work was going better and increasing by the weeks and money was pouring in but Jeanne was not happy (mainly because she didn't have a life) and now she wanted me to meet her parents. A dinner party was arranged at their house and I had to go. Sicilians are supposed to be very friendly and so they were. They spoke only a few words in Italian but the rest was their dialect that I could not understand so Jeanne would translate for me.

It was a simple two-story house, more like two long trailers. In the lower apartment there was her brother. The backyard was very small with grapes growing on an arbor and her father assured he was getting at least 80 bottles of red wine a year.

Dinner was spicy! I had no idea that Sicilian food was so hot! And I really don't like spicy food.

The surprise came after I was introduced to her parents: they knew my last name! One of my ancestors, Roberto, left the city of Orvieto in the year 1193 and followed king Pietro II to Noto in Sicily where he was the captain of the guards. Since then the descendents gained glory and wealth ending up in the small town of Villarosa and gaining the titles of Barons in the year 1365, and

Marquis of Camporotondo in 1637, making it one of the most famous families in the island. I had always been aware of that but I never told a soul even because the king in Italy left in 1946 and the nobility was no more. Nevertheless they were flattered to have a celebrity visiting their home. I have never been to Sicily but at this point I made a point to go there before I die and check it out.

Jeanne's interest had drastically grown overnight and she became even more demanding of spending time together.

Mr. Locati was coming to visit us for one week to make sure everything would go smooth before the Christmas holiday. That was one of the busiest months of the year for shipping because all the orders for 1983 had to be evaded. I was often in touch with Giorgio who was a direct dependent of Mr. Conti. A busy week was ahead dense with courtesy calls to important customers, business lunches and dinners and a lot of driving in the chaotic traffic. Jeanne was always a pain in the neck because she wanted to include herself in every after hour meeting.

On morning after a sale call with the Ferragamo on their Fifth Avenue office Mr. Locati asked me to take him shopping to Tiffany where he bought some expensive jewelry for his wife. There was nothing strange about that with the exception that I had to use 4000$ of our petty cash. Thinking he would somehow reimburse before leaving New York I was puzzled when he asked me to cover up that expense with fake invoices. When I called Giorgio to ask for advice, he suggested, with my full approval, to tell Mr. Conti what had happened and so I did a couple of days later. The reaction was reassuring and even surprising: we wired the whole amount and told me not to worry about it. That was a strange company but if the owner wanted to keep quiet about it…well…he was the owner! Another surprise came when I got paid double for the month of December like if I were working in Italy.

2007

Christmas and New Year were very relaxing. The city was splendid with all those lights. Even the top of the Empire State had a different light at night. The tree at the Rockefeller Center was humongous and a huge snowflake was hanging at the corner of Madison and 57th. Those were some of the coldest and windy days, so cold that I had to buy a pair of earmuffs and walk around wearing Tom's bear fur coat.

Proud of my photographic equipment I was using the telephoto and the wide angular lenses taking shots all over. I bought myself a cute Watchman, a pocket size black and white TV and the latest anti skip Walkman. I asked my sister to put some more clothes and some books in a trunk and call Mercurio to ship it over. I was missing several things that I was using during my life in Milano.

On the other hand I was uncertain about my future in the USA and didn't want to start buying a lot of stuff to replace the one I already had overseas.

I involved Jeanne and Marianne in some of the afternoon visits to the city but kept my nights free to party with Jimmy, Dairo, and other friends that I had met. Parties were going on everywhere and people were extremely friendly. There was a disco that I liked very much, the Limelight, an old desecrated church with gorgeous stain glass windows.

Tom was always staying home enjoying several TV programs, especially those by the public TV 13. A couple of hours a day there was RAI USA transmitting the news and an old Italian movie.

Martha called from San Antonio to tell that her son was going to graduate at Notre Dame University in may and my presence was required.

The new year seemed very promising for my job. Jeanne was taking care of all the office work while it seemed easy enough for me to gain some new customers. My idea was also to start some traffic in export to Italy by using the weekly consolidation of Panda at very competitive rates. In doing that I started targeting some old Emery customers.

On the AIDS epidemic there were also some news coming from the French labs: they had isolated the virus (some terrible jokes on that started circulating among straight people) and it seemed then clear that it was transmitted only through sexual contacts with an exchange of body fluids. Poppers resurfaced in many gay stores while the media started a big campaign on the use of condoms. Several clubs were offering them for free. It was still not clear if oral sex was somewhat safe or not; with that doubt most people did abstain.

At Breadstick I met a guy who was going to my gym so we started working out together. He had a boyfriend but he openly admitted he was cheating on him if there was a chance, and the chance happened on a rainy Saturday afternoon when his friend had to go out of town. Most of the sexual stories were kind of "hit and run" in clubs like the Anvil, JR or in the basement of the bookstore in the village. I seldom was meeting some nice guy at Uncle Charlie's downtown or at the Monster. I remember one night when at JR there was a midget giving head to a huge 7' tall guy. That was really some show that lasted for almost half an hour. Not all the bathhouses had closed down because of AIDS; some were still open even if sex was going on insides the cubicles with the doors shut. Before there used to be dark rooms with several beds where everything was going on. Back then I remember asking and being asked if we knew of somebody who was HIV positive while the media were reporting several deaths, mostly in North America.

With the fact that I had been infected by syphilis in Brighton, I was always afraid of venereal diseases and I was regularly having my blood checked at the gay clinic at the Greenwich. For some reason once the test came back "inconclusive" so I insisted with the nurse to use one of those powerful penicillin shots that I had kept "just in case". He obviously was not skilled enough because a few hours after I started feeling very sick with high fever and vomit. I didn't sleep that night and I had to call in sick on the next day. In the afternoon I decided to go see a doctor and the response was what I had feared: the injection had hit a vein! I had 1.200.000 units of antibiotic in my blood system and I had risked my life, or so the doctor told me. It took me three days to recuperate.

Of course I told Tom that I had just some fever because of indigestion.

Two weeks later I turned 37 with a small party at the office and several phone calls from my family and friends from overseas. Jeanne wanted to celebrate that night but I succeeded in avoiding her date and go party with Jimmy and Dairo at the Saint.

Carla, my ex colleague from Sochital, called to let me know she wanted to come to New York with her mother to visit. That was the first of numerous visits that my friends were going to pay to me in the U.S.

There was no room in our flat to accommodate them so Jeanne offered her parent's garage apartment and I started taking them around for the grand tour. I was always managing to spend several hours with my friends because I was scheduling my calls in the city. Each call didn't take more than 30 minutes and I only had to make five or six a day. For the first time I managed to take them on the ship that goes around Manhattan so I was able to take several good photographs. We also got some tickets for one of the last memorable performances of Yul Brinner in "The king and I". Even Jeanne came to the theater that night but she did not believe that it was a fiction; she swore the event took really place in Siam.

After Carla and her mother left, Jeanne started bothering me again with going out to dinner and to dance. She too became friend of Robert, who was engaged to be married with a Spanish girl and wanted the three of us to go out together. I really tried to explain to her that my taste was kind of different and that I did not appreciate her walking "arm in arm" with me. It was like talking to a wall. We went to the most gay section of town, the Village, where were living most of my friends. The fact that some of them were walking by saying "hi" and kissing me goodbye apparently didn't change her mind. Gay was a concept that was absolutely not clear in her brain. The frosting on the cake came when she insisted that I go to some Italian party in Astoria with a few people, Marianne and her parents were part of the crowd. It turned out to be an unbelievable dinner party with 500 2nd-3rd generation Italians that spoke different dialects or a very bad English. The food was very americanized, and there was an orchestra playing ancient Italian songs, mostly from Naples. When we finally left I made her swear she would not ask me to go to such a party ever again.

My ex colleague Enrico came to New York for work and stayed at my flat sharing the big room with Tom and I for a few nights. His competence about electronics made me decide to buy a more sophisticated stereo equipment and my very first video recorder. I already had a vast collection of cassettes but now I could start collecting movies and recording whatever I wanted from the TV. Our favorites were the documentaries and the vintage movies courtesy of public TV without commercial interruptions.

I had underestimated Jeanne on her way to impose herself out of the office. She was always trying to get me involved in her restricted circle of social events with relatives and with Italian/Americans that she knew and that I really didn't want to mingle with. Giving up the hopes of seeing Tom dating her best friend, she was calling me for all kind of silly problems to get my opinion. She wanted so desperately spend time with me that she decided to join my gym. Unfortunately for her I was going to work out late at night when she was already in bed. The time we were spending together at the office, mostly on Friday, she was she was trying to talk about cultural subjects in which she was not competent so I started giving her lectures on history, music, opera and life in general. Sex was one subject she was absolutely not knowledgeable in that seemed to interest her more. If I was reluctant to answer her silly questions she had no hesitation to go two offices down the hall to ask Robert.

When I was working in Manhattan I got into the habit of going to a nice piano bar called Bogart at the foot of the Queensboro Bridge. There were many good-looking businessmen stopping by for a drink and an old black lady playing some jazz in a very pleasant way. I got very friendly with one of the bartenders and he started to introduce me to some of the customers. The crowd was friendlier than the one at Breadstick and I started dating a few guys. If I wanted some quick sex there was another place in Astoria called the "Adult Fair", a movie theater with several dark back rooms where everything was going on. Buddy on Queen's Boulevard was the closest disco to go on a weekend. Every night I was never going home before 1am and on Friday and Saturday nights 3 or 4am were the normal time.

I was finding out that New York was really not an expensive town to live in. I had to eat in different restaurants and diners for lunch, but that was during working hours and it was fully refunded by the company. Tom or I always prepared dinners and I certainly did not spare money on food. Jeanne introduced me to the "Meat Market", a huge grocery store with specialties from all over the world at prices so low that Milano was way overpriced in comparison. It was delightful shopping there. Even more: there was fruit and vegetable from every corner of the world, some that I had never seen before. Finally I could go shopping at any time without worrying about stores being closed.

February was an extremely cold month but the days were beautiful, sunny and windy. Jeanne told me that the employees of Alitalia had scheduled a weekend in a mountain lodge in the Catskill. She wanted to go but she insisted that I should go with her. I had never gone to ski in the U.S. so I decided to go to see what kind of slopes there were and also because I figured that in the lodge I could spot some cute guy and have a good time.

We left on a Friday afternoon on a special bus. The trip lasted only three hours and we arrived after dark in this huge secluded hotel. There was no snow on the ground and the wind had a sub zero factor. It took a while to check in and finally I could take a hot shower and put on some warm mountain clothes. I was sure that among all those guys there were a few gays but it was kind of difficult to spot them, besides Jeanne was like my shadow. We ended up in the disco and finally we went to bed in our own rooms. In the morning after a rich breakfast we went out to explore the area: the snow was not around but the wind was blowing at such a high speed that not even an Eskimo would have resisted. So we went back inside killing time playing cards and waiting for lunch. In the afternoon I decided to go to work out and then to the pool. Jeanne followed me like a puppy dog. After the pool I was going back to my room to shower and change. I thought she was going to take a nap. I was just getting out of the shower when somebody was knocking at the door. Thinking it could have been a guy working there I wrapped myself in the towel in a sexy way and opened the door. It was not the guy of my dreams; it was Jeanne who was coming to visit!

I really didn't want to become involved in a relationship with her. It was a cold afternoon, my libido was high, there was no chance of finding somebody in the lodge because of the very straight environment and it would have taken more than a few hours to achieve my goal. At that point even Jeanne was a kind of sexual "prey" and she had started the game! I started joking about her being fully dressed and one thing lead to another: our lips met for the very first time and I started kissing her passionately, even more than I had intended to. All my experience started surfacing. Years of sexual encounters, preferences, the knowledge of the most erotic spots of a human body, the way to kiss, touch and using the tongue in the most accurate way were all aces up my sleeve. The poor girl had never slept with another guy before with the exception of a five minutes intercourse that happened in a hotel in Torino once she was there for work when some not better identified ex colleague went to pick her up. In that occurrence she didn't even have time to feel anything since he pulled out immediately while he was coming.

I started undressing her so slowly that the whole operation took at least 30 minutes, then I finally let go of my towel and there we were, not having sex, making love for the following three hours. I know she reached orgasm at least 5 times. I was almost to the same point for a couple of times but I did not want to give her the satisfaction of displaying such an intimate image of myself. At some point she was so loud moaning that I had to turn up the music that was playing in the background. At the end of the tenzon she was exhausted yet radiant resting in my arms. I couldn't wait to get in the shower and clean up.

At dinner her usual attitude had changed. She was now looking at me like a hero sprang out of some idyllic poem of an ancient mythology. I knew she had desperately felled in love with me but I wasn't sure if I had to be pleased or sorry about it.

We were in the bus returning to New York and while she was holding my hand on her breast I was thinking what I was going to tell Tom since I knew my life was going to change drastically by spending more time with Jeanne than with my regular friends. I made it clear that I was not in love with her. That was just an isolated episode that did not bind us. I told her my preferences were for the guys, but it didn't seem to meet the objective: she was sure that we could be a perfect couple, besides she definitely wanted to repeat that sexual experience over and over in the future. The idea of getting married had been floating in her mind but it was now gaining more strength and possibly becoming a certainty. To be honest I had thought of such a possibility but it seemed very unrealistic. And now she was constantly pushing me in that direction. I had to talk to Tom and see what he was thinking. Of course, in case of a wedding, there were several things to take into consideration. Jeanne knew that Tom and I were roommates but she had no idea that my goal was to get a green card to live in the country so that Tom and I could finally live together without fear.

That weekend had become a milestone because Jeanne started calling me every day. She was asking for more sex but, fortunately for me, there was no place to do it and her parents never left the house. She was so exasperating on a Friday afternoon that I had to lock the door of the office and have a quickie on the desk. I felt sorry for her discovering the pleasure of sex at 34!

The days were getting longer and the temperature was finally rising. It had been a nice winter but we also had some snow in the city and that was not pleasant. Mr. Locati was busy in Europe and I was mainly dealing with the manager of the Milano branch. The problem was with Panda because the space in the warehouse reserved to us was too small to accommodate some of our large shipments. Jeanne started to look around for a bigger office and for a company that would guarantee more efficiency. She knew two brothers that owned a medium size company just one mile away. After making all the necessary arrangements at the end of March we moved into our new office at Horizon Airfreight.

In April I had to go to Milano for a meeting and that was the occasion that Jeanne was waiting for: she wanted to come to meet my family.

I thought things were rushing too much. I had all these thoughts on my mind and the first had to do with Tom. I did not want to be separated from him and on the other hand I could not impose his presence to Jeanne living in the same flat in case we really got married. Then there was the issue of the actual wedding. Did I want to get involved in something that I had carefully evaluated but that I didn't want to go on forever? Of course I had been very honest from the beginning telling Jeanne I did not love her and, if there were going to be such a strong commitment, we would need a bigger flat granting full privacy to her and myself. I did not want to stop seeing my friends and would not give up my nightlife. At the Adult Fair I had met Carlos, a nice guy from Colombia, and we had started dating on and off. He was living with his parents in Astoria therefore, to have sex; we were going to the West End bathhouse and rent a room. Jeanne had met him but it was far from her mind that we had a story going on. That was typical of her thinking. Anyway the departure date was near, so she made arrangements to take two days off and to meet me in Milano on a Friday morning, spend the week end in Lugano, and go back to New York on the following Monday.

I arrived at Malpensa airport and went straight to one of the business meetings where we spent all day. It was after seven p.m. when I got to my flat, took a shower, changed and went to the grocery store to buy some food for my dinner. All the stores closed at 7,30 but I was not in the state of mind to remember that since I was used to go shopping at any time. Disappointed and mad for not thinking in advance I had to go to a pizzeria. The next day we had to go to Firenze for a meeting with the company's owner (and also to face Mr. Locati for the first time after reporting him for the petty cash spent in the U.S.). Back in Milano that night at dinner with my sister and Bruno I told them out of the blue that I was going to be married and that my bride to be was arriving in two days to meet them. We called our parents and Wilma gave them the news. I'm sure my dad was surprised but he didn't say anything. My mom's comment was: "I hope you are not getting married because she's expecting a baby..." I promptly reassured that was not the case and she was relieved.

With a lot of curiosity Wilma came to the airport to meet Jeanne. During the short trip she asked a lot of questions. I know she didn't want me to get involved in something that I would not be in a position to handle. Her doubts disappeared when she finally met the girl: my description was fitting right in.

All my brother in law relatives, living in the same building in several apartments all connected, gave a big dinner party in Jeanne's honor that Friday night. There has always been a huge table in one of the several dining room where the whole family would banquet on occasions like that, combining one of their cook and numerous maids.

Jeanne did not expect such a welcome and was overcome by the big display of wealth and the big variety of food available. She asked if aristocrats live like that on every day life. On the Saturday we went to Lugano where my parents were expecting us for lunch. My mother was cordial, as usual, and was testing Jeanne's behaviors with some specific questions about her backgrounds, family, studies and inclinations from religious to political matters. She told me years later that her impression was not too positive. After lunch she called me to her room and said that if I was going to marry I had to provide an engagement ring so, with the pretext of a walk downtown, we went by the bank to check the safety box with the family jewels. The first ring that came on display was a small brilliant of one carat that had belonged to my grandmother: Jeanne loved it at first sight! My mother closed the box and I gave it to my new fiancée who put it on her ring with proud.

That night we slept in separate rooms as it used to happen in all old-fashioned families and on Sunday we want back to Milano. Her plane was leaving on Monday morning while I had to go out on sales calls with my Milanese colleague.

I spent the remaining three nights partying with my old friends and going to some new clubs in Milano. I also met a cutie with whom I spent the last night before flying back.

By the way, all my friends and family didn't think much about the wedding, they all knew that was just a move to stay in the U.S.

Back in New York I just went on with the usual life, Breadstick on Wednesday night, some sex with Carlos and a few drinks at Bogart's where, on a sunny but cold afternoon, I met somebody who captured my interest who would have an impact on my future life: Barry.

He was one of the few people that could talk for hours about different subjects. A manager in his father's company with some big responsibilities and a huge yearly salary, he was living in a fancy flat on the Upper East Side. His company was supplying wearing apparel to Saks 5th Avenue and Bloomingdale all over the company. It was amazing the fact that we had a friend in common, an Italian designer named Egon von Furstenberg. Barry only problem was that he liked to drink too much and when he was buzzed he was not able to reason and he would fall asleep not necessarily on his bed.

I started telling Tom about the recent events and the prospective that I could get married. Being very insecure, he started going on a rampage and it took me a few days to calm him down. He also realized we could not all live together like a happy family. While Jeanne was looking for a residence in the neighborhood, I was looking for a small flat, not too far, where Tom could be safe and happy. He was a loner anyway but he had the assurance that this arrangement was going to be temporary.

The date of Andrea's graduation at Notre Dame was approaching. Jeanne decided she wanted to come too and the arrangements were done with Martha. We got a plane ticket with the cheapest airline on the market: People Express. In Chicago we rented a car and drove to South Bend to join the Quaroni on the campus. Those two days were full of events. The university was interesting to visit. We spent the night in one of the rooms they had reserved for relatives and friends. Several personalities were present like the heavily guarded president of El Salvador, Napoleon Duarte, and our Italian ex Prime Minister Giulio Andreotti, personal friend of Martha with whom we had a nice chat.

It was sunny but rather cold so Martha loaned Jeanne a beautiful mink coat. I remember vividly how she was proudly wearing it while we were taking some pictures.

The graduation ceremony was held in the auditorium and it was interesting. Now that Andrea had graduated and wanted to start a career in dentistry, his sister Vittoria had one more year to go. Martha's efforts to move to divorce her husband move to the States to give a secure future to her children was paying off. But at that point she had spent far more money that she had anticipated. A V.I.P. visa is costly.

We drove back to Chicago in the morning, went around town and tried to have a walk in a park by the lake. The wind was too cold and we were happy to be back in old New York early that evening.

My job, friends and other things apparently took me, but my mind was constantly thinking about the wedding and the chances that some unforeseen problem could go wrong. Robert who had married a Spanish girl in Spain, who did not yet have the permit to join him in the States, gave me some very important tips including an album with dated photographs of Jeanne and me to exhibit to the immigration officers in case they would question me on the subject. Fortunately we had several pictures together in the U.S., Switzerland and Italy. I just rearranged the dates to make it look like we had been dating for a couple of years.

I asked Wilma to get my birth certificate and the document stating that I was a single man from the city hall in Venezia. Another thing that had to be done was the blood test so I made an appointment and in one week I got the results nice and clean. The wedding date was set for June the 16th at the city hall in Manhattan. I had to convince Jeanne not to have a party: just her family and two witnesses; hers was going to be Marianne.

In may my sister and her husband decided to make a trip to the United States stopping in New York, San Antonio to visit Martha and in Houston for some medical tests. I made sure their permanence was the most enjoyable and took a couple of days off work. It was a must to introduce them to Jeanne's family so one evening was dedicated to them. The second day we were all invited for dinner at North by North East by Barry who couldn't wait to meet my sister and gossip about the Italian fashion designers. Before they left I took them to eat the famous steaks at Gallagher's.

When they were boarding the flight to Texas they gave me 1000 $ to buy whatever present for my wedding.

News came to me from Giorgio that Mr. Locati was leaving the company (or maybe was forced to leave?). I was not so sure that business was going to be as usual besides in Firenze they were not doing anything to renew my visa and that was making me nervous. Through my custom broker friend in Milano I heard that a big Italian shipping company was looking for an airfreight manager in New York. The job was stable, paid almost as much as I was making, offered company car, all expenses paid, four full weeks vacation and also medical. Jeanne could take care of Mercurio needs by herself, but that was my big opportunity to make a jump in quality. I asked and obtained an interview strong of the fact that if I was going to marry and I practically had the green card in my hands to be able to work. It was strange that the president of the American branch of Merzario was a Japanese guy who did not know much about shipping. After only one chat and thanks to the references from my previous employers, I got the job with the starting date two weeks after my wedding.

Now I had to call Mr. Conti and resign from my position. The satisfaction was that I opened the office and in those few months we made more than enough money to pay for our salaries, the office expenses and to have a margin of profit in the bank.

One week before the wedding Jeanne informed me she had found the perfect apartment located in a very quiet area of Middle Village, just five blocks away from Marianne's house. It was three bedrooms, two baths, brand new, on the top floor of a three story duplex. The asking rent was only 850$ a month that would be split in two. I had to go through a realtor to find quickly a studio for Tom and I did find one just one mile away for 400$. We were going to put our furniture in it since Jeanne wanted to buy everything new.

This was the first time that Tom and I were going to live in the same city sleeping under different roofs. I was already missing him.

Everything was ready for the big day. I was wearing a black suit and she had to go to Abraham&Strauss to find a fancy gown. Her parents had booked the pizzeria of a friend on Queen's Boulevard for lunch and they had bought Champagne.

The ceremony lasted only ten minutes. I recall seeing Marianne taking pictures but I never saw them printed. As we walked out of city hall we went by the social security office with the marriage certificate and I got my SSN valid for working. The second step was the green card but that was a different office.

We had one of the most squalid pizza-wedding banquet and by three we were back at the office as husband and wife!

At the Green Acres Mall in Long Island we had spotted some cheap yet cute puzzle furniture. Borrowing the huge Buick station wagon from Marianne's sister we went to pick them up. There was a huge sectional corner sofa, two twin size sofa beds and a coffee table. The dining table with the chairs was bought at Seaman's Furniture and Jeanne bought in the Village a nice modern queen-size bed for her master suite.

With some of my sister money I bought a stain glass lamp that I had seen in a shop for a long time.

When I had to go apply for the green card they did ask me a bunch of questions about how and when I met my wife. Just in case I had brought the photo album with a lot of pictures taken in Europe and in New York. Under each picture there was a date, the oldest was from august 1980.

Our good friend Robert, who was always waiting for his wife to join him from Spain because they made the mistake of getting married there, advised me not to leave the country while I was waiting for the green card: they would let me out…but they wouldn't let me back in. Needless to say that I took that very seriously.

My parents and friends called to congratulate and my father made then the big promise to buy me a house in the States if I got the residency. That was just what I had hoped for.

So I left Mercurio and I started working for Merzario, a much bigger company with offices and agents all over the world. Jeanne was all alone handling everything in the small office at Horizon, by the airport, while I was commuting to my new fancy office located on Battery Place, at the very tip of Manhattan. It was on the 16th floor of an old building overlooking the west river and the heliport. I could see Ellis Island, New Jersey, and, in a distance, the statue of Liberty. My secretary was Robin, a really tall, really sweet lady from Winnipeg. My other colleagues were also nice. Alex, another Italian from Genova, and Bill were the salesmen for ocean. Rita, a Sicilian lady, was their secretary, and the rest were all Americans with the exception of the president and his vice that were from… Japan! The guy that I was going to substitute was going back to his native Milano to manage the airfreight department at the headquarters. The day he left he gave me the keys of the company car, a Chrysler Fifth Avenue leased from Hertz. I had a very vast territory to cover, basically the whole country. That meant I had to make frequent trips by plane and also be gone for days, but first I had to get familiar with the local agents and the many small and big customers in the city and the neighboring states.

It was a very challenging job but I knew that with my experience I could take care of it. The efficiency of Robin was very precious. Alex and I became very good friends. Ten years my junior, we had gone to the same Maritime high school in Genova. His girlfriend, a beautiful blonde, was an actress in several off Broadway shows and had been a pupil of the famous Geraldine Page.

Going back and forth from Queens to Manhattan I experimented different roads. The 295 was the fastest but traffic could be really bad, so I learned how to cut through Brooklyn and to go across that bridge. We had spots reserved at the Katz Parking, next to the office, making it really easy. Since the car didn't belong to me I used to carry the Italian driver license just in case the cops would stop me. I figured they would warn me but not give me a ticket. That happened a few times.

Every morning I would get up, get ready, and go have breakfast with Tom. Then I would go visit customers, eat lunch in different places, go on with my visits, have several phone calls with Robin to check what was going on at the office, and around five I would go to spend a couple of hours with Tom and have dinner with him. Around 7,30-8pm I would go home to change and go out with my friends or with Carlos. Fridays were always dedicated to the office work.

Jeanne was very nice and patient. I knew she wanted more but I was not going to give up my freedom and I was maintaining my word on how our lives were going to be: minding our own business. At least once a month we had to go to dinner at her parents and once in a while she was inviting her relatives and her best friend Marianne over. In her mind we had to give the idea of the perfect couple. Sex was happening once every two or three weeks but it was going to be short and then I was going back to my room to sleep. The only time I came on her bed while having sex, and some sperm went on the sheets, after she went to take a shower and I had gone back to my room to go to sleep, I heard noise in the hallway. I opened the door and saw Jeanne putting her bedding in the washer. When I asked her why she was washing that late at night, she told me it was because I had come on her sheets and she didn't want to risk getting pregnant!!! No, she was not joking.

I had started shopping around for premium electronic gadgets. In Italy the telephone company had two standard models of phone, in the USA we were flooded with all kind of different shapes. AT&T became my favorite company. They were way ahead with all kind of different services and their rates were much cheaper than the European.

I remember calling my sister in Milano and my mom in Lugano at the same time. My sister had been warned, by my mom could not figure out if I was in Milano or my sister was visiting me in New York.

The summer was slowly coming to an end when a shocking story started unveiling on the news: Rock Hudson was taken to Paris on a private plane because he was ill. The cause was AIDS and the Pasteur Institute was the most advanced for the research. One of the best-kept secrets of Hollywood was out. Everybody knew about Liberace...but Rock?

He had recently been on some episodes of Dynasty, even kissing Linda Evans. Could she have been infected? There was a big turmoil while the myth of an era was drastically coming to an end.

To go meet our agent in California I planned a trip to San Francisco for a whole week. I flew out on American Airlines and for the first time during the five boring hours they showed on the big screen the projection of the plane over the land, the speed, the altitude and all the data. I found that very interesting. These days it's normal routine on long flights.

San Francisco in the fall of 1984 was not the live gay city that I had discovered almost ten years earlier. The Castro was kind of dead, the discos were empty and on the streets there were fewer people. I remember going to four different bars in one night and counting maybe 30 guys. Many hustlers were walking down Polk Street and the famous Brothel Hotel was no more. The whole atmosphere that had filled the days of Harvey Milk and George Moscone was gone forever.

I managed to spend at least one night in a gay hotel at Fell and I had my share of fun with another guy that was there on business. Unfortunately the morning after when I reached for my coat of arms ring that I had put in the drawer of the nightstand I discovered that my sex partner had stolen it. I really got mad but it was too late to try to do something then. These things happen.

At least when I got back home Giorgio called me with the wonderful news that Ghena was going to sing Turandot at the Metropolitan, the same production that had opened the season of La Scala in Milano, directed by Zeffirelli. Ghena with her husband were going to arrive in October and spend there several weeks for the rehearsal.

I was so happy to be out of Milano and living in the big apple. There was something new to discover every day. The city that never sleeps was up to its name. Often I would go to work out at the gym very late at night and then eat something at its restaurant. Grocery shopping was also a pleasure because I was discovering food, fruits and veggies from all over the world, some that I had never seen before. Experimenting in the kitchen I enjoyed inviting for dinner my friends and some colleagues. With Dairo we would spend hours in Central Park riding the bike or roller-skating. The pollution was definitely less than in Milano probably because of the winds. On top of everything some of my best friends were planning to come visit.

The first occasion happened when a famous Italian sculptor, friend of a friend, had to come to New York for an art exhibit and was in need of finding a place to stay for a couple of weeks. I was very glad to invite him to stay at my place and Jeanne was thrilled to have a celebrity over. He was a very pleasant and simple guy. I showed him around and I also introduced him to Robin who could speak Italian quite well. Before going back to Milano, he made five drawings of very modern art that represent the state of mind of a man in New York City. Three were for me, and two for Robin, who had been so kind with him. Mine are nicely framed and are still hanging in my house.

Ghena and her husband Giorgio arrived and took a nice apartment at the Essex House behind the Plaza. It was wonderful to see them again and to spend many evenings together trying out all the restaurants in the area and also walking around in some freezing weather.

Enrico and his wife, Serena, came to spend one week during one of the coldest waves. We had a very good time but I understood that their wedding was going through some rough times and probably it was going to end pretty soon. Thank God they didn't have any kids.

My wedding was going on all right with some highs and some lows. Jeanne was getting on my nerves sometimes but I did not want to do or say anything because, after all, she was my passport to the States. Three months went by when I finally got my green card that I proudly kept together with my passport.

Being at the head of the airfreight department I was entitled to ask and obtain free plane tickets to the major airlines that we were using for our shipments. Since I had a few days vacation coming up

I decided to take that opportunity to fly for free and see my family and friends and also to show my father the green card that was worth his promise to buy me a house. Of course Jeanne wanted to join me but she didn't have any days off and she had to stay home with my joy. Tom was the one who didn't want to stay for ten days without seeing me.

My trip was nice and refreshing. All my friends thought I was ready to go back to Milano but I quickly had to dissuade them. I loved to go visit for a little while but I was happier to go back, especially now that I had the residency.

I went to visit my Masonic lodge where my brothers gave me a very warm welcome. I had reached there the 27th degree in the Scottish Rite and I was still paying the annual dues.

I spent a few hours in my usual clothing store to renew my wardrobe, and then I went to buy several pairs of shoes.

I loaded a big trunk with clothes, books and several personal items I had collected during my trips, and had it picked up and shipped to New York by our Malpensa office. I went to visit my ex colleagues at Emery, organized a dinner the night before my departure and left on the Alitalia flight getting an upgrade to business class after we became airborne.

Glad to be back with some of my belongings, I started filling the apartment with some nice art and some I took to Tom's place, after all that was his stuff too.

Jeanne became accustomed to see Carlos coming to pick me up, what she didn't know is that we were going to the baths to rent a room. Sometimes she was coming with my other friends for a walk in Central Park where she was feeding the squirrels. I cannot say she was getting on my nerves, except when she was trying to expose her strange thoughts about life in general or political opinions in particular. I did not want to offend her or start an argument. With Tom there was always the perfect understanding. He spent hours reading and watching the most interesting programs on TV.

There were rumors at the office that Mr. Tanizumi was going to be fired for some wrongdoing that was never disclosed. The fact that he destroyed the company car in an accident was the final drop. He was fired and replaced by Claudio, a guy from Milano, who had left the same position in the Johannesburg branch. Claudio was about my age, had a beautiful wife who was working for our ocean agents in the World Trade Center, and we became very good friends having many things in common.

Apparently Mr. Tanizumi's management had gone overboard with the expenses. Our fleet of cars was costing way too much and also other things had to be reviewed. I was lucky because they got rid of the Fifth Avenue and they leased a new Honda Prelude, my favorite color, blue. I loved it because it was sportier and more manageable in the heavy traffic.

Every night I was having dinner with Tom, and then, kissed him goodnight, I was going home, change and go to Manhattan to hit the clubs or to Astoria to Billy the Kid or to The Magic Touch. There was a Latino guy there who was always trying to pick me up but his manners were too feminine for my taste. During that period a killer who had not been identified had murdered a few gays under torture.

It was a few days later when I read in the paper that the same Latino had been tortured chained on a chair and murdered. That made a big sensation all over Jackson Heights.

Bogart's was always one of my favorites for a drink in the late afternoon. The piano player was great and the company was also very pleasant. Barry was very nice too, except when he was drinking too much and I had to take him home and make sure he would hit the bed. If the weather was bad during the weekends I loved to go to his apartment to watch movies and also to cook something Italian.

There were always good performances at the Metropolitan and also at the Carnegie Hall. The best way to get discounted tickets was in the lobby of the World Trade Center.

Thanks to my Masonic passport I was going to visit different lodges in Manhattan and a small one in Forest Hill. Their work was kind of dull so I started introducing more interesting talks about symbols and esoteric subjects. Eventually I asked my Lodge in Milano to transfer my papers to the States because the dues were only a few Dollars a year while in Italy it had risen to almost 500 $. Dear old Pietro sent everything in a short time and took me off the list of the Krishna.

Martha decided she had enough of San Antonio and asked if we could host her for a few days while she was looking for a place to stay. I was happy that she was going to move so close; I had always considered her like part of the family. Vittoria was graduating from Notre Dame and wanted to see about getting a job in New York.

Jeanne was flattered to have a countess in our guestroom. The only problem is that Martha smoked like a chimney and the whole flat smelled bad while smoke was impregnating clothes and beddings.

The few days she was supposed to stay turned in weeks and months. Our life was totally turned around, or, I should say, my life. Jeanne adjusted to Martha's presence and she also started smoking early in the morning while having breakfast. That smell around the house was getting on my nerves. The only nice think was a variation in the regualr diet with the introduction of some different Romanian dishes. It was during that time that one day at the gym, for some stupid idea, I started going on the stair machine. Apparently one day I overdid it and my knees resented so bad that for a few days i could hardly walk around.

Andrea came for the Christmas holiday and stayed at the apartment. He was studying hard for his graduation that was going to be in april. Joanne and I promised we would attend in Notre Dame. He was going to be a dentist.

I organized a small Christmas party and a nice crowd showed up, all the Italians from my office and my local friends.

The days were going by fast, working lightly during the day, going to party at night sometimes around Jackson Heights, sometimes in Manhattan at the Gree Parrot, the Limelight, the Anvil and a few quick visits to the Adult's Fair in Astoria. There I met Carlos, a nice cute nurse from Colombia. We started dating.

In the morning I would go have breakfast at Tom's, then to visit a few customers, lunch wherever, visit a few more customers and hitting the gym. Dinner would be consumed at Tom's and usually I would take a shower there. Then home to change and out to party.

Making love to Carlos was nice and relaxing, he was not the type that rushed to the natural conclusion of the deal. Still we did not get together as often as I wanted so I was still going around cruising for more in all the odd places like the Apollo on 6th Ave. or the Bijou in the east village. Eventually I was also going to a theater were two guys were performing live on stage.

Fridays were days that I would dedicate to the office. Robin, my secretary, was one of the most efficient person I had ever met. We were having lunch together at the Kompass or at a vegetarian restaurant close to the twin towers. The afternoon was dedicated to making the appointments for the following week.

Spending time with my close friends in New York was always a pleasure. There was not one single weekend when we got bored. Central park, rollers skating, bycicle riding, Broadway shows, movies or playing cards if the weather was miserable. Winter of 1984 had been a particularly cold one. Freezing wind and quite some snow messed up the city streets. Fortunately it didn't turn into the dirty mess that I was used to see in Milano. A couple of times I got stuck with the car.

Talking about cars... I had started by driving a rental Citation for a couple of weeks, to lease a new Buick Lesabre while working for Mercurio. Joanne was driving her old piece of junk Nova. Fortunately the cost of gas was always around 1,15 $ per gallon.

With Merzario I got a Chrysler Fifth Avenue which was considered a luxury car but this one had the problem that the engine was stopping when it was overheating and the power stearing was defective. So once the car stopped on the FDR during rush hour and another time the power stearing gave up while I was coming down from the 5th floor of the Katz parking lot by the office.

The manager was driving a very sporty Honda Prelude that happened to be of my favorite color, blue. When he got fired...I got that car making me a very happy guy.

Not that I was driving much in Manhattan, but to go around the five boroughs the car was necessary and to find a parking space was relatively easy. In the city, after 6pm, it was not a problem either.

I found a gymn that was open 24/7 and Joanne joined too, but she was going there during a totally different time. I saw that after midnight there were mostly asians probably working out after their shifts at restaurants.

I started taking advantages from my position. Dealing with the airlines that we were using for cargo transportation I was entitled to free plane tickets to Italy with the excuse of meeting with customers to increase the present traffic or to gain some new or just because there were important meetings at my headquarters that required my presence. Needless to say that I was going there for shopping, visiting my friends and family and taking a break from the very busy New York life.

Enrico and his wife were coming regularly to visit me. Joanne also became a friend and confident of Serena and it's that way I found out that their marriage was in a deep crisis.

My sister and Bruno decided it was time to cross the big pond and visit. They did not stay too long in New York, only one week. I had no idea then that the real purpose of the trip was to go to Houston for an accurate oncological test because her cancer was slowly coming back, but I wasn't aware of what was going on back then, for some reasons my family was keeping me out of it.

Anyway, I made sure they had the best possible time. They met Barry who invited us to have dinner at North by Northwest. We went to see a beautiful performance of the King and I with Yul Brynner, not knowing that was going to be one of his last performances before he died.

When I took them to Kennedy airport at the end of their trip I was feeling that something was not right but I was not going to investigate any further.

New York was a pleasant discovery every day. It was just enough to think about something different that it would be appearing at the horizon. I did not find the city "expensive". Knowing the where about I was able to find anything at a very affordable price. The "meat market" was just a few miles from home and had the best supplies from all over the world. It was rumored to belong to the New York mafia families.

I was going to the Masonic Temples in Queens and also at the headquarters in Manhattan but I couldn't say that was too satisfactory because we were not really talking about interesting subjects. It was all about business, charity and money. A couple of times they let me give a lecture about symbols, but then everything would fall back on business.

I started to look for something else. For a while I went to the North Pole Temple, and a few times I went to the Ganesh Temple in Flushing. Then I heard about a gay coven that was meeting twice a month and was performing white magic.

The leader, or High Priest, was a handsome black guy who had been instructed by a Master from Haiti. The group was based on a Minoyan rite worshiping the Mother Earth. The ritual, consisting in bathing, annointing, opening and closing the works, was performed under the direction of the High Priest. We were all naked, all males, sometimes we were raising power by masturbation ejaculating on the pentagram. Occasionally we would get together with guys from different groups, performing all together. That was a very interesting way to meet more people, very handsome guys too, and have some kind of fun during times in which sexual habits had changed drastically because of the AIDS epidemic. More discoveries about the virus were reported every month and some stupid jokes were told by ignorant people that believed that just being in the proximity of gays one could get infected.

It was in October of 1985 when one of the most famous star of Hollywood was flown to Paris on a rented jet to seek a cure for HIV. He had played a small part in Dynasty where during an episode he had kissed the actress Lynda Evans. The fear was great.

Stars of the caliber of Doris Day and Elizabeth Taylor went public to support him and people that were sick. The death of Rock Hudson on 12.2.1985 signed a turning point for the government that had to acknowledge the fact that the problem had become so big that could not be further ignored.

It was considered a "homosexual plague" so straight people thought they could not be affected. Obviously, they don't realize that a lot of guys are bisexual by nature and a lot of them marry just because they do not want to be known as gay.

In Europe it was considered to be the "disease coming from America" and everybody started to boycott American people and American products. The use of poppers that had been very popular in discos, bathhouses and during sexual encounters almost stopped completely because they thought it was one of the causes. In New York people were suddenly dying like flies. Soon enough everybody had friends that were sick and the cure did simply not exist.

That 1985 was reserving another bitter surprise. Out of the blue we got the news that Rock Hudson was flown to Paris on a private jet to undergo some tests in Paris at the famous Pasteur Institute, which was involved in the AIDS research.

I knew Rock was gay because I had met him in a notorious bookstore off Santa Monica Boulevard in Los Angeles back in '75 but some people, especially older women, could not believe their ears. Everybody knew about Liberace… but Rock was too much because there were important meetings at my headquarters that required my presence. Needless to say that I was going there for shopping, visiting my friends and family and taking a break from the very busy New York life.

Enrico and his wife were coming regularly to visit me. Joanne also became a friend and confident of Serena and it's that way I found out that their marriage was in a deep crisis.

My sister and Bruno decided it was time to cross the big pond and visit. They did not stay too long in New York, only one week. I had no idea then that the real purpose of the trip was to go to Houston for an accurate oncological test because her cancer was slowly coming back, but I wasn't aware of what was going on back then, for some reasons my family was keeping me out of it.

Anyway, I made sure they had the best possible time. They met Barry who invited us to

have dinner at North by Northwest. We went to see a beautiful performance of the King and I with Yul Brynner, not knowing that was going to be one of his last performances before he died.

When I took them to Kennedy airport at the end of their trip I was feeling that something was not right but I was not going to investigate any further.

New York was a pleasant discovery every day. It was just enough to think about something different that it would be appearing at the horizon. I did not find the city "expensive". Knowing the where about I was able to find anything at a very affordable price. The "meat market" was just a few miles from home and had the best supplies from all over the world. It was rumored to belong to the New York mafia families.

I was going to the Masonic Temples in Queens and also at the headquarters in Manhattan but I couldn't say that was too satisfactory because we were not really talking about interesting subjects. It was all about business, charity and money. A couple of times they let me give a lecture about symbols, but then everything would fall back on business.

I started to look for something else. For a while I went to the North Pole Temple, and a few times I went to the Ganesh Temple in Flushing. Then I heard about a gay coven that was meeting twice a month and was performing white magic.

The leader, or High Priest, was a handsome black guy who had been instructed by a Master from Haiti. The group was based on a Minoan rite worshiping the Mother Earth. The ritual, consisting in bathing, anointing, opening and closing the works, was performed under the direction of the High Priest. We were all naked, all males, sometimes we were raising power by masturbation ejaculating on the pentagram. Occasionally we would get together with guys from different groups, performing all together. That was a very interesting way to meet more people, very handsome guys too, and have some kind of fun during times in which sexual habits had changed drastically because of the AIDS epidemic. More discoveries about the virus were reported every month and ignorant people that believed that just being in the proximity of gays one could get infected told some stupid jokes.

It was in October of 1985 when one of the most famous stars of Hollywood was flown to Paris on a rented jet to seek a cure for HIV. He had played a small part in Dynasty where during an episode he had kissed the actress Lynda Evans. The fear was great. Stars of the caliber of Doris Day and Elizabeth Taylor went public to support him and people that were sick. The death of Rock Hudson on 12.2.1985 signed a turning point for the government that had to acknowledge the fact that the problem had become so big that could not be further ignored.

It was considered a "homosexual plague" so straight people thought they could not be affected. Obviously they don't realize that a lot of guys are bisexual by nature and a lot of them marry just because they do not want to be known as gay.

In Europe it was considered to be the "disease coming from America" and everybody started to boycott American people and American products. The use of poppers that had been very popular in discos, bathhouses and during sexual encounters almost stopped completely because they thought it was one of the causes. In New York people were suddenly dying like flies. Soon enough everybody had friends that were sick and the cure did simply not exist.

1985 was reserving another bitter surprise. Out of the blue we got the news that Rock Hudson was flown to Paris on a private jet to undergo some tests in Paris at the famous Pasteur Institute, which was involved in the AIDS research.

I knew Rock was gay because I had met him in a notorious bookstore off Santa Monica Boulevard in Los Angeles back in '75 but some people, specially older women, could not believe their ears. Everybody knew about Liberace… but Rock was too much.

Famous stars came on TV to talk about the AIDS problem and to give a big support to Rock.

His last appearance as an actor was in the fortunate serial "Dynasty" co-star with Linda Evans who he had to kiss. The question suddenly was: is she going to result positive to the HIV test? That didn't happen and I know that a lot of people were relieved by the news.

We had a common séance with other witchcraft groups in New York to raise power to help the people with AIDS.

The announcement of Rock's death on October 12th did not come as a surprise.

Liz Taylor remembered him on TV and she informed about the foundation of AMFAR, an organization to raise founds for people with AIDS and to raise money for the research. President Reagan acknowledged there was a spread epidemic and we finally got bombarded by leaflets and TV ads. Even the big bathhouses chains were forced to shut down. The one Carlos and I were using remained open and "people were still having sex", just like the lyrics of a famous song.

That summer when I went to visit Italy I found out that a couple of friends had passed away. One was an employee of TWA and Giuliano was the steward for Qantas who I knew was sleeping around with anybody. In Lugano, while my parents were in Lavarone, I met a very famous songwriter wondering in the park. Invited him home but we ended up talking about music, Mina, Ornella Vanoni and we did not manage to find out if we were sexually compatible. Or, maybe, we were afraid of doing something to avoid dangerous contacts. I also met a very cute and nice guy at the Venere Imperiale, one of the two gay clubs in town, but our became a nice sex free friendship. He was an architect and he gave me the idea of opening an arch in the kitchen ending on the counter, thing that, years later, I would develop in my house in Pensacola.

His name was Davide: bright, cute and solar, with a beautiful smile. I could have easily fall for him but, even though I knew he liked me a lot, he always kept me at a certain distance giving me the idea that he had AIDS. As a matter of fact a few months later when I called his house his mother answered and told me he had passed away. That was the beginning of a long list of dear friends and many acquaintances.

The months were passing by and nothing special was happening except Joanne was getting on my nerves not because of her attitude but because she was so naïve.

We had as a guest for 15 days a famous Italian sculptor who was exposing some works in a gallery. One night, while I was cooking a risotto in the pressure cooker, she decided to check the status of the rice and she opened the pot while it was under pressure! Her hands seriously burned to the point she had to run to the emergency room. That was the first and last time she dealt with that pot.

I was getting up at about the same time she did in the morning, getting dressed and go to see Tom in his apartment just a few blocks away. There I was having breakfast, and then go to visit customers or go by the office to see what was new and if Robin needed me there. I had a parking place reserved at Katz, downtown; just 2 minutes walk from my office. Traffic in Manhattan could be bad but I seldom found jams.

After work I was going to Tom's to take a shower and change clothes, then I was going home ready to hit the clubs or go to see friends. I was always clean and Joanne started thinking I was not from this earth but coming from another planet where apparently they never showered or shaved.

We had another guest, a famous Italian pianist, who was going to have a concert at the annex of the Carnegie Hall. He gave us a set of tickets so I invited Robin, jimmy, Dairo and, of course, my wife and her best friend, Adriana aka as "the monster". We were supposed to meet in front of the Russian Tearoom half an hour before the concert. Joanne and Adriana were not in sight. We waited until five minutes before the beginning and then gave up and went in. Suddenly they appeared from the entrance of the Carnegic Hall screaming and shouting because we were late and they had waited for us for an hour. They were so sure that we were not coming that they also bought the tickets… to the Carnegie Hall, where they were going to have Handel's Messiah! Nothing to do with a piano concerto… They finally came in during the intermission because in the meantime they had to find someone that bought their tickets, for less money, of course.

My mother came to visit for a couple of weeks with her friend Eda. She brought a present for Joanne, a necklace and a bracelet of Mikimoto pearls she had bought in Hong Kong. My wife was in seventh Heaven! With the diamond ring and the pearls she had quite a jewelry collection. I went to Tiffany and bought her matching earrings and a ring with real pearls. After we had divorced she forgot the real pearls in Boston at a friend's and she had them shipped in a very small package via mail without insurance to New York. They never arrived. Their value was twice the one of the other cultured pearls!

I regret not taking notes of all the things she did or said because some could have been so funny to make a difficult audience like the Apollo theater laugh.

With my mother and Eda we planned a little trip to Boston, Philadelphia and Washington. Needless to say that after dinner, when they were retiring in their rooms, I was going to the clubs to see what the night was reserving for me. Nothing special came out from all that cruising.

After my mother was gone back to Lugano, Ettore's mother came to New York to visit her sister who lived very close to my house. Over and over I had several friends visiting from Europe and that was making me feel very special. Even Paolo, which I introduced as my godchild, spent a couple of weeks with me. He was a 17-year-old boy when I first met him in Milano at the famous cinema "Alce". He was into older guys probably because he didn't have a father figure in his life. Still these days he loves me very much and hopes for a durable relationship.

The statue of Liberty had been covered for months undergoing a major "face lifting". Everything was getting ready for the big celebration for the 4th of July when they would uncover the statue and celebrate the bicentennial of the USA.

My boss decided to have a party at the office on that day inviting some of the most important customers. It was the perfect location: we were on the 16th floor of the building on the corner of Battery Park. The view was going from the Verrazano Bridge to Battery Park City. Ellis Island was right in front of my window and, of course, New Jersey is just on the other side of the Hudson.

We arrived at the office bright and early, around 9am, to make sure we could walk around the area that was getting extremely crowded by people coming from all over the country. A catering company delivered a big variety of food and beverages. In all there were 32 people.

In the bay there were over 4000 boats and an aircraft carrier with President and Mrs. Reagan and then there were the tall ships coming from all over the world. The Italian "Vespucci" was by far the most magnificent. Going up the Hudson the sails were all hoisted, coming back they were al down.

Too bad I did not have a camcorder back then, but I had my precious camera with wide angle and telephoto lenses so I could take memorable pictures.

During the whole day the show was great. Looking down on the streets the crowd was huge and the noise was reaching us.

At exactly 9pm they started the fireworks from several barges in the bay. The show went on until midnight when some of the most magnificent fires lit up the sky. It was a weekend to remember and after all these years I must say I was happy to be there.

Vacation time came and with Tom we decided to drive to Pensacola. I could have used the company car but I decided to rent a bigger one to be more comfortable.

We drove through the Appalachian Mountains and in two days we reached our destination.

It was always so good to be around the best beaches of Florida. I never liked the Mediterranean Sea because of its cold waters, but in the Gulf I could spend endless hours swimming. We took a room at a fashionable motel in the walking distance from the best gay club in town, the "Fancy Free" that was split in a restaurant, a cruise bar and a disco.

During the Summer Pensacola was still the gay capital of the Emerald Coast attracting people from all the surrounding areas, including New Orleans.

The days of the San Carlos were definitely gone. They had given up the idea to transform it into a place for retired old people, the building had been closed down and also stripped of marble, chandeliers, door handles and everything they could get. Such a luxury old style hotel! It was a pity. Even the old Red Garter disco had burned down and it was reopened across the street from the landmark that used to be "Trader John". It was more fancy but did not have the character of the original. That's why Fancy Free and Faces were more successful.

The old area around the civic center, at the end of Palafox, was a notorious cruising spot but also a place where some people were going to fish, especially during the night.

During the day we would go to the gay beach, in the hearth of the National Sea Shore Park. I was staying on the gulf side, while Tom, always very shy, was going on the sound side among the dunes and the sea oats.

The guys were very friendly. Some were trying to go skinny-dipping but it was always risky because the rigid law of the county did not allow that.

Once in the water some games were going on but it was at night that there were all the concrete contacts. Even though there were plenty of cute guys, sometimes one could not decide with who and where to play. Walking back to the motel, probably 200 yards, there was always somebody stopping to ask if I wanted a lift. The few times I accepted because the guy was appealing, I was always lucky and had a good time.

Going back to New York we drove to Jacksonville and then we stopped in Savannah and Charleston to get a taste of the old south. The first was nice, very green, with big old mansions, nice squares and… a lot of mosquitoes. The second was beautiful, a bit decadent in some areas, but one of my favorite cities in the US. We took a room in a nice hotel right after the big bridge entering the historical area. The downtown market, the restaurants and bars and the "Battery" where everybody was just walking around like in any European city.

We stayed only one night in Charleston and I managed to go to the only gay club there but to my surprise there were very few people. Back to the hotel I saw a guy by the pool, so I hurried up and got in my bathing suit and went, fully dressed, near the spot where he was. Two minutes later we were chatting like old friends until he invited me to drink a beer in his room. He was on leave from the Citadel, the military school. He told me how difficult it was for him to be gay with the fear to be discovered and get a dishonorable discharge. We had only that one nightstand but I regret not being there to get to know him better. When physical waves work it is always sad to part.

We went to Atlanta through the green countryside of South Carolina and Georgia. The city was changing rapidly soon to became a metropolis. When I first went there in 1976 the airport was small and the downtown area had a few high rises. North of Peachtree Street there were a few residential areas, but nothing special. After the death of Harvey Milk in San Francisco and the AIDS virus I heard that a lot of gays moved to Atlanta. In the area around Piedmont Park there were a few gay flags hanging by the front doors.

Left Atlanta we drove North towards Norfolk Virginia and then through Chesapeake Bay.

Tom was happy about the whole trip, but we were back to the usual routine and now we could only take short trips during the weekend. One of our favorites was going upstate to West Point area.

My colleague Alex, who was also from Italy, moved from Manhattan to my neighborhood in Queens, as a matter of fact just one block away. He had married Laura, a beautiful American-Irish girl who had Geraldine Page as acting teacher. She was very talented performing in plays off Broadway and also in soaps on national TV.

Ettore and Luciana started coming regularly to New York and we were having a great time going around to visit museums, see the world headquarter of the Jehovah's Witnesses, the Hassidic Jews that were wearing thick dark coats and big hats even in summer, and going shopping on 42nd Street. The gym was always part of my daily routine where I was making sure my body was toned. One day I over did it with cardio and my knees got really fucked up. For a couple of weeks I was hardly able to walk.

Vittoria, Martha's daughter, had found a good job in New York. Her college sweetheart moved also to Queens and joined my gym. I had a very cute work out buddy! That was giving me more motivation.

Chapter 20

It was during 1986 that a famous Italian show woman, Raffaella Carra', came to New York City to make a program for the Italian network RAI.

Joanne, who was always sociable and meeting everybody she could lay eyes on, became friend with Cinzia, a very pretty girl who was the daughter of a member of the orchestra.

She came home, one night, enthusiastic about her new friend who, obviously, was there temporarily because the show was going to last for a couple of months.

Of course I didn't object to this new friendship, as a matter of fact I was quite happy if she had these new interests. Our home became a place where we would occasionally meet after work, for brief time, then I was off to Tom's to have dinner and she was off to the Sheraton on 6th Ave. where the Italian crew was lodging.

One night she told me they were going to Chinatown to have dinner at a famous restaurant and she asked me if I would have liked to join. Since the place is very close to Greenwich Village, I said I would meet them there around eight, and so I did, parking my car around the corner, on Orchard Street.

I never really liked to mingle with Italian people abroad, especially in New York, but I must admit I was curious to see what kind of individuals were accepting Joanne as a friend, and so I was introduced to Cinzia. She was a very cute, well-shaped 25-year-old girl with a beautiful smile and very expressive eyes. She had a good sense of humor and was "playing" so to speak, with Joanne who usually had no clue about what was going on because of her candid naivety.

Cinzia was sitting at my left at the head of the table and Joanne was sitting in front of me, then there were another three people. My wife was trying to be brilliant the way she was among other people but it was obvious that nobody was really taking her into consideration. Some of her smart remarks were dead even before she could finish the sentence because the chat was leading elsewhere. Then she asked Cinzia what she thought about me and even if she found me to be enough attractive to be her husband.

Cinzia was very diplomatic but there was something going on under the table. We were now on the end of the main course and debating about having some dessert. I felt the light pressure of a shoe against mine and I was not sure if it was Joanne's or, by accident, Cinzia's. It became clear that it was not accidental by some looks that I got. At that point I played along just to see where the whole thing would lead.

Guys have always attracted me more, but if a girl would pay attention to me I would certainly not turn her down. I never knew how to approach the matter therefore I was thrilled that she was doing it for me. It also meant she was finding me sexually appealing as much as she was to me. The idea of a mutual exploration of a body was always making me horny enough to go on and show the female what a nice body and what a nice tool I was concealing under my clothes.

We left the restaurant and started walking around a semi-deserted Little Italy with Cinzia grabbing my arm and chatting with me. Of course Joanne was more interested in being the guide telling the other people about stores and Italian cafes in the area. Then while she was offering a lift to take everybody back to the Sheraton in her car, she insisted that Cinzia came with me because her car couldn't fit more than four and mine, being a sport car, couldn't fit more that 1 passenger. So I did.

During the short trip we exchanged several points of view about New York and continued chatting at the hotel bar for another hour or so. She told me clearly that she had liked me from the moment we met and I told her that, even if I was gay, I thought she was very smart and pretty. She did not look surprised. Many of her friends in Rome were gay or bisexual and she had slept with both without any problem.

We made a point to see each other very soon.

The next day Joanne asked me: "Don't you think this girl I nice? I think she likes you too, maybe we should invite her for dinner… she is the youngest there and I'm sure she prefers to be in our company".

Friday evening, out of the office, I went to pick Cinzia up and I drove home through the Midtown tunnel. Joanne was preparing one of her famous dinners with my recommendation to keep it free of hot pepper.

After a pleasant dinner we decided to go out around the area, specifically Forest Hill, and ended up at the Lemon Tree, a cute little disco. Joanne was tired because she had a very busy day at work so she decided to call the night telling Cinzia that she was welcome to spend the night at the apartment instead of going back to Manhattan.

Of course I was sleeping in the small room in my double bed while the lady of the house was occupying the master bedroom, the guestroom was adjacent to hers.

We got back quite late, after 2, then spent some time chatting on the sofa in the living room. We had many things in common and on top of that we were both Aquarians. Then she asked me if I was really in love with my wife because from what she had seen so far it didn't really appear that way.

1987

We convened that she was a nice girl who tried hard to be liked by people and who tried to emerge from some anonymity that otherwise would have let her gone unnoticed. Since I had acquired more confidence I told Cinzia that our marriage was really for convenience: mine because I could achieve residence status, her because she didn't want to be right under the supervision of her family. I think her mother had given the advice not to marry me because something was telling her that was the case. Wise woman!

I also told Cinzia that I was mostly gay, that I had been living with Tom since 1972, that I was not going to leave him for any reason, even if we had not been lovers in the true sense for many years.

One thing led to another and we finally started kidding on the sofa and landed in bed where we made passionate love until dawn. That was probably the best sexual encounter I had with a girl at that point in life. She was not inhibited like women usually are. She knew how to stimulate all the erogenous areas and she was a great kisser.

We finally laid back and relaxed when, surprise…surprise, Joanne opened the door of the room and, naked as her mother had made her, laid next to us in that already small bed!

We were both feeling uncomfortable while my wife was trying to make some conversation but not about the fact that we had spent the night in bed.

Needless to say that not even a few minutes were spent sleeping. Around 11 we were once again sitting on the sofa drinking some coffee and thinking how we were going to spend the rest of the day.

Cinzia and I became inseparable for the rest of her staying in New York. I think Joanne started realizing what was really going on only a few days later when she became very hostile. So she didn't really mind me going out with Carlos or dating other guys but she was jealous about this now "ex friend" who was stealing the attention of her husband.

The day Cinzia went back to Rome with the whole crew of Raffaella Carra' was a great day for Joanne and was a sad day for me because I didn't know if I would have seen her again. The "Eternal City" was never on my schedule.

The atmosphere at home was kind of tense and I had not slept with my wife for over to months. Usually I would do that every fortnight or so.

I made it up to her treating her to the Rainbow Room, going to the Limelight to dance and having passionate sex (I didn't say "love") for about one hour before going back to sleep in my room. Contrary to any other time I was so horny that I ejaculated on her bed.

I was just turning off the light when I heard some noise in the hallway. Curious, I went to check what was going on: Joanne had taken the sheets of her bed and was going to put them in the washing machine. When asked why she was doing that at such hour of the night, she replied: "Well, you came on my sheets and I certainly wouldn't like to get pregnant"…

The month wasn't over when I got a call from Cinzia who was back in New York to visit a friend. The story could go on!

My friend Carlos was a very nice guy. He liked to be with me but he was never possessive and was never asking questions about what I was doing during the time we were not spending together at the baths.

Time was flying since there was always something to do. The gym was my night kingdom since I preferred to go there after midnight, even with the idea (always on the back of my mind) to make some interesting encounter. That would never materialize except for once towards the end of my permanence in New York.

Cinzia was a very nice girl and we had fun being together but soon she had to go back to Roma and I went back to my routine. I managed to go to visit her a couple of times but by then she had started a longtime relationship with some guy and she was expecting a baby.

My father was getting older and I wanted him to fulfill the promise to buy me a house in Pensacola since I had won the bet to get the so-called green card.

Besides the numerous visits of my Italian friends and my frequent trips to Italy I was getting tired of working for the same company, visiting the usual customers and going to the usual places like Philadelphia, Boston and Washington. I started looking for customers in other areas of the United States and increased the collaboration with our Californian agents Consolidated Freightways.

I never really liked Los Angeles, but going there and spending more time in that city made me change my mind. Even San Francisco was a mine of potential customers for the fashion industry but that city was no longer the gay Mecca that it had been during the famous times of Harvey Milk and the golden times of the Castro.

So I found myself waking around the area with a fewer people and more hustler than ever. I picked up a cute guy that I took to dinner and then, as a dessert, to my room, but he turned out to be a hustler as well and he stole my golden ring with the crest of my family.

The trip was however successful because I managed to get a couple of good customers importing from Italy.

Back in New York I searched for a white magic group and I got in touch with a very handsome black guy from Puerto Rico who lived in the East Village. He was the great priest of a whole male coven and I figured out all the members had to be gay, just what I was looking for. After having some fun with its founder, I started having meetings twice a month with the whole group. Not many, just nine, but a couple were really hot guys and none except two were coupled.

We were meeting at the apartment of Kevin, the high priest, taking a bath, anointing our bodies and seat, naked, in a circle. The ritual was always the same, then we were proceeding to raise power in different ways, sometimes masturbating each others and ejaculating on the copper pentacle. We would also exchange muffins and drink some juice. That was taking place during some Saturday or Sunday afternoons. Carlos was never a part of it, I don't think he would have understood the whole thing.

Joanne, on the other hand, started to believe that I was coming from a different planet due to the fact that in the morning I was getting up, get dressed, go to have breakfast with Don at his apartment, go to work or about my business, then around 6 I would go back to Don, take a shower, have dinner with him and watch some TV and finally go home and change, ready to hit the clubs in the city until late night.

If Carlos would join me we would get a room at the Westside baths near 65th Street or we would go to other clubs like the Monster, the Anvil or even the bookstore all located in the Greenwich Village, the heart of the gay district. Joanne seldom saw me eating or taking a shower at home, therefore she was really thinking I was "something else" or… coming from a different part of the universe.

During the late 1986 my friend Barry started feeling some discomfort on his legs and changed his habits about going out to party. The only thing he did not reduce was his drinking habit and smoking. A famous chiropractor was coming to his apartment but the treatment didn't seem to help much. His condition did not change his attitude towards other people that we would encounter on the walks around his neighborhood. Once I remember being on line at a teller because he needed to get some cash. There was an older lady who got away with a 20$ bill and she left the slip falling on the floor. Barry looked at her complaining about the cheap "Walmart dress" she was wearing and the slippers on her feet. The guy who was next in line and before Barry picked up the slip of the old lady, then showed it to us: her balance was over 9 million $! Barry could not believe his eyes. And for the next day that was on his mind.

Another rather embarrassing time was when we went to one of his favorite restaurants, East by North West, and the guy next table asked for the check. When he saw that he was paying with a regular green American Express, Barry called the owner of the restaurant just to ask him how came they gave us a table next to such cheap people. Needless to say ha was carrying a platinum American Express with unlimited amount.

On the wall of his living room was hanging a really funny big painting with three fat women drinking a tiny cup of espresso and visibly gossiping. I liked that so I took a picture of it and I asked Don if he could replicate it. Don has always had some good drawing skills. That painting, in reduced dimension, is now hanging in our home.

Life with Joanne was becoming increasingly difficult because she wanted more out of our very fragile relationship. Alex and his wife had moved from Manhattan to Forest Hill just a block away from us. Even though she did not have much to share with them, she started going to visit quite often and one evening, after we had a small fight, she confided Laura that our marriage was all a lie and that I was really gay. All that in order to gain some sympathy. She didn't know that they had known that for a long time, besides the fact that Laura's sister was a lesbian too and nobody had any prejudice about the whole matter. Alex told me the next day and we were laughing about the episode.

One night Joanne insisted in coming to the Limelight with Carlos and me. To prove that she was able to meet somebody she disappeared in the crowd and returned after a couple of hours with an Italian guy she had met on the dance floor. She was so proud to introduce him to me and I believe he did not understand that we were married just in name and that I couldn't care less if she had an adventure or even someone else to go to bed with on a steady way. This guy was from Italy, working at a "pizzeria" and speaking a very bad English. His Italian was also very "tinted" with a lot of dialect profanities, I believe from the southern region called Calabria. However he did tell me that under the clothes of Joanne there was a lot of "good stuff". That really made me smile.

That night she did not come home and the next afternoon, when she finally appeared, she had a funny look on her face. I did not investigate any further, but after all I was happy she had got some, if she did… After a few days when I asked if she had seen the guy again, she answered with a laconic "stupid"!

The conditions of Barry were starting to worry me and I began to suspect his illness was more than a common condition. I started thinking that it had to do with AIDS. Another dear friend of mine, Jimmy, who was dating a cute latino guy named Claudio, was also getting ill but would not admit he was affected by the disease of the century. AZT was the only known possible remedy but it was difficult to find and very costly, especially for people that did not have free medical assistance.

For thanks giving weekend of that 1986 I decided to go to Pensacola to escape the harsh weather of New York for a few days. Joanne wanted to come bad and I also invited Dairo to go with us.

We left from La Guardia on a Tuesday, flew to Birmingham Alabama, then rented a car and drove to the Florida Panhandle. We were going to be hosted by my longtime friend Bill who had a "new" lover and had rented a house downtown.

The weather turned out to be nice and we spent most of the time sailing around the inner coastal waterways. Finally we could get a tan being totally out of season and swim in the still warm water of the Mexican Gulf. Of course at night we hit the clubs. To my surprise there were a couple that had recently open, Faces and Fancy Free. Joanne looked like she was having a good time too, even if she was only around a bunch of gay guys.

The funny thing was when she suddenly appeared, completely naked, at the door of Bill's room and asked him what he thought about her body. Obviously her intention was to have a sexual encounter with my ex boyfriend who had never touched a girl in his whole life.

We had a great time going around the new clubs.

The music in those years was really dynamic and I always enjoyed dancing because there was a good rhythm. Joanne didn't really have a great time at night because she was trying to chat with all the wrong people like guys that were too interested in cruising other guys or girls that were probably interested in hooking up with her. Pensacola, having a very large Navy base was home to a lot of lesbians.

The trip back home was a little more adventurous because our plane couldn't lend at La Guardia and we were forced to spend the night in Philadelphia at the expenses of the airline. We finally arrived at our final destination on the late Monday morning and everybody resumed the usual routine. At least we had a very nice tan to show off for a few days while freezing wind was blowing all over New York.

The city was fun while I was participating to our witchcraft covens, going to the clubs, meetings interesting guys almost every night, sleeping my usual 6-7 hours per night and spending time at the office only on Fridays afternoons. The weeks were flying. It seemed it was always Monday morning and suddenly Friday evenings.

One time that I didn't drive the car to Manhattan because I had stuff to do at the office, I left right at 5pm during the classic rush hour. Waiting for the subway to go to the Greenwich Village there was a cute couple next to me waiting for the train. She was the typical pretty secretary of some firm, he was a very good-looking guy with a killer smile, in his mid twenties, wearing a suit. I envied that girl and I really figured out he was a straight guy. She was very obviously hitting at him, trying to find out what his plans were for the weekend. Suddenly one of her friends tapped on her shoulder and when she turned to him she greeted him with a hug, then she introduced her friend to the new comer and from that time on, almost forgetting she was there, they started chatting and smiling to each other. The train arrived and we all boarded it. There was a big crowd but I was only a couple of feet away from them and I could hear what the guys were talking about. A few minutes and they got off at Sheridan Square without saying goodbye to the girl who looked very disappointed. I followed them for a few yards enough to see they were going inside Uncle Charlie Downtown, a famous gay bar.

These scenes were quite common in New York. While I lived there, besides the fear of AIDS, everything was happening in parks, subway, around the docks off the FDR and in the numerous clubs all over Manhattan. I think after Koch ended his term as Mayor, things changed and the city got a much cleaner look.

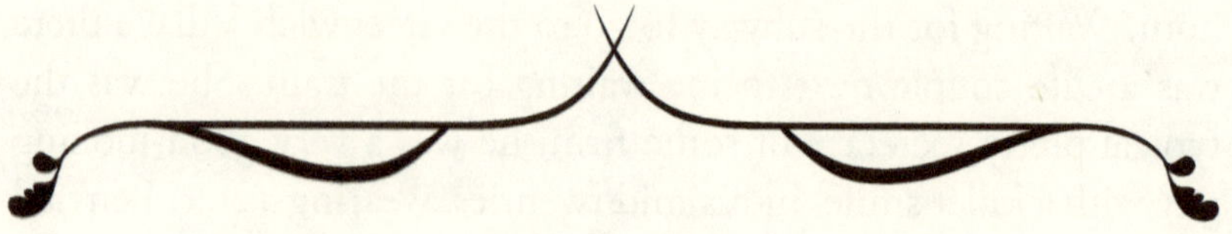

Chapter 21

Life in New York was fun, lots of friends were always coming to visit and each neighborhood offered something different. But during the winter, if the wind was blowing, the temperature was dropping to levels that were unimaginable for Europeans, not even London was so bad.

My job was fine, but, as it happened when I was working for Emery in Milano, going round to visit customers all the time was becoming routine and I started looking for something different.

There was an Italian custom broker that was a consolidator for a much smaller company than Merzario who was always trying to join his team.

I started taking care more about my business, which meant I was spending more time having fun, going to the gym or going shopping. During the weekends I was spending more time at Barry's apartment watching movies, cooking or ordering meals from fancy restaurants to be delivered to us.

Sometimes Egon, a famous Italian stylist, was popping by, entertaining us with his detailed accounts of his adventures with black guys extremely well endowed met in really scary places and taken to very scary hotels.

We had exhausted all the places to go visit with Tom. Sometimes we would take a ride to Lon Island where I had found a farm to buy duck eggs.

We hosted for a fortnight an Italian sculptor who had an exhibit in a gallery. When he left he painted 3 very interesting paintings that are still hanging in my living room.

My mother came to visit again with her dear friend Eda and Martha made sure they knew that I was gay and I was mistreating my poor wife Joanne. Fortunately my mother always misunderstood this aspect of my life, it was like her mind would not register. I know she never asked me anything about girls or if I was eventually going to have a normal family with kids. She did definitely not have patience with children.

She had brought a necklace and a matching bracelet of pearls for Joanne who was very happy to wear like they were extremely precious.

It was during a nice spring day that Joanne suddenly moved out and into a small one bedroom apartment just a couple of blocks away. When I got home, it was on a Friday afternoon, I found the master bedroom, the dining room and the living room completely empty. At that point I really got furious because I had bought the huge sectional sofa myself and she had no right to take it all. I traced her and told her I was going to take half of the sectional back to my apartment, for the rest I didn't care because the furniture was cheap and not exactly my style.

Having paid for half the rent and for the entire rent of Don's apartment did not change my financial situation because now that I was alone again Don could move back with me and we could go back to our normal life after three and a half years.

I used my job to get a free ticket to Europe to gather more stuff from home and to pick up Loreto, our parrot, from Lugano. I knew it was possible to bring one animal in the cabin on Swissair, but I had to book it in advance. The other problem was the quarantine in the USA. Through my friends at Kennedy airport I found out the best service for my pet: an acclimatized car would pick it up at my arrival and would take it to the quarantine site that was located out of the city. I could call there anytime and get up to date information about him.

I shipped a trunk full of books, clothes and personal effects to New York because at this point I was pretty sure I was staying in the country for good. Back in town I went shopping for a dining room table, chairs and a few other furniture. I didn't want to go overboard because, after all, my goal was to move to Pensacola and that was some 1200 miles south.

I had a chat with my father about the promise to buy me a house if I would get US residency and he told me he would keep his word.

I decided it was time for me to buy a car because I could not relay on the company forever. I decided to get a Honda, but when I went to the dealer and I wanted to build some credit paying 50% and financing the rest, I was told they would not approve it because I had no debts! Therefore there was no guarantee that I would keep paying the monthly due.

At that point I flew to Pensacola, shopped around for a good used car, and bought one, cash. Then I drove back to New York. That was a damn long drive so I stopped for the night somewhere in North Carolina and checked the motel out to see if there could be somebody cruising, but I had no luck.

When I start working for a new company it seems everything goes smooth and the events that take place are always exciting because of the new environment, new colleagues and a different field of potential customers to explore. After a few years of this experience, everything becomes a routine and that's when I usually get bored with my life. That was slowly but inexorably happening to me at that point. New York was getting on my nerves, the traffic, the crowds, the long lines on the Long Island Expressway or on the BQE. Even the very cold weather in winter or the very hot steamy temperature during the summer.

I started dreaming of a different kind of work, maybe more challenging, but that would leave me time to take care of my daily needs like the gym, cooking, entertaining and, of course, cruising.

There was an Italian guy who owned a small forwarding company near Kennedy airport and he had asked me several times to go work for him, it seemed challenging enough but it was certainly nothing compared to Merzario. I decided to take a leave of absence and give it a try but after the first week it appeared that he was up to no good trying to cheat on weights and to overcharge customers. I told him what I thought and left in bad terms.

Things at home were not going to well either. Joanne was getting on my nerves and I was really thinking that the breakage was going to be inevitable. After all I had got what I had aimed for and I wanted to get back to my previous life with Don and my freedom.

Robin, my secretary, was hoping that I would not rush into something that I would regret, but the urge for a change was too strong.

Some furniture was in Tom's apartment and I went to buy a round dining table and some chairs. Needless to say that Tom moved back with me, he took the master bedroom and I kept my small but comfortable bedroom. The guestroom had just a queen size bed, a night stand and, of course, the closet. That was good because my mother was supposed to come visit shortly and then Ettore and his wife were scheduled to be over for a whole month in may.

I had a long phone talk with my father and told him it was time to fulfill his promise to buy me a house as we had agreed if I would get my US residency.

A head-hunter called me because there was a company interested in my services. It was an international freight forwarder with its headquarter on the 40th floor of the world trade center. Most of the work was done by the clerk and I had to get in touch with the airline companies, get the best deals on rates and schedule the fastest transit time. They were not offering a company car, but I didn't have to go around town or the state to visit customers. The salary was not as high as with Merzario, but I couldn't expect it to be, still they were offering something short of 80.000 $ a year. I took the job but was not sure I would keep it for long. New York had started to bore me: excessive cold in the winter, hot and humid in the summer, bad traffic and even the quality of the air was not good.

The fact that I had to spend at the office most of the day from 9 till 5, going back and forth in the subway, not been able to go to the gym whenever I wanted, took over me and three months later I was ready to quit.

I flew to Pensacola and with the help of Tom who hooked me up with Elizabeth, a nice real estate agent; I started looking for the house that would be my home in the place I wanted to settle.

The area I always liked was the same where my friend Tony had been living for years, in Myrtle Grove, on the west side of town.

Fortunately Elizabeth showed me different areas in the east side, by the bay, that were much nicer and even very affordable. The choice fell on a house that had been vacant for 2 years off Scenic Hwy, a small 3 bedrooms 2 bathrooms and garage in a cul de sac with a big corner lot. It had belonged to a member of the Gambino family and it was repossessed by the VA. It needed some work but the price was only 44.000$.

There I made my first big mistake: instead of paying it in full I put 1000$ down and got a 15 years mortgage thinking that I would get a job, and pay for the restructuring with the money my father had given me. Things do seldom work the way one figures them out.

I went back to New York, the deal of the house got through, I got in the car with Don and Loreto, and we drove to Pensacola stopping in North Carolina for the night.

The plan was to take possession of the house, get it ready to be habitable, leave Tom and Loreto, fly back to New York, get the rest of the furniture and drive the truck back to Pensacola.

The first night was obviously spent at a motel. That evening in an effort to show the house to Don we drove to the subdivision. It was dark but the moon was shining and it was possible to have an idea of the location. His response was totally negative. While I had seen the potential of the construction, he thought the house had too much work to be done and he didn't want to inspect any further blaming me for choosing such a neighborhood and sitting back in the car. I tried to explain that I had envisioned much more but it was useless.

Anyway I had the utilities turned on, got an inflatable mattress, moved in and spent the first night.

There was a chirping noise every now and then and we thought there was a bird trapped in the house, only the next morning we found out that the smoke detectors were running out of batteries and that was the noise they were making.

I went to buy a fridge, some necessary supplies, then I flew back to New York to get the rest of the furniture.

Fortunately I managed to get a telephone line because in those days cellular phones were just starting and not many areas were covered.

With the help of some friends we managed to load the truck. The most bulky things were the sofa and the dining table. One does not realize how much stuff there is in a house until everything has been taken out of the closets! I even eliminated some because I found it totally useless. By 11 am I left Queens starting my journey of 1170 miles to Florida that would take almost 2 days stopping in a motel in S. Carolina. I arrived in Pensacola for teatime and found Tom a little bit more satisfied than before because he had inspected the yard and found it of his liking.

The first thing to do was to get rid of the awful greenish carpet throughout the house and get an estimate to have some hardwood floor installed in the living room and the corridor.

Then we started to paint the rooms with different colors, got cable tv, went to the flea market to browse and see how to make the house more livable. Joanne had got most of the stuff but that was ok because everything for me up to that point was cheap and temporary. Now I was starting to buy things according to my taste and certainly not cheap. In the bank I had more than 40,000$ and great projects in my mind.

The new appliances gave a different aspect to the kitchen and plants bought at the nursery were slowly turning the bare backyard into a greener place making Tom a happier guy.

I got acquainted with some of the neighbors and they all seem very nice, specially a lady who was from Denmark two houses down.

My old friend Tom Hay who was the local agent for Emery loaned me a truck to howl the debris to the landfill. It was such a pleasure to go there and unload the ugly carpet and a lot of other unwanted stuff that was scattered all over the front and back yard.

We needed a privacy fence to replace the low metal one. Tom wanted and got a poster bed while I was still sleeping in the sectional sofa we had in New York.

I let him have the master bedroom while I picked the smaller of the 3 bedrooms closer to the entrance and across from the second bathroom. It bothered me that didn't have a window, so I had a skylight installed making the ceiling much higher.

From the kitchen to the backyard there was a double sliding glass door and out there a concrete platform some 20 by 15 feet. That was a good base for a so called "Florida room".

I really wasn't using the garage for the car because I thought it was a waste of time to open and close the door, eventually I would have used the garage space to enlarge the house.

In the meantime I started going to the clubs, the beach and even to a Masonic lodge that was right on Scenic Hwy. I became more acquainted with people that counted in town. Jack Pace, the local millionaire, was a great help and also a lot of fun. The only problem with him was his drinking habit. After a certain time his mind was not connecting properly and that was a shame for such a brilliant men.

It took a couple of months to make the house more likeable. Even Tom was starting to appreciate my choice.

My long time Bill was always pursuing his ideas for grandeur looking for the perfect love and possibly somebody with means. Sometimes he was getting on my nerves. His brother Ronnie was so hot but so in love with his third boyfriend, a totally different kind of guy. Sometimes we were all going to Mobile, just 40 minutes away, for a change of scene. There were 4 gay clubs in the same block and they stayed open much later than those in Pensacola, one didn't close at all. I met some guys over there and I was having a lot of fun while Tom, I thought, was staying home all the time even though the Bluff, very cruising spot in Pensacola, was just a half mile away.

In those days the city administration was not too much concerned about gays. The gay beach had been used since the 1920's and family oriented beaches were more to the East, like Fort Walton and Destin. Ours was the best-kept secret in Florida until… the mid 1990's when everything started to change.

Anyway there were places like Trader John, an institution, and Rosie O'Grady, a complex of 9 bars/restaurants and discos, packed by large crowds almost every night of the week, and there were our 9 gay clubs with people coming from places as far as Panama City and even New Orleans.

One afternoon I just went to a very quiet bar to see what was going on. There were just a dozen customers but this cute young guy who was chatting with an older skinny queen drew my attention. When he remained alone I noticed we was crying. I said nothing but I wrote this note on a piece of paper "you are too nice to be so upset… if you want to talk call me at this number…." And I gave it to him, and then I left.

I had forgot about this episode when, a day later, the phone rang and it was him!

That was David, a 20-year-old sailor stationed in Pensacola on the Lexington, an ancient aircraft carrier.

We met that afternoon because he had a couple of days leave. I couldn't take him home because Tom would have not been a very happy camper, so I got him a room in a motel and he told me why he was in that state of mind: there was an older guy he had met and they saw each other for a few times until he found out this guy had a lover who was working on an oil rig. They had a falling out and David got very hurt by this matter that could not get out of his mind.

I took him to dinner and by the end of the day he was feeling much better, so much better that we ended up in bed together having one of the best time since I had moved to Pensacola.

We started seeing each other and somehow I managed to sneak him into my room at night taking off the screen from the window and letting him out at dawn, while Tom was still asleep.

David was from Bonyfay, a small town 120 miles East, by the border with Alabama. His dad was a retired navy officer, he was the only son but he had 2 older step brothers.

He hated the day he decided to enlist in the navy and he didn't like the Lexington. But he had at least another 2 years to go before getting discharged.

To see him every time he was off duty became the rule. I never dated somebody so much younger before, but that was not bothering me and it seemed we were getting along great and always having a good time. Due to the fact he was under 21 he could not go to the clubs, but the owners of the Fantasy club apparently liked him and had no problem to let him in. We both liked to dance but he also liked to drink quite a bit. It didn't seem that was affecting his state of mind. Needless to say I was paying for everything, but that was certainly not a problem. The real problem was to tell Tom that I had found someone I was very comfortable with and to introduce him. I had to work on Tom state of mind to make him feel sorry about this young guy who was young, in the military, far from home and very unhappy. It was kind of rough on him, but in the end he agreed to meet him.

The second step was to let David stay at the house whenever he was off duty, and even this was accomplished without too much drama. I always hated drama. Of course Tom was like a brother to me, and our relationship was not going to change regardless of my possible lovers.

So David's car was parked in our driveway and he had the possibility of seeping over every time he was off duty, meaning 3 day a week.

Tom was very much a homebody, going to the stores very early in the morning, working on the garden planting plants I was getting at the nursery and making him very happy. Of course he was not eating with us, but always in his room, away from indiscreet eyes. Then he had the beloved TV with all the programs he so much loved.

My little Honda started having mechanical problems when it was approaching the 100.000 miles, so I decided to get rid of it and David, who knew much more about cars, came with me to the dealers. The choice fell on a Pulsar that had T tops and looked very sporty, the ideal for a beach town like Pensacola.

We were having a blast! I always liked to go to the clubs until late, dance, socialize with my friends, not having to cruise looking for other guys to have sex with and the fact that David was in the navy and he was tested for vds and AIDS was a security for me. Our sex was always without protection while people were starting to die all over because in those early days of the epidemic the only drug available, AZT, was not really doing much for anybody, in fact it was making things worse.

So I learned that my dear friend in New York, Barry, had died and my other friend Jimmy was very sick while his lover Claudio, 24 years old, was in the hospital with Kaposi sarcoma and other diseases. Even Dairo was now on AZT and trying all kind of different therapies, including the "urine therapy" already practiced by Ghandy.

The days were passing fast and so were the weeks and months. Did not have any worries, money in the bank, and always thinking there would be plenty of time to search for a job. I also provided David with an additional American Express card with no spending limit, thinking he would use it responsibly; after all he had been living alone and far from his family and on a budget. He certainly liked to drink! Even though he could not being still under 21. I saw him "happy" several times but even then he was still very much in control and had a clear mind.

On his 21st birthday we celebrated with an evening at the Fantasy Club with a bunch of friends. I had a couple of drinks while he had several. Leaving the club right around closing time, at 2am, he insisted in driving back home. I really didn't want that, but being his birthday, I finally allowed it. Back then, the safety belts were not an enforced law in Florida and we were never using them (they always bothered me).

Going up Scenic Highway, instead of turning on Newton to the house, he kept driving forward reaching and passing the Bluffs. He had probably in mind to go all the way to the chimney, famous cruising spot to see who was there. Suddenly he started playing with the steering wheel while I was asking to stop that. It happened in a fraction of a second when he turned the wheel right and the car went on the edge of the road, tilted to the right and felt down the hill for about 200 feet, banging on trees and rotating over bushes and shrubs and ending near the railroad with the car leaning on the right side. I do remember going out of the road, but I certainly don't remember falling all the way down. I came out of the passenger window and in the pale light of the moon I saw David's head and torso sticking out of the driver's window, while the T-top was resting on his belly and the rest of his body was trapped inside the car. He appeared not to be breathing and I was almost sure he had been crushed by the weight of the car. I tried to push the car to make it fall on its 4 wheels but it was too heavy. Then I tried to do mouth to mouth respiration to David and thanks god he started coughing and opened his eyes. He appeared to be allright with a few bruises on the face and a concussion on his head. He could also move his legs, but he could not free himself from that position.

Going down we had also destroyed a wooden staircase, so I reached out and climbed to the top of the road to call for help. Due to the late hour it took me almost 30 minutes to stop a car and give the alarm. Finally the police arrived around 3,30 am, they moved the car releasing David from his position and they called an helicopter from Baptist hospital to pick up David and to fly him to the emergency room, but before doing that they took a sample of his blood for testing. I couldn't say I was driving because he was the one trapped on the driver's side. He was charged with DUI since the content of alcohol in his blood was 3 times over the limit.

I had a few bruises on my legs and arms, but on the whole nothing dramatic had happened. They wanted me to go to the emergency room but I refused and a policeman gave me a lift to the house.

Tom of course was very mad and more concerned about the status of the car that was obviously totaled than the fact that I was shocked for what had happened and that David was recovered in the hospital. At dawn I called his parents and told them what had happened and they rushed to Pensacola from Bonifay and we all went to the hospital to see what were his conditions: Just a light concussion, he could leave the hospital in the afternoon.

The car was recuperated and taken to a junk yard to be examined by the insurance agent, but I knew the result would have been not reparable. Now we did not have transportation with the exception of David's Gran Prix and I was in need of buying another car as soon as possible.

I did not follow anybody's advice and my choice felt on a very cheap and new Geo Metro. For me it was just basic transportation and nothing else. State Farm reimbursed me for the value of the Pulsar and paid for the expenses of David's recovery and hospital bills, but then they dropped me leaving me with the task of finding another insurance. It was then that I started my longtime relationship with Nationwide.

The accident was soon forgotten but the DUI charges remained and coasted some 3000$ plus some restrictions on David's driving. After that he became more careful about drinking relying more on my driving.

I started looking for a job and I found one through an agency in Fort Walton, but the location was not going to be Pensacola after all, I got a position as a night manager at a German restaurant in Niceville, some 35 miles to the east. I had to leave the house around 3pm and work until closing, sometimes as late as 1am, sometimes a little earlier. The restaurant was a very nice one and quite big. It could accommodate about 200 customers and I had a crew of 16 waiters, 2 chefs and some kitchen helpers. In that area there were several German people vacationing on the Emerald Coast but many customers were military personnel that had stationed in American bases in Germany and that had liked that kind of food.

Going back and forth to the restaurant was a little annoying, but after all the salary was good and I did not have to get up early in the morning, thing that I never liked to do. And we still had time to go to the clubs two times a week to enjoy time with our friends and to dance. Back in those days the music was still good, not like the crap that they play now. Madonna, Michael Jackson and many other groups were extremely popular, at least music had a good rhythm.

Sometimes we would go to the beach to swim and get sun. Once David had his feet exposed in such a way that when we got back to the house they were burned so much he was not able to wear shoes and walk for a couple of days. Everybody was teasing him for that.

The weeks were passing fast and the money was going fast too. I made the mistake of giving an American Express card to David with no limit. I thought he was using it wisely but by Christmas the balance he had put on it reached 17.000$! What could I do but ask for help to my parents? My father wired me enough to cover the card and some money to put in the bank, but at that point it was necessary for me to find a job fast. He occasion came from an old friend of mine who owned a restaurant downtown: I started as a waiter during lunch and, since he was only open during the day, we agreed that I would open in the evening. The schedule was: German food for lunch, Italian food for dinner. The place was very cozy and had just 14 tables that could accommodate about 60 people. Lunch was usually very busy and the tips were split between me and Jerry, the other waiter, For dinner I had to build my clientele but fortunately, by word of mouth, knowing many people in town, I succeeded to fill the restaurant every night. I did not have many items on the menu because I wanted to serve real Italian food and stuff that was not available in the "So called" Italian restaurants in the area. As a matter of fact there was one just next door that provided a good service but mostly Americanized bastard food. We gained several customers that were going to "Scotto" during the 7 months that followed. Mark, the owner, was providing with the supplies, David was serving and Tom was cleaning up and washing the dishes. Besides the tips we were making 40% of the total bills.

David was not happy to be in the Navy, with one and a half year to go to the end of his service, and to gain the 20.000$ that he would get for college after an honorable discharge, he decided to take a step that would getting him out for good, without even discussing the matter with me: he was a boiler technician on board of the old aircraft carrier Lexington, always anchored at the NAS base. One morning he pretended he got insane and tried to jump overboard! One week later he was released with a disonorable discharge. Out of his principal job and with his car to maintain, a Montecarlo that had several engine problems, he managed to get a part time job at a burger joint, Hardees. When he was coming home after his shift he had to take a shower because the smell of fried was all over him.

It was during that time that I metTim, a very cute guy who liked me very much, but there was no chemistry from my part. He introduced me to Janet, his roommate, and to Ella, their landlady who was running a cleaning company serving offices and churches in the area. It was with her that Tom found a job that would keep him occupied during 4 or 5 hours in the evening. That was the perfect combination because, being agrophobic and having the fear of working among other people, was allowing him to work by himself in empty places. Driving to and back was not a problem. Sometimes I would take him there, sometimes was David.

One night, going to pick him up I went through I-110. After the ramp, going at speed limit (in those days it was 55mph) an other car was trying to pass me. I accelerated and so did he. In other words I didn't want him to pass me. My speed reached almost 80 mph when, suddenly the unmarked car turned the lights on and I realized I was racing with an under covered cop!

I pulled on the side of the highway and stopped, then I waited for the cop to approach me with his flashlight and I told him that

I was Italian, they had kidnapped me on a highway in Italy in the same way, passing me and forcing to stop my car, and that was like reviving the whole scene all over again scaring me to the point that I was trying to escape and reach a less isolated place downtown.

He checked my driver license and car registration, then he apologised and let me go! I could have landed in jail for something like that! Don't even know how that explanation came out of my mouth so fast and so convincing, probably thanks to my Italian accent.

Time was passing by and we were spending money like crazy. My idea to find a job was slowly fading away. I had made a curriculum that I was passing around, but a call was never coming. I started to fear about paying the mortgage of the house. Tom was doing his best to make some money; David was only good to spend it. My big mistake was to give him an American express card that had no limit… too late I realized he had charged almost 17.000 $ buying stuff we didn't need, going to restaurants etc. The only thing I could do was turn to my parents for help.

Of course I knew they wouldn't let me down, the money transfer arrived in a couple of days and all the bills were paid. In the meantime I started working for Rainbow carpet cleaning company going around houses and apartments together with the owner who would come pick me up in the early morning and drop me home around 4. It wasn't too bad of a job, not really too hard and interesting. The money was paying the expenses and we even had some left over.

After a few months, while we were cleaning dome condo in Perdido, I received a phone call from my brother in law: my sister had died in Lugano, the funeral was going to be the next day! That was a very sad news. I knew she had been sick but my family didn't tell me how really bad she was, fighting cancer, in a clinic for the last 4 months.

I really don't care about death, that's just a passage from a stage to another, but the fact that she suffered so much was really hurting. She was 53.

One day I had a talk with Mark Meyer, he was the owner of the German restaurant "Bodenheimer" in the center of town, Seville square. He was only open for lunch and had a very busy crowd. I got an idea and proposed him to open at night for Italian food. Considering that next door there was a pseudo Italian restaurant "Scotto" the matter appeared really challenging. We decided I would open up around 5pm, David would seat the customers, take the orders and serve, Tom would come in after his cleaning work to wash dishes and clean the kitchen. I prepared a menu with about 18 different dishes, all 100% Italian. The news went fast around my numerous friends in Pensacola and the first week wasn't even over that the restaurant got filled very quickly. There were only 16 tables sitting a total of 70-80 people. Mark was ordering all the food that I was asking for, the bread was coming from the renound French bakery "Napoleon" and I was preparing a few different desserts like "tiramisu', zabaglione, panna cotta, montebianco etc."

Biggest reward is that we never had a complaint, never a dish returned with some food left over and many customers of Scotto started coming over! David was happy because he was getting good tips, Tom was working for the glory and sometimes, when there was too much to do, Jerry, who was the waiter during lunch, was coming to help too.

Now I could really say I was getting experience in restaurant management. I liked to cook and the appreciation of the customers was a big reward.

We had agreed that I would get 40% of the net income and Mark was keeping his word on that.

Still, after about 8 months of this hard work, I got contacted byan employment agency in Fort Walton Beach: there was a position for night manager at a very important German restaurant in Niceville, some 40 miles away.

I went to talk to Mr. Fennel who explained to me what the work would consist in. There was a staff of 8 chefs and a crew of 18 servers and busboys, my duty was to take over around 5pm and stay until closing around midnight. The salary was going to be around 400$ a week! More than I was making at Bodenheimer. Mark was sorry to see me go, but he understood that was more proficuous for me.

So I started going to Niceville 6 days a week, putting miles on the car that I had just bought. One doesn't realize how quickly the mileage goes up. Gas was no problems since the price back then was around $1,20 per gallon.

I had to wear a suit and tie every day. With my wide collection of Italian clothes that was certainly not a problem. David had found some work at Hardees flipping burgers and when he was getting home at night he had to jump in the shower and change because the smell of the fried food wa really awful. Tom was always going to clean offices from 6 to 10 and he had managed to get around by car in Pensacola.

Niceville is a beach resort on the Emerald coast very close to Eglin airforce base. Many military stationed there had been to American bases in Germany so they liked German food. Heidelberg Hause was owned by Germans and Mr. Fennel was part owner and manager. The food was strictly authentic and not Americanized. We were busy every night, sometimes with over 300 customers. Of course if some waiters were not needed it was my duty to send them home… everything to reduce costs. A computerized program was helping me to determine that. Before closing I had to deposit all the cash in the safe, make sure that everything had been cleaned and in order, turn on the alarm system and close down.

On the highway connecting the interstate I-10 I would sometimes stop to a rest area that looked cruisy and sometimes I would get lucky in picking up somebody cute for some quick sex. Once I even found a very hot guy that I had noticed before eating at the restaurant. Tom was sound asleep when I was getting home but David was seldom there. We had met this guy named Wayne who was in his late thirties, working at Sacred Heart hospital as an anesthesiologist. His house in East Hill was a gay heaven. A lot a guys were stopping by to drink, smoke pot, socialize and… have sex if chemistry was right, sometimes even 3 or 4ways on the same bed. David had befriended this not too cute skinny long haired (I do not like guys with long hair) named Billy. This close friendship was really getting on my nerves but I wasn't saying anything. It was allright to have some fun with other partners but with the same one all the times it meant there was something more going on and jealousy was sparkling up.

A young Pilipino arrived in town and, of course, was hosted by Wayne. He was too cute to be left alone and everybody had him. At the beginning he seemed quite masculine, but soon enough he revealed his true nature: he became one of the main attraction in the drag queen show at the "Office", the new gay disco in town. Later on he moved to Chicago where he became quite famous under the assumed name of Regine Phillips, some of his shows can be seen on YouTube.

I had stopped going to the Masonic lodge because talking about business and how they were employing the charity money was not really interesting, besides after the meetings they would go to the bars to have drinks until they dropped.

The gay beach was the Sunday afternoon pastime, swimming, getting tan, relaxing on the white sand and walking up and down to see who was there. Some would lay down in the nude keeping an eye on the rangers that did not allow nudity.

The round up was the usual stop on the way back home after sunset and then there were different choices of clubs to spend the night. The Fantasy club, the Office, the Grocery Store, Fancy Free, Faces and, of course, the new Red Garter were the busy and favorite spots. Some guys would also go to the Rosie o'Grady complex to look for straight condescending guys, mostly military. The opening of "Sluggo" changed the habits of most people that were going to cuise at the chimney or by the waterfront area around the auditorium after 2am when all the clubs were closed. This was, and still is, a "byob" club, bring your own bottle, open until 5am on weekends.

Things were going quite smooth and could not last forever. So, one evening, while I was on duty, Mr Fennel informed me my services were no longer needed because the restaurant was going to close, the Germans had decided not to renew the leasing of the premises and would let everybody go! So, back to square one. I would get a severance of a full month salary and the task to look for another job that was not easy. In a way I was glad not to be driving back and forth every day, but certainly the money wouldn't last long so I started to look for something in the restaurant business, reducing my curriculum to my last 2 experiences. Whataburger called me and offered the position of assistant manager with a starting salary of 250$ a week. That wasn't bad, 5 working days, 6am to 3pm, the burger place was just 5 miles away, and lunch was included. I had to go through a week training and learn to use the computer program that was very similar to the one of the restaurant.

Working in a burger joint could be very stressful depending on the time of the day. Breakfast and lunch were extremely busy and during the other time the crew needed to restock the kitchen, clean up, mop the floor and make sure the next customer didn't have a long wait. If it would get slow it was up to me to reduce the personnel sending somebody home. The team leader was giving a great support, she had been working at that location for 3 years. The manager was usually coming in around 11am and he expected everything to be perfect. This place was just 3 miles away from the naval air station, on Fridays, when the military were getting paid, we would sell food for over 30.000 $! I remember there was a couple with two kids, all short and very overweight, that was coming in for breakfast and for lunch every day eating everything from salad to turnovers and would get a jumbo diet coke because regular coke would have too many calories!

One thing I have to say about these burger places is that the frying oil turns brown after 2 or 3 days, it's shocked with some white powder to clear it up and it's finally changed every other week. The used oil, together with the grease from the cooked meat, is dumped in a big metal reservoir in the back of the building that a truck is picking up every other week. The smell is not pleasant...

My Whataburger adventure lasted about 6 months. I had to fire a cashier by the order of the manager because she was 3$ short. She needed the job and she was crying, but there was nothing I could do to help her. The final stroke came a few days later when, during breakfast, a lady in a Jaguar started cursing the team leader at the drive through because the service was too slow. I intervened and told the lady to take her business somewhere else and not to insult my colleague calling her names. The customer called Whataburger headquarter from the car phone complaining and when the manager arrived he was furious for what had happened. I sent him to hell and left on the spot.

Of course I was going to do that anyway since my ex colleague from New York, Alex, asked me to open their branch office in Atlanta.

I was back in the shipping business!

So now I had to go to Atlanta, find a location for the office. I asked my friend Tom if he had a correspondent there and he put me in touch with Atlanta Custom Broker: the office was found, the place to live too because a dear friend of ours who was living in Pensacola had moved to Atlanta and had a very large house. That was a very good opportunity for David too because he could work at the office and start a career in the freight forwarding and import export.

At that time I had to buy another car and leave the Geo in Pensacola to allow Tom to go to work and to go shopping. The choice fell on a Ford Tempo, used, of course, but big enough for our needs. The day we left Pensacola was on a Saturday right after lunch but, arrived in Flomaton, just across the Alabama border, the car stalled and the only mechanic told us it was a computer chip that could not be replaced until the following Monday morning! The only alternative was to stop in the only motel available and spend the two nights there, in the middle of nowhere. Flomaton is definitely not a very happening place, not even during a weekend. A prostitute and her pimp occupied the room next door and there was some movement until early morning. Finally, the car being repaired, we proceeded to Roswell Georgia where our friend Larry welcomed us in his big house.

The place was nice, surrounded by woods, in a very quiet neighborhood but only one mile and a half away from the interstate. The office, located by the airport, was a straight shot south that would take about 20 minutes even in heavy traffic rush.

Of course during the weekends we would go back to Pensacola even though that was 300 miles away but, being the boss, we could leave right after lunch on a Friday.

So during the week I was going around visiting existing customers and several prospects that had business to and from Europe.

Atlanta is a very large city but it certainly doesn't compare to New York or Chicago. All the clubs were located in midtown, including the "Cove", the only one open 24/7. For David this was a very interesting and happening place because living between Alabama and Florida he had never experienced something like that. I must also say that after the big epidemic of AIDS happened a lot of guys moved from San Fancisco and Los Angeles to Atlanta making it the new gay center besides New York and Miami. Everywhere there were the rainbow flags posted in front of houses and business, our favorite places soon became Berkhard, Buddy and Bulldog. Occasionally we would go to the Eagle but the guys there were a little too weird for our taste. At the office we became good friends of Donna who had a partner named Kathy. Not that we liked to mingle with a bunch of lesbians, but them and their friends were really cool.

It was at Burkhard that David befriended this guy names Jerry, first playing pool and then also dancing together. We had always cruised together, but this time, for some reason, I thought the matter was going beyond what I liked.

For a few weeks nothing really happened, on my side I met other guys that were quite interesting. One night I was in a club notorious for hustlers when I met a really nice guy named Tim. At first I thought he was just a very cute hustler trying to pick me up, but it turned out to be a wealthy young man, living in a big house in midtown. He didn't have any particular job but we were into remodeling his home and landscaping his yard, he had the so called green thumb.

David was seldom going out with me, always with this Jerry guy. Of course, not having a car, he was depending on him to get around. Needless to say he was not allowed to spend the night out.

Larry, our roommate, met a guy in a club and decided to let him move in the house without even asking our opinion. This drove David mad so I had the task to find another accommodation. I found an apartment in a nice complex very close to the airport and off we moved. There was also a gym in the premises making my life easier, David said he wanted to work out with me, but that didn't last long. He was getting on my nerves because then he did not want to go to Pensacola for the weekend. The 4to5 hours drive was becoming too annoying by myself besides I did not trust that car too much after the water pump broke. I always like the shape of the Probe, so I went to Ford and exchanged the Geo and the Tempo with 2 semi-new Probe, one silver and one burgundy, I left this one with Tom.

My patience with David reached the limit when he did not come home one night, nor did he call me. He showed up around noon the next day to find all his belongings on the lawn in front of our building. I told him he could go and live with Jerry because I didn't want him under the same roof.

At that point I was single again and I was resolute to enjoy myself meeting other gays and eventually dating them but not for a long time, just for fun. My new friend Tim asked me if I wanted to be his roommate in his huge house in midtown and I accepted even because it was very close to all the clubs and even to my gym.

Tim vas a "party popper" and many times he had a lot of friends over for dinner or even to spend the night with. His taste was usually not matching mine, but I was pretty successful in meeting interesting people.

During the weekends I was always going to Pensacola, sometimes with friends that wanted to go to the beach. Wade was a very cute guy I had met at the "Phoenix" who was married and separated with 2 kids. We became very close friends and also slept together a few times. He was a plumber during the day but at night he made a living challenging other guys at the bar playing pool, betting, and usually winning.

The Cove was another club open 24 hours and according to the time of the day one could find interesting people to hang with. Very late at night the drunks were poring in and, as I could see from their eyes, drugs like ecstasy were circulating freely.

Sometimes I would plan a trip to different cities in neighborhood states where there were some potential customers to be acquired. Charleston and Savannah were my favorite even because there were some gay guesthouses. One town that I found very ugly, overbuilt and of no interest at all was Myrtle Beach.

So one morning of September 1991 when I went to the office I found a fax sent by my friend in Genova announcing that my father had been taken ill in Lugano. When I called home I was told that when my parents came back from Lavarone on the Sunday afternoon, he had gone out for a walk but shortly after he went back home feeling sick and asking my mother to call an ambulance. Rushed to the hospital he remained unconscious until Thursday morning when he passed away for cardiac arrest.

My nephew informed me the funeral had been disposed for the next morning, Friday, but I told him to hold it until I would be there. That evening I boarded the flight to Milano and by 9am I was in Alberto's car going to Switzerland.

This is when the real nature of my nephew came to the surface.

After telling me he was sorry for my father's death he said he had preferred my mother had died instead. Then he asked me if he could have my dad's golden watch and he handed me an envelope with 12 million Italian lire: he had already gone to Lavarone to withdraw almost all the money in the bank from my parents account and was going to divide it with me. There was no way to get the rest of the money back because he had already spent it.

Sunday morning there was my dad's funeral held by his Masonic brothers of the Lugano lodge. My nephew and his wife came wearing jeans and T-Shirt.

I must say my mother took the departure in a very quiet way. I had always wondered what would happen if one of them had died after over 50 years of life in common.

My week was very busy. I had to go to Lavarone, close the account at the bank and reopen one in my name so that my nephew would not interfere again, then I went to one of the banks in Lugano and took the whole content of the safety box. Some 300 golden coins were missing and so where the golden Parker pens with my father's name engraved. Probably more was taken by my nephew but I had no way to know it because there was not an inventory available.

I arranged for all the utilities payments to be made through the bank and provided my mother with a bank card in case she needed money. Fortunately one of those nights I ran into a very handsome blonde guy who was an attorney who started taking care of all the legal aspects that needed to fulfilled and also about the transfer of my dad's 3 pensions to my mother.

I flew back to Atlanta after spending a couple of weeks between Italy and Switzerland. With me I brought back all the content of the safe box and a lump sum of money in cash. It was my intention to give 5000$ to Joanne to pay her credit cards, but that never happened because she did not show up at Kennedy airport nor she Ever called me again and I lost track of her.

At this point I really didn't have any reason to go on working in Atlanta so I gave my resignation and went back to Pensacola for good.

I had arranged an open account from one of the Swiss banks to my Pensacola bank so whenever I needed cash I could get it wired with a simple call.

I started buying houses to rent. The real estate market then was booming. Paying cash I could get very good deals and the revenue was quite high, over 8% on a yearly basis after paying for insurances and property taxes. I was buying very nice houses in the best areas of tow, houses that didn't need much work and were basically ready to move in. By the end of 1991 I owned 4 plus the one Tom and I were living in. On this one I added a second master bedroom, converted the garage in a big storage area, pantry and a very cute living room with bar area, very convenient for the parties that I like to throw frequently. On the back of the house I had built a large Florida room, a kind of heated and air-conditioned all glass room with stain glass skylights. I also had several sun tunnels installed in my home and also in the rentals.

My friends Antonio and Fiorella and also Ettore with Luciana were frequently coming to visit. Even they started checking out the possibilities of buying houses in Pensacola for investment, after all I was living there and I could take care of their properties. So Ettore bought 2 in my same neighborhood and Antonio one in Gulf Breeze.

It was then that Fiorella introduced me to an Italian couple, he was a retired co-pilot from Alitalia and his wife, originally from Trieste, had been living in Pensacola for many years. They Introduced me to other Italians resident in the area and to the famous Italian Cultural Society that was meeting once a month for eating, drinking and cultural events.

Tom was still working for the cleaning company and there was no way to make him stop.

I had got tired of the Probe and had set my eyes on an older model of Corvette, but after driving it for a couple of weeks I decided it was really a gas consuming piece of crap, so I settled for a blue Stealth 3000GT, best car I ever had and very powerful.

Then I bought a Ninja motorcycle to go running around in my shorts and T, going to the beach or to the gym.

The nights were spent between the Round Up, the Office or even going skinny dipping at the gay beach with friends. Occasionally going to Fort Walton, Mobile or even New Orleans for a change of scene, this latter I could not take it for more than a couple of days because everything was just too much.

Time was coming for my mother to go spend summer in Lavarone, so I got the usual ticket on Swissair and left for Zurich and Lugano.

Her friend Rosita had already met my mother and we were ready to drive to the mountain, but before I went to the banks to see the situation of all the accounts. It's there that I found a very unpleasant surprise: money had been withdrawn from 3 of them on different occasions, and they were not really small amounts. When I asked my mother if she had taking all that money for specific reasons, she said she had not withdrawn much besides what she needed for the normal house expenses, but she confirmed that my nephew Alberto had visited quite often, taking her out to lunch, and telling her she had to go to the bank to sign some documents. Obviously he had tricked her and in most cases, since the accounts were invested in stocks and bonds, the bank had to sell some to free some money, also applying some penalties. In all the damage had been consistent around 150.000 Swiss Francs!

I had to close all the accounts and re-open them, always in my mother's name, but with my only signature.

I did not bring up this matter with my nephew but for that Summer my mother told him they could not spend any time at the house with the pretext that they just had a baby who was too small and she did not want children around.

When I went back to Lugano spent a few days there relaxing and meeting occasional friends and having a really good time. I also spent a day in Zurich in a hotel in the old district spending the night at a club where they had an excellent drag queen show and where I met the cutest Hungarian guy that ended up in my bed. In the morning I boarded the 747 back to Atlanta and Pensacola.

After that summer of '91, when I went back to pick up my mother in the mountain a very tragic news struck me: Ghena's husband, Giorgio, had died in a car accident while he was driving his Volvo in Sofia. The guy who never wanted to fly because was afraid of planes had been hit by a big truck. Ghena was devastated but she went on with her performances around the world.

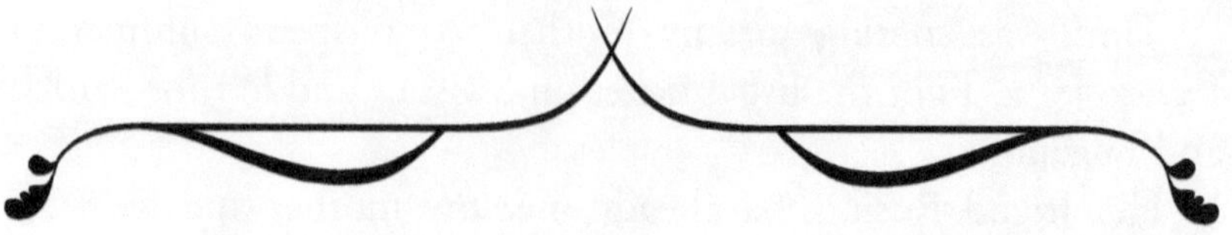

Chapter 22

The year 1992 had started with a big "bang" and everything was just going well.

Ettore and Luciana had bough a couple of houses in my area and Antonio and Fiorella had bought a house in Gulf Breeze. My dear friend Ron Nelson told me there was a small condo available at the Mirador, the oldest and classic apartment building on the bayou near downtown Pensacola. I bought that 50/50 with my friends always transfering money from one of the Swiss accounts.

Not really surprising was a letter that I got from the IRS requesting an "audit". When I went there they wanted to know where was all that money coming from . Being a resident alien and since the transfers were officially sent by my mother, it emerged there was no limit on she was giving me, but, of course, I would have to pay taxes on the revenues that those investments would produce in the USA.

The rentals were producing enough to live comfortably, but intresting half of the properties to Don, was going to cut the revenue in half and, counting the maintenance expenses, keeping the receipts that were deductable from the taxes, I was able not to pay taxes, or, if any, very little.

One day coming back from the beach I met a handsome blond guy named Amon who was in the air force at NAS, he was from a little town in Arkansas and had a wife and 2 children that were living somewhere in Texas.

We started dating and were having the most enjoyable time together. Besides the fact that he liked to drink a lot and when he was drunk he could be quite abnoctious, we were going places together and we met some other couples and also single guys. We were partying almost every night and at a certain point he moved in my house. At first Don was kind of mad about it, but after he came to know him better and saw that, after all, he was a nice guy, they became good friends.

Talking almost every day with my mother and also with her neighbors, I realized that it could become a problem for her living alone in Lugano, buying food, cooking and cleaning the house so I decided it was best for me to go there and check things out.

I managed to take off with Amon for a couple of weeks and go to have a little tour of Italy and to Lugano to see what I could do about my mother. Although he had spent sometimes in an American base in Wiesbaden, he didn't know much of Europe. It was also pleasant to show him around.

I convinced mother to come to Pensacola to help me at the house and while time was passing by she was not talking about going home soon, she will spend the last 3 years of her life with me and in the company of Don who was her "buddy".

Not much to say about the following years when life was flowing smooth including the usual trips to Italy and Switzerland until I met through gay.com a Peruvian guy named Felipe. We did not talk about sex and it looked like he was trying to find out about himself, in other words he was interested in friendship making frequent questions about gay life but we had a very important subject that would keep us busy for hours on the chat, and that was Inca, Aztec, Maya history so towards the end of 1998 I decided to go to Lima to meet him in person so I could explore the megalithic constructions that are dated much before the Inca period that started around the 15th century.

Felipe was a very nice and intelligent young man, we sympathized immediately and spent a couple of weeks going to Nazca, Ollaintaytambo, Sachsayhuaman, Pisac, and Arequipa. The most important thing was to see the Nazca lines from the small Cessna that scared Felipe who had never flown before. Turbulence over the desert was quite strong but he survived and was happy about the new experience. Cuzco was the stunning capital of the pre-Inca civilization in part destructed by the followers of Pizarro adducing the fact that those megalithic constructions couldn't have been built without the help of the Devil (the conquistadores were always followed by ignorant bigot priests that had the idea to convert the natives to the Christian religion). They also imported illnesses unknown to the populations of central and South America that caused the death of millions of natives.

Around these sites there were guys playing the flute de pan and their music was blending in perfect harmony with the surroundings.

The end of my journey was sad for me but also for Felipe who had grown very affectionate and wanted to know if we would see each other soon. I kept my affirmative promise because I was back in Lima three months later. This time we spent more days in Machu Picchu, Cajamarca an d Trujillo with the citadel of Chan Chan and the pyramids of the moon and the sun where I managed to get a couple of ancient figurines dug out by two workers that were excavating the site, they ended together with my Etruscan potteries, old family heirlooms.

The night before I left Felipe told me, crying, that he was thinking he was gay and that he wanted to be with me. At that point we made Love for hours. At the airport I invited him to come to Pensacola at his early convenience. He would not be able to come unless I wrote a letter saying that I would take care of him during the two weeks he was planning to stay and he had to open a bank account in a Peruvian bank to prove that he would go back into the country.

So a couple of months later I drove to Houston to pick him up and on the way to Florida we stopped in New Orleans where he had a blast. After spending a few days in Pensacola we went to Orlando to Disneyworld, cape Canaveral, Miami and land's end, Key West.

The fortnight went fast and when I drove him back to Houston the sadness was sovereign. But he was a student of mechanical engineering and his duty was to end the university and took over his father who owned a small factory, never than less to marry, very customary in the Peruvian society like we saw in the first gay movie "no se lo digas a nadie" watched in a cinema in Lima.

We kept in touch but we would never see each other again. Eventually he got married after graduation and he has now a child.

My story with Amon had ended because he was drinking too much and somehow managed to get infected with the Aids virus. He was under the supervision of the military hospital in Pensacola but they transferred him to Houston and that was too far for a stable relationship. Eventually he got out of the military and moved to Denver where I saw him a couple of years later and that was then last time I heard of him, I think he died there all alone and I feel sorry about that, but that has been the tragedy of more of 88 friends of mine in New York, San Francisco, Los Angeles, Atlanta, Mobile, Dallas and Miami. I stopped counting by the end of the century, it has been very heartbreaking because, besides many acquaintances, some were good friends and remembering them makes me feel very sad.

On the whole my life in the USA has been very happy, relaxing, I met wonderful people, may be starting with some sex adventures but with some it became real friendship that still goes on at this time.

The last guy that I met on the 20th of December 1999 was Spencer. He was living in New York visiting his parents for Christmas. I wasn't looking for anyone in particular but when I saw his profile on gay.com I just wrote "we are the same height, weight, same green eyes, I have brown hair and you have it red"… One hour later I got a message from him who wanted to meet me. We did meet the same night over at the Round Up and that was a "coup de foudre" (bolt of lightning). He went back to New York, settled his business and moved to Pensacola in his (adopted) parents home where he lived for about a month and then he moved to my house. We will stay together for 19 years. We got married in Vancouver in 2006 because in the US gay marriages were not allowed, then in Boston when they approved the law in Massachusetts in 2012.

1999

Spencer started working as a car salesman for Volkswagen and at the same time managed my rentals. When a tenant was leaving he was remodeling the house because he was very skilled in electric, plumbing and construction, easy in a country where houses are built with wood and sheetrock while the bricks are just like a veneer surrounding the perimeter. He managed to increase the value of the properties that during the previous years had largely paid themselves with the rents. Most people in America buy with a mortgage and that can stretch for up to 30 years, that way they pay the house 3 times more. There are only a few people that really own the property but the majority move around selling and buying somewhere else pocketing the equity matured and starting another mortgage, never ending paying and many times losing the property that is repossessed by the bank. People that work in the medical field, attorneys at law and big managers or CEOs, the large majority live on small by monthly paychecks that disappears when they have to pay the minimum dues on the numerous credit cards that everybody has in their wallet. In most families there are at least two people working. The interests they have to pay on the credit cards are up to 15%. Spencer's parents still don't own a house and they are living in a double mobile house paying a rent on the land occupied by the trailer park. These parks are scattered all over the US except near the downtown areas. The electric cables are surrounding the whole country hanging from millions of wooden poles giving the impression of a third world country. Some newer areas have the cables underground. Certainly if you are visiting New York or any major city you will not see this, but it's enough to go to the suburbs. That's why when there are tornadoes, hurricanes, floods, thousands of homes remain without power, sometimes for several days, the fall of a tree can result in a loss of power for the whole street and so can be the walk of a squirrel touching the transformers that are like barrels on top of the poles.

In August 2005 the Gulf coast got hit by hurricane Katrina that caused billions of damage in Louisiana, Mississippi, Alabama and NW Florida. Spencer went to work for a remediation company to restore what was left of the houses. We had 4 properties partly damaged but the insurance paid everything and then they raised the premiums.

Previous hurricanes happened in 1995, Erin, witnessed from my Florida room, but that was only force 1. Then we had Ivan in September 2004. Dennis in July 2005.

By that time we had enough and Spencer suggested we should move to a site more inland. The choice fell on San Antonio in Texas where Don had been for boot camp during his military service, Spencer went on a temporary exploration and he found the right house. We bought it and went back and forward there for 5 times, 8 hours drive one way. We had some remodeling to do and after 3 months we were able to move with our 6 cats, the pick up truck, my car, Spencer's car and the little trailer that Spencer was using working in Louisiana. The house was stunning in a very nice area, cables buried, big yard, had marble floor, double garage, two master bedrooms, 1 guest room and 3 baths with bidets (uncommon in the US). I wanted an induction stove to eliminate the

gas and that's the best way to cook. My mania to have phone in every room including bathrooms, big screen tvs and a large patio. Don fixed the yard with all the plants making it in a botanical garden. The fence was raised 2 meters so that the cats, that were all declawed, would not be able to roam in other's people yards. San Antonio is located at the beginning of the desert, the climate is warm and seldom humid, perfect for a big variety of plants. The city has miles of river walk giving the idea of a different kind of Venice it's the river channeled through downtown, furthermore the area was site of 5 different Franciscan missions, the most famous of which is the Alamo that it's the destination of tourists all year round.
Through the chat line I met a few local people that became our good friends.
I can adapt well in a different environment as long as the weather is nice and it doesn't get too cold. San Antonio had the perfect climate

Last Chapter

After the death of Spencer my life took a totally different turn because I was in a state of deep depression and I did not know what I would have done next so for the first thing I went back to Pensacola but my house had been sold it and I was a guest of Ella for a few days but I did not feel right so I went to San Antonio where I found Mandy and her girlfriend that were taking care of the Airbnb. Apparently Mandy did not like the fact that I was back and she acted like she was the owner of the place asking me to make a will in her favor because she said that she spent too much time and she was making too little money to run the run the place. I got even more aggravated when she pretended to own armchairs and furniture that I had previously bought and with her girlfriend they put everything in a pick up truck and left.

I saw it was a lost cause and I didn't want to have a big fight for my rights so I decided to put the building for sale. It sold within one week, I put the money in the bank and went back to Cartama where I found a builder to finish the beautiful bathroom the way Spencer would have done. Apparently I did not feel right living in the house, it was still under remodeling and much too my regrets I decided to put the house for sale I took all the possible values that could be sold in a flea market and I sold everything that could be sold. Some items I gave to my neighbors that loved them. It didn't take long for the house to be sold and in the meantime I rented an apartment near Torremolinos to start a new life.

Amedeo, an acquainted friend of a friend of mine from the old days in Atlanta, came to visit and convinced me to go to London to stay in his flat help him to pay the rent and get over my problems. I really don't think London is the best place to go, I find the city kind of boring maybe because of its citizens but after all I decided to go maybe for a few months. My British mother Terry lived in Brighton which is only one hour away from London, Brighton is gonna be different place where there are university students from all over the world and it's a live city, London it's kind of dead specially in the evening because everybody goes to the pub to get drunk and there is no dialogue there. So we packed five suitcases and brought all the stuff that I salvaged from the house and from the flea market and went on the plane to London Heathrow.

Amedeo's flat was in the section of the Brixton in the east side that used to be a very nice area and now it's kind of run down looking and not very nice people live there. That Flat was a mess, my room was small and filled with all kind of stuff. The closet was small and a bunch of rags were upright in a corner. I didn't have all the space I needed and I had to keep some packed suitcases under the bed. Amedeo had a very wreckage life. On his days off two or three a week depending on where he was flying to he was spending his time on grinder looking for big macho black guys. This did not bother me even if he asked me not to leave my room while he was with somebody in his room but I would see some of the people that were coming to the house, from the top window I could see the gate, some where scary, I didn't see anybody that I would fancy, as a matter of fact I was always afraid that some guy would attack him and stab him, or harm him like in the movie cruising with Al Pacino but the silence reigned sovereign and the whole action would usually last 20 to 30 minutes, sometimes somebody else was coming over in the same evening. That was certainly not the kind of a life that I was looking for. I know London in and out and besides the museums and the big buildings there is not really much to see, it has beautiful parks one can go from one section of town all the way to Windsor. I must say that a lot of people are in the parks unless you go to Soho. During the week nights everything was quiet all day on Friday and Saturday night that were more people going around than usual but even then pubs would close around 1 o'clock. More people go to private parties after hours and have more drinks and probably get drunk until 3- 4 o'clock in the morning before going home. I don't drink and I spend most of the time at home on the Internet reading everything interesting that I could find and watching very interesting documentaries on YouTube. With the advent of Whatsapp I can get in touch with all my friends around the world without any problem and avoiding all the big expenses of the telephone. I always keep in touch with my friends on a weekly or monthly basis on my Facebook the sun never sets. I don't sleep much, about 4 to 5 hours a night but sometimes I will spend the whole night talking to some friends. That gives me pleasure and makes me feel close to them, I need to know how they are doing. So one night I was talking online with somebody named Abdul, he is an Algerian escaped from his country because he was threatened by his father and brothers; they would kill him because he is gay. He asked for political asylum and that he was under the care of the home office waiting for residency. Of course he was feeling very lonely because he didn't know anybody so we started a kind of dating and I decided I was going to take care of him the best I could. Amedeo did not like this and he did everything to get in the way of this friendship. I will understand the reason later on when he decided to go to Israel with one of his colleagues for three days. He loves hassidic Jews and he was going to have some adventure with them in Tel Aviv he got home one morning from Toulouse and he was very excited, I said OK go and enjoy yourself so I could have a few days by myself in peace.

I didn't hear from him until Tuesday evening when he came back and he was all excited and happy because he met somebody really interesting in Tel Aviv. I said great! good for you I hope you hook up and that you can find a lover for the rest of your life.

A few days later he came back from Milan and he was having the kitchen remodeled. He said he could not move from London until everything was done and that I should take the chance and go to Pensacola to find out how to work on line with my account.

He got me a ticket and he took me to the airport on the subway and all the way to the concourse kissing me goodbye before the security gate. He had got me a first class ticket with the return in two weeks. When I got to Atlanta I sent him a WhatsApp saying I am here everything is fine lunch over the plane was really good thank you for getting me in first class now I'm going to wait for the plane to Pensacola where I will arrive around 11 tonight. He never saw the message or if he did he didn't mark it as read. The next day I didn't hear from him. I touched base with some longtime friends of mine and I spend the night over at the round up. On Monday morning I finally went to the bank and I talk to the manager and she explain to me how to check my accounts online. After that I asked the balance of my two accounts and she said the big account it's 25 I said what 25,000? She said no! 25cents! I said that's impossible there are at least hundreds of thousands of dollars in it! And she said yes, but Amedeo send some money to a bank in England! I said how did he do that he could not work online and the account was not active… how much is in my small account and she said $650 I say even though they were thousands How? When? During the previous week …so instead of going to Israel he went to Pensacola wiped off my accounts and came back to London on the next day! He had no problem in doing that because of his flight attendant status!!!

I was totally frozen, this was one of my worst moments in life. All that we had been working for years had disappeared in a heartbeat. It was definitely my fault because I put him on my accounts and now I was basically penniless all I had in my account was $450 plus the 600 and something that he left on the small account. No way I could get in touch with him, he would not answer the phone or Whatsup. I got an email from him saying that we are no friends anymore and that I would have not go back to London but I could take it easy going to my house in the mountains or stay in Pensacola, just stay out of his life.

I was devastated, I called Ella in Copenhagen and told her what had happened, she could not believe it but that was the tragic reality where I got my trying to have somebody who needed a new car, a new, kitchen I had offered to pay his lst 35,000 debt for trying to start a company producing scarves or so he said… never believe anything he say. I had to borrow some money to get back to London because I had all my stuff in his flat including family heirlooms valuables silvers paintings the famous Piranesi prints that would have been my anchor in case I would need money. It was kind of difficult to get a $1500 loan from Piero, Antonio from Rome had to call him and reassure him that he would have the money back in three days. As I had thought what is the ticket to Atlanta still good because it was paid in full and not part of the British Airways deal so when I arrived in Atlanta I called my friend John who was not at home but he was in Columbia, then I called my friend and ex colleague Donna who promptly came to pick me up at the airport because the ticket to London had been canceled by Mr. Amedeo.

I spent three days at Donna and Kathy's house and I got myself a ticket from Atlanta to Newark and London. When I arrived at Heathrow I got a subway and I went with my freedom card to Brixton. The locks had been changed. I could not go into the flat. I went straight to the police to denounce the problem just to hear that they couldn't do anything and I had to go through an attorney but, of course, I did not have the money to hire an attorney at that point. I asked my cousin and his wife if I could go and stay with them living in the outskirts of London. I stayed there for a few days they have a garage apartment that I could use. I found an attorney that was helping people like me that could not pay a fee. He wrote an official letter to Amedeo asking him to return my stuff. The letter was picked up signed by him but nothing else happened even when I gave it to the police and they had an open case against him. I reported the case to the police in Pensacola and after a long while they called me to say they couldn't do anything about it because the value of the goods that were stolen was not over $300,000. I would not leave England empty-handed and I went to Brighton to stay with my friend Paula, I was thinking what could I do next.

She came up with a great idea to put me in touch with a company that was looking for living in carers. I could get a place to stay and work just a few hours a week keeping company to one person who had mobility problems and some kind of Alzheimer. At the end did not amount to anything because all I could get back was the silver and other valuables but the paintings in the prints and everything else was gone probably sold in some auction. I managed to sell my stuff on a very good auction in Brighton and I made some 8000 pounds. I could survive, my colleague working in the same house was from Australia. We became good friends and we are still friends today so when I go to visit I can stay in his flat in Ealing. Working for the agency Share and Care gave me the idea wanted to do now is taking care of all the indigent people man or a woman with love and compassion and be happy if I see them smiling and laughing and so that they know that somebody really cares about them. After the two years spent in London Covid came around and that I did not really stay there to die so I decided to go back to Pensacola which is after all my favorite spot. In August 2020 I left London and I started working for another carer agency in Pensacola. This was kind of different because they were telling me where to go how to take care. to do that kind of job which is not really stressing or anything like it but it's taking care of people they have been forgotten with have different pathologies and that they really care about the effort that you're putting into it. One of my patient happened to be the son of our Emery air freight agent that I had met in Pensacola when he was just a teenager and now, not too old, he was relegated to a bed affected by diabetes. He had already lost a leg and he could not walk. How to remember him playing pool at a specific tournament where he was probably the best. He did not last long, he died a few months later and he was only 42. I looked after a writer who was relegated to a wheelchair and after a psychiatrist in an advanced state of Parkinson's,

To be in touch with so many patients and so many different kind of illnesses it's very sad and sad it's realizing how this people get to the end of their life in pain.

Since I started going to the United States with my parents back in the early 60s and subsequently growing by myself in the 70s 80s I saw the American people changing a lot. Then there was a middle class and now the middle class is basically gone. There are very rich people but the majority are very poor. They live in houses built with wood and sheet rock, mostly barracks. Out of the city centers the country roads are old and the lights are on leaning wood poles with a bunch of cables hanging in there with some barrels holding transformers and electrical equipment. If a squirrel walks on it it gets immediately electrocuted, the power goes off on the entire street and Gulf Power might take hours to restore it. Seems more like Europe was before the second world war. It's not nice to see all these cables hanging all over the country side and all over the villages, they do not bury them unless they build a new subdivision. Most houses do not have a basement and have an insulation between the wood and the bricks. Termites could be a calamity so that pest companies are thriving all over costing a pretty penny for a lot of people that are on minimum wage meaning $10 an hour gross. The health care insurance is quite expensive the best insurance covers about 80% of the cost but the 20% it's in charge of the patient... the problem is that the cure and the medicines are very very expensive. The multi national pharmaceutical companies charge what ever they want and the costs are astronomical. On TV they bombard the people with spots about new medicines that are coming out every other day,   medicines for pathologies that you never heard of, one that I remember is this "are you tired of being tired" we have a medicine for this. If you have diabetes, obesity's, high blood pressure ect don't take it! The list of the side effects is announced at a very high incomprehensible speed...sometimes the last word is DEATH! Tell your doctor about this medicine... Some of my patients take up to 15 and more pills a day and I assure you they have most of the side effects that this medicines cause. Obesity is a real plague among young people. Monsanto is producing genetically modified crops, tons of transgenic foods are consumed every day and some shows are on TV all the time showing people eating tons of shrimps, hamburgers and other goodies when there are people starving to death because they cannot afford to buy food.

The school system is very poor and what they teach in school it's not what one would expect. Unless somebody has a lot of money and can go to private schools. high schools are more or less like the medium schools in Europe they do not make people think they do not make people exercise they give some thought information and they live people in total ignorance. It's difficult to have a regular conversation with somebody who goes to a public school. Of course people that go to college t have a totally different education in certain subjects but not in general science. Most people don't know anything about geography history. College could cost a lot of money and some people get grants that they have to repay in the future making them liable for low interests.

Usually a family gives a credit card to a teenager with a maximum spending of $1000 the teenager goes to spend the money almost immediately and then he starts paying the minimum payment every month which could be $15. A few months later he will receive an increase of limit or a different card with the offer with a maximum spending of $3000 and that goes on and on and on by the time they are in their early 20s they already have debts with different credit cards that would be getting paid by minimum amounts every month. If they don't have this kind of debits then they do not have credit and if they don't have credit they cannot buy a car or anything else on the monthly payment. The more debits one has and the more credit he has. God forbid if somebody has to go to a hospital to seek cures, a friend of mine 36 years old owns almost $3 million to the hospitals because he has a cancer, he may repay that in his next life if he makes enough money to do so.

Multinational companies are really running the United States of America they have powerful lobbies and they pay minimum taxes. The government and the president can only take some actions, but not much. The US have been destabilizing several countries around the world starting with Iraq, Libia, Yemen, Afghanistan, instigating different ethnic groups that want to take the supremacy in the country. Then the multinational companies will go there and rebuild the countries. China is doing pretty much the same but on a different silent level in Africa and South America. We know the objective of China is to dominate the world, their flag with the 5 points star speaks clearly.

Due to the fact that the 2 most important persons in my life have died I decided to take care of indigent old people neglected by their families and I started a career in caregiver. I did that in London for two years taking care of an older Muslim Indian man named Yunus. He was living in a big house in Ealing, his son and his daughter-in-law were leaving in a different area of London and were coming to see him may be a couple of times a month for only a few minutes. I had a colleague Kim, from Australia, who had been there long before me, we became good friends. Yunus didn't speak much. They were saying that he had dementia. If his younger sister was coming to visit he was talking to her in Hindi without any problems. I started to talk to him in Hindi using the translator on my cell phone and he told me that he shut himself to everybody because he was fed up, he lost his wife seven years before and he did not want to cope with other people. There was another carer coming in the morning to get him up and give him a shower and then I would give him breakfast and take him over to his beautiful armchair where he would spend almost the whole day watching TV. With me he started watching movies and documentaries on YouTube and we had very good conversations. I would cook him lunch and give him a snack around 5 o'clock, dinner was at eight and then he would go to bed around 10. He liked British comedy like Are you been served, Keeping up appearances, and The golden girls.

Through the chatline I met a couple of friends that were living in the neighborhood and sometimes we were going out for a long walk in the parks, sometimes all the way to Windsor along the canals.

Yunus died last April in his sleep. I was very sad because I liked the guy but he was certainly out of his misery with the kind of family that he had.

The Covid pandemic had started in London, everybody was going around with the mask that was mandatory in the buses and on the subway. This situation became quite annoying and the usually empty streets of Ealing became even more deserted then. I was going to the stores at night and I couldn't go to the gym because it was temporarily shut. Before it was too late I decided to go back to the United States. It took me a while to understand the rules to go on the plane and take the Covid test nothing was clear the news kept changing day by day, finally I boarded the flight at Heathrow and I made it back to Pensacola. In Atlanta I called a friend of mine and I found out that he had died of Covid a couple of weeks before. That was Wayne, he was coming often to visit me to go to the beach and so far the only one that died of Covid. I was wondering how many friends I would lose because of this pandemic and that made me really sad. I have been calling everybody on a weekly basis to make sure that they are all right. And I had a friend that got hit by Covid in Bergamo, he was in the hospital for a month but now he has to carry some oxygen because he can hardly breathe. I joined an agency that was sending me to different patients in Pensacola and I was there for a few months until it became unbearable because the price of gas line up and what I was making on minimum wage was not enough to pay my rent, car insurance and all the other expenses. With much regret of the two people that I was taking care of I decided to leave the United States and retire in my house in the mountains of the north east of Italy, at least I won't have to pay rent.

When I was in London hi did not go out much. To people over 65 is given a freedom card that allows to go freely on the subway on the buses and to have big discounts on train tickets. That was great because I was saving a whole lot of money, the prices of the tickets were quite high. One of my favorite places to go walking is Soho, in a cold afternoon on Dean Street my sight encountered the eyes of a guy that was walking on the other side, he noticed me too and after proceeding further we look back at each other and smiled. I always thought that "coups de foudre" could happen but they are extremely rare. There was something in the eyes of this guys that caught my attention like I could see his soul and I was deeply touched by his beautiful smile with a point of sadness. He was visiting London for shopping from Dubai and was going to leave in a couple of days. He came to see me in Ealing and I made a point to accompany him to the airport when he was leaving. We have been in touch ever since by telephone. He is Lebanese has a very nice voice, I believe he is Muslim but we never really talked about religion, not that it matters because I'm Buddhist and open to any kind of faith. I did not have in mind to date somebody after the death of Spencer but this guy was just too sweet, too good to be true, intelligent and handsome. He had some bad experiences in the past.

I have a few things that I need to take care in Italy and up I'm planning to go to Lavarone check on the house and and eventually spend a few months there. Hamza told me he's dreaming of a house in the country with an orchard and some animals. So my house would be ideal for that but the fact that winter is very cold up at 1200 m. and we get a lot of snow I'm not sure that somebody living near the equator would like such change of climate. He watched some documentaries of the dolomites and he's coming to check up the place in a couple of months. If he likes it I will be back in a relationship even though I'm much older than he is and I am afraid that I will be gone in a very few years leaving him alone.

Pensacola Beach

Malaga Alcazaba